DOCUMENTS ON AMERICAN FOREIGN RELATIONS 1970

DOCUMENTS ON AMERICAN FOREIGN RELATIONS 1970

Edited by ELAINE P. ADAM
and WILLIAM P. LINEBERRY

Published for the Council on Foreign Relations
by Simon and Schuster / New York

The Council on Foreign Relations is a non-profit institution devoted to the study of political, economic, and strategic problems
as related to American foreign policy. It takes no stand, expressed
or implied, on American policy.

The authors of books published under the auspices of the
Council are responsible for their statements of fact and expressions of opinion. The Council is responsible only for determining
that they should be presented to the public.

For a partial list of Council publications see pages 509–11.

First printing
SBN 671-21459-4
Library of Congress Catalog Card Number: 39-28987
Manufactured in the United States of America

PREFACE

With this volume covering the year 1970, the Council on Foreign Relations continues publication of its annual series of documentary materials relating to United States foreign policy, a series initiated by the World Peace Foundation in 1939 and carried forward by the Council since 1952. The purpose of the series has been and remains the compilation in convenient reference form of the most important documents bearing on U.S. diplomacy in any given year. As such, the volume is designed to provide less a narrative account of American policy in its global setting than a concise documentary record of the key speeches, reports, communiqués, agreements, and treaties that serve as signposts on the nation's international passage from one year to the next. Although most of the documents contained herein have previously appeared in such publications as *The Department of State Bulletin* and *The Weekly Compilation of Presidential Documents,* it is hoped that their presentation here in orderly sequence and with suitable annotations will prove a particularly useful reference aid for scholars, editors, writers, and other serious students of American foreign policy.

As might be expected, documents emanating from the executive branch of the federal government—and specifically from the White House and the Department of State—compose the major source of materials included in the volume. But the reader may note that the appearance of an occasional congressional resolution also testifies to the growing concern of Congress with the foreign policy process and that the inclusion of such items as the complete text of the Bonn-Moscow treaty of August 12, 1970 or the extensive excerpts from the "International Development Strategy for the Second United Nations Development Decade" points up the growing impact of other centers of world power on America's dealings abroad. Indeed, of all the documents brought to the attention of American policy-makers in 1970, few could claim the immediate importance or the long-term significance of the pact signed in Moscow by Chancellor Willy Brandt of the Federal

Republic of Germany and Premier Aleksei Kosygin of the U.S.S.R.

The plan of this volume, like those of past years, moves from the general to the specific and was designed primarily with ease of reference in mind. All documents are numbered consecutively, their appropriate serial number appearing, together with a brief identification of the document, at the head of each right-hand page. Footnotes are also numbered consecutively within chapters and often refer to the parallel Council on Foreign Relations volume, *The United States in World Affairs, 1970* (New York: Simon & Schuster, 1972), a descriptive, narrative account of U.S. diplomacy that provides the context for a broader understanding of the material included here. Other footnotes refer to earlier volumes in this series or in *The United States in World Affairs* series. Editorial treatment of the documents themselves has been limited to the correction of occasional typographical errors and the insertion within brackets of supplementary information where greater accuracy or fuller comprehension require it. For additional information and clarification, the reader's attention is directed to the five-year Cumulative Index covering all volumes in this series from 1966 to 1970, inclusive.

No compilation of this sort is possible without the assistance and cooperation of numerous individuals and institutions. The editors are especially indebted to Donald Wasson, Librarian, and to Janet Rigney, Assistant Librarian, of the Council on Foreign Relations Library, as well as other members of the library staff, for their generous support and help. They are grateful for the guidance afforded them by Richard P. Stebbins, a Senior Fellow of the Council and the editor of these volumes for many years past. And their appreciation is also due to Grace Darling Griffin, Production and Promotion Manager for the Council, for her generous cooperation throughout the editorial process and to Prudence Crowther for help with the proofs. The White House, the Department of State, and the United Nations deserve a note of thanks for the use made of their publications, as do *The New York Times* and the Press and Information Office of the German Federal Republic. For the selection of documents and their manner of presentation, of course, the editors themselves assume full responsibility.

CONTENTS

I. WORLD AFFAIRS THROUGH AMERICAN EYES

II. EAST-WEST RELATIONS: ARMS CONTROL AND DISARMAMENT

F. Chemical and Biological Warfare

G. Disarmament at the Twenty-Fifth Regular Session of the United Nations General Assembly, September 15–December 17, 1970

III. THE ATLANTIC COMMUNITY

A. Security and *Détente*

IV. AMERICAN POLICY IN ASIA: THE MIDDLE EAST

V. AMERICAN POLICY IN ASIA: THE WAR IN INDOCHINA

A. The Communist Offensive in Laos

VIII. INTER-AMERICAN AFFAIRS

A. The Organization of American States

B. Economic and Social Problems

IX. THE UNITED NATIONS AND INTERNATIONAL COOPERATION

SOURCES FREQUENTLY CITED

Department of State Bulletin (Washington: G.P.O., weekly)

Documents on American Foreign Relations (annual volumes):

Volumes prior to 1952—Princeton: Princeton University Press, for the World Peace Foundation

Volumes for 1952–1966 inclusive—New York: Harper & Row, for the Council on Foreign Relations

Volumes for 1967–1970 inclusive—New York: Simon and Schuster, for the Council on Foreign Relations

U.S. Arms Control and Disarmament Agency (ACDA):

Documents on Disarmament (annual volumes)—
1967 (ACDA Publication 46; Washington: G.P.O., 1968)
1969 (ACDA Publication 55; Washington: G.P.O., 1970)
1970 (ACDA Publication 60; Washington: G.P.O., 1971)

U.S. Foreign Policy for the 1970's: A New Strategy for Peace—A Report to the Congress by Richard Nixon, President of the United States, February 18, 1970 (Washington: G.P.O., 1970)

(Also appears in *Department of State Bulletin,* March 9, 1970, pp. 273–332, and in *New York Times,* February 19, 1970)

The United States in World Affairs (annual volumes):

Volumes prior to 1967—New York: Harper & Row, for the Council on Foreign Relations

Volumes for 1967 and 1970—New York: Simon and Schuster, for the Council on Foreign Relations

Weekly Compilation of Presidential Documents (Washington: G.P.O., weekly)

(Most presidential documents also appear in definitive text in *Public Papers of the Presidents of the United States: Richard Nixon, 1969* [Washington: G.P.O., 1971] and *Richard Nixon, 1970* [Washington: G.P.O., 1972])

(The abbreviation G.P.O., as used in the foregoing list and in the footnotes, refers invariably to the United States Government Printing Office)

DOCUMENTS ON
AMERICAN
FOREIGN RELATIONS
1970

I.
WORLD AFFAIRS THROUGH AMERICAN EYES

A. American World Policy.

(1) The State of the Union: Message Delivered by President Richard M. Nixon Before a Joint Session of the Congress, January 22, 1970.[1]

(Excerpts)

* * *

To address a joint session of the Congress in this great chamber in which I was once privileged to serve is an honor for which I am deeply grateful.

The State of the Union Address is traditionally an occasion for a lengthy and detailed account by the President of what he has accomplished in the past, what he wants the Congress to do in the future, and, in an election year, to lay the basis for the political issues which might be decisive in the fall.

Occasionally there comes a time when profound and far-reaching events command a break with tradition.

This is such a time.

I say this not only because 1970 marks the beginning of a new decade in which America will celebrate its 200th birthday. I say it because new knowledge and hard experience argue persuasively that both our programs and our institutions in America need to be reformed.

The moment has arrived to harness the vast energies and abundance of this land to the creation of a new American experience, an experience richer and deeper and more truly a reflection of the goodness and grace of the human spirit.

[1] Text from *Weekly Compilation of Presidential Documents*, January 26, 1970, pp. 58–66. For the context see *The United States in World Affairs, 1970*, Introduction to Chapter 1.

1

The seventies will be a time of new beginnings, a time of exploring both on the earth and in the heavens, a time of discovery. But the time has also come for emphasis on developing better ways of managing what we have and of completing what man's genius has begun but left unfinished.

Our land, this land that is ours together, is a great and a good land. It is also an unfinished land, and the challenge of perfecting it is the summons of the seventies.

It is in that spirit that I address myself to those great issues facing our Nation which are above partisanship.

When we speak of America's priorities the first priority must always be peace for America and the world.

The major immediate goal of our foreign policy is to bring an end to the war in Vietnam in a way that our generation will be remembered not so much as the generation that suffered in war, but more for the fact that we had the courage and character to win the kind of a just peace that the next generation was able to keep.

We are making progress toward that goal.

The prospects for peace are far greater today than they were a year ago.

A major part of the credit for this development goes to the Members of this Congress who, despite their differences on the conduct of the war, have overwhelmingly indicated their support of a just peace.[2] By this action, you have completely demolished the enemy's hopes that they can gain in Washington the victory our fighting men have denied them in Vietnam.

No goal could be greater than to make the next generation the first in this century in which America was at peace with every nation in the world.

I shall discuss in detail the new concepts and programs designed to achieve this goal in a separate report on foreign policy, which I shall submit to the Congress at a later date.[3]

Today, let me describe the directions of our new policies.

We have based our policies on an evaluation of the world as it is, not as it was 25 years ago at the conclusion of World War II. Many of the policies which were necessary and right then are obsolete today.

Then, because of America's overwhelming military and economic strength, because of the weakness of other major free world powers and the inability of scores of newly independent nations to defend, or even govern, themselves, America had to

2 House Resolution 613, 91st Congress, adopted December 2, 1969. For the context see *Congressional Record*, December 2, 1969, pp. 36459-36538.
3 Document 2.

assume the major burden for the defense of freedom in the world.

In two wars, first in Korea and now in Vietnam, we furnished most of the money, most of the arms, most of the men to help other nations defend their freedom.

Today the great industrial nations of Europe, as well as Japan, have regained their economic strength, and the nations of Latin America—and many of the nations who acquired their freedom from colonialism after World War II in Asia and Africa —have a new sense of pride and dignity, and a determination to assume the responsibility for their own defense.

That is the basis of the doctrine I announced at Guam.[4]

Neither the defense nor the development of other nations can be exclusively or primarily an American undertaking.

The nations of each part of the world should assume the primary responsibility for their own well-being; and they themselves should determine the terms of that well-being.

We shall be faithful to our treaty commitments, but we shall reduce our involvement and our presence in other nations' affairs.

To insist that other nations play a role is not a retreat from responsibility; it is a sharing of responsibility.

The result of this new policy has been not to weaken our alliances, but to give them new life, new strength, a new sense of common purpose.

Relations with our European allies are once again strong and healthy, based on mutual consultation and mutual responsibility.

We have initiated a new approach to Latin America, in which we deal with those nations as partners rather than patrons.

The new partnership concept has been welcomed in Asia. We have developed an historic new basis for Japanese-American friendship and cooperation, which is the linchpin for peace in the Pacific.

If we are to have peace in the last third of the century, a major factor will be the development of a new relationship between the United States and the Soviet Union.

I would not underestimate our differences, but we are moving with precision and purpose from an era of confrontation to an era of negotiation.

Our negotiations on strategic arms limitations [5] and in other areas will have far greater chance for success if both sides enter

4 *Public Papers of the Presidents of the United States: Richard Nixon, 1969* (Washington: G.P.O., 1971), pp. 545–549; excerpts in *Documents, 1968–69*, pp. 329–334.
5 Documents 10–11.

them motivated by mutual self-interest rather than naive sentimentality.

It is with this same spirit that we have resumed discussions with Communist China in our talks at Warsaw.[6]

Our concern in our relations with both these nations is to avoid a catastrophic collision and to build a solid basis for peaceful settlement of our differences.

I would be the last to suggest that the road to peace is not difficult and dangerous, but I believe our new policies have contributed to the prospect that America may have the best chance since World War II to enjoy a generation of uninterrupted peace. And that chance will be enormously increased if we continue to have a relationship between Congress and the Executive in which, despite differences in detail, where the security of America and the peace of mankind are concerned, we act not as Republicans, not as Democrats—but as Americans.

As we move into the decade of the seventies, we have the greatest opportunity for progress at home of any people in world history.

Our gross national product will increase by $500 billion in the next 10 years. This increase alone is greater than the entire growth of the American economy from 1790 to 1950.

The critical question is not whether we will grow, but how we will use that growth.

*   *   *

In the majesty of this great Chamber we hear the echoes of America's history, of debates that rocked the Union and those that repaired it, of the summons to war and the search for peace, of the uniting of the people, the building of a nation.

Those echoes of history remind us of our roots and our strengths.

They remind us also of that special genius of American democracy, which at one critical turning point after another has led us to spot the new road to the future and given us the wisdom and the courage to take it.

As I look down that new road which I have tried to map out today, I see a new America as we celebrate our 200th anniversary 6 years from now.

I see an America in which we have abolished hunger, provided the means for every family in the Nation to obtain a minimum income, made enormous progress in providing better housing, faster transportation, improved health, and superior education.

6 Documents 50–51.

I see an America in which we have checked inflation, and waged a winning war against crime.

I see an America in which we have made great strides in stopping the pollution of our air, cleaning up our water, opening up our parks, continuing to explore in space.

Most important, I see an America at peace with all the nations of the world.

This is not an impossible dream. These goals are all within our reach.

In times past, our forefathers had the vision but not the means to achieve such goals.

Let it not be recorded that we were the first American generation that had the means but not the vision to make this dream come true.

But let us, above all, recognize a fundamental truth. We can be the best clothed, best fed, best housed people in the world, enjoying clean air, clean water, beautiful parks, but we could still be the unhappiest people in the world without an indefinable spirit—the lift of a driving dream which has made America from its beginning the hope of the world.

Two hundred years ago this was a new nation of 3 million people, weak militarily, poor economically. But America meant something to the world then which could not be measured in dollars, something far more important than military might.

Listen to President Thomas Jefferson in 1802: We act not "for ourselves alone, but for the whole human race."

We had a spiritual quality then which caught the imagination of millions of people in the world.

Today, when we are the richest and strongest nation in the world, let it not be recorded that we lack the moral and spiritual idealism which made us the hope of the world at the time of our birth.

The demands of us in 1976 are even greater than in 1776.

It is no longer enough to live and let live. Now we must live and help live.

We need a fresh climate in America, one in which a person can breathe freely and breathe in freedom.

Our recognition of the truth that wealth and happiness are not the same thing requires us to measure success or failure by new criteria.

Even more than the programs I have described today, what this Nation needs is an example from its elected leaders in providing the spiritual and moral leadership which no programs for material progress can satisfy.

Above all, let us inspire young Americans with a sense of excitement, a sense of destiny, a sense of involvement in meeting the challenges we face in this great period of our history. Only then are they going to have any sense of satisfaction in their lives. The greatest privilege an individual can have is to serve in a cause bigger than himself. We have such a cause.

How we seize the opportunities I have described today will determine not only our future, but the future of peace and freedom in this world in the last third of the century.

May God give us the wisdom, the strength, and, above all, the idealism to be worthy of that challenge, so that America can fulfill its destiny of being the world's best hope for liberty, for opportunity, for progress and peace for all peoples.

(2)   The State of the World: First Annual Report by President Nixon Transmitted to the Congress February 18, 1970.[7]

(Excerpt)

UNITED STATES FOREIGN POLICY FOR THE 1970'S: A NEW STRATEGY FOR PEACE

INTRODUCTION

"A nation needs many qualities, but it needs faith and confidence above all. Skeptics do not build societies; the idealists are the builders. Only societies that believe in themselves can rise to their challenges. Let us not, then, pose a false choice between meeting our responsibilities abroad and meeting the needs of our people at home. We shall meet both or we shall meet neither." [8]

When I took office, the most immediate problem facing our nation was the war in Vietnam. No question has more occupied our thoughts and energies during this past year.

---

[7] *U.S. Foreign Policy for the 1970's: A New Strategy for Peace—A Report to the Congress by Richard Nixon, President of the United States, February 18, 1970* (Washington: G.P.O., 1970); text from *Weekly Compilation of Presidential Documents,* February 23, 1970, pp. 194–239. For the context see *The United States in World Affairs, 1970,* Section 3 and *passim.*
[8] *Documents, 1968–69,* p. 46.

Yet the fundamental task confronting us was more profound. We could see that the whole pattern of international politics was changing. Our challenge was to understand that change, to define America's goals for the next period, and to set in motion policies to achieve them. For all Americans must understand that because of its strength, its history and its concern for human dignity, this nation occupies a special place in the world. Peace and progress are impossible without a major American role.

This first annual report on U.S. foreign policy is more than a record of one year. It is this Administration's statement of a new approach to foreign policy, to match a new era of international relations.

A NEW ERA

The postwar period in international relations has ended.

Then, we were the only great power whose society and economy had escaped World War II's massive destruction. Today, the ravages of that war have been overcome. Western Europe and Japan have recovered their economic strength, their political vitality, and their national self-confidence. Once the recipients of American aid, they have now begun to share their growing resources with the developing world. Once almost totally dependent on American military power, our European allies now play a greater role in our common policies, commensurate with their growing strength.

Then, new nations were being born, often in turmoil and uncertainty. Today, these nations have a new spirit and a growing strength of independence. Once, many feared that they would become simply a battleground of cold-war rivalry and fertile ground for Communist penetration. But this fear misjudged their pride in their national identities and their determination to preserve their newly won sovereignty.

Then, we were confronted by a monolithic Communist world. Today, the nature of that world has changed—the power of individual Communist nations has grown, but international Communist unity has been shattered. Once a unified bloc, its solidarity has been broken by the powerful forces of nationalism. The Soviet Union and Communist China, once bound by an alliance of friendship, had become bitter adversaries by the mid-1960's. The only times the Soviet Union has used the Red Army since World War II have been against its own allies—in East Germany in 1953,[9] in Hungary in 1956,[10] and in Czechoslovakia

9 Same, *1953,* pp. 170–178.
10 Same, *1956,* pp. 255–261.

in 1968.[11] The Marxist dream of international Communist unity has disintegrated.

Then, the United States had a monopoly or overwhelming superiority of nuclear weapons. Today, a revolution in the technology of war has altered the nature of the military balance of power. New types of weapons present new dangers. Communist China has acquired thermonuclear weapons. Both the Soviet Union and the United States have acquired the ability to inflict unacceptable damage on the other, no matter which strikes first. There can be no gain and certainly no victory for the power that provokes a thermonuclear exchange. Thus, both sides have recognized a vital mutual interest in halting the dangerous momentum of the nuclear arms race.[12]

Then, the slogans formed in the past century were the ideological accessories of the intellectual debate. Today, the "isms" have lost their vitality—indeed the restlessness of youth on both sides of the dividing line testifies to the need for a new idealism and deeper purposes.

This is the challenge and the opportunity before America as it enters the 1970's.

THE FRAMEWORK FOR A DURABLE PEACE

In the first postwar decades, American energies were absorbed in coping with a cycle of recurrent crises, whose fundamental origins lay in the destruction of World War II and the tensions attending the emergence of scores of new nations. Our opportunity today—and challenge—is to get at the causes of crises, to take a longer view, and to help build the international relationships that will provide the framework of a durable peace.

I have often reflected on the meaning of "peace," and have reached one certain conclusion: Peace must be far more than the absence of war. Peace must provide a durable structure of international relationships which inhibits or removes the causes of war. Building a lasting peace requires a foreign policy guided by three basic principles:

— Peace requires *partnership*. Its obligations, like its benefits, must be shared. This concept of partnership guides our relations with all friendly nations.

— Peace requires *strength*. So long as there are those who would threaten our vital interests and those of our allies with military force, we must be strong. American weakness could tempt would-be aggressors to make dangerous miscalculations. At the same time, our own strength is im-

---

[11] Same, *1968–69,* pp. 134–138.
[12] Cf. note 5 to Document 1.

portant only in relation to the strength of others. We—like others—must place high priority on enhancing our security through cooperative arms control.

—Peace requires a *willingness to negotiate*. All nations—and we are no exception—have important national interests to protect. But the most fundamental interest of all nations lies in building the structure of peace. In partnership with our allies, secure in our own strength, we will seek those areas in which we can agree among ourselves and with others to accommodate conflicts and overcome rivalries. We are working toward the day when *all* nations will have a stake in peace, and will therefore be partners in its maintenance.

Within such a structure, international disputes can be settled and clashes contained. The insecurity of nations, out of which so much conflict arises, will be eased, and the habits of moderation and compromise will be nurtured. Most important, a durable peace will give full opportunity to the powerful forces driving toward economic change and social justice.

This vision of a peace built on partnership, strength and willingness to negotiate is the unifying theme of this report. In the sections that follow, the first steps we have taken during this past year—the policies we have devised and the programs we have initiated to realize this vision—are placed in the context of these three principles.

1. Peace Through Partnership—The Nixon Doctrine

As I said in my address of November 3, "We Americans are a do-it-yourself people—an impatient people. Instead of teaching someone else to do a job, we like to do it ourselves. This trait has been carried over into our foreign policy." [13]

The postwar era of American foreign policy began in this vein in 1947 with the proclamation of the Truman Doctrine and the Marshall Plan, offering American economic and military assistance to countries threatened by aggression. Our policy held that democracy and prosperity, buttressed by American military strength and organized in a worldwide network of American-led alliances, would insure stability and peace. In the formative years of the postwar period, this great effort of international political and economic reconstruction was a triumph of American leadership and imagination, especially in Europe.

For two decades after the end of the Second World War, our foreign policy was guided by such a vision and inspired by its success. The vision was based on the fact that the United States

[13] *Documents, 1968–69*, p. 282.

was the richest and most stable country, without whose initiative and resources little security or progress was possible.

This impulse carried us through into the 1960's. The United States conceived programs and ran them, We devised strategies, and proposed them to our allies. We discerned dangers, and acted directly to combat them.

The world has dramatically changed since the days of the Marshall Plan. We deal now with a world of stronger allies, a community of independent developing nations, and a Communist world still hostile but now divided.

Others now have the ability and responsibility to deal with local disputes which once might have required our intervention. Our contribution and success will depend not on the frequency of our involvement in the affairs of others, but on the stamina of our policies. This is the approach which will best encourage other nations to do their part, and will most genuinely enlist the support of the American people.

This is the message of the doctrine I announced at Guam [14]— the "Nixon Doctrine." Its central thesis is that the United States will participate in the defense and development of allies and friends, but that America cannot—and will not—conceive *all* the plans, design *all* the programs, execute *all* the decisions and undertake *all* the defense of the free nations of the world. We will help where it makes a real difference and is considered in our interest.

America cannot live in isolation if it expects to live in peace. We have no intention of withdrawing from the world. The only issue before us is how we can be most effective in meeting our responsibilities, protecting our interests, and thereby building peace.

A more responsible participation by our foreign friends in their own defense and progress means a more effective common effort toward the goals we all seek. Peace in the world will continue to require us to maintain our commitments—and we will. As I said at the United Nations,[15] "It is not my belief that the way to peace is by giving up our friends or letting down our allies." But a more balanced and realistic American role in the world is essential if American commitments are to be sustained over the long pull. In my State of the Union Address,[16] I affirmed that "to insist that other nations play a role is not a retreat from responsibility; it is a sharing of responsibility." This is not a way for America to withdraw from its indispen-

14 Cf. note 4 to Document 1.
15 *Documents, 1968–69*, p. 469.
16 Document 1.

sable role in the world. It is a way—the only way—we can carry out our responsibilities.

It is misleading, moreover, to pose the fundamental question so largely in terms of commitments. Our objective, in the first instance, is to support our *interests* over the long run with a sound foreign policy. The more that policy is based on a realistic assessment of our and others' interests, the more effective our role in the world can be. We are not involved in the world because we have commitments; we have commitments because we are involved. Our interests must shape our commitments, rather than the other way around.

We will view new commitments in the light of a careful assessment of our own national interests and those of other countries, of the specific threats to those interests, and of our capacity to counter those threats at an acceptable risk and cost.

We have been guided by these concepts during the past year in our dealings with free nations throughout the world.

—In Europe, our policies embody precisely the three principles of a durable peace: partnership, continued strength to defend our common interests when challenged, and willingness to negotiate differences with adversaries.

—Here in the Western Hemisphere we seek to strengthen our special relationship with our sister republics through a new program of action for progress in which all voices are heard and none predominates.

—In Asia, where the Nixon Doctrine was enunciated, partnership will have special meaning for our policies—as evidenced by our strengthened ties with Japan. Our cooperation with Asian nations will be enhanced as they cooperate with one another and develop regional institutions.

—In Vietnam, we seek a just settlement which all parties to the conflict, and all Americans, can support. We are working closely with the South Vietnamese to strengthen their ability to defend themselves. As South Vietnam grows stronger, the other side will, we hope, soon realize that it becomes ever more in their interest to negotiate a just peace.

—In the Middle East, we shall continue to work with others to establish a possible framework within which the parties to the Arab-Israeli conflict can negotiate the complicated and difficult questions at issue. Others must join us in recognizing that a settlement will require sacrifices and restraints by all concerned.

—Africa, with its historic ties to so many of our own citizens, must always retain a significant place in our partnership with the new nations. Africans will play the major role in fulfilling their just aspirations—an end to racialism, the building of new nations, freedom from outside interference, and cooperative economic development. But we will add our efforts to theirs to help realize Africa's great potential.

—In an ever more interdependent world economy, American foreign policy will emphasize the freer flow of capital and goods between nations. We are proud to have participated in the successful cooperative effort which created Special Drawing Rights,[17] a form of international money which will help insure the stability of the monetary structure on which the continued expansion of trade depends.

—The great effort of economic development must engage the cooperation of all nations. We are carefully studying the specific goals of our economic assistance programs, and how most effectively to reach them.[18]

—Unprecedented scientific and technological advances as well as explosions in population, communications, and knowledge require new forms of international cooperation. The United Nations, the symbol of international partnership, will receive our continued strong support as it marks its 25th Anniversary.[19]

2. America's Strength

The second element of a durable peace must be America's strength. Peace, we have learned, cannot be gained by good will alone.

In determining the strength of our defenses, we must make precise and crucial judgments. We should spend no more than is necessary. But there is an irreducible minimum of essential military security: for if we are less strong than necessary, and if the worst happens, there will be no domestic society to look after. The magnitude of such a catastrophe, and the reality of the opposing military power that could threaten it, present a risk which requires of any President the most searching and careful attention to the state of our defenses.

The changes in the world since 1945 have altered the context and requirements of our defense policy. In this area, perhaps more than in any other, the need to re-examine our approaches is urgent and constant.

---

[17] For background of the agreement on special drawing rights see *Documents, 1965*, pp. 419–435; same, *1966*, pp. 459–467; same, *1967*, pp. 458–461; same, *1968–69*, pp. 509–515.
[18] Cf. Documents 95, 97–98.
[19] Cf. Documents 73–74.

The last 25 years have seen a revolution in the nature of military power. In fact, there has been a series of transformations—from the atomic to the thermonuclear weapon, from the strategic bomber to the intercontinental ballistic missile, from the surface missile to the hardened silo and the missile-carrying submarine, from the single to the multiple warhead, and from air defense to missile defense. We are now entering an era in which the sophistication and destructiveness of weapons present more formidable and complex issues affecting our strategic posture.

The last 25 years have also seen an important change in the relative balance of strategic power. From 1945 to 1949, we were the only nation in the world possessing an arsenal of atomic weapons. From 1950 to 1966, we possessed an overwhelming superiority in strategic weapons. From 1967 to 1969, we retained a significant superiority. Today, the Soviet Union possesses a powerful and sophisticated strategic force approaching our own. We must consider, too, that Communist China will deploy its own intercontinental missiles during the coming decade, introducing new and complicating factors for our strategic planning and diplomacy.

In the light of these fateful changes, the Administration undertook a comprehensive and far-reaching reconsideration of the premises and procedures for designing our forces. We sought—and I believe we have achieved—a rational and coherent formulation of our defense strategy and requirements for the 1970's.

The importance of comprehensive planning of policy and objective scrutiny of programs is clear:

—Because of the lead-time in building new strategic systems, the decisions we make today substantially determine our military posture—and thus our security—five years from now. This places a premium on foresight and planning.

—Because the allocation of national resources between defense programs and other national programs is itself an issue of policy, it must be considered on a systematic basis at the early stages of the national security planning process.

—Because we are a leader of the Atlantic Alliance, our doctrine and forces are crucial to the policy and planning of NATO [North Atlantic Treaty Organization]. The mutual confidence that holds the allies together depends on understanding, agreement, and coordination among the 15 sovereign nations of the Treaty.

—Because our security depends not only on our own strategic strength, but also on cooperative efforts to provide greater security for everyone through arms control, planning weapons systems and planning for arms control negotiations must be closely integrated.

For these reasons, this Administration has established procedures for the intensive scrutiny of defense issues in the light of overall national priorities.[20] We have re-examined our strategic forces; we have reassessed our general purpose forces; and we have engaged in the most painstaking preparation ever undertaken by the United States Government for arms control negotiations.

3. *Willingness to Negotiate—An Era of Negotiation*

Partnership and strength are two of the pillars of the structure of a durable peace. Negotiation is the third. For our commitment to peace is most convincingly demonstrated in our willingness to negotiate our points of difference in a fair and businesslike manner with the Communist countries.

We are under no illusions. We know that there are enduring ideological differences. We are aware of the difficulty in moderating tensions that arise from the clash of national interests. These differences will not be dissipated by changes of atmosphere or dissolved in cordial personal relations between statesmen. They involve strong convictions and contrary philosophies, necessities of national security, and the deep-seated differences of perspectives formed by geography and history.

The United States, like any other nation, has interests of its own, and will defend those interests. But any nation today must define its interests with special concern for the interests of others. If some nations define their security in a manner that means insecurity for other nations, then peace is threatened and the security of all is diminished. This obligation is particularly great for the nuclear superpowers on whose decisions the survival of mankind may well depend.

The United States is confident that tensions can be eased and the danger of war reduced by patient and precise efforts to reconcile conflicting interests on concrete issues. Coexistence demands more than a spirit of good will. It requires the definition of positive goals which can be sought and achieved cooperatively. It requires real progress toward resolution of specific differences. This is our objective.

As the Secretary of State said on December 6: [21]

---

[20] Cf. Document 4.
[21] *Documents, 1968–69*, p. 177.

"We will continue to probe every available opening that offers a prospect for better East-West relations, for the resolution of problems large or small, for greater security for all.

"In this the United States will continue to play an active role in concert with our allies."

This is the spirit in which the United States ratified the Non-Proliferation Treaty [22] and entered into negotiation with the Soviet Union on control of the military use of the seabeds,[23] on the framework of a settlement in the Middle East,[24] and on limitation of strategic arms. This is the basis on which we and our Atlantic allies have offered to negotiate on concrete issues affecting the security and future of Europe, and on which the United States took steps last year to improve our relations with nations of Eastern Europe. This is also the spirit in which we have resumed formal talks in Warsaw with Communist China.[25] No nation need be our permanent enemy.

AMERICA'S PURPOSE

These policies were conceived as a result of change, and we know they will be tested by the change that lies ahead. The world of 1970 was not predicted a decade ago, and we can be certain that the world of 1980 will render many current views obsolete.

The source of America's historic greatness has been our ability to see what had to be done, and then to do it. I believe America now has the chance to move the world closer to a durable peace. And I know that Americans working with each other and with other nations can make our vision real.

*   *   *

---

[22] Cf. note 5 to Document 7.
[23] Documents 13–14.
[24] Document 29.
[25] Cf. note 6 to Document 1.

(3) *Continuity and Change: Address by Secretary of State William P. Rogers Before the National Foreign Policy Conference for Editors and Broadcasters, Washington, D.C., January 15, 1970.*[26]

(Complete Text)

In this first year the Nixon administration has put its own stamp on United States foreign policy. It is a mix of continuity and change.

There is a necessity for continuity in our foreign policy which derives from the fact that we are the world's greatest power. Nothing can relieve us of the inescapable responsibilities that go with that status. Certainly one of the most stabilizing influences in world affairs today is that other nations, friendly and not so friendly, take it for granted that the United States will live up to its obligations. Without the element of continuity in basic United States foreign policy, world affairs would be much more unstable and dangerous.

Yet there must be change, too, because world events require a dynamic foreign policy. When this administration took office, our participation in the war in Viet-Nam had come to pervade and color the whole of our foreign policy. In fact, it consumed much of the time and energy of our top leaders. The alternatives seemed to be either to negotiate a settlement or to go on fighting indefinitely.

It was clear that we needed another approach. President Nixon decided that our policy should be to negotiate a settlement or, if that were not possible, to transfer the responsibility for combat activities to the South Vietnamese in a way which would assist them to achieve self-determination. As you know, that has come to be known as Vietnamization, and we are cautiously optimistic about its success. It will be carried out until all combat forces and ultimately other forces have been withdrawn or until Hanoi decides to work out a peace through negotiation which will give the people of South Viet-Nam the right of free choice.

President Nixon's program to end American participation in combat in Viet-Nam is irreversible. We are training and equipping the forces of the Republic of Viet-Nam to take care of themselves as we transfer to them the whole of the combat role. There is a growing confidence in South Viet-Nam that this can be done. Assuming its success—and our policy makes this assumption—the result will be valuable for the future security of the area: a feeling of independence and self-reliance not just in South Viet-Nam but in Southeast Asia as a whole.

We believe we are on the right track toward national release from total preoccupation with this one area of foreign affairs.

If United States foreign policy a year ago was overly concentrated on Viet-Nam, the foreign policy of the Soviet Union was equally preoccupied with the quarrel with Communist China. As far as we can see this is still the case, and there is no reason to believe that it is likely to change dramatically in the near future.

It therefore seemed wise to us to make known what our position was with respect to the Sino-Soviet border dispute and the general tensions between those Governments. This we have done.

We have made it clear that we have no intention of attempting to exploit their differences.

We intend to negotiate with the Soviet Union, hopefully in a meaningful way, in pursuit of common ground and mutual advantage.

We also intend to seek ways to have better relations with Communist China. Consequently, we are pleased that we now have an agreement to meet in Warsaw on January 20.[27]

To have better relations with the Soviet Union and with Communist China, we believe, would be in our national interest, and our policy is to seek sensible ways to accomplish this. The fact that a Sino-Soviet conflict exists is strictly their affair, but it should not be a restraint on our efforts to improve relations with both.

I think I should mention two other powerful nations in the world which are making new contributions to the dynamics of world affairs.

The first is Japan. Japan has become the third industrial power of the world. She is ready to play a part in the affairs of the Asian and Pacific community of nations more commensurate with that status. In recognition of this fact our administration decided to return Okinawa to Japan in 1972.[28] This historic decision should be looked upon as the closing act of the postwar period of United States–Japanese relations. Our relations with Japan now enter a new stage of close and friendly cooperation at the beginning of a new decade.

The Pacific community provides a bright picture. The highest

27 Cf. note 6 to Document 1.
28 Cf. *Documents, 1968–69*, pp. 336–341.

rates of sustained economic growth in the world are found today in Japan, Korea, Taiwan, and Thailand. The picture in Indonesia is most encouraging. Cooperative regional organizations in the Pacific area have come into being; and as I have indicated, the new strength and energy of Japan is an outstanding factor in that regional picture.

The fourth most productive economy in the world is the Federal Republic of Germany. There is a new government in Bonn [29] with which we have excellent relations, both bilaterally and within NATO.

The German Government is seeking in every practical way to reduce the tensions that made the German question the most dangerous of the cold-war issues. The North Atlantic Council serves as a good forum for close consultation on policies and methods of improving relationships with the countries of Eastern Europe. But if East-West relations are to return to a more normal state, Germany obviously must play a major role in that process. The present German Government is engaged in an effort to do this in consultation with, and with the support of, its allies, including, of course, the United States.[30]

These brief remarks serve to highlight the fact that in this next decade glacial changes will undoubtedly occur. The Nixon administration's general approach to foreign policy as we enter the decade of the seventies is:

First, to try to move from stalemated confrontations to active negotiations on outstanding issues with the Soviet Union and others;

Second, to encourage other more developed nations, and especially in the framework of regional organizations, to assume greater responsibility for leadership and initiative in the affairs of the major regions of the world;

Third, to lower our voice and our visibility on the world stage to accord with what we intend to be a more moderate dialogue and a greater degree of partnership with our friends and allies; and

Fourth, to make it clear that the United States has no intention of renouncing its treaty obligations, of withdrawing from the international scene, or of failing to play a proper and active role in the constant search for security and for a better life for all of mankind.

---

[29] A two-party coalition government, headed by Social Democrat Willy Brandt, was inducted October 22, 1969 following the Bundestag elections held September 28, 1969.
[30] Cf. Document 23.

On the negotiating front, we have successfully launched the strategic arms limitations talks; [31] we have agreed with the Soviet Union on a draft treaty banning the emplacement of weapons of mass destruction on the ocean floor; [32] we are seeking to discuss arrangements to normalize access to Berlin; [33] we have negotiated intensively, but with disappointing results so far, to find a framework on which the parties may negotiate a lasting settlement in the Middle East; [34] and we have indicated a willingness to negotiate with the Warsaw Pact nations on mutual and balanced reduction of forces in Europe. [35]

We shall make some proposals next week to the Communist Chinese in Warsaw in the hope that we can improve relations with them.

On the second point—encouraging greater responsibility for regional leadership by the nations of the area—we have moved forward in Europe, Asia, and Latin America.

To our NATO allies, President Nixon has offered to consult more on subjects of mutual concern. [36] This has eliminated the fear of unilateral action, and our Western allies are appreciative.

In Asia our friends and allies have agreed that henceforth, if it should be required, they will provide the necessary military forces to cope with subversion, both internally and externally promoted, with the United States providing appropriate support by way of equipment and training, et cetera. We have agreed, too, that the proper role of the United States is that of partner and participant in regional activities, for which Pacific and Asian countries will undertake initiatives and provide leadership. This is the way we want it and the way the Asians want it.

In Latin America a comparable development has taken place. In accord with our neighbors to the south, we are proceeding on the basis of a more mature and a more equal partnership. Our hemisphere friends have accepted responsibility for providing a leading voice in inter-American affairs and in setting their own course in the struggle for economic development and social reform.

I have not mentioned Africa, but next month I shall visit Africa. [37] I will in particular discuss with African leaders their views on how best to find a steady, long-term basis for relating

---

[31] Cf. note 5 to Document 1.
[32] Document 13.
[33] *Documents, 1968–69*, p. 157, note 65; see further note 9 to Document 20.
[34] Cf. Document 29.
[35] *Documents, 1968–69*, pp. 133–134.
[36] Same, p. 144.
[37] Document 55.

our interest in helping them raise standards of living to their own efforts.

Overall, I believe that the United States, under the leadership of President Nixon, has had a successful year in the conduct of its foreign affairs.

Finally, I want to underscore that the foreign policy of this administration cannot be characterized as tending toward isolationism—as a curtailment of interests or a shedding of responsibility in world affairs. We cannot retreat from a world in which we will increasingly be involved, however longingly some might glance in that direction.

What we *can* do and what we propose to do is to alter the character of our involvement, to make that involvement more consistent with present-day realities, to give it a sound footing for the long term. We can be less intrusive and less domineering. We can have a lower profile. We can speak with a less strident voice. By working more effectively with other nations, by conducting our international affairs with a bit more modesty, we hope that we may become more successful and effective partners in the search for peace and security in the world during this last third of the 20th century.

B. Foreign Policy and the National Budget.

(4) The Budget for Fiscal Year 1971: Message by President Nixon to the Congress, February 2, 1970.[38]

(Excerpts)

To the Congress of the United States:

I have pledged to the American people that I would submit a balanced budget for 1971. This is particularly necessary because the cost of living has been rising rapidly for the past five years.

The budget I send to you today—the first for which I bear full responsibility as President—fulfills that pledge.

Outlays are estimated at $200.8 billion, with receipts at $202.1 billion, yielding a surplus of $1.3 billion.

This anti-inflationary budget begins the necessary process of reordering our national priorities. For the first time in two full

---

[38] House Document 91–240, Part 1, 91st Congress, 2nd session; text from *Weekly Compilation of Presidential Documents*, February 9, 1970, pp. 106–119. For the context see *The United States in World Affairs, 1970*, Introduction to Chapter 10.

decades, the Federal Government will spend more money on human resource programs than on national defense.

A budget must be a blueprint for the future. In the 1971 budget, I seek not only to address today's needs, but also to anticipate tomorrow's challenges. Only with a plan that looks to the years ahead can we gain control over the long-range use of our resources, and mark a clear course for meeting national goals. Most worthwhile objectives are costly. Therefore, we must pursue our purposes in an orderly fashion, measuring our efforts to accord with the budget resources likely to be available.

A balanced plan for resource allocation does not require Federal domination. On the contrary, by placing greater reliance on private initiative and State and local governments, we can more effectively mobilize our total resources to achieve national purposes over the long run.

This comprehensive perspective was instrumental in shaping the 1971 budget.

With this budget we will move ahead to:

—Meet our *international responsibilities* by seeking an honorable peace in Vietnam, by maintaining sufficient military power to deter potential aggressors, by exploring with the Soviet Union possible limitations on strategic arms, and by encouraging multilateral aid, expanded trade, and a greater measure of economic self-help for developing nations of the world.

—Help restore *economic stability* by holding down spending in order to provide another budget surplus and to relieve pressure on prices—and to achieve that surplus without income or excise tax increases.

—Launch a major effort to improve *environmental quality* by attacking air and water pollution, by providing more recreation opportunities, and by developing a better understanding of our environment and man's impact upon it.

—Inaugurate the *Family Assistance Program,* fundamentally reforming outmoded welfare programs, by encouraging family stability and providing incentives for work and training.

—Provide major advances in our programs to *reduce crime.*

—Foster *basic reforms* in Government programs and processes by making entire program systems operate more effectively, and by encouraging responsible decentralization of decision-making.

The proposals in this budget are important steps toward these goals. Even so, taking these steps requires difficult choices.

The need to choose among alternative uses of our resources is a basic fact of budgetary life. In the past few years, too many hard choices were avoided. Inflation was permitted to steal purchasing power from us all, and to work particular hardship on the poor and the millions of Americans who live on fixed incomes, as well as on the housing industry, small businesses, and State and local governments.

Indeed, the willingness to make hard choices is the driving force behind my 1971 budget proposals.

*   *   *

A STRATEGY FOR THE SEVENTIES

I am pleased to present a budget that demonstrates a shift in priorities; we now begin to turn in new directions.

CHANGING PRIORITIES.—About 41% of estimated outlays in the 1971 budget will be devoted to human resources—spending for education and manpower, health, income security, and veterans benefits and services. Spending for national defense, despite continued improvements in our military forces, will claim a smaller percentage of the budget than in any year since 1950. Although still comparatively small, other major programs of this Administration—pollution control, crime reduction, transportation, and housing—are planned to grow substantially in the years ahead.

*   *   *

THE SEARCH FOR PEACE

We seek a world in which all men can live in peace, freedom, and dignity.

PEACE AND NATIONAL SECURITY.—The best way to achieve this goal is through maintaining sufficient strength to deter aggression—and cope with it where necessary—supported by effective and verifiable international agreements, and by collective security and cooperation.

One of my first official acts as President was to direct a comprehensive and orderly review of our national security policies and the programs required to carry them out.[39] This was the most thorough re-examination of its type ever undertaken, designed to bring our strategies, forces, and priorities into proper balance.

This budget reflects the transition from old policies and strategies to the new ones stemming from our review. I have:

[39] Cf. White House announcement, February 7, 1969, in *Weekly Compilation of Presidential Documents,* February 10, 1969, pp. 232–233.

—Initiated a plan designed to bring a just and honorable peace to Vietnam. Our approach involves a two-pronged effort to negotiate in Paris and to effect an orderly transfer to the South Vietnamese of the major responsibilities the United States has assumed in that country.[40] We will do so in a manner that will help maintain that country's right of self-determination. While negotiations have been disappointing, progress in Vietnamization has been encouraging and has enabled Vietnamese forces to assume a greater burden on the battlefield. In accord with this plan, I have already announced a series of troop withdrawals that will reduce our authorized forces in Vietnam by 115,500 below that existing when this Administration took office.[41]

—Begun strategic arms limitations talks with the Soviet Union.[42]

—Signed the Nuclear Nonproliferation Treaty.[43]

—Begun construction of the Safeguard missile defense system, intended to protect the United States from limited nuclear attacks, including an accidental missile launch, and to protect some of our retaliatory forces.[44]

—Renounced biological weapons and initiated disposal of existing bacteriological weapons.[45]

—Appointed an advisory commission to develop a comprehensive plan for eliminating the draft and moving toward an all-volunteer military force.[46]

—Signed into law my proposal for draft reform, to shorten the maximum period of draft vulnerability to one year, thereby reducing uncertainty for millions of our young men.[47]

Looking to the future, both our strategy and forces must be designed to honor our international commitments and to insure our national security. We must make realistic and continuing assessments of the programs required to support these objectives.

[40] *Documents, 1968–69,* pp. 261–263.
[41] Same, p. 290.
[42] Cf. note 5 to Document 1.
[43] Cf. note 5 to Document 12.
[44] Cf. *Documents, 1968–69,* pp. 83–87.
[45] Same, pp. 106–109; see further Document 15, below.
[46] The report of the President's Commission on an All-Volunteer Armed Force, headed by former Defense Secretary Thomas S. Gates, was released February 21, 1970. Text of President Nixon's message to Congress, April 23, 1970, outlining draft reforms in *Weekly Compilation of Presidential Documents,* April 27, 1970, pp. 571–575.
[47] Selective Service Amendment Act of 1969 (Public Law 91–125, approved November 26, 1969).

The strategy of this Administration, as I stated at Guam,[48] is based on the expectation that our allies will shoulder substantial responsibility for their own defense. With this posture, we can safely meet our defense requirements with fewer resources.

International Relations.—Early in my Administration, we sought to identify more effective ways to encourage international development and stability with a limited availability of Government funds.

I have concluded that the answers lie in greater initiative by the countries we assist, more trade, a larger role for private enterprise, and increased reliance on cooperative, multilateral efforts. I strongly support international organizations as effective channels for development assistance.

We are urging all industrialized countries to reduce trade barriers against products of special importance to developing countries. I urge enactment of trade legislation now before the Congress that would reduce trade barriers and provide more equitable adjustment assistance to industries, companies, and workers injured by import competition.[49]

We are encouraging private enterprise, both locally based and American, to bring its dynamism to the challenge of economic development. To enlarge the role of private enterprise still further, I will establish the Overseas Private Investment Corporation—a recommendation already approved by the Congress.[50]

Trade and private enterprise by themselves are not sufficient. I am also proposing budget authority of $1.8 billion for the Agency for International Development to provide direct aid to developing countries. I will make further proposals to strengthen our aid programs based on a review by my task force on foreign aid.[51]

*   *   *

Space.—Man has ventured to the moon and returned—an awesome achievement.

In determining the proper pace for future space activities, we must carefully weigh the potential benefits of:

[48] Cf. note 4 to Document 1.
[49] Cf. Document 91. For President Nixon's message on the proposed Trade Act of 1969 see *Documents, 1968–69*, pp. 522–530.
[50] In the Foreign Assistance Act of 1969 (Public Law 91–175, approved December 30, 1969); text of the President's foreign aid message of May 28, 1969 in *Documents, 1968–69*, pp. 543–551.
[51] Document 95.

- Scientific research by unmanned spacecraft;
- Continued exploration of the solar system, including manned exploration of the planets; and
- The application of space and aeronautics technology to the direct benefit of mankind.

I have reviewed many exciting alternatives for the future. Consistent with other national priorities, we shall seek to extend our capability in space—both manned and unmanned. I intend to do this within total space outlays 12% smaller than in 1970. In our current efforts, we will continue to stress additional uses of space technology. Our actions will make it possible to begin plans for a manned expedition to Mars.

*   *   *

Conclusion

We have begun to travel a new road.

I am confident that this new road will lead us to an honorable peace in Southeast Asia and toward peace and freedom in the years ahead. As we travel that road of responsibility, our economy will overcome its inflationary fever and return to a sustainable rate of growth.

Domestic programs are being reshaped and revitalized to reach and involve the individual American. Guiding us in this effort are five central themes, which are essential elements of the New Federalism:

—An awareness of the growing desire for fairness and equal opportunity in every facet of American life;

—A recognition of the importance of the interests of the individual in the decisions that determine his destiny;

—An emphasis on restructuring basic program systems to ensure that Government efforts deliver the full measure of their promise;

—An understanding that national unity is needed for the setting of goals, and national diversity must be respected in the administration of services; and

—A willingness to return power to the people and dignity to the individual, through financial help to State and local governments and renewed reliance on private, voluntary action.

This budget reflects these principles; it expresses the *shared purposes* of the Nation.

This budget imparts to our goals a sense of timing and commit-

ment appropriate to a vigorous, free people seeking constantly
to expand the Nation's potential and improve its performance.

Richard Nixon

February 2, 1970

(5) *Defense Requirements and National Priorities: Statement
by Secretary of Defense Melvin R. Laird Before a Joint
Session of the Senate Armed Services Committee and the
Senate Subcommitte on Department of Defense Appropriations, February 20, 1970.*[52]

(Excerpts)

*   *   *

F. approach to the FY 1971 defense program and budget

The programs we are proposing for FY 1971 are essentially
designed to preserve our own military capabilities and flexibility
during the transition period financed by the FY 1971 Defense
budget. We have made no irrevocable decisions on the future
composition of our strategic, general purpose, or mobility forces.
We know that under any kind of sensible national security program, we will need major portions of the forces that are already
in existence. The precise mix of those forces depends on many
uncertain factors; some of them are subject to our control,
others are outside our influence. SALT [Strategic Arms Limitation Talks] [53] and the Paris Peace Talks [54] are the most obvious
factors that contribute to this uncertainty. Other factors include:

(1) The progress of our Vietnamization policy;
(2) The need for detailed consultations with our allies; and
(3) The need to conclude additional wide-ranging studies on
such matters as the balance of forces between NATO and the
Warsaw Pact.

During the coming year, we will continue to review what
adjustments in military strength will be required for ourselves

---

[52] *Fiscal Year 1971 Defense Program and Budget: A Statement by Secretary
of Defense Melvin R. Laird, February 20, 1970* (U.S. Department of Defense Press Release, Washington: G.P.O., 1970), pp. 1–167; quoted material,
pp. 13–20.
[53] Cf. note 5 to Document 1.
[54] Cf. Document 44.

and our allies to make our new strategy effective. Many of these adjustments will be reflected in our five-year Defense program next year.

As I indicated earlier, a number of significant changes are being made in our PPBS procedures and, although we have not found it feasible in this Defense Report to project our proposed forces and programs beyond FY 1971, we have already started the FY 1972–76 PPBS cycle. We confidently expect to be in a position next year to present to the Congress our proposed five-year Defense program.[55]

An important change under the new PPBS (Planning-Programming-Budgeting System) concerns the role of the Joint Chiefs of Staff (JCS) and the Services. In contrast to the practice of the preceding Administration, we are now providing the JCS and the Services explicit strategy and fiscal guidance, prior to the submission of their final force recommendations for the forthcoming five-year program and annual budget. In the past, they were placed in a position where they had to submit their force recommendations without reference to any explicit fiscal guidance. This, in large part, explains why, in the past, the JCS proposals always cost $20 to $30 billion more than the annual Defense budgets recommended by the Secretary of Defense and approved by the President.

The wide divergency between the JCS recommendations and the annual Defense budget had long troubled me as a member of the Congress. It was perfectly clear to me that the JCS and the Secretary of Defense were proceeding on two entirely different planning assumptions. As a result, the efforts of the JCS in the preparation of their recommendations were largely wasted as far as the final budget submitted to the Congress was concerned. It seemed to me that the work of the JCS had to be more fully integrated into the entire PPB System, particularly in relating our military strategy and force plans to the overall fiscal objectives of the Government. I believe that the new PPB procedures will help accomplish this purpose, since they will enable the JCS and the Services to make timely adjustments in their initial force recommendations in light of our fiscal guidance. The final JCS and Service proposals can then serve as a realistic basis for the preparation of the next five-year Defense program and annual budget.

[55] *Toward a National Security Strategy of Realistic Deterrence: Statement by Secretary of Defense Melvin R. Laird Before the Senate Armed Services Committee on the FY 1972–1976 Defense Program and the 1972 Defense Budget, March 15, 1971* (U.S. Department of Defense Press Release, March 1, 1971, Washington: G.P.O., 1971).

Pending the full implementation of the new PPB System, which will be completed this year, we have had to adopt some interim arrangements for the development of the FY 1971 Defense program and budget. It became evident by the late summer of last year that major reductions would have to be made in the FY 1970 Budget, and that the conditions which made these reductions necessary would also affect the FY 1971 Budget. Those conditions included:

(1) The determination of President Nixon to reorder our allocation of Federal resources to bring them in line with changing national priorities;

(2) The crucial need to bring inflation under control and the President's dedication to this objective; and

(3) The clear intent of Congress to make major reductions in Defense spending.

Therefore, we modified the FY 1971 segment of the previously-approved five-year Defense program to reflect all adjustments the Department and Congress were expected to make in the FY 1970 Budget. We then estimated the cost of the modified FY 1971 program. The results were provided to the Army, Navy, Air Force, Marine Corps, and the Defense Agencies as fiscal guidance for preparing their FY 1971 Budget requests. In addition, each of the Military Departments was given tentative force objectives for FY 1971. It was understood that the Departments could propose changes in force levels within the fiscal guidance.

The Military Departments and Defense Agencies submitted their program proposals and budget estimates to the Office of the Secretary of Defense in early October 1969, together with their proposed force changes. The budget estimates were reviewed jointly by my staff and the Bureau of the Budget staff, as has been the practice for many years. The force changes were reviewed by the Joint Chiefs of Staff and by elements of my own staff. Mr. [David] Packard [Deputy Secretary of Defense] and I, in full consultation with all of our principal military and civilian advisors, then reviewed the outstanding issues and made final decisions on our FY 1971 program and budget recommendations.

These recommendations, plus those of the Defense Program Review Committee on major issues involved in the FY 1971 Defense program and budget, were submitted directly to the President. The President, of course, made the final decisions.

The FY 1971 Defense Budget transmitted to the Congress by the President totals $71.3 billion in New Obligational Authority (NOA) and $71.8 billion in outlays, excluding any pay increases that may be enacted by the present session of the Congress. This is $11.9 billion in NOA and $9.8 billion in outlays below that requested by the Johnson Administration last year for FY 1970 (including the pay raise effective July 1, 1969).

It is interesting to note that on a Total Obligational Authority basis, the FY 1971 Defense Budget recommended by the President is only $5.4 billion less than the amount requested by the Military Departments and Defense Agencies under the fiscal guidance I discussed earlier. The Military Services did not make substantially larger requests such as frequently advanced in past years under their prevailing guidance. You may recall that I told some of the Congressional Committees last year that I might well go down in history as the Secretary of Defense who made the smallest reduction in the Service requests, at least in the last decade. In fact, under my guidance the Services and Defense Agencies prepared programs which cost less for FY 1971 than the Johnson Administration asked of Congress for the FY 1970 Budget. I believe it is fair to say that this new and more realistic approach has produced as sound and reasonable a Defense Budget as any in the last decade, and without the wasted effort.

As I pointed out in my first appearance as Secretary of Defense before a Congressional Committee last year, I understand the role of the Congress and its Committees in overseeing the vast enterprise of the Executive Branch, and I will do everything in my power to cooperate with the Committees in the discharge of their responsibilities. Accordingly, throughout the preparation of the FY 1971 program and Budget, we tried to take into account all of the views and judgments expressed by the Congress last year in the FY 1970 Defense Authorization and Appropriations Acts [56] and the related Committee reports.

Many of the more important issues raised by the Congress are discussed in following sections of this report. Others will be discussed by subsequent Defense Department and Service witnesses, or in supporting documents furnished directly to the Committee. These include, for example, the creation of a new position of an Assistant Secretary for Health and Environmental Affairs. Regardless of where these issues may be discussed, I can assure the Committee that the Defense Department will take appropriate action on each of the matters set forth in last year's legislation and the accompanying reports, or be prepared to explain why no action can be taken. I have asked the Service Secretaries and the Directors of Defense Agencies to personally monitor our responses to issues raised by Congress in their respective areas of

[56] Public Law 91–171, approved December 30, 1969.

responsibility. Mr. Packard and I will personally review all important policy matters pertaining to the Defense Department as a whole. Follow-up action has already been started, but because of the late enactment of much of this legislation only preliminary progress reports are as yet available on many of these items.

*   *   *

I welcome the increased public interest in national security and defense activities, reflected by the increasing attention these matters now receive from Congress. Public criticism frequently improves efficiency. Some public criticism in certain areas, however, sometimes inhibits progress toward the very goals the critics profess to support.

Let me give one example: The Nixon Doctrine [57] is designed to shift our contribution to the defense of our friends in Asia to greater material rather than manpower support from the United States. These changes must be effected with the understanding of the allies with whom we have these obligations. Yet public demands for United States renunciation of its obligations, or abandonment of them forthwith, make it quite difficult to convince our allies that our change in policy is a move toward further sharing of burdens, and not, in fact, an abandonment of our obligations. Thus, criticism and exposure of the details of particular United States obligations to other nations can sometimes inhibit the very changes we are attempting to make—changes which would more nearly conform to the objectives the critics themselves seek.

I also should mention the effect of the lengthy authorization-appropriations process on defense operations. I fully appreciate the necessity of careful and thorough consideration of Defense authorization and appropriations requests. But I also feel an obligation to mention the serious concern that I frequently expressed as a member of Congress and that I continue to have about the difficulties created by late appropriations. They severely complicate both defense management and planning. They also add to our costs. Defense programs stretch over many years. It is extremely difficult to prepare budget requests for January presentation to Congress for the fiscal year to follow when, in the middle of the previous December, we still do not have the current year's budget approved. We have an added complication under the Nixon Doctrine. We are endeavoring to reduce the need for American ground combat support by shifting the emphasis to military assistance programs. In this case we did

[57] Cf. note 4 to Document 1.

not even know what Congress would finally approve for the fiscal year 1970 military assistance programs at the time we were submitting the fiscal year 1971 defense budget to Congress.

Unfortunately, "continuing resolutions" are not a substitute for regular appropriations. They impact not only on management and planning, but also on costs. In the early years of a development program, the costs increase markedly from one year to the next, sometimes doubling or tripling. To scale down the program in mid-development to the level of effort of the previous year, as required by continuing resolutions, can disrupt programs and increase total costs. Reprogramming funds later is only a limited remedy because lengthening periods under continuing resolutions severely constrict even this amount of flexibility.

I know that the Members of this Committee and other Members of Congress are aware of these problems and are seeking ways to shorten the authorization-appropriation process or to lengthen the period for which authorizations and appropriations are granted. I hope that as we move into the decade of the 1970s, we can together devise better means for meeting our joint and separate responsibilities for more effective utilization of the defense dollar.

As a final note, Mr. Chairman [John C. Stennis], let me restate to the Committee my conviction that, given the staggering challenges that confronted us one year ago, I believe we have made significant progress in attempting to meet them.

Vietnamization, SALT, and the development of a new national security strategy are concrete manifestations of major progress. The threats from abroad, though growing, continue to be contained for the present at less expense than in recent years, and a new, vigorous attack on our domestic problems has been set in motion.

Furthermore, we have established new machinery that promises to produce more rational decisions in foreign and national security policy, in urban and domestic affairs, and in restoring and maintaining a proper balance between defense and non-defense needs.

Given a sufficiently tranquil world, the Defense Department's objective in the 1970s concerning fiscal matters will be to keep defense spending at such a level that: (1) additional resources will become available for domestic programs; and (2) we will do our share in turning the tide against inflation. In doing this, we must and we will maintain sufficient strength to ensure our ability to deter aggression and meet our Defense needs.

I believe it is obvious that a new balance between defense

and non-defense spending cannot be achieved in one year, or even in two. Transition to a new equilibrium will take time. We made a beginning in 1969 and are continuing the transition into calendar year 1970. We consider our fiscal year 1971 budget another building block in that transition.

The Nixon Administration's program for winding down inflationary defense spending and for reallocating resources to domestic needs have no doubt had an effect on the mood of the country. Not all of the challenges we encountered last year have been met. In the coming year, I hope that closer working relationships with Congress will help us find better, less costly means for meeting our joint and separate responsibilities.

In summary, Mr. Chairman, we have not solved all the hard problems before us as we proceed to implement the programs which we deem necessary for the security of our country in the 1970s. And, of course, we must realize that there is some risk attached to our lowered defense budget at a time when there has not been a similar reduction in the threats we face. As Secretary of Defense, however, I want to assure this Committee that I will not hesitate to recommend any action that may be required to ensure the security of our country and our people should the degree of risk become unacceptable.

We have made a determined effort in planning the FY 1971 Defense budget to be fiscally responsible, to maintain our current basic capability with modernization as appropriate, and to provide the foundation for our work ahead—that of reshaping our military establishment to support our new strategy and our revised national priorities.

Finally, I must state that this is a rock-bottom budget. I believe that the national security would be jeopardized by any further reductions in our FY 1971 Defense budget request. In our testimony throughout the authorization and appropriations processes in the House and Senate, I hope we can convince the Congress that the program presented to you is the right program for the first year of this new decade.

*   *   *

C. Streamlining the Instruments of Diplomacy.

(6) *Diplomacy for the Seventies: A Program of Management Reform for the Department of State.*[58]

    (a) *Report of the Department of State's Task Forces Transmitted by William B. Macomber, Deputy Under Secretary for Administration, to Secretary of State Rogers November 20, 1970.*[59]

(Excerpts)

*   *   *

AN AGENDA OF REFORM

Candor compels the admission that in spite of outstanding achievements by individual officers at all levels, the Department as an organization has sometimes been disappointing in its performance of this important role. The principal cause of this has been its weakness in the area of management capability. Because of the diversity and complexity of our overseas activities, effective coordination calls for a wide range of management skills and management tools. The traditional reliance of Foreign Service officers on experience and intuition is no longer good enough. The diplomacy of the seventies requires a new breed of diplomat-manager, just as able as the best of the old school, but equipped with up-to-date techniques and backed by a Department organized on modern management principles.

In the past, with some notable exceptions, State Department and Foreign Service officers were slow to accept this view. They believed that modern management principles, however essential they might be to the effective operation of other large organizations, were of doubtful applicability to the practice of diplomacy. Consequently, they have not developed the corps of adequately trained and experienced managers and the modern management systems which this role called for, preferring instead to continue relying, often with distinction, on the talent of their gifted personnel. Although their performance in the management of short-term crises has frequently been superb, they have been resistant to efforts to give them a more systematic capacity for determining long-range strategies through an orderly and thorough assess-

[58] For the context see *The United States in World Affairs, 1970,* Section 4.
[59] *Diplomacy for the 70's* (Department of State publication 8551; Washington: G.P.O., 1970); text from *Department of State Bulletin,* December 28, 1970, pp. 775–802.

ment of our national interests and for directing the allocation of our resources in accordance with these strategies.

More recently, a new argument against the need to develop modern diplomat-managers has been advanced. Its proponents assert that even if a need for foreign policy coordination has existed up to now, the new trend toward a reduced U.S. presence abroad reduces this need. Therefore, in undertaking an ambitious program for developing a corps of manager-diplomats, the Department would be meeting in the seventies the challenges of the fifties and sixties.

This argument fails to take account of the fact that, even after the desired reduction in the level of our presence abroad has taken place, the magnitude and multiplicity of our foreign interests will continue to be large. Moreover, with the rapid advance of technology constantly widening the agenda of diplomacy, these interests are likely to be increasingly complex and the necessity of supporting them with limited resources will require difficult decisions among competing interests. There will thus be at least as much need for the State Department to play a strong directing and coordinating role in the seventies as at any time in the past. And since the central task of foreign policy coordination is allocation of resources among competing interests—a key management function—this will place a high premium on strengthening the Department's managerial effectiveness.

It is not only its past failure to develop managers and management systems which has limited the Department's effectiveness as the director and coordinator of our overseas activities. It has relied too long on the "generalist" and has been slow to recruit and develop officers with the wide range of special aptitudes, skills and knowledge which the new diplomacy requires. Too many officers have been reluctant to master the intricacies of the new activities—agriculture, labor, commerce, finance, development economics, science, information and the like—which have become a standard part of our diplomatic operations abroad, and the Department has not done enough to encourage them to do so. This has eroded the confidence of other Federal agencies in the Department's ability to exercise leadership in the conduct of foreign policy.

And while the Department has not adequately mastered the new skills which the new diplomacy calls for, the task forces found that the traditional skills of the old diplomacy were also receiving less emphasis than they deserved. These "core" skills —the ability to negotiate, to observe carefully and report accurately and precisely, to analyze and synthesize—are as critically important today as they ever were. The task forces believed that a stronger effort to improve them was needed.

Finally, despite its efforts to do so, the Department has never entirely succeeded in overcoming the strong pressures toward conformity which have dulled its creative impulse. Like all major bureaucracies, it has sometimes been guilty of excessive caution and a tendency to defend established policy and programs even when their time may have passed. Nor has it always been able adequately to surmount the spirit of parochialism which has tended to isolate it from the main currents of our national life.

These shortcomings were recognized by the task forces as the principal causes of the Department's weakness in the area of management capability. They therefore became the principal items on the agenda of reform which guided the task forces in their work.

*   *   *

SUMMARY

This, in broad outline, is the program which the task forces have proposed for the modernization of the Department of State. What will the Department look like after these reforms have been carried out? In purely organizational terms, the task forces do not envisage that it will look a great deal different than it does now. They have not called for a radical overhaul of the present structure but for more effective use of it.

On the Management Side

To recapitulate: on the management side, they envisage the reorganization of the two key decisionmaking levels in the Department (the Secretary and the Assistant Secretaries) into management centers in which the decisionmaking and management functions are combined. To support the Secretary and the Under Secretaries, there would be a Strategic Management Center incorporating the Department's top officials together with the staffs and the facilities necessary to fulfill the Department's major roles: decisionmaking, management of internal resources, interagency leadership, and evaluation. The Center would have a capacity for providing information and managing its flow; a capacity for investigating and applying new analytical techniques; a planning capacity which would allow it to develop and maintain an "issue bank" on long-term issues, put forth alternatives to bureau recommendations, examine ongoing policies, and relate resource allocation to policy; and a capacity for policy and program evaluation. No new staff units would be required but there would probably have to be some expansion and consolidation of existing units.

To support the Assistant Secretaries, there would be Bureau Management Centers with the same general capacity as the Strategic Management Center but with responsibilities limited to regional and functional matters. In particular, these Bureau Management Centers would have the capacity to coordinate policy and resource allocation and to present alternatives to both existing and proposed policies. To perform these functions, the bureaus would probably need additional staff.

THE PERSONNEL STRUCTURE

The end product of the personnel recommendations of the task forces would be a Foreign Service of the United States commanding a range of skills wide enough to permit it to represent the interests of a broad spectrum of Federal agencies. The personnel system proposed by the task forces envisages a career pattern which would begin with entry after selection through written and oral examination. Before entry, the applicant would have chosen a field of specialization. New officers would be admitted in accordance with more systematically anticipated needs of the Service and the number of officers admitted to each cone would be proportional to the relative size of the cones. New officers would serve in non-tenured status for a period of 2 to 4 years, with at least one assignment abroad during that period in the cone they have chosen. A large majority of the junior officers would then be selected into the Foreign Service officer corps.

Between Class 6 and Class 3, promotion would be essentially semiautomatic. After Class 3, promotion would be by Selection Board. Many careers would end at the FSO-3 level with retirement after 20 years of service, regardless of age. Between Class 6 and Class 3 most assignments would be in the officer's cone of specialization but there would be broadening assignments, especially for those officers with executive potential. The executive potential of all officers would be carefully reviewed at the FSO-4 level and those with a confirmed potential for executive leadership would qualify for executive training at the FSO-3 level.

At the Class 2 and Class 1 levels, most assignments would be to the so-called interfunctional positions, including program direction and executive positions such as deputy chief of mission and country director. There would also be a few assignments to senior specialist positions (economic and political counselors in large missions).

The number of officers promoted and the frequency of promotions would be controlled so that in time the personal rank structure of the Service would be virtually identical with the position structure. The structure of the Foreign Service officer corps, which is now topheavy, would, after a transition period of several years, more nearly approximate a pyramid as the result of reclassification downward of many FSO positions.

Officer positions in the Department and abroad would be under the Foreign Service Act and would be designated for staffing by Foreign Affairs Specialists or Foreign Service officers. The former category would include positions both at home and abroad calling for a high degree of specialization; it would also include, in the Department, positions calling for greater continuity than can be met by a normal Washington duty tour. By the end of the transition period, the Foreign Service Staff officer category would disappear and Foreign Service Staff officers would be converted either to FAS or FSO status. The Foreign Service Staff category would be retained for clerical and other non-officer positions.

Assignments and position classification would be under centralized control. Assignments would be made in closer accord than is possible today with needs dictated by an agreed concept of foreign policy priorities, as well as with the career aspirations of individual officers.

The system would be less rigid and bureaucratic than is now the case. There would be less emphasis on an officer's position in the hierarchy and more on the specialized knowledge that he could bring to the solution of a specific problem. There would be less isolation of the Service from the outside world with personnel moving more freely in and out of the Service. There would be greater emphasis on creativity and on independent expression of views.

BUILDING ON THE PRESENT STRUCTURE

As noted earlier, the task forces have not attempted to reorganize the Department from top to bottom. Indeed, they see no necessity for such drastic surgery. They believe that the present structure of the Department is fundamentally sound and that what is needed is not a new structure but the application of a number of practical measures to make the present structure function more effectively.

The task forces have also carefully avoided recommending

major additions of staff. With a few exceptions, they believe that their recommendations can be carried out with existing staff. What they have sought to do is to set more relevant priorities for existing staff, to place modern management tools in their hands, and to give management greater flexibility in the use of present personnel resources.

REFORM WITHIN THE FOREIGN SERVICE ACT

No major changes in legislation have been proposed. Instead, the recommendations have been cast entirely within the framework of the Foreign Service Act of 1946.[60] The task forces believe that this Act is still fundamentally sound and just as appropriate for the problems of the seventies as it was for the problems of the fifties. Indeed, the versatility of the Act is striking testimony to the farsightedness of its authors.

In some respects, however, the recommendations constitute a departure from the concept of a closed career system and an elite corps of generalists which lies at the heart of the Foreign Service Act of 1946 and which a growing number of Foreign Service officers consider inappropriate in today's world. This fact is particularly evident in the recommendations on openness and in the full acceptance by the task forces of the necessity for a service of specialists.

A NEW SPIRIT IN THE DEPARTMENT

The task forces believe that none of these reforms will mean very much if they are not matched by a new spirit in the Department. What is needed, as one of the reports put it, is "a tremendous effort by all of us to shake off old habits, old ways of doing things, old ways of dealing with each other. What we are proposing is a change of outlook and method." It is not enough to have an increased ability to carry out the President's wishes. Ability must be matched by determination. The traditional mode of reflection and detachment cultivated by diplomats trained in the old school must be reinforced by a more dynamic and aggressive style if the Department is to play the role which the President expects of it.

*   *   *

---

[60] Public Law 724, 79th Congress, 2nd session, approved August 13, 1946; excerpts and related material in *Documents, 1945–1946,* pp. 81–104.

(b) *Statement by Secretary of State Rogers on the Recommendations of the Department of State's Task Forces, Made Public December 8, 1970.*[61]

(Complete Text)

We face a wide variety of daily crises in this building, and obviously the way we deal with them is of very great importance. Yet almost from the beginning of my stewardship I have been convinced that if we can leave behind us an improved and modernized system for dealing with this country's future foreign policy problems, this could well be a more lasting and significant contribution than success in handling of many of the more transitory matters which necessarily occupy most of your attention and mine.

We are fortunate indeed to have such an able group of career professionals in the Department and the Foreign Service. Their dedication and capabilities are unsurpassed by any group I know of anywhere. I concluded that the best way to improve our system was to draw on their unique knowledge of the organization's strengths and weaknesses, and so I called on them to prescribe the remedies.

I am delighted to release today the reports of 13 task forces composed of more than 250 career professionals. They have looked deeply at the problems of our Department, have consulted widely with their colleagues and outside experts, and have recommended a far-reaching program to deal with them.

I believe that the adoption of this program will greatly strengthen the Department of State's ability to deal with the challenges which will surely come in the years ahead.

The next step, therefore, is to see that concrete actions are taken as a result of these recommendations. I have given instructions to start on this task immediately and I shall continue to give this effort my close attention and active support.

[61] Department of State Press Release 339, December 8, 1970; text from *Department of State Bulletin*, December 28, 1970, p. 794.

II.
EAST-WEST RELATIONS:
ARMS CONTROL AND DISARMAMENT

A. United States-Soviet Relations: An Overview.

(7) *Controlling Local Conflicts: Address by Under Secretary of State Elliot L. Richardson Before the Second National Convocation on the Challenge of Building Peace, New York, N.Y., April 29, 1970.*[1]

(Excerpt)

*   *   *

There are many questions on which the United States and the Soviet Union disagree. We are likely to continue to disagree. There is nothing to be gained by pretending that this is not the case. Despite these differences we also have areas of common interest. I should like to concentrate today on how we can maximize one of those areas of common interest: how we can most effectively insulate ourselves against the escalation of local conflicts. Whatever strengthens and promotes this common interest will also serve the cause of peace. To this end I would like to suggest three simultaneous and complementary forms of action.

The first involves acknowledging and developing what I shall refer to as "spheres of restraint"; the second calls for encouraging regional self-policing and the development of regional institutions and capabilities; and the third requires strengthening United Nations mechanisms so that they can more effectively cope with local conflicts.

As I look at the world situation that now seems to be emerging, I see an uneasy equilibrium at the center in which the

[1] Department of State Press Release 133, April 29, 1970; text from *Department of State Bulletin,* May 18, 1970, pp. 628–631. For the context see *The United States in World Affairs, 1970,* Section 8.

crucial element is the U.S.–U.S.S.R. bilateral strategic relationship. In recent years we have both come to recognize the need to give this strategic relationship greater stability.

Significant headway has already been made. Agreements on a partial test ban treaty,[2] the banning of nuclear weapons from Antarctica [3] and from outer space,[4] and the Nuclear Non-proliferation Treaty [5] have been followed by a draft treaty barring weapons of mass destruction from the seabed.[6] The strategic arms limitation talks now underway in Vienna have even greater potential for stabilizing our strategic relationship.[7] Extremely sensitive and complex matters touching upon the vital security of each side are at stake. But if solutions continue to be pursued in the same serious manner in which the talks have begun, we are confident that ways can be found to limit the dangers and costs of the strategic arms race.

Beyond this central strategic equilibrium and destined, I believe, to become increasingly important are complex new configurations of power involving other countries and, in some cases, new regional groupings. In some areas of the world the power of the United States is involved in the local balance; in some areas Soviet power is involved; in other regions we are both involved, directly or indirectly.

Certain regions where both of us are now deeply involved are so important to the central configuration of power that accommodations will require a careful process of negotiation on outstanding issues. Central Europe, for which the NATO ministerial meeting recently proposed mutual and balanced force reductions, is the outstanding example.[8]

---

[2] Treaty Banning Nuclear Weapon Tests in the Atmosphere, in Outer Space and Under Water, signed in Moscow August 5, 1963 and entered into force October 10, 1963. Text in *Documents, 1963*, pp. 130–132.

[3] The Antarctic Treaty, signed in Washington December 1, 1959 and entered into force June 23, 1961; text in *Documents, 1959*, pp. 528–535.

[4] Treaty on Principles Governing the Activities of States in the Exploration and Use of Outer Space, Including the Moon and other Celestial Bodies, opened for signature in Washington, London, and Moscow January 27, 1967 and entered into force October 10, 1967; text in *Documents, 1966*, pp. 391–398.

[5] Treaty on the Non-Proliferation of Nuclear Weapons, signed in Washington, London and Moscow July 1, 1968 and entered into force March 5, 1970; text in *Documents, 1968–69*, pp. 62–68. For President Nixon's remarks on entry into force of the treaty, see Document 12.

[6] Document 13; for text of the U.S.-U.S.S.R. revised draft treaty of October 30, 1969, see *Documents, 1968–69*, pp. 102–106.

[7] Documents 10–11.

[8] *Documents, 1968–69*, pp. 166–173.

Development of "Spheres of Restraint"

In other areas, however, where neither of us is now so heavily committed, progress can be made toward reducing the danger of expanded local conflict by deliberately limiting our involvement. This does not require that we agree on the origin and merits of the conflict in question nor that we forgo all interest in the area. What is required is that we do agree, either tacitly or explicitly, to refrain from any action, direct or indirect, which might disturb its internal equilibrium.

Since the world of the 1970's is not likely to be a placid one, this will not be an easy task. Experience has shown that the process of modernization is inevitably accompanied by convulsion and dislocation. Turmoil and turbulence are thus unfortunately likely to continue to accompany rapid social change in large parts of the world. Peaceful development—economic or political—is a process that has thus far eluded much of mankind.

The temptations, the impatience, and the anger which will be stirred by continuing eruptions and violence in developing areas emphasize the need for major-power abstention. The development of spheres of restraint will require that both major powers recognize that their long-term interests are not furthered by attempts to gain short-term—and often fleeting—advantage.

Each side has its own views as to what constitute current examples of such attempts. I believe, for instance, that the Soviet Union should realize that any immediate gains it might make by attempting to take advantage of the troubled Middle East situation are far outweighed by the danger of stirring up a wider conflict. When in such an area one of us—in this case the U.S.S.R. —involves itself militarily, it is inevitable that the other will take notice and react.

We in the United States, meanwhile, must come to terms with the fact that violent upheaval, however repugnant to our preference for orderly and peaceful change, is going to continue to occur. We must realize that in most such situations U.S. power is neither a desirable nor an effective prescription.

In addition to realizing that we have neither a moral right nor a duty to intervene in every local quarrel, both the United States and the U.S.S.R. must also recognize that our power to deal with such disputes is sharply circumscribed by the new confidence and strength of many of the smaller nations. In many cases, to be sure, our participation—together with such leverage as we can usefully exercise—can help the parties find an acceptable formula for a settlement. This is what we are seeking to do in our discussions on the Middle East. But such efforts should not lead us to believe that an imposed solution, even where we can agree on its basic elements, is a lasting solution. Where persuasion fails, coercion is not an acceptable option.

These perceptions are reflected in the way the Nixon administration is attempting to remold U.S. foreign policy. They can be seen in the more precise manner in which we are now setting the limits of our obligations. As President Nixon has put it, ". . . we have commitments because we are involved. Our interests must shape our commitments, rather than the other way around." [9] Accordingly, we are being more exact in the delineation of those U.S. interests which, when threatened, must call forth a response.

We hope that the Soviet Union is also undertaking a new look at its own real interests around the world to see whether they, too, might not, to advantage, be defined more narrowly. To the extent it does so, the development of spheres of restraint will become an easier task.

*   *   *

B. The Conference of the Committee on Disarmament, Geneva, February-September 1970.

(8) *Report of the Conference of the Committee on Disarmament to the United Nations General Assembly and the United Nations Disarmament Commission, September 11, 1970.*[10]

(Excerpts)

INTRODUCTION

1. The Conference of the Committee on Disarmament submits to the United Nations General Assembly and to the United Nations Disarmament Commission a progress report on the Committee's deliberations on all questions before it for the period 17 February to 3 September 1970, together with the pertinent documents and records.

2. Included in this report is a detailed account of the negotia-

[9] Document 2.
[10] Text from U.N. Document A/8059 (DC/233), September 11, 1970. Annexes not reprinted here, but most of the working papers and statements referred to are reprinted in *Documents on Disarmament, 1970.* For the context see *The United States in World Affairs, 1970,* Section 8.

tions, to which the Committee devoted an important part of its work during 1970, regarding a draft Treaty on the Prohibition of the Emplacement of Nuclear Weapons and Other Weapons of Mass Destruction on the Sea-Bed and the Ocean Floor and in the Subsoil Thereof. The text of the final draft of the Treaty is contained in annex A.[11]

3. This report also includes accounts of the Committee's work during 1970 on the question of a treaty banning underground nuclear weapon tests, the question of chemical and bacteriological (biological) weapons, the question of general and complete disarmament, and other questions.

I. ORGANIZATION OF THE CONFERENCE

A. PROCEDURAL ARRANGEMENTS

4. The Conference reconvened on 17 February 1970.

5. Two sessions were held, the first from 17 February to 30 April 1970 and the second from 16 June to 3 September 1970. During this period the Committee held forty-six formal plenary meetings during which members set forth their Governments' views and recommendations for progress on the questions before the Committee. The Committee also held five informal plenary meetings without records.

6. In addition to the plenary meetings described above, members of the Committee met frequently for informal multilateral consultations on disarmament questions of common interest.

7. The representatives of the Union of Soviet Socialist Republics and the United States of America, in their capacity as Co-Chairmen of the Committee, also held meetings to discuss procedural and substantive questions before the Committee.

B. PARTICIPANTS IN THE CONFERENCE

8. Representatives of the following States continued their participation in the work of the Committee: Argentina, Brazil, Bulgaria, Burma, Canada, Czechoslovakia, Ethiopia, Hungary, India, Italy, Japan, Mexico, Mongolia, Morocco, Netherlands Nigeria, Pakistan, Poland, Romania, Sweden, Union of Soviet Socialist Republics, United Arab Republic, United Kingdom of Great Britain and Northern Ireland, United States of America and Yugoslavia.

---

[11] Document 13.

II. WORK OF THE COMMITTEE DURING 1970

9. In a letter dated 30 January 1970, the Secretary-General of the United Nations transmitted to the Conference of the Committee on Disarmament the following resolutions adopted at the twenty-fourth session of the General Assembly:

Resolution 2602 (XXIV)—Question of general and complete disarmament; [12]

Resolution 2603 (XXIV)—Question of chemical and bacteriological (biological) weapons; [13]

Resolution 2604 (XXIV)—Urgent need for suspension of nuclear and thermonuclear tests; [14]

and also the following resolutions which dealt with disarmament matters:

Resolution 2499 (XXIV)—Celebration of the twenty-fifth anniversary of the United Nations; [15]

Resolution 2605 (XXIV)—Conference of Non-Nuclear-Weapon States.

Members of the Committee were assisted in their examination and analysis of possible disarmament measures by numerous messages, working papers, and other documents that were submitted to the Conference (annexes B and C), and by the plenary statements of Committee members (annex D).

10. The Secretary-General of the United Nations [U Thant] addressed the Conference on 18 February 1970 and called attention to the resolutions adopted by the General Assembly at its twenty-fourth session, the urgent tasks it had entrusted to the Conference and the important role of the Conference in achieving agreement on disarmament measures.

11. In accordance with its provisional agenda, the Committee continued work on the following measures in the field of disarmament:

(a) Further effective measures relating to the cessation of the nuclear arms race at an early date and to nuclear disarmament;

(b) Non-nuclear measures;

(c) Other collateral measures;

(d) General and complete disarmament under strict and effective international control.

[12] *Documents, 1968–69,* pp. 109–115
[13] Same, pp. 119–122.
[14] Same, pp. 122–123.
[15] Same, pp. 477–480.

A. FURTHER EFFECTIVE MEASURES RELATING TO THE CESSATION
OF THE NUCLEAR ARMS RACE AT AN EARLY DATE AND
TO NUCLEAR DISARMAMENT

Special report on the question of a treaty banning underground nuclear weapon tests

12. Having in mind the recommendations of General Assembly resolution 2604 B, members of the Committee continued to work on the question of a treaty banning underground nuclear weapon tests.

13. The great importance of this measure was recognized by members of the Committee in their opening plenary statements.

14. The delegation of the United Kingdom submitted a working paper (CCD/296) on verification of a comprehensive test ban treaty aimed at determining what detection and identification capability could be achieved in support of a comprehensive test ban treaty given the present state of the art in seismology.

15. The United States delegation submitted a working paper (CCD/298) on data from the underground nuclear explosion for peaceful purposes (Project RULISON) which was utilized collaterally for seismic investigation purposes.

16. The Secretary-General circulated to members of the Committee responses to his request, pursuant to General Assembly resolution 2604 A, concerning the provision of certain information in the context of a proposal for the creation of a world-wide exchange of seismological data which would facilitate the achievement of a comprehensive test ban.

17. On 12 August 1970, at the request of the Canadian delegation, the Committee held an informal meeting on the cessation of testing.

18. The delegation of Canada submitted a working paper (CCD/305) on 10 August 1970 which assessed the responses circulated to Committee members by the Secretary-General and analyzed seismological capabilities for detecting and identifying underground nuclear explosions.

19. On 12 August 1970 the delegation of Sweden presented a working paper (CCD/306) on a comparison of two systems for verification of a comprehensive test ban.

20. The delegation of Sweden expressed the belief that while Strategic Arms Limitation Talks (SALT) negotiations continue,[16] the Conference of the Committee on Disarmament should proceed with preparatory work towards a ban on underground testing of nuclear weapons, noting the advisability of

16 Cf. note 5 to Document 1.

underpinning, through such a ban, arms limitation measures that might be achieved through SALT (CCD/PV.487).

21. The United States delegation made clear (CCD/PV.449) its continued support for a comprehensive ban on the testing of nuclear weapons, adequately verified, including provisions for on-site inspection, and reaffirmed its desire to contribute to international co-operation in the improvement of seismic detection and identification capabilities.

22. The Soviet delegation emphasized (CCD/PV.494) the importance of a political decision regarding this measure and pointed out that the Soviet position is based on the belief that the use of a national means of detection for the purpose of control over the prohibition of underground nuclear testing is adequate.

Other measures

23. Many members of the Committee welcomed the entry into force of the Treaty on the Non-Proliferation of Nuclear Weapons on 5 March 1970, and expressed the hope that additional countries would adhere to this Treaty.[17] The representatives of the Union of Soviet Socialist Republics, the United Kingdom and the United States of America submitted as Committee working papers the statements made by the heads of their respective Governments at the ceremonies marking the entry into force of this Treaty (CCD/279/Rev.1, CCD/280 and CCD/281). A statement by the Secretary-General of the United Nations was also submitted (CCD/282).

24. On 10 March 1970 the delegation of Yugoslavia submitted as a working paper (CCD/278) the declaration made by its Government in connexion with the ratification of the Treaty on the Non-Proliferation of Nuclear Weapons.

25. A number of delegations stressed the importance of full implementation of the provisions of the Treaty on the Non-Proliferation of Nuclear Weapons, in particular article VI concerning further negotiations on effective measures relating to cessation of the nuclear arms race and to nuclear disarmament. Delegations noted the importance of the bilateral discussions between the Governments of the Union of Soviet Socialist Republics and the United States of America on the limitation of offensive strategic nuclear weapons delivery systems and systems of defence against ballistic missiles. The delegations of Sweden and Mexico suggested that the Conference of the Committee on Disarmament should consider the nature and contents of a spe-

17 Cf. note 5 to Document 7.

cial international agreement or agreements to be concluded pursuant to the provisions of article V of the Treaty (CCD/PV.450 and 487).

26. Having in mind General Assembly resolution 2602 C, which invited the Conference of the Committee on Disarmament to consider effective methods of control against the use of radiological methods of warfare conducted independently of nuclear explosions and the need for effective methods of control of nuclear weapons that maximize radio-active effects, the Netherlands delegation submitted a working paper (CCD/291) on this subject on 14 July 1970. This paper concluded on the basis of available information that possibilities of radiological warfare do exist theoretically, but do not seem to be of much or even of any practical significance; therefore, it is difficult to see the practical usefulness of discussing measures related to radiological warfare.

B. NON-NUCLEAR MEASURES

Question of chemical and bacteriological (biological) weapons

27. Members of the Committee continued their work with a view to achieving progress on all aspects of the problem of the elimination of chemical and bacteriological (biological) weapons. They took into consideration General Assembly resolution 2603 B, which requested the Conference of the Committee on Disarmament to give urgent consideration to reaching agreement on the prohibitions and other measures referred to in the draft Convention on the Prohibition of the Development, Production and Stockpiling of Chemical and Bacteriological (Biological) Weapons and on the Destruction of Such Weapons submitted to the General Assembly by the delegations of Bulgaria, the Byelorussian Soviet Socialist Republic, Czechoslovakia, Hungary, Mongolia, Poland, Romania, the Ukrainian Soviet Socialist Republic and the Union of Soviet Socialist Republics,[18] the draft Convention for the Prohibition of Biological Methods of Warfare submitted to the Conference by the United Kingdom of Great Britain and Northern Ireland, as well as other proposals.[19]

28. In addition to plenary meetings, informal meetings on this question were held on 22 April, at the request of the delegation of Sweden, and on 5 August 1970, at the request of the delegations

---

[18] Text, dated September 19, 1969, in U.N. Document A/7665, September 19, 1969 (reprinted in *Documents on Disarmament, 1969*, pp. 455–457). For key articles see *Documents, 1968–69*, p. 116 at note 157.

[19] Text, dated August 26, 1969, in *Documents on Disarmament, 1969*, pp. 431–433. For language of key articles see *Documents, 1968–69*, p. 108 at note 136.

of Argentina, Canada, Italy, Japan, the Netherlands, Pakistan and Sweden.

29. The following amendments to the two conventions mentioned above were proposed to the Conference of the Committee on Disarmament:

The delegations of Hungary, Mongolia and Poland suggested amendments (CCD/285) to the socialist delegations' draft Convention providing for complaints of possible violations of its prohibitions to be reported to the United Nations Security Council which would undertake necessary measures to investigate complaints, and submitted a draft Security Council resolution.

The United States delegation proposed (CCD/290) that toxins be added to the agents covered by the prohibitions of the United Kingdom draft Convention.

The delegation of the United Kingdom subsequently introduced a revised text of its draft Convention and accompanying draft Security Council resolution (CCD/255/Rev.2), which took into account the proposal of the United States and a suggestion (CCD/PV.458) made by the Netherlands delegation together with minor drafting amendments.

30. The following proposals were also presented to the Committee:

The delegation of Yugoslavia proposed that all countries consider the possibility of placing, by law, all institutions engaged in chemical and biological weapons research, development and production under civilian administration (CCD/PV.456).

The delegation of Japan suggested (CCD/PV.456) a complaints procedure and an arrangement for investigation by the Secretary-General of the United Nations with the co-operation of international experts. For chemical weapons verification, it proposed procedures based on possible check points in the production cycle (CCD/288) and on statistical reporting and a possible technical method of on-site inspection (CCD/301).

The Swedish delegation suggested (CCD/PV.463) an international verification system for the prohibition of C and B weapon production based on open information with obligatory reporting regarding C and B agents to international agencies and verification by challenge.

The delegation of Mongolia proposed that special government agencies might be established to enforce compliance with prohibitions on C and B weapons in a manner similar to that in the 1961 Single Convention on Narcotic Drugs,[20] and suggested adding to the socialist

[20] Department of State, *United States Treaties and Other International Agreements*, No. 6298, done at New York, March 30, 1961; in force for the United States June 24, 1967.

draft Convention a provision regarding a review conference (CCD/PV.464).

The delegation of Morocco suggested in a working paper (CCD/295) that C and B weapons should be jointly prohibited and their destruction provided for by one instrument; verification procedures for B weapons would be defined in this instrument and B weapons would be totally eliminated on its entry into force; this instrument would define the manner and time-limit for negotiation of a supplementary document on verification procedures for C weapons which would put into effect the prohibition on these weapons.

The Yugoslav delegation presented a working paper (CCD/302) elaborating a control system combining national legislative measures of renunciation and self-control, and measures of international control supplemented by a procedure in case of suspicion of violation.

31. In addition, the following steps were recommended:

The Japanese delegation proposed (CCD/PV.456) that a group of experts study technical aspects of verification for the prohibition of C and B weapons.

The Italian delegation presented a working paper (CCD/289) containing suggestions on the possible convening of a group of experts to study the problems of controls over chemical weapons and the way in which such a group would function. It also introduced an additional working paper (CCD/304) raising a certain number of technical questions.

The United States delegation presented working papers on the relationship between the production of chemical agents for war and the production of chemicals for peaceful purposes by the commercial chemical industry (CCD/283); on toxins (CCD/286); on the problem of differentiating through off-site observation nerve agent production facilities from civilian chemical production facilities (CCD/293); and on economic data monitoring as a means of verifying compliance with a ban on chemical weapons (CCD/311).

The delegation of Canada submitted an analysis (CCD/300) of various proposals regarding verification of prohibitions on the development, production, stockpiling and the use of C and B weapons and a number of questions concerning additional information on national policy and controls, the production and stockpiling of chemicals, and research and development.

The delegation of Czechoslovakia presented a working paper on the prohibition of the development, production and stockpiling of C and B weapons and on their destruction (CCD/299), which concluded that national self-inspection and supervision seem to be the most suitable fundamental method of verification.

The delegation of the Soviet Union submitted a working paper on the complete prohibition of C and B weapons (CCD/303) which emphasized the necessity of a full prohibition of C and B weapons, the danger of approaching separately the prohibition of C and B means of warfare, and the practical advisability of the use of national means of control over the prohibition of these weapons with appropriate procedures for submitting complaints to the Security Council in cases of violation of the agreement.

A working paper examining certain of the problems involved in meeting the verification requirements for an acceptable CW agreement was submitted by the United Kingdom delegation (CCD/308).

At the conclusion of the 1970 session the delegations of Argentina, Brazil, Burma, Ethiopia, India, Mexico, Morocco, Nigeria, Pakistan, Sweden, the United Arab Republic and Yugoslavia presented a joint memorandum (CCD/310) on the question of C and B methods of warfare. This memorandum expressed the consensus of these delegations that it is essential that both chemical and bacteriological (biological) weapons should continue to be dealt with together in taking steps towards the prohibition of their development, production and stockpiling and their effective elimination from the arsenals of all States, and that the issue of verification is important in this field, as indeed adequate verification is also essential in regard to the success of any measure in the field of disarmament. It also expressed the hope that the basic approach outlined in this paper would receive general acceptance so that an early solution could be found in regard to the prohibition of the production, development and stockpiling of such weapons and their effective elimination from the arsenals of all States.

The delegation of the United States emphasized the inherent differences between chemical and biological weapons from the standpoint of arms limitations, underlined advantages of reaching early agreement to the greatest extent possible, and urged that there should be immediate negotiation of a convention along the lines of that proposed by the United Kingdom prohibiting production and stockpiling of all biological weapons and toxins, while study proceeds on the problems which must be resolved in order to make progress towards further prohibitions regarding chemical weapons (CCD/PV.491).

The delegation of the United Arab Republic submitted a working paper concerning suggestions on measures of verification of a ban on chemical and biological weapons (CCD/314).

The delegations of Hungary, Mongolia and Poland submitted a working document concerning the introduction of a safeguard clause—CCD/285—to the draft Convention on the Prohibition of the Development, Production and Stockpiling of Chemical and Bacteriological (Biological) Weapons and on the Destruction of Such Weapons [21]

[21] Text in *Documents on Disarmament, 1969*, pp. 455–457.

made by Mr. J. Winiewicz, Deputy Minister for Foreign Affairs of the Polish People's Republic, at the 464th plenary meeting of the Conference of the Committee on Disarmament (CCD/315).

32. The USSR delegation emphasized the necessity of an urgent prohibition both of bacteriological (biological) and chemical weapons. The Soviet delegation pointed out the strict logic and soundness of the approach to this problem of those delegations which urge that these types of weapons be prohibited together (CCD/PV.493).

33. A number of delegations made statements regarding their Governments' unilateral renunciations of one or both of these weapons and comments were made by Committee members with regard to these statements. Several delegations emphasized that unilateral renunciations should not be regarded as a solution of the problem of prohibiting chemical and bacteriological (biological) weapons.

34. Members of the Committee believe that the time and effort they devoted to this question contributed to a better understanding of the views and concerns of all participants, and to a deeper knowledge of the problems involved.

35. The Conference of the Committee on Disarmament, convinced of the need to give urgent consideration to the question of chemical and bacteriological (biological) weapons, intends to continue intensive work in this field with the aim of reaching agreement on the prohibitions and other measures referred to in General Assembly resolution 2603 B and other relevant proposals.

36. Many members of the Committee welcomed the statements by the delegations of Brazil, Japan and Morocco concerning ratification of the Protocol for the Prohibition of the Use in War of Asphyxiating, Poisonous or Other Gases, and of Bacteriological Methods of Warfare, signed at Geneva on 17 June 1925,[22] and expressed the hope that additional countries would adhere to this instrument in the near future. The delegations of Mexico, Sweden, Mongolia, India, the United Arab Republic and Yugoslavia (CCD/PV.449, 480, 489, 490) emphasized the importance of General Assembly resolution 2603 A (XXIV) regarding the Geneva Protocol of 1925.

37. The delegations of Mongolia and Hungary emphasized (CCD/PV.455, 456) the importance of implementing General Assembly resolution 2603 B (XXIV), inviting all States which have not yet done so to accede to or ratify the Geneva Protocol

[22] Cf. *Documents, 1968–69*, p. 107 at note 135. See also Documents 15–16, below.

in the course of 1970 in commemoration of the forty-fifth anniversary of its signing and the twenty-fifth anniversary of the United Nations.

38. The Italian delegation reaffirmed (CCD/PV.453, 474) its view that parties to the Geneva Protocol of 1925 should withdraw the reservation that the Protocol is only binding as regards States which have signed and ratified the Protocol. The delegation of Japan expressed the hope that those States which have attached reservations to the 1925 Geneva Protocol would withdraw their reservations as early as possible (CCD/PV.471). Several delegations emphasized that reservations to the 1925 Geneva Protocol have played an important positive role in gaining wide adherence to the Protocol and in preventing the use of chemical and biological weapons in the Second World War.

Other measures

39. Certain delegations expressed in plenary statements different views regarding the question of conventional armaments. A working paper (CCD/307) on possible principles that might assist in the development of approaches to this subject was submitted by the United States delegation.

C. OTHER COLLATERAL MEASURES

Draft Treaty on the Prohibition of the Emplacement of Nuclear Weapons and Other Weapons of Mass Destruction on the Sea-Bed and the Ocean Floor and in the Subsoil Thereof

40. Having in mind the recommendations of General Assembly resolution 2602 F (XXIV), the Conference of the Committee on Disarmament continued its work on the draft Treaty on the Prohibition of the Emplacement of Nuclear Weapons and Other Weapons of Mass Destruction on the Sea-Bed and the Ocean Floor and in the Subsoil Thereof.[23]

41. When addressing the Conference of the Committee on Disarmament at the beginning of its 1970 session, the Secretary-General of the United Nations expressed the view that the elaboration and submission to the General Assembly of an agreed draft treaty on this subject would constitute an important step in preventing the danger of the spread of the nuclear arms race to a vast area of our planet (CCD/PV.450).

42. In commenting on this question in their opening statements, many members of the Committee expressed the view that certain amendments and more precise language should be incorporated in the draft Treaty which was reported to the twenty-

[23] Text of draft treaty in *Documents, 1968–69*, pp. 102–106.

fourth session of the General Assembly. After careful consideration of the views of Committee members and all the proposals and suggestions made at the General Assembly, the representatives of the Soviet Union and the United States tabled a second revised joint draft Treaty on 23 April 1970 (CCD/269/Rev.2).

43. Articles I and II of this draft contained new language designed to reconcile a number of suggestions about how the area covered by the Treaty should be defined. The new draft of these articles took into account points raised at various times by the delegations of Argentina, Ethiopia, India, Morocco, Nigeria, Pakistan and the United Arab Republic; the text was essentially that proposed by the delegation of Argentina in working paper A/C.1/997.

44. The amended text of article III represented a synthesis of the views and positions of many countries regarding the verification provisions of the Treaty, largely as these were reflected in working paper A/C.1/992 submitted by the delegation of Canada. With respect to article III, statements were made by the delegations of the Soviet Union and the United States regarding the right of States Parties to apply directly to the Security Council in accordance with the Charter of the United Nations (CCD/PV.467 and 492).

45. In response to proposals of Argentina, India, Morocco, Pakistan and the United Arab Republic, the disclaimer provision was broadened and was given the status of a separate article IV as it appeared in the working paper of Argentina (A/C.1/997).

46. In response to a proposal by the delegation of Mexico in a working paper (A/C.1/995), an amendment making clear that the Treaty would in no way affect the obligations of parties under international instruments establishing zones free from nuclear weapons was incorporated in the new draft as article VIII.

47. A number of minor editorial changes suggested by various delegations in the General Assembly and at the Conference of the Committee on Disarmament were also included.

48. During subsequent discussions, a number of delegations expressed their complete satisfaction with the second revised draft of the Treaty. A number of other delegations suggested that the Treaty might still be improved and its provisions further clarified through certain additional amendments.

49. On 18 June 1970 the Polish delegation proposed that the question of the prevention of an arms race on the sea-bed remain on the agenda of the Committee (CCD/PV.471). General support was expressed for this proposal.

50. On 25 June 1970 the delegation of Brazil suggested a number of amendments regarding the verification provisions of article III (CCD/PV.473). On 3 July 1970 the delegation of Argentina proposed changes in paragraphs 1, 2, 3 and 6 of article III regarding verification activities (CCD/PV.475/Add.1).

51. On 7 July 1970 the delegation of the United Arab Republic suggested that article VIII should be expanded to include other agreements on disarmament and in particular the Treaty on the Non-Proliferation of Nuclear Weapons (CCD/PV.476). Statements by the delegations of the Soviet Union and the United States made clear that the Treaty does not affect obligations assumed under other arms control treaties, including the non-proliferation treaty and the partial test ban treaty (CCD/PV.492). On 21 July 1970 the delegation of Mexico proposed that a second paragraph be added to article VIII of the draft Treaty (CCD/294). On 30 July 1970 two further amendments to article III and a new article V were recommended in a working paper (CCD/297) submitted by the delegations of Burma, Ethiopia, Mexico, Morocco, Nigeria, Pakistan, Sweden, the United Arab Republic and Yugoslavia.

52. The substance of the amendments contained in the latter paper and suggestions put forward in plenary statements and in consultations with many delegations were incorporated in a third revised draft of the treaty. The representatives of the Soviet Union and the United States consulted extensively with all members of the Committee concerning the precise formulation of the text of this draft, which was tabled on 1 September 1970.[24] On this occasion the delegations of the Soviet Union and the United States made statements with explanations of the provisions of the revised draft Treaty. A number of delegations took note of these statements. The Argentine and Brazilian delegations made interpretative declarations in this respect (CCD/PV. 492, 494).

53. Delegations expressed satisfaction with the general consensus achieved and the spirit of compromise which resulted in the inclusion in this draft of amendments responsive to their suggestions. Hope was widely expressed that the draft Treaty would be commended by the General Assembly and opened for signature at an early date.[25]

*   *   *

[24] Cf. note 11, above.
[25] Document 14.

Other measures

55. The representatives of Bulgaria, Czechoslovakia, Hungary, Poland, Romania and the Union of Soviet Socialist Republics made statements concerning the problem of European security.

56. General Assembly resolution 2602 D recommended that the Conference of the Committee on Disarmament give consideration to the military implications of laser technology. An examination of this question, contained in a working paper (CCD/292) submitted by the Netherlands delegation, concluded that the highly speculative character of the conceivable military applications of laser technology for weapons purposes did not seem to substantiate the need for arms control consideration at this time, although further developments in this field should be followed attentively.

D. GENERAL AND COMPLETE DISARMAMENT

57. During its 1970 sessions the Conference of the Committee on Disarmament gave detailed attention to the recommendation of General Assembly resolution 2602 E. The possibilities of preparing a generally acceptable programme dealing with all aspects of the problem of the cessation of the arms race and general and complete disarmament under effective international control were carefully studied in considering this question. Members of the Committee were particularly aware of the need to encourage activities directed toward systematic progress in solving the complex problems of disarmament.

58. During the discussions of this question, all members of the Committee stated their positions on the issues involved. The discussion took into account General Assembly resolutions 1378 (XIV),[26] 1722 (XVI) [27] and 2602 (XXIV), the agreed principles for disarmament negotiations contained in the 1961 Joint Statement of the Soviet Union and the United States [28] which was approved by the United Nations General Assembly at its sixteenth session, the Committee agenda adopted in 1968, and treaties and agreements on disarmament questions already in force, which in the opinion of Committee members should serve as a point of departure for continued negotiations on the question of general and complete disarmament.

59. In the course of considering this matter, members of the Committee stated their positions on:

[26] *Documents, 1959,* pp. 308–309.
[27] Same, *1961,* pp. 229–230.
[28] Same, pp. 200–203.

The interdependence of disarmament problems and questions of international peace and security;

The relationship of partial disarmament measures to general and complete disarmament;

The priority of nuclear disarmament, and disarmament regarding other weapons of mass destruction;

The need to give due consideration to maintaining a balance among various measures to prevent armament, to limit armament, and of disarmament;

The need to assure that no State or group of States gains military advantages at any stage of disarmament measures;

The need to associate all militarily important States, in particular all nuclear weapon Powers, with the process of disarmament in order to achieve a full measure of success in the efforts to contain the nuclear arms race and to reduce and eliminate all armaments;

The importance of full implementation of and wide adherence to treaties and agreements already in force in the field of disarmament;

The role of political and technical factors in determining appropriate methods for effectively verifying disarmament measures;

The need for flexibility;

The importance of converting resources released by disarmament to peaceful uses;

The role of regional disarmament measures;

The need to intensify efforts in the field of disarmament in general.

60. Many delegations stressed the urgent necessity of resuming work on general and complete disarmament. A number of plenary statements were devoted exclusively to a review of the way in which the question of general and complete disarmament has been approached in the past and to proposals for further progress in this field. Many delegations devoted their statements to the elaboration of a comprehensive programme of disarmament referred to in General Assembly resolution 2602 E.[29]

61. On 9 July 1970 the Foreign Minister of Brazil, in addressing the Conference of the Committee on Disarmament on this subject, suggested certain principles for disarmament negotiations, including the need to ensure that disarmament measures do not affect adversely economic, scientific and technological development, or prejudge or prejudice unresolved juridical and other questions in any outside field (CCD/PV.477).

62. The following working papers and proposals were submitted on this subject:

The Netherlands delegation submitted an analysis (CCD/276) of steps toward a comprehensive disarmament programme.

29 Enumeration omitted; cf. note 10.

The Mexican delegation stated its position in a working paper submitted on 5 March 1970 (CCD/277).

The Romanian delegation presented to the Committee proposals for further specific steps leading to disarmament (CCD/PV.455) including a proposal aiming at the establishment of a nuclear free zone in the Balkans. In a subsequent statement (CCD/PV.485) the Romanian delegation elaborated its ideas on the contents of a programme for the Disarmament Decade.

The delegation of Sweden presented a working paper (CCD/287) on ways in which verification has been dealt with in various arms control and disarmament treaties and proposals.

The delegation of India suggested that the Joint Statement of Agreed Principles for Disarmament Negotiations (ENDC/5) could be elaborated into a comprehensive programme of disarmament, taking into account the various comments and suggestions which had been put forward in the Committee (CCD/PV.488).

The delegation of Italy submitted a working paper (CCD/309) which recalled the report it had made following an exchange of views with a number of delegations regarding a possible approach to a comprehensive programme of disarmament, its goal, principles and mandates, main elements and related general considerations (CCD/PV.475). In the same working paper the delegation of Italy submitted proposals on initiating programmes of studies relating to the question of the reduction of armed forces and conventional disarmament, in the framework of a comprehensive programme of disarmament, and on an undertaking to begin negotiations of these reductions.

On 27 August 1970 the delegations of Mexico, Sweden and Yugoslavia submitted a draft comprehensive programme of disarmament (CCD/313), which contains principles and proposals as to elements and phases of the programme and procedures for its implementation, and states that the aim of this comprehensive programme is to achieve tangible progress in order that the goal of general and complete disarmament under effective international control may become a reality in a world in which international peace and security prevail, and economic and social progress are attained.

63. Members of the Committee believe that the wide discussion of these problems which took place at the Conference of the Committee on Disarmament during 1970 will contribute to progress in this field.

64. Since the questions related to general and complete disarmament are matters of great importance and complexity and in view of the fact that in the course of its discussions a number of concrete considerations and proposals were put forward which merit broad and thorough study by Governments and further

discussion in the Committee, the Conference of the Committee on Disarmament intends to continue its discussions of general and complete disarmament during 1971.

65. The Committee agreed to reconvene on a day to be established by the co-chairmen in consultation with all members of the Committee.

66. This report is transmitted by the co-chairmen on behalf of the Conference of the Committee on Disarmament.

(*Signed*) A. A. ROSHCHIN   (*Signed*) James F. LEONARD
Union of Soviet Socialist Republics   United States of America

C. The Strategic Arms Limitation Talks (SALT), April-December 1970.[30]

(9) *Call for a Missile Moratorium: Senate Resolution 211, 91st Congress, Adopted by the United States Senate April 9, 1970.*[31]

(*Complete Text*)

Whereas the competition to develop and deploy strategic weapons has reached a new and dangerous phase, which threatens to frustrate attempts at negotiating significant arms limitations and to weaken the stability of nuclear deterrence as a barrier to war;

Whereas development of multiple independently targetable reentry vehicles by both the United States and the Soviet Union represents a fundamental and radical challenge to such stability;

Whereas the possibility of agreed controls over strategic forces appears likely to diminish greatly if testing and deployment of multiple independently targetable reentry vehicles proceed;

Whereas a suspension of flight tests of multiple independently targetable reentry vehicles promises to forestall deployment of such provocative weapons; and

Whereas a suspension of such tests could contribute substantially to the success of the strategic arms limitations talks between the United States and the Soviet Union:[32] Now, therefore, be it

---

[30] For the context of this group of documents see *The United States in World Affairs, 1970,* Introduction to Chapter 3; Sections 9 and 10.
[31] Text from *Congressional Record* (Daily Edition), April 9, 1970, p. S 5509; adopted by a vote of 72–6.
[32] Documents 10–11.

Resolved, That it is the sense of the Senate that prompt negotiations between the Governments of the United States of
America and of the Union of Soviet Socialist Republics to seek
agreed limitations of both offensive and defensive strategic weapons should be urgently pursued; and

Resolved further, That the President should propose to the
Government of the Union of Soviet Socialist Republics an
immediate suspension by the United States and by the Union
of Soviet Socialist Republics of the further deployment of all
offensive and defensive nuclear strategic weapons systems, subject to national verification or such other measures of observation and inspection as may be appropriate.

(10) Phase Two, Vienna, April 16-August 14, 1970.

(a) United States Statement by Ambassador Gerard C. Smith, August 14, 1970.[33]

(Complete Text)

Foreign Minister [of Austria Rudolf] Kirchschlaeger, Minister Semenov, ladies and gentlemen:

Today we conclude the second phase of talks between the
United States and the Soviet Union on limiting strategic arms.[34]
For the past 4 months the delegations of the United States and
the U.S.S.R. have continued their efforts toward achieving a
strategic arms limitation agreement which would benefit both
countries and the entire world. I believe that both sides can agree
that important progress has been made. The work we have done
here in Vienna should provide a sound basis for the next phase
of our talks starting November 2 in Helsinki.

In his message which I read at our opening session last April,
President Nixon emphasized his firm commitment to the search
for an early, equitable, and verifiable agreement on the limitation and eventual reduction of the strategic arsenals of the two
countries.[35] Such an agreement would enhance international
security by maintaining a stable strategic relationship between
the Soviet Union and the United States. Limiting strategic arms

[33] Text from *Department of State Bulletin,* August 31, 1970, p. 245.
[34] For documentation on Phase One of SALT, held in Helsinki November
17–December 22, 1969, see *Documents, 1968–69,* pp. 125–127.
[35] Text of President Nixon's message, April 16, 1970, in *Department of State
Bulletin,* May 4, 1970, pp. 572–573.

should assist in reducing the tensions and uncertainties which exist in the world today.

Minister Semenov, I should like once again to express my appreciation to you and your delegation for the courtesies you have offered me and my delegation during our negotiations here.

Minister Kirchschlaeger, on behalf of the entire United States delegation, I should like to express through you our sincere appreciation to the Austrian people and their Government for the gracious hospitality shown us here and for the many ways in which our negotiations have been facilitated. I hope that you will enjoy your visit to the United States in September half as much as we have enjoyed our stay here. Your country's neutrality, its beautiful scenery and outstanding cultural facilities, and its warmhearted, friendly people have made your capital city a favorite site for international conferences. In common with all others who have engaged in such international conferences here in Vienna, we have greatly enjoyed our stay in your uniquely attractive and warmly hospitable capital, Vienna.

(b) Soviet Statement by Deputy Foreign Minister V.S. Semenov, August 14, 1970.[36]

(Complete Text)

Minister Kirchschlaeger, Ambassador Smith, ladies and gentlemen:

On behalf of the delegation of the Soviet Union, I express its gratitude to the President of the Austrian Republic [Franz Jonas], the Federal Government, and the Austrian authorities for creating favorable conditions for our work here and for their generous hospitality. We feel gratified by the fact that the Austrian public displayed a positive attitude toward the negotiations. We take this as a confirmation of the desire of the Austrian people for strengthening peace and international security and for the implementation of a policy of permanent neutrality of their country.

The negotiations between the delegations of the U.S.S.R. and the U.S.A. were devoted to the task of limiting strategic armaments of the sides. The Soviet Government attaches great importance to an appropriate solution of this problem, which would have an impact not only on the development of relations

36 Text from same, August 31, 1970, pp. 245–246.

between the Soviet Union and the United States but also on strengthening peace and international security. It is from this premise that the U.S.S.R. delegation proceeded in its work here.

I can say that the negotiations proceeded in a businesslike, calm, and frank atmosphere. Substantial and useful work was accomplished during the 4 months in Vienna. Naturally, it would be erroneous to underestimate the complexity of the problem under discussion and the difficulties which continue to exist here. Despite their difficulty, the Soviet Union intends to continue the negotiations and seek the necessary results. This, of course, requires efforts on both sides.

The two sides have agreed to resume the talks on November 2, 1970, in the capital of Finland, the city of Helsinki.[37]

In conclusion, I would like to express our gratitude to the delegation of the United States, its head, Mr. Smith, to the members of the delegation, and to the advisers and experts for the joint work accomplished here.

(c) Joint United States-Soviet Communiqué, August 14, 1970.[38]

(Complete Text)

In accordance with the agreement between the Governments of the United States of America and the Soviet Union negotiations took place in Vienna from April 16 to August 14, 1970, on the question of limiting strategic armaments.

The U.S. Delegation was headed by the Director of the Arms Control and Disarmament Agency, Gerard Smith. Members of the delegation included J. Graham Parsons, Paul Nitze, Llewellyn Thompson, Harold Brown and Royal Allison.

The USSR Delegation was headed by the Deputy Minister of Foreign Affairs of the USSR, V. S. Semenov. Members of the delegation included N. V. Ogarkov, P. S. Pleshakov, A. N. Shchukin, and N. N. Alekseev.

The delegations were accompanied by advisors and experts.

In the course of the negotiations a wide range of questions dealing with the problem of limiting strategic offensive and defensive armaments was thoroughly considered. The exchange was useful for both sides and made it possible to increase the degree of mutual understanding on a number of aspects of the matters discussed.

---

37 Document 11.
38 Text from *Department of State Bulletin*, August 31, 1970, p. 246.

Both delegations expressed their determination to pursue the negotiations with the aim of limiting strategic armaments. Agreement was reached that negotiations between the U.S. and the USSR Delegations will be resumed on November 2, 1970, in Helsinki, Finland.

The two delegations express their appreciation to the Government of Austria for creating favorable conditions for holding the negotiations. They are grateful for the traditional Austrian hospitality which was extended to them.

(11) Phase Three, Helsinki, November 2-December 18, 1970.

(a) Statement by Ambassador Smith at the Opening Public Session, November 2, 1970.[39]

(Complete Text)

Foreign Minister [of Finland Vaino] Leskinen, Minister Semenov, ladies and gentlemen:

I want to express my appreciation and that of the other members of the American delegation for the gracious words of welcome expressed by you, Mr. Leskinen, and for the wishes you have expressed for the success of our work. On behalf of my delegation, I thank you, Mr. Foreign Minister, and the Government of Finland for the hospitality that once again is being extended to the SALT delegations. We recall with pleasure the friendly and gracious cooperation offered us last year by the Government and people of neutral Finland and by your charming city of Helsinki. We are most grateful.

On behalf of the American delegation, I would like to express to Minister Semenov and other members of the Soviet delegation our satisfaction in resuming the common task begun here last year and carried forward during the talks in Vienna.

Mr. Foreign Minister, Minister Semenov, 1 year ago at the opening of these talks, President Nixon said that the U.S. SALT delegation was embarking upon one of the most momentous negotiations ever entrusted to an American delegation.[40] During the past year, we have been fully conscious of the heavy responsibility placed upon us.

The nature of modern strategic weapons makes their limitation a complex endeavor. We have, however, during the course

39 Text from same, November 23, 1970, pp. 651–652.
40 *Documents, 1968–69*, p. 125.

of the past year's discussions been able to explore a wide range of questions relating to limiting both strategic offensive and defensive armaments and to increasing mutual understanding of some of the issues involved. From our initial general exploratory discussions here in Helsinki last year, we moved to more specific discussions in Vienna on strategic arms limitation.[41]

Today in Helsinki we resume the effort to translate objectives which all rational men must surely hold in common into agreed verifiable arrangements to limit strategic arms. The prize of success would not be small.

In his address before the General Assembly of the United Nations on October 23, President Nixon said: "There is no greater contribution which the United States and the Soviet Union together could make than to limit the world's capacity for self-destruction." [42] It is the profound hope of my Government that in this current session of our talks significant progress will be made in fashioning the contribution which the United States and the Soviet Union can make to that end. A SALT agreement would be a momentous contribution to international peace and well-being.

With hard work and a mutual recognition of the legitimate security interests of each side, we should be able to make a start in the limitation of arms and a redirection to more constructive ends of some of the resources and energies of our societies.

Let us hope that as a result of our efforts here in Finland, future generations will pass a favorable judgment on our work.

(b) Statement by Deputy Foreign Minister Semenov at the Opening Public Session, November 2, 1970.[43]

(Complete Text)

Esteemed Mr. Minister, esteemed Mr. Ambassador, ladies and gentlemen:

May I first of all express our gratitude to the Minister of Foreign Affairs of Finland, Mr. Leskinen, for the warm greetings and good wishes for success in our work.

We are profoundly grateful to the Government and people of Finland for the opportunity accorded to us of holding a new stage of the negotiations in the city of Helsinki, the capital of a friendly country whose peace-loving foreign policy commands respect in Europe and all over the world.

41 Cf. Document 10.
42 Document 73.
43 Text from *Department of State Bulletin,* November 23, 1970, p. 652.

The Soviet side attaches great importance to the negotiations on limiting strategic arms that are resumed in Helsinki today.

The Soviet Union has consistently come out in favor of the relaxation of tension in the world, the stopping of the arms race fanned up by certain imperialist circles, and the strengthening of international security. It is from these positions that we conduct these negotiations.

As was emphasized before, the Soviet Government hopes that eventually the Soviet-American negotiations on this question will produce positive results.

It is evident that the questions that we discuss are not simple ones. That is why a constructive and businesslike approach from both sides is all the more important to insure progress in this matter.

On behalf of the U.S.S.R. delegation I welcome the delegation of the United States headed by Ambassador Smith, its advisers and staff members.

In conclusion, I would like to say that the U.S.S.R. delegation is gratified that the negotiations will again take place in Helsinki. The cordiality and hospitality of this city are widely known, which has justly made it a recognized place for holding international conferences and negotiations. We avail ourselves of this opportunity to extend the best wishes to the people and the authorities of the city of Helsinki and all the Finnish people. Thank you.

(c) *Joint United States-Soviet Communiqué at the Conclusion of Phase Three, December 18, 1970.*[44]

(*Complete Text*)

In accordance with the agreement between the Governments of the United States of America and the Soviet Union, negotiations on the question of limiting strategic armaments continued in Helsinki from November 2 to December 18, 1970.

The US delegation was headed by the Director of the U.S. Arms Control and Disarmament Agency, Gerard Smith. Members of the delegation included J. Graham Parsons, Paul Nitze, Harold Brown, and Royal Allison.

The USSR delegation was headed by the Deputy Minister of Foreign Affairs of USSR, V. S. Semenov. Members of the delegation included N. V. Ogarkov, P. S. Pleshakov, A. N. Shchukin, and O. A. Grinevsky.

44 Text from same, January 11, 1971, p. 55.

The delegations were accompanied by advisors and experts.

In the continuing course of the negotiations a wide range of questions dealing with the problem of limiting strategic offensive and defensive armaments was considered. The exchange further clarified a number of aspects of the matters discussed. Both delegations expressed their determination to pursue the negotiations with the aim of limiting strategic offensive and defensive armaments.

Agreement was reached that negotiations between the U.S. and the USSR delegations will be resumed on March 15, 1971, in Vienna, Austria.[45]

The two delegations express their appreciation to the Government of Finland for assisting in establishing favorable conditions for holding the negotiations, and for the warm hospitality extended to them.

D. Treaty on the Non-Proliferation of Nuclear Weapons, Signed at Washington, London, and Moscow July 1, 1968.[46]

(12) Remarks by President Nixon on Entry Into Force of the Treaty, Washington, March 5, 1970.[47]

(Complete Text)

Mr. Secretary [of State William P. Rogers], Your Excellencies, the members of the diplomatic corps, Members of the Senate and the House, and our other distinguished guests:

With the completion of this ceremony,[48] this treaty is now in force and has become the law of the land.[49]

Mr. Secretary, I would like to be permitted something beyond that formal statement which puts the treaty in force.

I feel that on an occasion like this, an historic occasion, it is

[45] Phase Four of SALT took place March 15-May 28, 1971. For text of President Nixon's remarks, May 20, 1971, announcing a U.S.-U.S.S.R. agreement see *Weekly Compilation of Presidential Documents,* May 24, 1971, pp. 783–784.

[46] For the context see *The United States in World Affairs, 1970,* Introduction to Chapter 3.

[47] Text from *Weekly Compilation of Presidential Documents,* March 9, 1970, pp. 318–319.

[48] Parallel ceremonies were held in London and Moscow. For texts of statements by Secretary Rogers and Deparment of State Legal Adviser John R. Stevenson on deposit of ratifications, March 5, 1970, see *Department of State Bulletin,* March 30, 1970, pp. 410–411.

[49] Text in *Documents, 1968–69,* pp. 62–68.

well to pay tribute to some of those, both in our Government and in other governments, who have been responsible for the success in negotiating this treaty.

First, in our own Government, I should point out that the treaty spans three administrations—the Kennedy administration, the Johnson administration, and its completion in this administration.

It was primarily negotiated during the Johnson administration.[50] And we very much regret that he was unable to attend this ceremony due to an illness, which I understand will be certainly temporary. We trust that if he is looking on television that he has seen this ceremony and the culmination of, I know, what was one of his major objectives during his administration, the ratification of the Nonproliferation Treaty.

Having spoken of President Johnson and his administration, I think it is also appropriate to speak of the negotiating team. Seated at this table is William C. Foster. In speaking of him, I speak of all the men who worked with him.

I can speak with some experience in that respect. I remember on two occasions when I was in Geneva—when I was out of office with no influence in the administration in Washington and very little influence in my own party—Mr. Foster felt so strongly about this treaty that he took much of his time to explain it and also to present the facts in an effective way as to why the treaty was in the best interest of the United States, as well as the other nations involved. In other words, what was involved here was not only negotiation on his part and the other members of his team, but a very effective and necessary program of education.

And for that long and at times very frustrating and at times almost, it seemed, impossible task, we can congratulate him and all the members of the diplomatic corps who worked as he did for that treaty.

And on this occasion, too, I wish to pay respect to the Members of the House and the Senate that are here.

This treaty indicates both the continuity of American foreign policy in its search for a just peace, and it also indicates its bipartisan character; because without bipartisan support in the Senate, where the treaty received the consent of the Senate,[51] and bipartisan support in the House as well, this treaty could not go into effect as it has today.

And, finally, I wish to pay tribute and express appreciation to all the representatives of the other governments that are present here today.

50 Cf. same, pp. 52–62.
51 The Senate gave its advice and consent to ratification March 13, 1969.

The fact that so many governments have brought this treaty into effect is an indication of the immense desire that exists among all people in the world to reduce the danger of war and to find a way peacefully to settle our differences.

This is indeed an historic occasion. As I sit here today, I only hope that those of us who were fortunate enough to be present will look back one day and see that this was the first milestone on a road which led to reducing the danger of nuclear war and on a road which led to lasting peace among nations.

This milestone, as has already been indicated, results in non-proliferation of nuclear weapons to the extent that the nations participating in this ceremony and who have ratified the treaty have indicated.

The next milestone we trust will be the limitation of nuclear weapons, the historic strategic arms limitation talks which will enter their second phase on April 15 in Vienna.[52] And we noted the fact that when Prime Minister [Aleksei N.] Kosygin signed the treaty in Moscow today, reference was made to those talks.

We trust that on April 15 the climate for progress in those talks will be good and that we can at some time in the future look forward to a ceremony in which we note the ratification of that historic treaty.

And then finally, of course, we trust that the third milestone will be continued progress in reducing the political tensions, the differences between governments which make it necessary for us to consider that we must maintain armed forces to the degree that we maintain them.

This is the work of all of us, the work of the diplomats, the work of the men of peace, and all of us I think can be so described today.

And so, Mr. Secretary, on this historic occasion, let us trust that we will look back and say that this was one of the first and major steps in that process in which the nations of the world moved from a period of confrontation to a period of negotiation and a period of lasting peace.

52 Document 10.

E. Barring Nuclear Weapons from the Sea-Bed.

(13) *Second Revised Draft Treaty Submitted by Representatives of the United States and the Soviet Union to the Conference of the Committee on Disarmament at Geneva, September 1, 1970.*[53]

(*Complete Text*)

DRAFT TREATY ON THE PROHIBITION OF THE EMPLACEMENT OF NUCLEAR WEAPONS AND OTHER WEAPONS OF MASS DESTRUCTION ON THE SEABED AND THE OCEAN FLOOR AND IN THE SUBSOIL THEREOF

The States Parties to this Treaty,

Recognizing the common interest of mankind in the progress of the exploration and use of the seabed and the ocean floor for peaceful purposes,

Considering that the prevention of a nuclear arms race on the seabed and the ocean floor serves the interests of maintaining world peace, reduces international tensions, and strengthens friendly relations among States,

Convinced that this Treaty constitutes a step towards the exclusion of the seabed, the ocean floor and the subsoil thereof from the arms race,

Convinced that this Treaty constitutes a step towards a Treaty on general and complete diarmament under strict and effective international control, and determined to continue negotiations to this end,

Convinced that this Treaty will further the purposes and principles of the Charter of the United Nations, in a manner consistent with the principles of international law and without infringing the freedoms of the high seas,

Have agreed as follows:

ARTICLE I

1. The States Parties to this Treaty undertake not to emplant or emplace on the seabed and the ocean floor and in the subsoil thereof beyond the outer limit of a seabed zone as defined

---

[53] Text from U.N. document A/8059 (DC/233), September 11, 1970, Annex A (also issued as U.N. Document CCD/317, Annex A). Opened for signature at Washington, London, and Moscow February 11, 1971, the treaty was signed by 62 nations; cf. *Department of State Bulletin*, March 8, 1971, pp. 288–290. For the context of this and the following document see *The United States in World Affairs, 1970,* Section 41.

in Article II any nuclear weapons or any other types of weapons of mass destruction as well as structures, launching installations or any other facilities specifically designed for storing, testing or using such weapons.

2. The undertakings of paragraph 1 of this Article shall also apply to the seabed zone referred to in the same paragraph, except that within such seabed zone, they shall not apply either to the coastal State or to the seabed beneath its territorial waters.

3. The States Parties to this Treaty undertake not to assist, encourage or induce any State to carry out activities referred to in paragraph 1 of this Article and not to participate in any other way in such actions.

ARTICLE II

For the purpose of this Treaty the outer limit of the seabed zone referred to in Article 1 shall be coterminous with the twelve-mile outer limit of the zone referred to in Part II of the Convention on the Territorial Sea and the Contiguous Zone, signed in Geneva on 29 April 1958 [54] and shall be measured in accordance with the provisions of Part I, Section II, of this Convention and in accordance with international law.

ARTICLE III

1. In order to promote the objectives of and ensure compliance with the provisions of this Treaty, each State Party to the Treaty shall have the right to verify through observation the activities of other States Parties to the Treaty on the seabed and the ocean floor and in the subsoil thereof beyond the zone referred to in Article I, provided that observation does not interfere with such activities.

2. If after such observation reasonable doubts remain concerning the fulfilment of the obligations assumed under the Treaty, the State Party having such doubts and the State Party that is responsible for the activities giving rise to the doubts shall consult with a view to removing the doubts. If the doubts persist, the State Party having such doubts shall notify the other States Parties, and the Parties concerned shall co-operate on such further procedures for verification as may be agreed, including appropriate inspection of objects, structures, installations or other facilities that reasonably may be expected to be of a kind described in Article I. The Parties in the region of the activities, including any coastal State, and any other Party so requesting,

[54] Department of State, *Treaties and Other International Acts Series*, No. 5639; cf. *The United States in World Affairs, 1958*, pp. 555–561.

shall be entitled to participate in such consultation and co-operation. After completion of the further procedures for verification, an appropriate report shall be circulated to other Parties by the Party that initiated such procedures.

3. If the State responsible for the activities giving rise to the reasonable doubts is not identifiable by observation of the object, structure, installation or other facility, the State Party having such doubts shall notify and make appropriate inquiries of State Parties in the region of the activities and of any other State Party. If it is ascertained through these inquiries that a particular State Party is responsible for the activities, that State Party shall consult and co-operate with other Parties as provided in paragraph 2 of this Article. If the identity of the State responsible for the activities cannot be ascertained through these inquiries, then further verification procedures, including inspection, may be undertaken by the inquiring State Party, which shall invite the participation of the Parties in the region of the activities, including any coastal state, and of any other Party desiring to co-operate.

4. If consultation and co-operation pursuant to paragraphs 2 and 3 of this Article have not removed the doubts concerning the activities and there remains a serious question concerning fulfilment of the obligations assumed under this Treaty, a State Party may, in accordance with the provisions of the Charter of the United Nations, refer the matter to the Security Council, which may take action in accordance with the Charter.

5. Verification pursuant to this Article may be undertaken by any State Party using its own means, or with the full or partial assistance of any other State Party, or through appropriate international procedures within the framework of the United Nations and in accordance with its Charter.

6. Verification activities pursuant to this Treaty shall not interfere with activities of other States Parties and shall be conducted with due regard for rights recognized under international law including the freedoms of the high seas and the rights of coastal States with respect to the exploration and exploitation of their continental shelves.

Article IV

Nothing in this Treaty shall be interpreted as supporting or prejudicing the position of any State Party with respect to existing international conventions, including the 1958 Convention on the Territorial Sea and the Contiguous Zone, or with respect to rights or claims which such State Party may assert, or with respect to recognition or non-recognition of rights or claims asserted by any other State, related to waters off its coasts; including inter alia territorial seas and contiguous zones, or to the seabed and the ocean floor, including continental shelves.

Article V

The Parties to this Treaty undertake to continue negotiations in good faith concerning further measures in the field of disarmament for the prevention of an arms race on the seabed, the ocean floor, and the subsoil thereof.

Article VI

Any State Party may propose amendments to this Treaty. Amendments shall enter into force for each State Party accepting the amendments upon their acceptance by a majority of the States Parties to the Treaty and thereafter for each remaining State Party on the date of acceptance by it.

Article VII

Five years after the entry into force of this Treaty, a conference of Parties to the Treaty shall be held in Geneva, Switzerland, in order to review the operation of this Treaty with a view to assuring that the purposes of the preamble and the provisions of the Treaty are being realized. Such review shall take into account any relevant technological developments. The review conference shall determine in accordance with the views of a majority of those Parties attending whether and when an additional review conference shall be convened.

Article VIII

Each State Party to this Treaty shall in exercising its national sovereignty have the right to withdraw from this Treaty if it decides that extraordinary events related to the subject matter of this Treaty have jeopardized the supreme interests of its country. It shall give notice of such withdrawal to all other States Parties to the Treaty and to the United Nations Security Council three months in advance. Such notice shall include a statement of the extraordinary events it considers to have jeopardized its supreme interests.

Article IX

The provisions of this Treaty shall in no way affect the obligations assumed by States Parties to the Treaty under international instruments establishing zones free from nuclear weapons.

Article X

1. This Treaty shall be open for signature to all States. Any State which does not sign the Treaty before its entry into force in accordance with paragraph 3 of this Article may accede to it at any time.

2. This Treaty shall be subject to ratification by signatory States. Instruments of ratification and of accession shall be deposited with the Governments of _____ which are hereby designated the Depositary Governments.

3. This Treaty shall enter into force after the deposit of instruments of ratification by twenty-two Governments, including the Governments designated as Depositary Governments of this Treaty.

4. For States whose instruments of ratification or accession are deposited after the entry into force of this Treaty it shall enter into force on the date of the deposit of their instruments of ratification or accession.

5. The Depositary Governments shall promptly inform the Governments of all signatory and acceding States of the date of each signature, of the date of deposit of each instrument of ratification or of accession, of the date of the entry into force of this Treaty, and of the receipt of other notices.

6. This Treaty shall be registered by the Depositary Governments pursuant to Article 102 of the Charter of the United Nations.

Article XI

This Treaty, the Chinese, English, French, Russian and Spanish texts of which are equally authentic, shall be deposited in the archives of the Depositary Governments. Duly certified copies of this treaty shall be transmitted by the Depositary Governments to the Governments of the States signatory and acceding thereto.

In witness whereof the undersigned, being duly authorized thereto, have signed this Treaty.

Done in _____ at _____, this _____ day of _____, _____.

(14) Action by the United Nations General Assembly: Resolution 2660 (XXV), Adopted December 7, 1970.[55]

(Excerpt)

The General Assembly,

Recalling its resolution 2602 F (XXIV) of 16 December 1969,[56]

Convinced that the prevention of a nuclear arms race on the sea-bed and the ocean floor serves the interests of maintaining world peace, reducing international tensions and strengthening friendly relations among States,

Recognizing the common interest of mankind in the reservation of the sea-bed and the ocean floor exclusively for peaceful purposes,

Having considered the report of the Conference of the Committee on Disarmament,[57] dated 11 September 1970, and being appreciative of the work of the Conference on the draft Treaty on the Prohibition of the Emplacement of Nuclear Weapons and other Weapons of Mass Destruction on the Sea-Bed and the Ocean Floor and in the Subsoil Thereof,[58] annexed to the report,

Convinced that this Treaty will further the purposes and principles of the Charter of the United Nations,

1. *Commends* the Treaty on the Prohibition of the Emplacement of Nuclear Weapons and Other Weapons of Mass Destruction on the Sea-Bed and the Ocean Floor and in the Subsoil Thereof, the text of which is annexed to the present resolution;

2. *Requests* the depositary Governments to open the Treaty for signature and ratification at the earliest possible date;

3. *Expresses the hope* for the widest possible adherence to the Treaty.

*   *   *

[55] Text from U.N. General Assembly, *Official Records: 25th Session, Supplement No. 28* (A/8028), pp. 11–12; adopted by a vote of 104–2 with 2 abstentions.
[56] *Documents, 1968–69,* pp. 114–115.
[57] Document 8.
[58] Document 13.

F. Chemical and Biological Warfare.

(15) United States Renunciation of Toxins as a Method of Warfare: White House Announcement, Released at Key Biscayne, Florida, February 14, 1970.[59]

(Complete Text)

On November 25, 1969, the President renounced all offensive preparations for and any use by the United States of biological or bacteriological agents and weapons in war.[60] Since that decision, at the direction of the President, a comprehensive review of the United States policy and military programs concerning toxins has been in progress.

Toxins are chemical substances, not living organisms, and are so regarded by the U.N. Secretary General and the World Health Organization. Although the effects of some toxins are commonly described as disease, they are not capable of reproducing themselves and are not transmissible from one person to another.

However, the production of toxins in any significant quantity would require facilities similar to those needed for the production of biological agents. If the United States continued to operate such facilities, it would be difficult for others to know whether they were being used to produce only toxins but not biological agents. Moreover, though toxins of the type useful for military purposes could conceivably be produced by chemical synthesis in the future, the end products would be the same and their effects would be indistinguishable from toxins produced by bacteriological or other biological processes. Accordingly, the President has decided that:

—The United States renounces offensive preparations for and the use of toxins as a method of warfare;

—The United States will confine its military programs for toxins, whether produced by bacteriological or any other biological method or by chemical synthesis, to research for defensive purposes only, such as to improve techniques of immunization and medical therapy.

The President has further directed the destruction of all existing toxin weapons and of all existing stocks of toxins which are not required for a research program for defensive purposes only.

[59] Text from *Weekly Compilation of Presidential Documents,* February 16, 1970, pp. 179–180. For the context of this and the following document see *The United States in World Affairs, 1970,* Introduction to Chapter 3.
[60] *Documents, 1968–69,* pp. 106–109.

The United States will have no need to operate any facilities capable of producing toxins either bacteriologically or biologically in large quantities and therefore also capable of producing biological agents.

These decisions have been taken with full confidence that they are in accord with the overall security requirements of the United States. These decisions also underline the United States support for the principles and objectives of the United Kingdom Draft Convention for the Prohibition of Biological Methods of Warfare.[61]

The United States hopes that other nations will follow our example with respect to both biological and toxin weapons.

The renunciation of toxin weapons is another significant step, which we are willing to take unilaterally, to bring about arms control and to increase the prospects of peace.

(16) Resubmission of the Geneva Protocol of June 17, 1925: Message from President Nixon to the Senate Requesting Its Advice and Consent to Ratification, August 19, 1970.[62]

(Complete Text)

To the Senate of the United States:

With a view to receiving the advice and consent of the Senate to ratification, I transmit herewith the Protocol for the Prohibition of the Use in War of Asphyxiating, Poisonous or Other Gases, and of Bacteriological Methods of Warfare, signed at Geneva June 17, 1925.[63] I transmit also the report by the Secretary of State which sets forth the understandings and the proposed reservation of the United States with respect to the Protocol.[64]

[61] Text, dated August 26, 1969, in *Documents on Disarmament, 1969,* pp. 431–433. For the language of the key articles see *Documents, 1968–69,* p. 108 at note 137.

[62] Text from *Weekly Compilation of Presidential Documents,* August 24, 1970, pp. 1081–1082.

[63] Text in League of Nations, *Treaty Series,* vol. 94 (1929), no. 2138, pp. 65–74 (unofficial text in *Department of State Bulletin,* December 15, 1969, pp. 541–542).

[64] Text of Secretary Rogers' report, August 11, 1970, in *Department of State Bulletin,* September 7, 1970, pp. 273–275. The proposed U.S. reservation reads as follows: "That the said Protocol shall cease to be binding on the Government of the United States with respect to the use in war of asphyxiating, poisonous or other gases, and of all analogous liquids, materials or devices, in regard to an enemy State if such State or any of its allies fails to respect the prohibitions laid down in the Protocol."

In submitting this Protocol for approval, I consider it desirable and appropriate to make the following statements:

—The United States has renounced the first-use of lethal and incapacitating chemical weapons.

—The United States has renounced any use of biological and toxin weapons.

—Our biological and toxin programs will be confined to research for defensive purposes, strictly defined. By the example we set, we hope to contribute to an atmosphere of peace, understanding and confidence between nations and among men. The policy of the United States Government is to support international efforts to limit biological and toxin research programs to defensive purposes.

—The United States will seek further agreement on effective arms-control measures in the field of biological and chemical warfare.

Today, there are 85 parties, including all other major powers, to this basic international agreement which the United States proposed and signed in 1925. The United States always has observed the principles and objectives of this Protocol.

I consider it essential that the United States now become a party to this Protocol, and urge the Senate to give its advice and consent to ratification with the reservation set forth in the Secretary's report.

RICHARD NIXON

The White House
August 19, 1970

(17)   Action by the United Nations General Assembly: Resolution 2662 (XXV), Adopted December 7, 1970.[65]

(Complete Text)

The General Assembly,

Mindful of the increasing concern of the international community over developments in the field of chemical and bacteriological (biological) weapons,

Recalling its resolution 2454 A (XXIII) of 20 December 1968 [66] and 2603 B (XXIV) of 16 December 1969,[67]

[65] Text from U.N. General Assembly, *Official Records: 25th Session, Supplement No. 28* (A/8028), pp. 14–15; adopted by a vote of 113–0 with 2 abstentions.
[66] *Documents, 1968–69,* pp. 76–78.
[67] Same, pp. 119–122.

Having considered the report of the Conference of the Committee on Disarmament,[68]

Noting the report entitled *Chemical and Bacteriological (Biological) Weapons and the Effects of Their Possible Use,*[69] prepared by the Secretary-General in accordance with General Assembly resolution 2454 A (XXIII), with the assistance of consultant experts, and the report of the World Health Organization's group of consultants entitled *Health Aspects of Chemical and Biological Weapons,*[70]

Deeply convinced that the prospects for international peace and security, as well as the achievement of the goal of general and complete disarmament under effective international control, would be enhanced if the development, production and stockpiling of chemical and bacteriological (biological) agents for purposes of war were to end and if those agents were eliminated from all military arsenals,

Conscious of the need to maintain inviolate the Protocol for the Prohibition of the Use in War of Asphyxiating, Poisonous or Other Gases, and of Bacteriological Methods of Warfare, signed at Geneva on 17 June 1925,[71] and to ensure its universal applicability,

Conscious of the urgent need for all States that have not already done so to accede to the Geneva Protocol,

1. *Reaffirms* its resolution 2162 B (XXI) of 5 December 1966 [72] and calls anew for the strict observance by all States of the principles and objectives of the Protocol for the Prohibition of the Use in War of Asphyxiating, Poisonous or Other Gases, and of Bacteriological Methods of Warfare, signed at Geneva on 17 June 1925;

2. *Invites* all States that have not already done so to accede to or ratify the Geneva Protocol;

3. *Takes note* of:

(a) The revised draft Convention for the Prohibition of Biological Methods of Warfare,[73] submitted on 18 August 1970 to the Conference of the Committee on Disarmament by the United Kingdom of Great Britain and Northern Ireland;

[68] Document 8.
[69] U.N. Document A/7575 (S/9292), July 1, 1969 (U.N. Publication, Sales No.: E.69.I.24). Extracts reprinted in *Documents on Disarmament, 1969,* pp. 264–298.
[70] World Health Organization, *Health Aspects of Chemical and Biological Weapons: Report of a WHO Group of Consultants* (Geneva, 1970).
[71] Cf. note 63 to Document 16.
[72] U.N. General Assembly, *Official Records: 21st Session, Supplement No. 16* (A/6316), p. 11.
[73] CCD/255/Rev. 2; text in *Documents on Disarmament, 1970,* pp. 428–432.

(*b*) The revised draft Convention on the Prohibition of the Development, Production and Stockpiling of Chemical and Bacteriological (Biological) Weapons and on the Destruction of Such Weapons,[74] submitted on 23 October 1970 to the General Assembly by Bulgaria, the Byelorussian Soviet Socialist Republic, Czechoslovakia, Hungary, Mongolia, Poland, Romania, the Ukrainian Soviet Socialist Republic and the Union of Soviet Socialist Republics;

(*c*) The working papers, expert views and suggestions put forward in the Conference of the Committee on Disarmament and in the First Committee;

4. *Takes further note* of the joint memorandum on the question of chemical and bacteriological (biological) methods of warfare,[75] submitted on 25 August 1970 to the Conference of the Committee on Disarmament by Argentina, Brazil, Burma, Ethiopia, India, Mexico, Morocco, Nigeria, Pakistan, Sweden, the United Arab Republic and Yugoslavia;

5. *Commends* the following basic approach, contained in the joint memorandum, for reaching an effective solution to the problem of chemical and bacteriological (biological) methods of warfare;

(*a*) It is urgent and important to reach agreement on the problem of chemical and bacteriological (biological) methods of warfare;

(*b*) Both chemical and bacteriological (biological) weapons should continue to be dealt with together in taking steps towards the prohibition of their development, production and stockpiling and their effective elimination from the arsenals of all States;

(*c*) The issue of verification is important in the field of chemical and bacteriological (biological) weapons, and verification should be based on a combination of appropriate national and international measures, which would complement and supplement each other, thereby providing an acceptable system that would ensure the effective implementation of the prohibition;

6. *Requests* the Conference of the Committee on Disarmament to continue its consideration of the problem of chemical and bacteriological (biological) methods of warfare, with a view to prohibiting urgently the development, production and stockpiling of those weapons and to their elimination from the arsenals of all States;

7. *Requests* the Conference of the Committee on Disarmament to submit a report on the results achieved to the General Assembly at its twenty-sixth session;

[74] A/8136; text in *Documents on Disarmament, 1970*, pp. 533–537.
[75] CCD/310; text in *Documents on Disarmament, 1970*, pp. 453–455.

8. *Requests* the Secretary-General to transmit to the Conference of the Committee on Disarmament all documents and records of the First Committee relating to questions connected with the problem of chemical and bacteriological (biological) methods of warfare.

G. Disarmament at the Twenty-Fifth Regular Session of the United Nations General Assembly, September 15-December 17, 1970.

(18) Question of General and Complete Disarmament: Assembly Resolution 2661 (XXV), Adopted December 7, 1970.[76]

(Complete Text)

The General Assembly,

Convinced of the necessity, for the very survival of mankind, of bringing the nuclear arms race to an immediate halt,

Recalling its resolutions 2456 D (XXIII) of 20 December 1968 [77] and 2602 A (XXIV) of 16 December 1969,[78]

Noting with satisfaction the continuation of bilateral negotiations between the Governments of the Union of Soviet Socialist Republics and the United States of America on the limitation of offensive and defensive strategic nuclear-weapon systems,[79]

Believing that the possibilities for rapid success in these negotiations would increase if steps were taken now by the nuclear-weapon Powers to halt the development of new nuclear weapons,

Urges the Governments of the nuclear-weapon Powers to bring about an immediate halt in the nuclear arms race and to cease all testing as well as deployment of offensive and defensive nuclear-weapon systems.

B

The General Assembly,

Noting that all States have the inalienable right to develop research, production and use of nuclear energy for peaceful purposes without discrimination,

[76] Text from U.N. General Assembly, *Official Records: 25th Session, Supplement No. 28* (A/8028), pp. 13–14; Resolution A was adopted by a vote of 102–0 with 14 abstentions; Resolution B, by 107–0 with 7 abstentions; and Resolution C, by 106–0 with 10 abstentions.

[77] *Documents, 1968–69,* p. 81.

[78] Same, p. 109.

[79] Documents 10–11.

Aware of the development of new techniques for uranium enrichment,

Considering that these new techniques may contribute to the promotion of the use of nuclear energy for peaceful purposes,

Considering also that material produced by these new techniques may be diverted for weapons purposes unless subject to effective safeguards,

Noting that the International Atomic Energy Agency is engaged in the study of safeguards under the Treaty on the Non-Proliferation of Nuclear Weapons,[80]

1. *Requests* the International Atomic Energy Agency to pay attention also to the safeguards required with respect to new techniques for uranium enrichment;

2. *Further requests* the International Atomic Energy Agency to inform the General Assembly at its twenty-sixth session on its consideration of this subject.

C

The General Assembly,

Recalling its resolution 2602 E (XXIV) of 16 December 1969,[81]

Further recalling its resolution 1722 (XVI) of 20 December 1961,[82] by which it welcomed the joint statement of agreed principles for disarmament negotiations, submitted on 20 September 1961 by the Union of Soviet Socialist Republics and the United States of America,[83]

Reaffirming once again the responsibility of the United Nations in the attainment of general and complete disarmament, which is the most important question facing the world today,

Considering that it has declared the decade of the 1970s as the Disarmament Decade,

Having considered the working papers on a comprehensive programme of disarmament submitted by the Netherlands on 24 February 1970 [84] and by Italy on 19 August 1970,[85] and the draft comprehensive programme of disarmament submitted by Mexico, Sweden and Yugoslavia on 27 August 1970 [86] to the Conference of the Committee on Disarmament.

[80] Cf. note 5 to Document 7.
[81] *Documents, 1968–69,* pp. 111–114.
[82] Same, *1961,* pp. 229–230.
[83] Same, pp. 200–203.
[84] CCD/276; text in *Documents on Disarmament, 1970,* pp. 59–63.
[85] CCD/309; text in *Documents on Disarmament, 1970,* pp. 440–445.
[86] CCD/213; text in *Documents on Disarmament, 1970,* pp. 459–465.

Having considered also the opinions expressed in the debates of the Conference of the Committee on Disarmament and of the First Committee concerning the question of a comprehensive programme of disarmament,

1. *Urges* the Conference of the Committee on Disarmament to make more intensive efforts to bring about a faster pace towards the achievement of disarmament measures;

2. *Expresses its appreciation* of the important and constructive documents and views submitted at the Conference of the Committee on Disarmament, including the working papers on a comprehensive programme of disarmament submitted by the Netherlands on 24 February 1970 and by Italy on 19 August 1970, and the draft comprehensive programme of disarmament submitted by Mexico, Sweden and Yugoslavia on 27 August 1970, and of the comprehensive programme of disarmament submitted to the General Assembly by Ireland, Mexico, Morocco, Pakistan, Sweden and Yugoslavia on 1 December 1970; [87]

3. *Recommends* to the Conference of the Committee on Disarmament that it take into account in its further work and its negotiations the comprehensive programme of disarmament submitted on 1 December 1970, as well as other disarmament suggestions presented or to be presented in the future.

(19) Urgent Need for the Suspension of Nuclear and Thermonuclear Weapon Tests: Resolution 2663 B (XXV), Adopted December 7, 1970.[88]

(Excerpt)

*   *   *

The General Assembly,

Having considered the question of the urgent need for suspension of nuclear and thermonuclear tests and the report of the Conference of the Committee on Disarmament,[89]

Recalling its resolution 1762 (XVII) of 6 November 1962,[90] 1910 (XVIII) of 27 November 1963,[91] 2032 (XX) of 3 Decem-

[87] U.N. document A/8191 and Corr. 1, December 2, 1970; text in *Documents on Disarmament, 1970*, pp. 653–658.
[88] Text from U.N. General Assembly, *Official Records: 25th Session, Supplement No. 28* (A/8028), pp. 15–16; adopted by a vote of 112–0 with 1 abstention.
[89] Document 8.
[90] *Documents, 1962*, pp. 177–180.
[91] Same, *1963*, p. 158.

ber 1965,[92] 2163 (XXI) of 5 December 1966,[93] 2343 (XXII) of 19 December 1967, 2455 (XXIII) of 20 December 1968 [94] and 2604 B (XXIV) of 16 December 1969,[95]

Noting with regret that all States have not yet adhered to the Treaty Banning Nuclear Weapon Tests in the Atmosphere, in Outer Space and under Water, signed in Moscow on 5 August 1963,[96]

Noting with increasing concern that nuclear weapon tests in the atmosphere and underground are continuing,

Taking into account that several concrete suggestions have been set forth in the Conference of the Committee on Disarmament as to possible provisions in a treaty banning underground nuclear weapon tests,

1. *Urges* all States that have not yet done so to adhere without further delay to the Treaty Banning Nuclear Weapon Tests in the Atmosphere, in Outer Space and under Water;

2. *Calls upon* all nuclear-weapon States to suspend nuclear weapon tests in all environments;

3. *Requests* the Conference of the Committee on Disarmament to continue, as a matter of urgency, its deliberations on a treaty banning underground nuclear weapon tests, taking into account the proposals already made in the Conference as well as the views expressed at the current session of the General Assembly, and to submit to the Assembly at its twenty-sixth session a special report on the results of its deliberations.

---

[92] Same, *1965*, pp. 76–77.
[93] Same, *1966*, pp. 105–106.
[94] Same, *1968–69*, pp. 79–81.
[95] Same, p. 124.
[96] Cf. note 2 to Document 7.

III.
THE ATLANTIC COMMUNITY

A. Security and *Détente*.

(20) Ministerial Session of the North Atlantic Council, Rome, May 26–27, 1970.[1]

(a) Communiqué.[2]

(Complete Text)

The North Atlantic Council, meeting in Ministerial Session in Rome on 26th–27th May, 1970, reaffirmed that the Alliance remains indispensable to the security of its members and makes possible their common search for progress towards a more stable relationship between East and West in which outstanding issues dividing Europe can be resolved.

2. Ministers again stated their determination to resolve these problems through a process of negotiation. They recognised that, for their part, this search for peace must rest upon a spirit of genuine partnership, the maintenance of the defensive strength of the Alliance and the practice of full and timely consultation.

3. Ministers agreed that it will not be enough to talk of European security in the abstract. The causes of insecurity in Europe are specific, they are deeply rooted in conflicting perceptions of state interests, and their elimination will require patient endeavour. However, the Allies for their part, remain willing to negotiate, in any suitable forum, those concrete issues whose resolution would enhance the security of Europe. The success of efforts to pursue genuine relaxation of tension will be a test of the willingness of all interested countries to deal meaningfully with real issues of security.

[1] For the context see *The United States in World Affairs, 1970,* Sections 5 and 36.
[2] Department of State Press Release 163, May 28, 1970; text from *Department of State Bulletin,* June 22, 1970, pp. 772–775.

4. Ministers affirmed that to endure, peace must rest upon universal respect of the sovereign equality, political independence and territorial integrity of each European state, regardless of its political or social system, and for the right of its peoples to shape their own destinies, free of the threat of external intervention, coercion or constraint.

5. Ministers, recalling their earlier statements on the subject, examined and approved a report on the situation in the Mediterranean, prepared by the Council in Permanent Session which they had requested in their meeting of December, 1969.[3] Having regard to the conclusions presented in this report, they found reason to reiterate their concern with regard to the situation in the area. They stressed again the importance of full and frequent consultation among the Allies on this question and the necessity for continued vigilance. They instructed the Council in Permanent Session to continue their close review of the developing situation in the Mediterranean and to report fully thereon to Ministers.

6. At their April 1969 meeting in Washington,[4] Ministers agreed to explore with the Soviet Union and the other countries of Eastern Europe which concrete issues best lend themselves to fruitful negotiations in order to reduce tension and promote co-operations in Europe and to take constructive actions to this end. The Council therafter conducted a detailed study of those issues, and at their meeting in December 1969, Ministers declared that Allied Governments would continue and intensify their contacts, discussions or negotiations through all appropriate channels, bilateral or multilateral, and that they remained receptive to signs of willingness on the part of the Soviet Union and other Eastern European countries to engage in such discussions.[5] Progress, they said, in these discussions and negotiations would help to ensure the success of any eventual conference, in which of course, the North American members of the Alliance would participate, to discuss and negotiate substantial problems of co-operation and security in Europe.

7. Ministers expressed satisfaction over the launching or continuation of the whole range of talks and negotiations, initiated by members of the Alliance, which they have been actively promoting during the six months since December 1969. At the same time, numerous other East-West contacts have been pursued. The Allies have consulted and will continue to consult closely on all these initiatives and contacts.

3 *Documents, 1968–69,* p. 166–173.
4 Same, pp. 154–158.
5 Same, pp. 172–173.

8. With the support and understanding of its Allies, the Federal Republic of Germany has initiated talks with the Soviet Union,[6] Poland [7] and GDR [German Democratic Republic] [8] in order to improve the situation in Central Europe. The Allies consider this to be encouraging. They express the hope that these talks will yield results and will not be compromised by the presentation of unacceptable demands. The efforts being made to solve outstanding problems and to achieve a modus vivendi in Germany which would take account of the special features of the German situation, represent an important contribution to security and co-operation in Europe. The Ministers express the hope that all governments desiring to contribute to a policy of relaxation of tension in Europe will, to the extent possible, facilitate a negotiated settlement of the relationship between the two parts of Germany and the development of communications between the populations.

9. The Ministers noted with satisfaction that the Four Powers, in the framework of their rights and responsibilities for Berlin and Germany as a whole began discussions on 26th March about improving the situation with regard to Berlin and free access to the city. They express the hope that the difficulties which exist at this especially sensitive area of the East-West relationship could be overcome by practical measures and that Berlin would be enabled to make its full contribution to economic and cultural exchanges.[9]

10. The conversations between the United States and the Soviet Union aiming at the limitation of strategic armaments, which began last November at Helsinki,[10] have been continued at Vienna in April.[11] Ministers welcome these talks, the outcome

---

6 Document 23.

7 On December 7, 1970, Poland and West Germany signed a treaty at Warsaw "on the bases for normalizing relations" between the two governments. Under the treaty West Germany recognized the existing Polish-German frontier and renounced all territorial claims; cf. *The United States in World Affairs, 1970*, Sections 5 and 35.

8 A reference to intermittent exchanges between the heads of government of East and West Germany, initiated in 1967, with reference to a possible meeting of heads of government and other steps to normalize the situation in Germany.

9 Four-power discussions on Berlin were begun March 1970 as a result of a proposal, August 7, 1969, from the three Western powers. The first phase of the talks was concluded September 3, 1971 with the signing of a four-power agreement on Berlin; text and related material in *Department of State Bulletin*, September 27, 1971, pp. 318–324.

10 *Documents, 1968–69*, pp. 125–127.

11 Documents 10–11.

of which is so important for the security of Europe and the future of humanity.

11. On the occasion of the coming into force of the Non-Proliferation Treaty,[12] Ministers reemphasised the importance they attach to limiting the spread of nuclear weapons as well as to measures for genuine nuclear disarmament. They noted with interest the efforts now under way to exclude mass destruction weapons from the seabed [13] and to deal with the problem of control of biological and chemical weapons.[14] They expressed the hope that further progress on disarmament measures, with appropriate safeguards, can reduce the arms burdens borne by all.

12. The members of the North Atlantic Alliance have, over a number of years, proclaimed their interest in arms control and disarmament measures which facilitate a gradual elimination of the military confrontation in Europe. Ministers recalled the declarations issued at Reykjavik in 1968,[15] and at Brussels in 1969.[16] They noted that up to now these declarations had led to no meaningful reply.

13. The Allies have nevertheless carried out intensive studies on mutual force reductions in accordance with the directions given by Ministers in December 1969. Ministers examined the detailed report presented to them by the North Atlantic Council in Permanent Session. This has been of great value in clarifying the complex issues involved. Ministers gave instructions for further relevant studies which would guide policies and explorations in this field.

14. Ministers, having examined all these developments, both positive and negative and having taken note of the Report on the Procedures for Negotiation which they had commissioned from the Permanent Council, stated that they were ready to multiply exploratory conversations with all interested parties on all questions affecting peace.

15. In so far as progress is recorded as a result of these talks and in the on-going talks—in particular on Germany and Berlin —the Allied Governments state that they would be ready to enter into multilateral contacts with all interested governments. One of the main purposes of such contacts would be to explore when it will be possible to convene a conference, or a series of confer-

---

[12] Document 12; cf. note 5 to Document 7.
[13] Documents 13–14.
[14] Documents 15–16.
[15] *Documents, 1968–69,* pp. 133–134.
[16] Same, pp. 169–173.

ences on European security and co-operation. The establishment of a permanent body could be envisaged as one means, among others, of embarking upon multilateral negotiations in due course.

16. Among the subjects to be explored, affecting security and co-operation in Europe, are included in particular:

(a) The principles which should govern relations between states, including the renunciation of force;

(b) the development of international relations with a view to contributing to the freer movement of people, ideas and information and to developing co-operation in the cultural, economic, technical and scientific fields as well as in the field of human environment.

17. In addition, Ministers representing countries participating in NATO's integrated defence programme attach particular importance to further exploration with other interested parties of the possibility of mutual and balanced force reductions and have therefore issued a declaration on this subject.[17]

18. As a first step, Ministers requested the Foreign Minister of Italy [Aldo Moro] to transmit this communiqué on their behalf through diplomatic channels to all other interested parties including neutral and non-aligned governments. They further agree that member governments would seek reactions of other governments to the initiation of the comprehensive programme of exploration and negotiation which they envisage.

19. Ministers reviewed the first report from NATO's Committee on the Challenges of Modern Society and welcomed the progress made in the six months since the Committee was established as a demonstration of the value of allied co-operation on the urgent problems of human environment. Intensive studies now in progress will contribute to national and international action on a broad range of environmental issues, including such pressing concerns as air and water pollution.[18]

20. Ministers reaffirmed the view that the benefit of the Alliance's work in Mankind's environment particularly could become a basis for broader co-operations between East and West in this field of ever-increasing importance. They considered that this could be ensured either through existing international organizations providing a useful framework for enhanced co-operations or by any other appropriate method.

17 Document 20 (b).
18 On the second meeting of the Committee on the Challenges of Modern Society, held in Brussels April 13–14, 1970, see *NATO Letter*, May 1970, pp. 8–16.

21. The next Ministerial Sessions of the North Atlantic Council will be held in Brussels in December 1970.[19]

(b) Declaration on Mutual and Balanced Force Reductions.[20]

(Complete Text)

DECLARATION ON MUTUAL AND BALANCED FORCE REDUCTIONS

1. Meeting at Rome on 26th and 27th May, 1970, the Ministers representing countries participating in NATO's Integrated Defence Programme recall and reaffirm the commitment of their nations to pursue effective policies directed towards a greater relaxation of tensions in their continuing search for a just and durable peace. They recall, in particular, the invitations they have previously addressed to the Soviet Union and other countries of Eastern Europe to join them in discussing the possibility of mutual and balanced force reductions.

2. The objective of the work on which their representatives have been engaged has been to prepare a realistic basis for active explorations between the interested parties at an early date and thereby to establish whether it could serve as a starting point for fruitful negotiation. Such exploratory talks would assist those concerned in developing in detail criteria and objectives for substantive negotiations to follow at the appropriate stage in a forum to be determined. They would also provide tangible evidence of the readiness to build confidence between East and West.

3. Ministers invite interested states to hold exploratory talks on mutual and balanced force reductions in Europe, with special reference to the Central Region. They agree that in such talks the Allies would put forward the following considerations:

(a) Mutual force reductions should be compatible with the vital security interests of the Alliance and should not operate to the military disadvantage of either side having regard for the differences arising from geographical and other considerations.

(b) Reductions should be on a basis of reciprocity, and phased and balanced as to their scope and timing.

(c) Reductions should include stationed and indigenous forces and their weapons systems in the area concerned.

[19] Document 22.
[20] Text from *Department of State Bulletin,* June 22, 1970, p. 775.

(d) There must be adequate verification and controls to ensure the observance of agreements on mutual and balanced force reductions.

4. As a first step Ministers requested the Foreign Minister of Italy to transmit this Declaration on their behalf through diplomatic channels to all other interested parties, including neutral and non-aligned governments. They further agreed that in the course of their normal bilateral and other contacts member governments would seek to obtain the responses and reactions of other governments. Members of the Alliance will consult further regarding the outcome of their soundings with a view to enabling the Alliance to determine what further individual or joint exploration might be useful.

(21) Remarks by President Nixon at NATO Southern Command Headquarters, Naples, September 30, 1970.[21]

(Excerpt)

Admiral [Horacio] Rivero [USN, Commander, Allied Forces Southern Europe], all of the officers, the distinguished guests, and the others associated with the NATO Southern Command:

I am very honored to be here on this occasion. And before I begin my formal remarks, if I could be permitted to say that I am very happy to see so many from the United States, the dependents, the wives, the children, and the rest, and I bring you the best greetings from all of your friends back home in the United States.

I know that you must have been as impressed as I was, and as moved as I was, by the pageantry that we have just witnessed, of the great nations that were represented by the forces that we saw pass in review.

I know, too, that you realize that that pageantry has something behind it. NATO is 21 years of age.[22] In fact, most of the people here in this audience were born since NATO came into being.

And when we consider NATO, we must realize that because of its strength and its purpose, Europe has enjoyed a generation of peace since it came into being.

---

21 Text from *Weekly Compilation of Presidential Documents,* October 5, 1970, pp. 1297–1298; for the context see *The United States in World Affairs, 1970,* Section 33.

22 Text of the North Atlantic Treaty, signed April 4, 1949, in *Documents, 1949,* pp. 612–615.

Now, at the present time, we live in a period of change. A period of change can be welcome. It can mean to this part of the world, to Europe, that we move from a period of confrontation to one of negotiation, that we move from a period in which Europe seems to be permanently divided by rigid blocs, to a period in which the nations and the peoples of Europe join together in cooperation and communication.

A period of change also can be one of very great danger, because in a time of change there is turmoil, there is also the lack of confidence that comes when instability seems to be the order of the day.

And the great question before us in NATO and in the free world today is whether in this period of change in Europe and in the world we shall be masters of change and masters of our fate, or whether we shall be the victims of change.

And that brings me back to this pageantry that we just saw and what it represents, what it represents not just to us from the United States, but from our friends in Europe and to our friends in Europe.

What we must realize is that in a period of instability, of uncertainty, and of possible lack of confidence, that what is needed is an institution that is stable, that men and women can hang onto, and NATO is such an institution.

It is strong, it is united, it represents the best of all of our people. It has power, but it is a power that exists for the purpose of peace, and because it exists for the purpose of peace, it serves the very best ideals of all of the great peoples that are proud to be members of the NATO organization.

My trip [23] as President of the United States to this NATO Command underlines the American commitment to a Mediterranean that will not be our sea, speaking of an American sea, but a sea that will belong to all people.

My trip, also, to this NATO Command represents a firm American commitment to this great institution, to which the credit must be given over these past 21 years for a period of peace in this continent of Europe, which has suffered so much from war in the past.

And I say particularly to all of you today, but if I could direct my remarks especially to the young people here today from

---

23 Other stops made by President Nixon on his trip to Europe included Italy (September 27–29), the Vatican (September 28), Yugoslavia (September 30–October 1), Spain (October 2–3), United Kingdom (October 3), and Ireland (October 3–5). For documentation see *Weekly Compilation of Presidential Documents,* October 5, 1970, pp. 1292–1300; same, October 12, 1970, pp. 1320–1342, 1359.

America, in our country we in America in this century have not known a full generation of peace. World War I, World War II, Korea, and now Vietnam.

The great goal that we have is to develop the policies that will provide the opportunity for your generation to experience that full generation of peace. I think it is possible. But it will be possible only if the United States remains strong and firm in its commitments to its alliances and particularly strong and firm in its commitments to the great alliance of NATO, perhaps the most successful in its purpose of any alliance in the history of the world.

I am proud to be here standing with our NATO allies and friends, and I say that this trip and my presence here speaks for a United States of America, united behind a great principle of strength, strength which exists for peace in Europe, and as it exists for peace in Europe which can contribute to that peace in the whole world that all of us want for ourselves and, most of all, for our children.

*   *   *

(22) Ministerial Session of the North Atlantic Council, Brussels, December 3–4, 1970.

(a) Communiqué.[24]

(Complete Text)

The North Atlantic Council met in Ministerial Session at Brussels on 3rd and 4th December, 1970. Foreign, Defence and Finance Ministers were present.

2. Ministers again stated that the political purpose of the Alliance is the common search for peace through initiatives aiming at the relaxation of tension and the establishment of a just and lasting peaceful order in Europe, accompanied by appropriate security guarantees.

3. The Council received a statement from President Nixon [25] which pledged that, given a similar approach by the other Allies, the United States would maintain and improve its own forces in Europe and would not reduce them except in the context of

---

24 Text from *Department of State Bulletin*, January 4, 1971, pp. 2–5; for the context see *The United States in World Affairs, 1970*, Sections 5 and 36.
25 Text in *Weekly Compilation of Presidential Documents,* December 7, 1970, pp. 1620–1621.

reciprocal East-West action. Ministers expressed their profound satisfaction at the reaffirmation of Alliance solidarity expressed in this statement.

4. Ministers reviewed the international situation as it had developed since their last meeting in May in Rome.[26] They noted that 1970 had been a year of extensive diplomatic activity by member governments of the Alliance to initiate or intensify contacts, discussions and negotiations with the members of the Warsaw Pact and with other European countries. Ministers paid particular attention to the Strategic Arms Limitations Talks,[27] the Treaties negotiated by the Federal Republic of Germany with the Soviet Union and Poland,[28] intra-German relations,[29] Berlin [30] and the situation in the Mediterranean.

5. Ministers welcomed the resumption at Helsinki in November of the negotiations between the United States and the USSR on Strategic Arms Limitations. They expressed the hope that the talks would lead, at an early date, to an agreement strengthening peace and security in Europe and in the world.

6. Ministers noted with satisfaction the signing of the Treaty between the Federal Republic of Germany and the USSR on 12th August, 1970, and the initialling of the treaty between the Federal Republic of Germany and the Polish People's Republic on 18th November, 1970. They welcomed these Treaties as contributions toward reduction of tensions in Europe and as important elements of the *modus vivendi* which the Federal Republic of Germany wishes to establish with its Eastern neighbours. Ministers noted the clarifications made in the context of the Treaties, and reflected in the exchange of notes between the Federal Republic of Germany and the Three Powers, to the effect that quadripartite rights and responsibilities for Berlin and Germany as a whole remain unaffected pending a peace settlement which would be based on the free decision of the German people and on the interests of European security. Ministers welcomed the beginning of an exchange of views between the Federal Republic of Germany and the GDR and expressed the hope that this exchange will prepare the ground for genuine negotiations between the two. Ministers reviewed the development of the quadripartite talks in Berlin.

7. In considering the situation with regard to Berlin and Germany, Ministers recalled their statement in the Brussels De-

[26] Document 20.
[27] Documents 10–11.
[28] Document 23 and note 7 to Document 20.
[29] Cf. note 8 to Document 20.
[30] Cf. note 9 to Document 20.

claration of 5th December, 1969 (paragraph 10) to the effect that concrete progress in both these fields would constitute an important contribution to peace and would have great weight in their evaluation of the prospects for improving East-West relations in Europe.[31] Indeed, these prospects would be put in question failing a satisfactory outcome to the current Berlin negotiations. With this in mind, Ministers stressed the importance of securing unhindered access to Berlin, improved circulation within Berlin and respect by all for the existing ties between the Western sectors of Berlin and the Federal Republic of Germany which have been established with the approval of the Three Powers. They underlined the need for an understanding between the Federal Republic of Germany and the GDR on a negotiated settlement of their mutual relations which would take account of the special features of the situation in Germany.

8. Ministers took note of a report on the situation in the Mediterranean prepared on their instructions by the Council in Permanent Session. They noted that the evolution of events in the area gives cause for concern and justifies careful vigilance on the part of the Allies. They recommended that consultations on this question should continue, and they invited the Council in Permanent Session to keep the situation under review and to report fully thereon at their next meeting.

9. As a result of their review of the international situation and its positive and negative aspects, Ministers emphasised that these developments in Europe and the Mediterranean all affect the Alliance directly or indirectly, and have a bearing on the possibilities of reducing tensions and promoting peace.

10. Ministers noted that the initiatives which had been taken by Allied Governments had already achieved certain results which constituted some progress in important fields of East-West relations. Nevertheless their hope had been that more substantial progress would have been recorded in bilateral exploratory contacts and in the on-going negotiations, so that active consideration could have been given to the institution of broad multilateral contacts which would deal with the substantial problems of security and co-operation in Europe. They affirmed the readiness of their governments, as soon as the talks on Berlin have reached a satisfactory conclusion and in so far as the other on-going talks are proceeding favourably, to enter into multilateral contacts with all interested governments to explore when it would be possible to convene a conference, or a series of conferences, on security and co-operation in Europe. In this event, the Council would give immediate attention to this question.

31 *Documents, 1968–69*, pp. 171–172.

11. In the meantime, the Council in Permanent Session will continue its study of the results which might be achieved at any such conference or series of conferences, and of the appropriate exploratory and preparatory procedures, including the proposals that have already been advanced. The Allied Governments will also pursue energetically their bilateral exploratory conversations with all interested states on questions affecting security and co-operation.

12. Ministers recalled that any genuine and lasting improvement in East-West relations in Europe must be based on the respect of the following principles which should govern relations between states and which would be included among the points to be explored: sovereign equality, political independence and territorial integrity of each European state; non-interference and non-intervention in the internal affairs of any state, regardless of its political or social system; and the right of the people of each European state to shape their own destinies free of external constraint. A common understanding and application of these principles, without condition or reservation, would give full meaning to any agreement on mutual renunciation of the use or threat of force.

13. In the field of international co-operation, the contacts mentioned in paragraph 10 might provide an opportunity to consider ways and means of ensuring closer co-operation between interested countries on the cultural, economic, technical and scientific levels, and on the question of human environment. Ministers reaffirmed that the freer movement of people, ideas and information is an essential element for the development of such co-operation.

14. Ministers noted that Alliance studies on the various aspects of the mutual and balanced force reductions question have further progressed since the Rome Meeting and instructed the Council in Permanent Session to pursue studies in this field.

15. Ministers representing countries participating in NATO's integrated Defence Programme re-emphasised the importance they attach to mutual and balanced force reductions as a means of reducing tensions and lessening the military confrontation in Europe and recalled the Declarations on this question issued at Reykjavik, in 1968 [32] and at Rome earlier this year.[33] They noted that the Warsaw Pact countries have not directly responded to these Declarations but have mentioned the possibility of a discussion at some future time of the question of reducing foreign armed forces on the territory of European states.

[32] Same, pp. 133–134.
[33] Document 20(b).

16. These Ministers renewed their invitation to interested states to hold exploratory talks on the basis of their Rome Declaration, and also indicated their readiness within this framework to examine different possibilities in the field of force reductions in the Central Region of Europe, including the possible mutual and balanced reduction of stationed forces, as part of an integral programme for the reduction of both stationed and indigenous forces.

17. Ministers reaffirmed their profound interest in genuine disarmament and arms control measures. In this connection, they expressed their satisfaction with progress towards a ban on the emplacement of weapons of mass destruction on the sea bed.[34] They further considered the pursuit of Allied efforts and studies in all fields related to disarmament to be essential, including those concerning biological and chemical weapons.[35] They invited the Council in Permanent Session to continue to examine these matters.

18. Ministers endorsed the recent Council recommendation to Allied Governments to start work at once in order to achieve, by 1975 if possible but not later than the end of the decade, the elimination of intentional discharges of oil and oily wastes into the sea. This and the other accomplishments of the Committee on the Challenges of Modern Society during the past year[36] were welcomed by Ministers as evidence that the Allies are effectively combining their resources to stimulate national and international action on environmental problems.

19. Ministers examined a report on the achievements of the Conference of National Armaments Directors and its subordinate bodies in the promotion of co-operation in research, development and production of military equipment during the four years of its existence. They noted that, in spite of the excellent progress that had been made in the exchange of information on defence equipment, it had proved possible to establish relatively few firm NATO projects for co-operative development and production of equipment. They recognised that more political support would be necessary to overcome the obstacles to greater co-operation. They agreed to the need for a more positive approach in order to achieve the financial and operational benefits of more widespread adoption of jointly developed and produced equipment.

20. Ministers of the countries participating in NATO's inte-

34 Documents 13–14.

35 Documents 15–17.

36 Cf. note 18 to Document 20. On the Third Plenary Session of the Committee on the Challenges of Modern Society, held in Brussels October 19–20, 1970, see *NATO Letter*, December 1970, pp. 9–12.

grated defence programme met as the Defence Planning Committee on 2nd December, 1970.

21. Ministers concentrated their discussion on a comprehensive study, which has been in progress since last May, of the defence programs which the Alliance will face in the 1970s. They approved for public release the text at Annex.[37]

22. Ministers confirmed that NATO's approach to security in the 1970s will continue to be based on the twin concepts of defence and détente. They reaffirmed the principle that the overall military capability of NATO should not be reduced except as part of a pattern of mutual force reductions balanced in scope and timing. They agreed that East-West negotiations can be expected to succeed only if NATO maintains an effective deterrent and defensive posture. Ministers confirmed the continued validity of the NATO strategy of flexibility in response, which includes forward defence, reinforcement of the flanks and capabilities for rapid mobilisation, and calls for the maintenance of military capabilities which are able to provide an appropriate counter to any aggression. They noted the continuous rise in Soviet defence and defence-related expenditure and the evidence that the USSR is continuing to strengthen still further its military establishment, including that in the maritime field where Soviet power and the range of its activity have markedly increased. They, therefore, emphasised the need for improvements in NATO's conventional deterrent, as well as the maintenance of a sufficient and modern tactical and strategic nuclear deterrent.

23. The security of NATO being indivisible, Ministers underlined the special military and political rôle of North American forces present in Europe as an irreplaceable contribution to the common defence. In parallel they welcomed the important decision of European member nations participating in NATO's integrated defence programme to make an increased common European effort to strengthen the defence capability of the Alliance. The establishment of a special European Defence Improvement Programme of substantial additional measures will significantly strengthen NATO's capacity for defence and for crisis management in fields, including communications, which have been identified in the "AD 70s" Study as having particular importance.

24. In respect of the above Study, Ministers invited the Defence Planning Committee in Permanent Session to draw up a suitable programme and to ensure that all possible progress is made.

25. Ministers noted the force commitments undertaken by

[37] Document 22(b).

member nations for the year 1971 and adopted the five-year NATO force plan covering the period 1971–1975. They gave directions for the development of a force plan for the next NATO planning period.

26. Ministers viewed with concern the evidence of continuing growth in Soviet military strength in the Mediterranean. Such developments, they felt, could constitute an increasingly significant threat to the security of the Alliance. Ministers commented with approval on steps which have been taken to improve the Alliance's defence posture in the Mediterranean. Referring to their Communiqué issued in Brussels on 11th June of this year,[38] Ministers directed that urgent attention be given to the development and implementation of further appropriate measures.

27. Within the field of crisis management, Ministers reviewed communications facilities for high level political consultation and for command and control; they agreed to a number of important measures designed to improve and expand these vital facilities. They encouraged further efforts in the field of civil preparedness and civil emergency planning. They noted progress made on various defence studies. They also noted that the trend towards more sophisticated equipment at increasing cost may well continue, and they stressed that forthcoming modernisation programmes would offer an opportunity for increased cooperation.

28. The Ministerial Meeting also provided the Defence Ministers comprising the Nuclear Defence Affairs Committee (Belgium, Canada, Denmark, Germany, Greece, Italy, Netherlands, Norway, Portugal, Turkey, United Kingdom and United States) with the occasion to review work recently in progress in the Nuclear Planning Group and plans for the future. Acting on the recommendation of the Nuclear Defence Affairs Committee, the Defence Planning Committee adopted the policy documents elaborated by the Nuclear Planning Group at their meeting in Venice last Spring[39] and finalised at Ottawa in October this year.[40] These documents are in consonance with NATO's strategy of flexibility in response.

29. The next Ministerial Meeting of the Defence Planning Committee will take place in the Spring of 1971.

---

[38] Text in *NATO Letter,* July-August 1970, pp. 20-21. A five-nation Naval On-Call Force Mediterranean (NAVOCFORMED) was activated April 27, 1970 and included 13 days of exercises and port calls in the Mediterranean; for details see *NATO Letter,* June 1970, pp. 28–29.

[39] The meeting was held June 8–9; text of communiqué in *NATO Letter,* July-August 1970, p. 20.

[40] Text in same, December 1970, p. 24.

30. The Spring Ministerial Meeting of the Council will be held in Lisbon on 3rd and 4th June, 1971.

31. Ministers requested the Foreign Minister [Pierre Harmel] of Belgium to transmit this Communiqué on their behalf through diplomatic channels to all other interested parties including neutral and non-aligned governments.

(b) Annex.[41]

(Complete Text)

ALLIANCE DEFENCE FOR THE SEVENTIES

The Allied countries participating in the integrated defence efforts decided at a meeting of the Defence Planning Committee in Permanent Session in May of this year to examine in depth NATO defence problems for the next decade.

2. The North Atlantic Alliance has made a practice over the years of periodically conducting major reviews and adapting its policies to accord with the changing circumstances of the times. A notable recent example was the study undertaken in 1967 which resulted in the Report on the Future Tasks of the Alliance establishing defence and détente as complementary pillars of its activities.[42] That report stated that "collective defence is a stabilising factor in world politics. It is the necessary condition for effective policies directed towards a greater relaxation of tensions." Against this background, governments earlier this year recognised the particular timeliness of a full and candid exchange of views among the Allies on their common defence over the next ten years. This examination of NATO's defence capability in the light of current and prospective military and political developments has now been completed.

3. NATO's approach to security in the 1970s will continue to be based on the twin concepts of defence and détente. Defence problems cannot be seen in isolation but must be viewed in the broader context of the Alliance's basic purpose of ensuring the security of its members. There is a close inter-relationship between the maintenance of adequate defensive strength and the negotiation of settlements affecting the security of the member states.

4. The 1970s could develop into an era of successful negotiations between members of the North Atlantic Alliance and

---

41 Text from *Department of State Bulletin*, January 4, 1971, pp. 5–6.
42 *Documents, 1967*, pp. 110–114; quoted passage, pp. 111–112.

those of the Warsaw Pact. On Western initiative, there are now negotiations under way between East and West which could lead to a real relaxation of tensions. It is hoped that there will be satisfactory progress in on-going talks on a limitation of strategic nuclear weapons and on an improvement of the situation in and around Berlin, and in other current negotiations between individual members of NATO and the Warsaw Pact. The Alliance will continue to seek improved East-West relations, and in the framework of this effort, one of its principal aims will be to engage the Soviet Union and its allies in meaningful talks on mutual and balanced force reductions and other disarmament measures. Progress in this field would facilitate dealing with the defence problems of the next decade. This period might also see convened one or more conferences on European security and co-operation.

5. On the other hand, the Allies cannot ignore certain disturbing features in the international situation. The evidence thus far suggests that the USSR, intent on extending and strengthening its political power, conducts its international relations on the basis of concepts some of which are not conducive to détente. In particular, its concept of sovereignty is clearly inconsistent with United Nations' principles. At the same time, Soviet military capablities, besides guaranteeing the USSR's security, continue to increase and provide formidable backing for the wide-ranging assertion of Soviet influence and presence, persistently raising questions regarding their intentions. In real terms, there has been a continuous rise in Soviet defence and defence-related expenditures between 1965 and 1969 of about 5% to 6% per year on average and the evidence is that the USSR is continuing to strengthen its military establishments still further. The contrast between these figures and the corresponding information relating to the Alliance may be seen from paragraph 10 below. Whether East-West relations can in these circumstances be significantly improved will depend mainly on the actions of the USSR and its Warsaw Pact allies, and on the attitudes they bring to negotiations now in progress or in prospect.

6. The position of the Alliance and its member countries during this period of exploration and negotiation, with special reference to European security and mutual force reductions, would be weakened if NATO were to reduce its forces unilaterally, especially those in the European area, and in particular at a time when it is confronted with a steady growth in Soviet military power, which manifests itself above all in the strategic nuclear and maritime fields. NATO member states must, therefore, maintain a sufficient level of conventional and nuclear

strength for defence as well as for deterrence, thus furnishing a sound basis from which to negotiate and underlining that negotiation is the only sensible road open. Progress towards a meaningful détente in an era of negotiation will, therefore, require the maintenance of a strong collective defence posture.

7. The present NATO defence strategy of deterrence and defence, with its constituent concepts of flexibility in response and forward defence, will remain valid. It will continue to require an appropriate mix of nuclear and conventional forces.

8. It is to be hoped that success in strategic arms limitation talks will be achieved. Allied strategic nuclear capability will in any event remain a key element in the security of the West during the 1970s. At the present time, adequate nuclear forces exist and it will be essential to ensure that this capability, which includes the continued commitment of theatre nuclear forces, is maintained.

9. The situation in the field of conventional forces is less satisfactory in view of certain imbalances between NATO and Warsaw Pact capabilities. Careful attention needs to be paid to priorities in improving NATO's conventional strength in the 1970s. In the allocation of resources, priority will be given to measures most critical to a balanced Alliance defence posture in terms of deterrent effect, ability to resist external political pressure, and the prompt availability or rapid enhancement of the forward defensive capability in a developing crisis. In addition to a capability to deter and counter major deliberate aggression, Allied forces should be so structured and organized as to be capable of dealing also with aggressions and incursions with more limited objectives associated with intimidation or the creation of faits accomplis, or with those aggressions which might be the result of accident or miscalculation. In short, Allied forces should be so structured and organized as to deter and counter any kind of aggression. Important areas in NATO's conventional defence posture to which attention should be paid in the next decade include: armour/anti-armour potential; the air situation including aircraft protection; overall maritime capabilities, with special reference to anti-submarine forces; the situation on NATO's flanks; the peacetime deployment of ground forces; further improvements in Allied mobilization and reinforcement capabilities as well as in NATO communications, for crisis management purposes.

10. The Alliance possesses the basic resources for adequate conventional strength. However, member countries are confronted with diverging trends in the pattern of expenditures and costs. On the other hand the cost of personnel and equipment

continues to mount and most NATO countries are faced with major re-equipment programmes. On the other, in many member countries the share of GNP devoted to defence has declined and, even if outlays in money terms have risen, outlays in real terms have diminished owing to inflation. In marked contrast with the trend in Warsaw Pact countries' military expenditure, defence expenditures of the NATO European countries taken as a whole and calculated in real terms went down by 4% from 1964 to 1969.

11. It is of paramount importance that there be close collaboration among all member states to ensure the most effective collective defence posture. It is equally important that the burden of maintaining the necessary military strength should be borne co-operatively with each member making an appropriate contribution.

12. The commitment of substantial North American forces deployed in Europe is essential both politically and militarily for effective deterrence and defence and to demonstrate the solidarity of NATO. Their replacement by European forces would be no substitute. At the same time their significance is closely related to an effective and improved European defence effort. Ten of the European countries have therefore consulted among themselves to determine how it would be possible for them individually and collectively to make a more substantial contribution to the overall defence of the Treaty area.

13. As a result the ten countries have decided to adopt a special European Defence Improvement Programme going well beyond previously existing plans and designed to improve Alliance capability in specific fields identified as of particular importance in the current study. This Programme will comprise:

(a) an additional collective contribution, in the order of $420 million over five years, to NATO common infrastructure to accelerate work on the NATO integrated communications system and on aircraft survival measures;

(b) numerous important additions and improvements to national forces, costing at least $450–500 million over the next five years plus very substantial further amounts thereafter; the forces concerned will all be committed to NATO;

(c) other significant financial measures to improve collective defence capability, costing $79 million over the next two years.

The United States and Canada have welcomed this Programme, and have reaffirmed their intention to maintain their forces in Europe at substantially their current levels.

14. After careful review of the proposals emerging from the examination of defence problems in the Seventies, the Defence

Planning Committee in Ministerial Session on 2nd December 1970, adopted concrete proposals aimed at improving NATO's defence capabilities.

B. The Federal Republic Looks East.

(23) Treaty Between the Federal Republic of Germany and the Soviet Union, Signed at Moscow August 12, 1970.[43]

(a) United States Note to the Federal Republic of Germany, August 11, 1970.[44]

(Complete Text)

The Government of the United States has the honor of informing the Government of the Federal Republic of Germany that it has received the note transmitted by the Government of the Federal Republic of Germany on August 7, 1970, containing the following text: [45]

The Government of the Federal Republic of Germany has the honor to report the following in connection with the imminent signing of a treaty between the Federal Republic of Germany and the Union of Soviet Socialist Republics.[46]

The Federal Minister of Foreign Affairs [Walter Scheel] has stated in connection with the negotiations the viewpoint of the Federal Republic concerning the rights and responsibilities of the Four Powers in relation to Germany as a whole and Berlin.

Since the settlement of a peace treaty is still outstanding, both sides take the position that the agreement under consideration does not affect the rights and responsibilities of the French Republic, the United Kingdom of Great Britain and Northern Ireland, the Union of Soviet Socialist Republics and the United States of America.

On August 6, 1970, the Federal Minister of Foreign Affairs stated in this connection:

[43] For the context see *The United States in World Affairs, 1970,* Section 5.
[44] Department of State Press Release 238, August 12, 1970; text from *Department of State Bulletin,* September 7, 1970, pp. 275–276.
[45] Identical notes were sent to France and the United Kingdom; complete text in Press and Information Office of the Federal Government, *The Treaty of August 12, 1970 Between the Federal Republic of Germany and the Union of Soviet Socialist Republics* (Wiesbaden, 1970), pp. 11–13.
[46] Document 23(b).

"The question of the rights of the Four Powers has no connection with the treaty that the Federal Republic of Germany and the USSR intend to conclude and will not be affected by it."

The Foreign Minister of the Union of Soviet Socialist Republics [Andrei A. Gromyko] has made the following statement:

"The question of the rights of the Four Powers was not a subject of the negotiations with the Federal Republic of Germany.

"The Soviet Government took the position that this question should not be discussed.

"The question of the rights of the Four Powers will also not be affected by the treaty which the USSR and the FRG intend to conclude.

"This is the position of the Soviet Government in this question."

The Government of the United States takes full cognizance of this note, including the declarations made by the Foreign Minister of the Federal Republic of Germany and the Foreign Minister of the Union of Soviet Socialist Republics as part of the negotiations prior to the initialing of the treaty which is to be concluded between the Federal Republic of Germany and the Soviet Union.

For its part, the Government of the United States also considers that the rights and responsibilities of the Four Powers for Berlin and Germany as a whole, which derive from the outcome of the Second World War and which are reflected in the London agreement of November 14, 1944 [47] and in the quadripartite declaration of June 5, 1945, [48] and in other wartime and postwar agreements are not and cannot be affected by a bilateral treaty between the Federal Republic of Germany and the Union of Soviet Socialist Republics, including the present treaty.

[47] United Kingdom, Secretary of State for Foreign Affairs, *Selected Documents on Germany and the Question of Berlin, 1944–1961* (Germany No. 2 [1961], Cmnd. 1552; London: H.M.S.O., 1961), pp. 31–33.
[48] *Documents, 1944–1948*, pp. 217–222.

(b) Treaty Between the Federal Republic of Germany and the Union of Soviet Socialist Republics, Signed at Moscow August 12, 1970.[49]

(Complete Text)

TREATY BETWEEN THE FEDERAL REPUBLIC OF GERMANY AND THE UNION OF SOVIET SOCIALIST REPUBLICS

The High Contracting Parties

Anxious to contribute to strengthening peace and security in Europe and the world,

Convinced that peaceful co-operation among States on the basis of the purposes and principles of the Charter of the United Nations complies with the ardent desire of nations and the general interests of international peace,

Appreciating the fact that the agreed measures previously implemented by them, in particular the conclusion of the Agreement of 13 September 1955 on the Establishment of Diplomatic Relations,[50] have created favourable conditions for new important steps destined to develop further and to strengthen their mutual relations,

Desiring to lend expression, in the form of a treaty, to their determination to improve and extend co-operation between them, including economic relations as well as scientific, technological and cultural contacts, in the interest of both States,

Have agreed as follows:

ARTICLE 1

The Federal Republic of Germany and the Union of Soviet Socialist Republics consider it an important objective of their policies to maintain international peace and achieve détente.

They affirm their endeavour to further the normalization of the situation in Europe and the development of peaceful relations among all European States, and in so doing proceed from the actual situation existing in this region.

ARTICLE 2

The Federal Republic of Germany and the Union of Soviet Socialist Republics shall in their mutual relations as well as in matters of ensuring European and international security be

[49] Text from Press and Information Office of the Federal Government (cited in note 45), pp. 7–9.
[50] Text of communiqué in *Documents, 1955,* pp. 107–108.

guided by the purposes and principles embodied in the Charter of the United Nations. Accordingly they shall settle their disputes exclusively by peaceful means and undertake to refrain from the threat or use of force, pursuant to Article 2 of the Charter of the United Nations, in any matters affecting security in Europe or international security, as well as in their mutual relations.

ARTICLE 3

In accordance with the foregoing purposes and principles the Federal Republic of Germany and the Union of Soviet Socialist Republics share the realization that peace can only be maintained in Europe if nobody disturbs the present frontiers.

—They undertake to respect without restriction the territorial integrity of all States in Europe within their present frontiers;

—they declare that they have no territorial claims against anybody nor will assert such claims in the future;

—they regard today and shall in future regard the frontiers of all States in Europe as inviolable such as they are on the date of signature of the present Treaty, including the Oder-Neisse line which forms the western frontier of the People's Republic of Poland and the frontier between the Federal Republic of Germany and the German Democratic Republic.

ARTICLE 4

The present Treaty between the Federal Republic of Germany and the Union of Soviet Socialist Republics shall not affect any bilateral or multilateral treaties or arrangements previously concluded by them.

ARTICLE 5

The present Treaty is subject to ratification and shall enter into force on the date of exchange of the instruments of ratification which shall take place in Bonn.

Done at Moscow on 12 August 1970 in two originals, each in the German and Russian languages, both texts being equally authentic.

For the Federal Republic of Germany:

WILLY BRANDT
WALTER SCHEEL

For the Union of Soviet Socialist Republics:

ALEXEI N. KOSYGIN
ANDREI A. GROMYKO

(c) Statement by Secretary of State Rogers, August 12, 1970.[51]

(Complete Text)

West German Chancellor Willy Brandt has today signed in Moscow a bilateral renunciation-of-force treaty with the Soviet Union.[52] The United States views this signing with satisfaction.

On several occasions during the long negotiating process, we have expressed confidence and support for the Federal Republic's efforts to reach new understandings with its East European neighbors. We wish today to reiterate that confidence and support. The Federal Republic has maintained close consultations with the British, French, and U.S. Governments on the treaty.

This consultation has led to an exchange of notes, which is published along with the treaty, affirming that the treaty cannot affect our continuing rights and responsibilities for Berlin and Germany as a whole.[53]

The United States shares the hope of the Federal Republic that its new treaty with the Soviets is but a first step in a process that will lead to an improved situation in Europe. We would hope that one of the next steps would be tangible evidence of Soviet cooperation toward bringing about substantial practical improvements for the people of Berlin.[54]

C. The Mediterranean

(24) United States-Spanish Agreement of Friendship and Cooperation, Signed at Washington, August 6, 1970.[55]

(a) Text of Agreement.[56]

(Excerpt)

*   *   *

Chapter VIII. Cooperation for Defense

The Governments of the United States and Spain are in agreement in considering that the threat to peace is the great-

[51] Department of State Press Release 237; text from *Department of State Bulletin*, September 7, 1970, p. 275.
[52] Document 23 (b).
[53] Cf. note 45 above.
[54] Cf. note 9 to Document 20.
[55] For the context see *The United States in World Affairs, 1970*, Section 33.
[56] Department of State, *Treaties and Other International Acts Series*, No. 6924; entered into force September 26, 1970 with exchange of notes and letters; text from *Department of State Bulletin*, August 31, 1970, pp. 237–242.

est problem faced by the modern world, and that it requires that both Governments remain vigilant and continue to develop their ability to defend themselves against such a threat. Consequently, both Governments, within the framework of their constitutional processes, and to the extent feasible and appropriate, will make compatible their respective defense policies in areas of mutual interest, and will grant each other reciprocal defense support as follows:

Article 30. Each Government will support the defense system of the other and make such contributions as are deemed necessary and appropriate to achieve the greatest possible effectiveness of those systems to meet possible contingencies, subject to the terms and conditions set forth hereinafter.

Article 31. The Government of the United States agrees to support Spanish defense efforts, as necessary and appropriate, by contributing to the modernization of Spanish defense industries, as well as granting military assistance to Spain, in accordance with applicable agreements. This support will be conditioned by the priorities and limitations created by the international commitments of the United States and the exigencies of the international situation and will be subject to the appropriation of funds by the Congress, whenever the case so requires, and to United States legislation.

Article 32. The Government of Spain, subject to Spanish constitutional provisions and legislation in force, will authorize the Government of the United States to use and maintain for military purposes certain facilities in Spanish military installations agreed upon by the two Governments.[57] Any major construction that may be necessary for the exercise of this use shall be subject to agreement between the two Governments in the Joint Committee created in Article 36 of this Chapter. The United States is further authorized to station and house the civilian and military personnel necessary for such use; to provide for their security, discipline, and welfare; to store and guard provisions, supplies, equipment and materiel; and to maintain the services necessary for such purposes. The exercise of the functions authorized herein shall be subject to such express terms and technical conditions as the two Governments may agree upon.

Article 33.

(a) The Government of Spain assumes the obligation of

[57] An agreement on the use of military facilities in Spain, implementing Chapter VIII of the Agreement of Friendship and Cooperation, was signed at Madrid September 25, 1970 and entered into force on the following day; text in Department of State, *Treaties and Other International Acts Series,* No. 6977.

adopting the security measures necessary for the exercise of the functions authorized in Article 32. The United States may exercise the necessary supervision and protection of its personnel, equipment and materiel.

(b) The above-mentioned use by the Government of the United States of facilities in Spanish military installations will be free of all taxes, charges and encumbrances. The Government of Spain will retain free of all charges the ownership of all permanent works constructed for the purpose of this Agreement.

(c) The Government of the United States may remove at any time nonpermanent constructions installed at its expense, as well as its personnel, property, equipment and materiel. However, any substantial removal prior to the expiration of this Agreement will be the subject of prior consultation of the two Governments in the Joint Committee. In the event that any such removal would bring about adverse security consequences, the two Governments will consult immediately in order to adopt appropriate measures.

(d) Whenever the Government of the United States relinquishes a facility authorized in this Chapter, either prior to or as a result of the expiration of the five or ten year period specified in Article 38, the Government of the United States shall not be obligated to leave such facility in the same state and condition it was in prior to its utilization by the Government of the United States, or to compensate Spain for not having returned it in such state, but shall leave the land and permanent constructions thereon in serviceable condition for use by Spanish authorities, provided that the Government of the United States shall incur no additional expense thereby.

(e) In normal circumstances any substantial increase in the personnel or military equipment of the United States in Spain, or any substantial increase in the use by the United States of facilities in Spanish military installations regulated by this Agreement, will be the subject of prior consultation in the Joint Committee and agreed upon between the two Governments through diplomatic channels.

Article 34. In the case of external threat or attack against the security of the West, the time and manner of the use by the United States of the facilities referred to in this Chapter to meet such threat or attack will be the subject of urgent consultations between the two Governments, and will be resolved by mutual agreement in light of the situation created. Such urgent consultations shall take place in the Joint Committee, but when the imminence of the danger so requires, the two Governments will establish direct contact in order to resolve the matter jointly. Each Government retains, however, the inherent right of self-defense.

Article 35. Both Governments consider it necessary and appropriate that the cooperation for defense regulated by this Chapter form a part of the security arrangements for the Atlantic and Mediterranean areas, and to that end they will endeavor to work out by common accord the liaison deemed advisable with the security arrangements for those areas.

Article 36. In order to establish the necessary coordination between the two Governments and to ensure greater effectiveness of the reciprocal defense support granted by the two Governments to each other, the Governments of the United States and Spain agree to establish a Joint Committee on defense matters. The Joint Committee will be the organ in which the two Governments normally will consult with each other and resolve matters that may arise in connection with the reciprocal defense support referred to in this Chapter. The Joint Committee will be organized and will function as specified in the Annex to this Agreement.

Article 37. The two Governments will determine by common accord, through an exchange of notes on this date, the facilities referred to in Article 32 of this Chapter, as well as the United States force levels in Spain and the assistance programs referred to in Article 31 of this Chapter. Thereafter any change in the number or extent of such facilities will be negotiated in the Joint Committee and agreed upon between the two Governments through an exchange of notes.

CHAPTER IX. FINAL PROVISIONS

Article 38. This Agreement shall enter into force on September 26, 1970, and will remain in force for five years, whereupon it may be extended, if both Governments agree, for another five years.

Article 39. In order to facilitate the withdrawal of the personnel, property, equipment and materiel of the Government of the United States located in Spain pursuant to Chapter VIII of this Agreement, a period of one year, during which the withdrawal must be completed, is provided. Such withdrawal shall be commenced immediately upon the expiration of the five year initial period, or, if the Agreement is extended, upon the expiration of the five year extension period. During the withdrawal period above mentioned, not to exceed one year, all of the rights, privileges and obligations deriving from Chapter

VIII of this Agreement shall remain in force as long as United States troops remain in Spain.

Article 40. The entry into force of this Agreement will in no way affect the validity or terms of any agreement existing between the Governments of the United States and Spain, with the exception of the Defense Agreement between the United States and Spain, dated September 26, 1953,[58] and its supplementary agreements which shall thereupon be superseded.

Done at Washington in duplicate, in the English and Spanish languages, each of which shall be equally authentic, this sixth day of August, 1970.

For the Government of the United States of America:

WILLIAM P. ROGERS

For the Government of Spain:

GREGORIO LOPEZ BRAVO

(b) United States Note Outlining Military Assistance Under the Agreement, August 6, 1970.[59]

(Complete Text)

Excellency:

I have the honor to refer to the Agreement of Friendship and Cooperation Between the United States of America and Spain signed today, August 6, 1970.[60] In accordance with Article 37 of the Agreement, I wish to advise you that the intentions of my Government regarding military assistance for Spain, pursuant to Article 31 of the Agreement, which I understand are acceptable to the Government of Spain, are as follows:

a. The United States Government is prepared to assist the Government of Spain to apply Export-Import Bank credits to the purchase of the following equipment:

36	F–4C Phantom fighter bomber aircraft including necessary accessories and ground equipment for 36 aircraft
2	KC–130 aircraft
3	P–3 aircraft
4	SH–3D helicopters

[58] *Documents, 1953,* pp. 283–285.
[59] Text from *Department of State Bulletin,* August 31, 1970, pp. 242–243.
[60] Document 24 (a).

4   Huey Cobra helicopters
6   C–130 A or B aircraft
    Equipment for the territorial command net of Spanish
    Army

b. The Government of the United States will seek to obtain from Congress the necessary funds for the following purposes:

(1) Coverage of 70% of the cost, which is not expected to exceed a total of $50 million, of modernizing and semi-automating the existing aircraft control and warning network in Spain.

(2) Training of Spanish personnel to operate and maintain the United States origin military equipment acquired by Spain.

(3) Military equipment for land forces:

1   battalion of M48 tanks (54)
2   battalions and 2 batteries of 105 MM Howitzer M108
    (48)
1   battalion of 155 MM Howitzer M109 (18)
1   battalion Armored Personnel Carriers
    —49 M113 Armored Personnel Carriers
    — 4 M106 Mortar Carriers
    — 7 M577 Command Post Carriers
16 Huey UH–1H helicopters
1   battalion of 175 MM Guns M107 (12)

c. The Government of the United States intends to loan to the Government of Spain the following vessels, subject, where necessary, to obtaining authorizing legislation:

Type	Quantity	Class of Ship
Submarines	2	Guppy 1A and 11A
Destroyers	5	Various: English, Sumner, Lavalette, Lloyd Thomas
Ocean Minesweepers	4	Aggressive
Landing Ships	3 LST	Chelan County
Auxiliaries	1 ammunition ship	Wrangell
	1 oiler	Cimarron

d. The Government of the United States is prepared to make available to Spain machine tools appropriate for use in the manufacture of munitions, subject to specific agreements with the Government of Spain.

e. The Government of the United States is prepared to relinquish to Spain the Rota-Zaragoza pipeline, subject to the provisions of a procedural annex.

f. The Government of the United States relinquishes any and all claims against the Government of Spain for the residual value of the permanent structures constructed under the Defense Agreement between the United States of America and Spain signed September 26, 1953.

I further wish to advise you that it is the understanding of my Government that the United States of America, subject to Spanish Constitutional provisions and legislation in force, is authorized to use and maintain for military purposes with the appropriate military personnel the facilities in or connected with the following Spanish military installations:

Torrejon Air Base
Zaragoza Air Base
Moron Air Base (standby)
Rota Naval Base
Cadiz-Zaragoza petroleum pipeline and pumping facilities
Petroleum and other storage facilities
Communications and navigational network support facilities

I should appreciate your confirmation of the foregoing understandings on behalf of the Government of Spain.

Accept, Excellency, the assurances of my highest consideration.

WILLIAM P. ROGERS
Secretary of State of the
United States of America

His Excellency
GREGORIO LOPEZ BRAVO
Minister of Foreign Affairs of Spain

(c) *Joint Statement by Secretary of State Rogers and Foreign Minister Gregorio López Bravo, August 6, 1970.*[61]

(Complete Text)

The Spanish Foreign Minister, Gregorio Lopez Bravo, and Secretary of State William P. Rogers today signed an Agreement of Friendship and Cooperation. This Agreement, which replaces the Defense Agreement of 1953 and extensions thereof,[62] initiates a new era in partnership between the United States and Spain.

The new accord comprehends various fields of existing co-

---

[61] Department of State Press Release 231, August 6, 1970; text from *Department of State Bulletin*, August 31, 1970, p. 237.
[62] Cf. note 58, above.

operation between the two countries. Among them are education, agriculture, environment, space, science and technology, as well as defense.

Such an agreement reflects the manner in which cooperation between the two countries has come to include new dimensions since the early 1950's. At that time, it was a matter of urgency to establish the joint-use bases in Spain to strengthen the defensive capability of the West. Under the new agreement, the United States will be permitted to use certain Spanish military facilities, which are still of great importance in Western defense. The United States will undertake to assist Spain in strengthening its own defense system.

In addition, the new agreement also takes into account the many nonmilitary fields in which both countries now have close mutual interest. An example of such an area is space; Spanish tracking stations, manned by personnel from both countries, have played an important role in the Apollo flights. The field of educational exchanges, having already become a fruitful area of cooperation, promises to assume an even greater importance with the adoption of an extensive educational reform program by the Government of Spain.

Both Governments intend this agreement, the text of which is being made public, to promote the well-being and progress of their peoples and, moreover, to make a positive contribution to world peace in accordance with the purposes and principles of the Charter of the United States.

(25) Resumption of Heavy Arms Shipments to Greece: Department of State Announcement, September 22, 1970.[63]

(Complete Text)

United States policy toward Greece has been under review by this administration for the past 18 months. During that time the United States has continued to withhold major items of equipment in the Military Aid Program for Greece, a policy established by the previous administration shortly after the coup in Greece in April 1967.[64]

The administration has now decided to resume normal military shipments to Greece. The resumption of such shipments

---

[63] Text from *Department of State Bulletin,* October 12, 1970, p. 413; for the context see *The United States in World Affairs, 1970,* Section 33.
[64] Cf. same, *1967,* pp. 214–217.

will enhance the ability of the Greek forces to carry out their
responsibilities in defense of the NATO area, and thus contribute importantly to the cohesion and strength of the southern
flank of NATO. Greece offers strategic advantages to the NATO
alliance and to the United States which are of great importance
to the security of the West. This importance has been sharply
underlined in recent months by events in the Eastern Mediterranean. The decision to resume the shipment of suspended items
rests entirely on these considerations.

Although the United States had hoped for a more rapid return
to representative government in Greece, the trend toward a constitutional order is established. Major sections of the Constitution have been implemented, and partial restoration of civil
rights has been accomplished. The Government of Greece has
stated that it intends to establish parliamentary democracy. The
United States shares the concern of its NATO allies for steady
progress toward restoring the country to political government.
This is a policy to which we remain firmly committed.

D. Europe and America in the Seventies

(26) Address Prepared for Delivery by Kenneth Rush, United States Ambassador to the Federal Republic of Germany, Before the Foreign Policy Society of Munich, October 20, 1970.[65]

(Complete Text)

A scant 10 years ahead lies the next decennial landmark: 1980.
In a time of accelerating technological and social change, one
must be prudent in risking predictions about the shape the
world will be in at that time. Yet it is not reckless to suggest
that a primary concern 10 years hence will be, as it is today, the
condition of the framework of peace and security among nations.
We hope it will be a sounder framework. Whether it is will be
determined in great part by our ability to cope with the problems
of 1970.

In the modern world, continuity and change mix in intricate
patterns. The title of my remarks tonight, "The New Era in
Europe and Its Meaning for America," refers both to the great

65 Text from *Department of State Bulletin*, December 7, 1970, pp. 691–697.
The address was read by U.S. Minister Russell Fessenden because Ambassador
Rush was detained in the U.S. on official business.

changes that have occurred in Europe and the continuity of America's vital interest in its relationship with Europe.

Twenty-five years ago the United States, assessing the tragic experience of two world conflicts, came to two fundamental conclusions which have guided it to the present day. The first was that peace in Europe is crucial to peace in the world. The second was that the United States could not again retreat behind shrunken oceans and leave to others the burdens of preserving the peace.

These convictions were translated into goals for policy, goals which have remained substantially unchanged through the administrations of five American Presidents.

The first is that the interests of both Americans and Europeans are best served through the creation and preservation of a climate of peace and stability and an order in which the right of peoples to choose their own paths is respected. Because we have identified our own security with that of Western Europe, we have committed powerful forces to the NATO alliance in order to maintain peace by deterring aggression.

We have from the beginning supported efforts in Western Europe to build a united Europe, in the belief that it would be in our interest to see emerge as our Atlantic neighbor an independent and united Europe. Finally, in the belief that the artificial division of Europe into two hostile camps is a source of tension and potential danger, we have supported efforts to heal this division.

As I suggested earlier, a notable feature of this set of policy goals has been America's constancy in its adherence to them. Moreover, in measuring achievements against our aspirations, we can find substantial ground for satisfaction. Peace in Europe has been kept. Great progress has been made toward European unity. The barrier across Europe has become somewhat more permeable.

I do not, of course, intend to suggest that this success is due entirely to American prescience and wisdom. For the fact is that America and Europe were partners in formulating these goals and in working toward them. They emerged from the North Atlantic community and have been the cement for the North Atlantic alliance. Without this commonality of purpose there could have been no question of success.

I am convinced, moreover, that these goals will continue to guide the alliance in the years ahead. They will do so because they are sound and valid expressions of the will of the individual partners. They will do so because the allies recognize the need to maintain peace and security, to continue the movement toward European unity, and to reduce the level of tension in Europe.

The Process of Change in Europe

While we agree on the continuity of our goals in Europe, we must also take into full account the changes in the environment in which policy is carried out. Europe today is a very different place than it was in the harsh years immediately following the war.

The most obvious change results from the historic economic recovery of Western Europe. Today this region has a combined gross national product exceeding $600 billion, a population of some 300 million, and a quarter share of the world's total industrial output. This is a measure both of strength and of a historic achievement of which this region can be justly proud. It also means that European recovery is complete, that indeed to speak of postwar Europe is to refer to an era now past.

Another great achievement, and another great change, is the movement of Europe toward unity. The Common Market [European Economic Community] has transformed Europe's economic life. Now negotiations are underway presaging the expansion of the Community.[66] While there remains a long way to travel before full economic and political unity is reached, the fact is that more progress has been made in the past 15 years in achieving unity than in the previous half millenium.

We also have seen important changes in the strategic balance as it affects Europe. A decade ago the United States had an overwhelming nuclear superiority over the Soviet Union. The growth during the 1960's of Soviet strategic forces has reduced that margin of superiority. This, of course, raises questions for defense planners.

We have also seen in recent years an evolution in attitudes toward the division of Europe. This development, of course, is not confined to Western Europe; it has taken place also in the United States. It represents a desire to move away from the rigidities of old positions and to probe for ways to reduce tension in Europe. This evolution arises from a number of sources. The sharp edges of ideological conflict have become duller. A new generation is coming of age, many of them impatient with what they consider the sterile conflicts of the past.

In Eastern Europe change, although different in pace and in

---

[66] The reference is to the negotiations that opened in Luxembourg on June 30, 1970 on the applications for Community membership of Denmark, Ireland, Norway and the United Kingdom; cf. *The United States in World Affairs, 1970*, Section 34.

form than in the West, has also occurred. Economic recovery has been slower; in recent years the pace of growth has lagged, as systemic rigidities and obsolete ideology have proved inadequate to the task of building modern economies. A growing interest has been manifest among the countries of Eastern Europe, recently including the Soviet Union itself, in economic cooperation with Western Europe. An important factor behind this interest is the desire to gain access to the sophisticated technology and organizational skill available only in the West.

Politically, in Eastern Europe, contradictory influences are at work. The Soviet Union has held in firm check pressures for liberalization. The invasion of Czechoslovakia in 1968 [67] demonstrated all too clearly that the Soviet Union does not intend to give up its role as arbiter and enforcer of "Socialist unity." What the future will hold for liberalization is uncertain. However, pressures for increased contact with the West continue to develop. The most striking sign of that trend is the effort to improve relations with the Federal Republic through important new political agreements.[68]

In filling this background, I have attempted to suggest two points. One is that fundamental changes have taken place in Europe. But they are changes of an evolutionary order, not sharp breaks with the recent past. They do not mean that the basic goals of American policy in Europe must be changed. Nor, I believe, do they mean that the essential harmony of American goals with those of its Western European allies has been altered. They do mean, however, that we will need to make adjustments in our postures in order that they remain relevant to the environment in which they operate.

There are three major fields of common concern among the United States and its Atlantic allies. These are Western European integration, the defense of our security, and negotiations with Eastern Europe. I should like to take them up at this point in some detail.

WESTERN EUROPEAN INTEGRATION

The first area I will discuss is that complex of questions arising from the movement toward Western European integration and its implications for European cooperation with the United States in areas other than defense.

Our support for the strengthening and broadening of the European Community continues. I believe that this support will remain strong in the years ahead. We consider it to be in our

[67] *Documents, 1968–1969*, pp. 134–143.
[68] Document 23.

interest that a unified, active, and strong European community emerge as a partner in a common quest for a peaceful and progressive world order. We recognize that the structure of Western European unity is a matter which must be settled by Europeans. However, we believe that we can render support to the process without becoming advocates of any single course toward this goal.

Thus, we welcome the opening of negotiations between the Community and Great Britain and three other applicants for membership. We hope they will be successful, and we stand ready to accept a reasonable economic burden to ease the entry of these nations into the EEC [European Economic Community].

The United States also has made known to the European Community its feeling that it would be inequitable to us if the Community were to be nothing more than a trading bloc. This would mean that we would suffer a loss in trade while continuing to carry an undue burden of the responsibility for political and military security in the world. In order to avoid the development of such a situation, we feel that steps should be taken toward political unity which would result in Europe's playing a larger role in the world. For the same reason, we have registered our opposition to agreements between the EEC and countries which seek association without accepting obligations of full membership and the goal of political unity.

We believe that we can in the 1970's build on the foundations of partnership which have been firmly established in the past. One area of great importance is that involving the developing countries of Latin America, Asia, and Africa. Unless we can find ways to help these areas—in which two out of three of the world's inhabitants live—through the painful problems of modernization, we cannot expect to achieve a secure and peaceful world community. Recent steps by President Nixon make clear his commitment to the principal of multilateralism in providing assistance to these areas.[69] We also are urging a liberal system of generalized tariff preferences for products of developing countries.[70] We believe that Europe and America must work together in this great task.

An issue which has recently come to demand our urgent attention is that of the protection of the human environment. In both Europe and the United States, with their great industrial systems and concentrations of urban populations, the problem of keeping our world a fit place in which to live is of increasingly

[69] Cf. Document 97.
[70] Cf. Document 92.

critical importance. Last year NATO, acting on a proposal by President Nixon, created the CCMS—the Committee on the Challenges of Modern Society.[71] This group has gone to work enthusiastically on the problem and has undertaken a number of projects. Indeed, a workshop on automobile safety is meeting tomorrow in Wolfsburg. However, in the area of environmental protection, we have scarcely begun to come to grips yet with the total problem. It represents a worthy challenge to the problem-solving skills and the talents for cooperation of our modern societies.

In our relationship to a Western Europe on the move toward integration, we recognize that conflicts will arise. Our interests inevitably will differ in some areas. At times friction will create some sparks. In this regard we will have to hope that the habits of partnership and the recognition of a larger identity of interest will allow us on both sides of the Atlantic to keep such problems in perspective.

Trade between the United States and the Community is of immense importance to both. Now totaling about $13 billion a year, it has tripled in volume since the Common Market was formed. This is due not only to the great productive capacities of the trading partners but also to the liberal trading environment which has developed under GATT [General Agreement on Tariffs and Trade]. Both sides have a great stake in the preservation of this environment; and, I believe, both recognize the gravity of the consequences which would arise if present problems were to escalate into a trade war. The problems to which I refer arise on both sides of the Atlantic. In my country, there are protectionist pressures which the executive branch of our Government is seeking to contain.[72] On this side, the Common Market's common agricultural policy has resulted in a severe downturn in U.S. exports of farm products to the market. This situation also has added fuel to protectionist fires in the United States, where it is cited as justification for raising trade barriers on our side. Both common sense and common interest suggest that the proper course is for parties on both sides to take those measures within their power to defuse protectionist pressures. My Government is seeking to do so, and we are hopeful that our Common Market friends also will. This situation also suggests the need for new and improved methods of consultation, an effort in which we stand ready to cooperate.

71 *Documents, 1968–69,* pp. 152–153.
72 Cf. Documents 90–91.

Defense of European-American Security

The second area of European-American relations I wish to discuss is that of our defense. I have already made clear my belief in the importance of maintaining the strength of our NATO alliance. The NATO system has provided and continues to provide the foundation of security which has made possible the great economic, political, and social progress of Western Europe. There is no reason to believe that in the 1970's this basic factor in European security will change substantially.

That this is so, I believe, is due to a fundamental fact about NATO: Its vigor and strength is of no less importance in a period of negotiation than it was during earlier periods of tension and danger. One of the great tasks of diplomacy during this decade will be to lessen tension in Europe through closer cooperation among the countries of Eastern and Western Europe without losing sight of the reality of Soviet power and without weakening the balance of relative security which NATO now provides.

The reasoning behind this is clear. If we have learned anything in the past 25 years it is that a posture of weakness does not contribute to the success of negotiations with those who measure the realities of power. It may be regrettable but it is nonetheless true that peaceful intentions and reasonable negotiating positions do not guarantee success at a bargaining table. As has been pointed out, "A kind heart is of little value at chess."

Moreover, prudence demands that we give greater weight in planning our defense to capabilities than to intentions. Our assessments of the intentions of the other side are inevitably flawed, in part because the processes by which they are formed are cloaked from our view. Moreover, intentions change. Capability, however, can be measured. And the fact is that the leaders of the Soviet Union persistently improve and expand their military power. This fact therefore must be the prime element in assessing the realities of the situation in Europe.

I believe that the members of our alliance fully appreciate that to relax our defense prematurely in anticipation of the benefits of a true detente would harm our efforts to negotiate and could lead to miscalculations on the Soviet side. President Nixon, in his recent visit to Europe, and to NATO's southern flank in the Mediterranean,[73] underlined America's commitment to NATO and to the principle that strength can contribute to peace. Chancellor Brandt has made it clear on repeated occasions that his

[73] Document 21.

government's Eastern policy is firmly anchored in its close ties with NATO and Western Europe.

America's commitment to NATO is firm. But we also believe that rethinking the pattern of relationships within the Western alliance is important to its continuing vitality. Thus we and our allies agree that NATO strategy and force structure should be reexamined from time to time. Such an examination is going on at the present time. We recognize that the American forces committed to NATO are vital to its strategy. We are committed to maintaining the present force level at least through mid-1971. This does not mean that we have decided to reduce our forces after that time; rather, we are determined to make every effort to maintain the present level. President Nixon made clear during his recent trip to Europe that the United States plans no unilateral reduction of its commitment to NATO.

I should like to repeat the President's words on this subject. He said in [Newmarket-on-Fergus], Ireland: [74]

I stated categorically to the NATO commanders, and I do here publicly again, that the United States will under no circumstances reduce unilaterally its commitment to NATO. Any reduction in NATO forces, if it occurs, will only take place on a multilateral basis and on the basis of what those who are lined up against the NATO forces—what they might do. In other words, it would have to be on a mutual basis.

We believe that the reality of Western Europe in 1970 suggests that the United States should play a less dominant role in the alliance than it has in the past, that NATO should be a more balanced association. This means for our part that we should consult with our allies more fully and more carefully. We also feel that it means that the European share of the burden of maintaining the alliance should be increased. You are, of course, aware of a widespread feeling in the United States that Western Europe has the capability of making a greater contribution to defense than it has in the past. The knowledge that Americans spend about twice the percentage of their gross national product on defense as do their European partners has undoubtedly contributed to the pressures in our Congress for the return home of some American troops. In this regard, we have welcomed the constructive initiatives that are being considered by our European allies toward improving their contribution to the common defense and hence sharing the burden more equitably. We believe that there is reason for optimism that an equitable solution to this problem can be found.

74 *Weekly Compilation of Presidential Documents*, October 12, 1970, p. 1333.

Negotiations With Eastern Europe

I should like to turn now to the third great question which concerns us, negotiations with the East. This is a vital concern to all partners of the alliance, but it perhaps has special significance for the United States and the Federal Republic.

President Nixon has identified as a principal concern of his administration the effort to end the era of confrontation and to move to an era of negotiation.[75] Here in the Federal Republic, the government of Chancellor Brandt has through its Eastern policy been seeking a normalization of its relations with its Eastern neighbors.[76] I have the privilege of knowing both President Nixon and Chancellor Brandt. I know the seriousness of purpose with which both approach this difficult undertaking. I know that they have measured the risks involved. Indeed, President Nixon has said: "I believe we must take risks for peace—but calculated risks, not foolish risks." [77]

Before discussing some of the negotiations now in progress or which may lie before us, I would like to make some general observations about the American view of negotiations with the East.

The first is that we consider that the reunion of Europe will come about through an extended process. It will not occur in a single spectacular negotiation. It may be useful to think of it as an organic process, through which objective conditions for peace are created and the sources of tension are allowed to wither. We do not underestimate the urgency of relaxing tensions, but we do not confuse urgency with haste.

We recognize that the tension which has existed in Europe for more than 20 years did not arise from superficial misunderstandings. We recognize the leaders of the Communist nations as serious and determined, and we mistake neither the depths of ideological disagreement nor the disparity between their interests and ours. Therefore, we believe it is not enough to have a superficial relaxation of tensions which does not get to the real issues between us.

We believe that negotiations and conferences should deal in concrete issues, not in abstractions, and that they should not be forums for cold-war rhetoric or ideological debate. This means that conferences must be preceded by careful preparation with the aim of achieving specific agreements which realistically accommodate competing interests.

[75] Documents, 1968–69, p. 41.
[76] Cf. notes 7–8 to Document 20.
[77] Documents, 1968–69, p. 49.

We do not believe that negotiations should be conducted as "zero sum" games, in which benefit to one side results in loss to the other. They should rather be synergistic, producing positive benefits for both sides. Indeed, the West has no reason and no need to accept less.

At this point I should like to discuss briefly some of the negotiations which are underway or contemplated with the East.

Regarding the *Ostpolitik* of the Federal Republic, I would make three points.

First, because the problem of Germany remains the key to East-West problems in Europe, we have welcomed the movement toward a normalization of relations between the Federal Republic and its neighbors to the East. We support the objectives of the Federal Republic in this effort, and we have full confidence in Chancellor Brandt and his government. We also have welcomed the treaty which was signed by the Federal Republic and the Soviet Union in August. With the Federal Republic, we hope that it is a first step toward a general improvement in East-West relations.

Second, we have been fully satisfied with the close consultations which we have carried on with the Federal Republic on this subject. We have agreed that it is important that negotiations not affect the continuing Four Power rights and responsibilities concerning Berlin and Germany as a whole, the maintenance of which is in the common interest of the Federal Republic and the Allies.

Finally, with respect to the treaty between the Federal Republic and the Soviet Union, we share the hope of the Federal Republic that its signature will now be followed by progress in the negotiations on Berlin.[78]

The Berlin negotiations are an opportunity for the Soviet Union to demonstrate a willingness to reach an agreement on specific and practical questions which would result in benefits to all concerned. A satisfactory agreement would result in improvements in the condition of access to the city and in circulation within the city, acceptance by the Soviets of ties between the Federal Republic and the Western sectors of the city, and a reduction in discrimination in the Soviet Union and Eastern Europe against Berliners and enterprises located in Berlin. Such an agreement would result in a reduction of the tensions over Berlin and would be a sign of genuine Soviet interest in a general improvement of relations in Europe.

Another major negotiation now underway, the Strategic Arms

---

[78] Cf. note 9 to Document 20.

Limitation Talks,[79] has important implications for the security not only of the United States and the Soviet Union but also for Europe as a whole. For that reason we carried on detailed and intensive consultations with our European allies in the months before the talks. These consultations have continued during the course of the talks so far and will go on in the future. Indeed this case is an excellent example of the importance which my Government attaches to the need for careful consultation with its allies. The course of the talks so far gives reason for optimism that a basis has been established on which agreement on limitations of at least some strategic weapons can be reached. The importance of these talks cannot be overestimated. A successful conclusion not only would serve to diminish the level of tension in the world but also would release for more productive purposes vast sums now expended on strategic arms. In the past 20 years the United States and the Soviet Union have spent some $600 billion on their strategic forces. We believe that we must find some better and more sensible way to preserve legitimate security interests other than to spend in the next 20 years an equal or greater amount.

The two alliance systems in Europe, NATO and the Warsaw Pact, have advanced proposals for negotiations.

The Warsaw Pact last year revived the idea of a conference on European security, proposing that it should take up two issues: renunciation of force and the threat of force and widened commercial, scientific, technical, and economic relations among European states.[80] While we welcome any constructive proposal to reduce tensions and are ready to negotiate, in any suitable forum, the issues which divide Europe, we do not believe that a conference which addresses security only in the abstract would be successful. Real problems would not be solved by such an approach. We feel that if progress is to be made, specific and substantive steps should be taken first toward ending the division of Europe, especially concerning Germany and Berlin.

The NATO initiative, taken in the May meeting in Rome,[81] proposed exploratory talks among interested states on mutual and balanced force reductions. This is a specific issue on which agreement could make an important contribution to easing East-West tension. We feel that this question, since it is a concrete issue, should be dealt with separately rather than being a single item on the agenda of a larger conference. We also believe progress in this area should take place before we move ahead to the

[79] Documents 10–11.
[80] Cf. *Documents, 1968–69*, p. 173, note 112.
[81] Document 20.

question of the convening of a general conference on European security. We do not have as yet any clear response from the East to this important initiative by NATO. We hope that it is being given serious study and that a positive response may be forthcoming.

All of the areas that I have discussed—defense, European integration, and negotiations with the East—are matched in their complexity only by their importance to the Western alliance. From the American perspective two common points emerge from this array to which I would call special attention.

First, there is no doubt of the importance which the United States attaches to its relations with Europe and particularly to its partners in the Atlantic alliance. President Nixon made this clear last year when he came to Europe during his first weeks in office.[82] Again, in his recent trip, he reaffirmed the American commitment to Europe and to the alliance.

The second point is the increasing importance which we attach to the principle of close and continuing consultation with our European allies. As our alliance evolves from the pattern of American predominance toward genuine partnership, the importance of consultation in harmonizing our policies is obvious. President Nixon has identified this as a central concern of his administration, and I believe that in the past 18 months we have achieved a good record in this area. I have referred to our consultations on SALT, on negotiations with the East, and on other questions. These have been constructive and useful. In other areas, including trade and economic issues, we need still to improve our processes.

In the 1970's the pace of change will present us with issues more subtle and more profound than those which our alliance has faced in the past 20 years. Eighteen months ago, before the North Atlantic Council, President Nixon defined the tasks before our alliance in these words:[83]

> I believe we must build an alliance strong enough to deter those who might threaten war, close enough to provide for continuous and far-reaching consultation, trusting enough to accept the diversity of views, realistic enough to deal with the world as it is, flexible enough to explore new channels of constructive cooperation.

This is an agenda of business which is realistic and urgent. Success in carrying it out offers us our best hope for the development of a peaceful order in Europe and in the world. I believe that we can succeed.

[82] Cf. *Documents, 1968–69*, pp. 144–148.
[83] Same, pp. 153–154.

IV.
AMERICAN POLICY IN ASIA:
THE MIDDLE EAST

A. Arabs and Israelis: The Shifting Balance of Power.[1]

(27) Status of the Problem: Statement by Joseph J. Sisco, Assistant Secretary for Near Eastern and South Asian Affairs, Washington, April 24, 1970.[2]

(Complete Text)

Before taking your questions, I want to give you a few preliminary observations regarding the Near East part of my trip.[3]

First, I accomplished 80 percent of what I set out to do, which was to have a direct exchange at the top with the leaders of the key countries concerned, both friendly and critical—to listen to their views, to learn of their concerns, and to answer clearly and frankly their questions about American policy. I did this in the U.A.R., Israel, Lebanon, and Saudi Arabia—four of the five countries in the Arab-Israel area which I had planned to visit.

I regret that the visit to Jordan had to be deferred.[4] It is in the mutual interest of Jordan and the United States that there be no long-range adverse effects on our close and mutually beneficial relations. There has been no interruption of our continuing discussions with Jordan.

Second, I wish I could say that I return with the impression

---

[1] For the context of this group of documents see *The United States in World Affairs, 1970*, Section 13.

[2] Department of State Press Release, April 25, 1970; text from *Department of State Bulletin*, June 1, 1970, p. 693.

[3] Assistant Secretary Sisco undertook a 17-day trip to the Middle East which included attendance at a conference of United States chiefs of mission at Tehran, Iran April 20–21, 1970.

[4] The Jordanian visit was cancelled because of protests by Palestinian commandos, who set fire to the U.S. Information Service center and stormed the U.S. Embassy in Amman.

127

that an early peaceful settlement is near. The clouds of suspicion and distrust still hang heavily over the area, and there remain fundamental differences between the parties. In my judgment, progress toward peace is unlikely unless both sides demonstrate a willingness to move from their maximum positions. This is another way of saying that, in my view, progress toward peace will require both sides to move in the direction of the kind of negotiating framework which Secretary Rogers outlined last December. 9.[5] That framework is firmly rooted in the Security Council resolution of November 22, 1967,[6] and provides a fair and balanced middle ground for getting negotiations started under Ambassador [Gunnar V.] Jarring's auspices.

While neither side has agreed to the framework outlined by the Secretary and set forth in the October 28 and December 18 proposals,[7] I stressed throughout my trip our continued firm adherence to them.

Third, our resolve must continue to be made clear in two ways: (1) that we will exhaust all avenues to help the parties achieve a peaceful solution; (2) that we will remain engaged and continue to make our presence manifest in order to discourage any who would seek unilateral advantage in the area.

Fourth, I return convinced that there is general recognition in the area that the United States has a decisive role to play in helping bring stability and a durable peace. The governments there with which we are in communication clearly want to continue talking to us. I believe our dialogue with those countries I visited, including the U.A.R., has been deepened. I have a better understanding of the views and positions of the governments and of the current trends in the area. I hope there is also a better understanding of our views and our position on their part.

Finally, I return reinforced in the belief that there can be no peace unless it takes account of the legitimate concerns of all in the area who are touched in their daily lives by the Palestine problem. As Secretary Rogers said on December 9, "There is a new consciousness among the young Palestinians who have grown up since 1948 which needs to be channeled away from bitterness and frustration toward hope and justice." While the Palestinians themselves speak with many voices, the United States

[5] *Documents, 1968–69*, pp. 212–219.

[6] Same, *1967*, pp. 169–170.

[7] The U.S. proposal of October 28, 1969, was not made public but its substance was reported in Secretary Rogers' address of December 9, 1969 (cf. note 5, above). On the U.S. note of December 18, 1969 see *United States Foreign Policy, 1969–1970: A Report of the Secretary of State* (Department of State Publication 8575; Washington: G.P.O., 1971), pp. 74–75.

is keenly aware of their sense of frustration and is as dedicated to the just solution of their problems foreseen in the November 1967 Security Council resolution as it is to all other parts of that resolution.

(28) The Military Balance: News Conference Statement by Secretary of State Rogers, March 23, 1970.[8]

(Excerpt)

Ladies and gentlemen:

My statement will deal with the Israeli requests both for military and economic assistance from the United States. The decisions I am announcing today are based on our present appraisal of the balance of power in the Middle East.

Last year, the Government of Israel asked the United States to sell it 25 additional Phantoms and 100 more Skyhawks. The Israeli request has been carefully and sympathetically considered in the light of the military situation in the area and of our policy of doing everything possible to achieve peace in the Middle East in accordance with the United Nations Security Council resolution of November 22, 1967.[9]

In our judgment, Israel's air capacity is sufficient to meet its needs for the time being. Consequently, the President has decided to hold in abeyance for now a decision with respect to Israel's request for additional aircraft. In doing so, he has instructed that close watch be kept on the military balance in the area. The United States will be in a position to provide additional as well as replacement aircraft promptly if the situation requires it. To this end the United States will remain in close consultation with those concerned.

In this connection, we have evidence that the U.S.S.R. has been taking recent steps to strengthen the air defense of the U.A.R. by introduction of SA–3 missiles and additional Soviet personnel. As the President indicated on Saturday [March 21], the situation bears and will receive close and careful scrutiny by us as well as continuous review and evaluation.[10]

On the economic side, the United States will respond affirmatively to certain of Israel's short-term financial requests while studying further its longer range needs. There will be an ex-

[8] Department of State Press Release 100, March 23, 1970; text from *Department of State Bulletin,* April 13, 1970, pp. 477–478.
[9] Cf. note 6 to Document 27.
[10] *Weekly Compilation of Presidential Documents,* March 23, 1970, p. 397.

panded P.L. 480 program for purchase of surplus food, principally wheat and feed-grains, under favorable credit arrangements. We will also extend credits to help cover the balance due on past military contracts.

These decisions are taken with the strong conviction that ultimate security for all concerned lies in peace. They are taken in the belief that the current trend of events must be reversed if the situation is to be stabilized and if progress toward peace is to begin. Restraint will be required on the part of other major suppliers to the Middle East. No nation can pursue a policy of seeking unilateral advantage in the area if peace is to be achieved.

In making this interim decision on aircraft, we have no intention of jeopardizing the security of Israel. If steps are taken which might upset the current balance or if in our judgment political developments warrant, the President will not hesitate to reconsider this matter.

We believe that our restraint will afford fresh opportunities for all concerned—in and outside the area—to diminish hostilities and enhance the prospects for peace. To this end, the United States will make renewed efforts in diplomatic channels to:

(1) encourage both sides to adhere fully to the U.N. cease-fire resolutions;

(2) call upon the parties to the conflict to reappraise positions which have become roadblocks to peace;

(3) urge all concerned to support proposals which would help Ambassador Jarring [Gunnar Jarring, U.N. Special Representative] launch a process of negotiation among the parties under his auspices; and

(4) engage the other major suppliers to the Middle East in early arms limitation talks.

These will be serious initiatives. We urge all concerned to respond to them with the sense of urgency which the present situation demands of all responsible governments.

*   *   *

B. The Cease-Fire and Standstill Agreement.

(29) The United States Peace Initiative.[11]

   (a) News Conference Statement by Secretary of State Rogers, June 25, 1970.[12]

(*Excerpt*)

*   *   *

Turning now to the Middle East, I would like to make a brief statement about the Middle East. Recent disquieting events in the Middle East led President Nixon, on April 29, to order a thorough review of all political and military aspects of this problem. That review has now been concluded.

As a consequence of the review, the United States has undertaken a political initiative, a major political initiative, the objective of which is to encourage the parties to stop shooting and start talking under the auspices of Ambassador Jarring [Gunnar Jarring, U.N. Special Representative] in accordance with the resolutions of the Security Council.

Our objective in launching this initiative has been to encourage the parties to move toward a just and lasting peace which takes fully into account the legitimate aspirations and concerns of all governments and of all peoples in the area.

In the light of that objective, we believe that it would not be useful, particularly because of the sensitive nature of the discussions now underway, the diplomatic discussions now underway, to disclose at this time the details of the political initiative or to discuss publicly military assistance for Israel.

We firmly believe that this is the time for such an initiative, which we have launched directly with the parties and with other interested powers. We are now in the process of having further discussions, getting the responses of other governments to this initiative, and we very seriously and profoundly hope that this initiative, taken together in collaboration with others, will result in the beginning of discussions which might lead to a peaceful solution of this problem that has plagued the Middle East for 20 years.

*   *   *

[11] For the context see *The United States in World Affairs, 1970,* Sections 13 and 15.

[12] Department of State Press Release 193, June 25, 1970; text from *Department of State Bulletin,* July 13, 1970, p. 26.

(b) Letter from Secretary of State Rogers to Foreign Minister Mahmoud Riad of the United Arab Republic, Dated June 19, 1970; Released July 22, 1970.[13]

(Complete Text)

JUNE 19, 1970

Dear Mr. Foreign Minister:

I have read carefully President [Gamal Abdel] Nasser's statement of May 1 and your subsequent remarks to Mr. Bergus [Donald C. Bergus, Counselor of Embassy and Consul General, U.S. Special Interests Section, Spanish Embassy, Cairo]. Mr. Sisco [Joseph J. Sisco, Assistant Secretary for Near Eastern and South Asian Affairs] has also reported fully on his conversations with President Nasser and you, and we have been giving serious thought to what can be done about the situation in the Near East. I agree that the situation is at a critical point and I think it is in our joint interest that the United States retain and strengthen friendly ties with all the peoples and states of the area. We hope this will prove possible and are prepared to do our part. We look to others concerned, and in particular to your government, which has so important a role to play, to move with us to seize this opportunity. If it is lost, we shall all suffer the consequences and we would regret such an outcome very much indeed. In this spirit, I urge that your government give the most careful consideration to the thoughts which I set forth below.

We are strongly interested in a lasting peace, and we would like to help the parties achieve it. We have made serious and practical proposals to that end, and we have counseled all parties on the need for compromise, and on the need to create an atmosphere in which peace is possible. By the latter we mean a reduction of tensions as well as clarifications of positions to give both Arabs and Israelis some confidence that the outcome will preserve their essential interests.

In our view, the most effective way to agree on a settlement would be for the parties to begin to work out under Ambassador Jarring's auspices the detailed steps necessary to carry out Security Council Resolution 242.[14] Foreign Minister [Abba] Eban of Israel has recently said that Israel would be prepared to make important concessions once talks got started. At the same time, Egyptian participation in such talks would go far towards overcoming Israeli doubts that your government does in fact seek to

---

[13] Text from *Department of State Bulletin,* August 10, 1970, pp. 178–179.
[14] *Documents, 1967,* pp. 169–170.

make peace with it. I understand the problems that direct negotiations pose for you, and we have made it clear from the beginning that we were not proposing such an arrangement be put
into effect at the outset, although, depending on the progress
of discussions, we believe the parties will find it necessary to meet
together at some point if peace is to be established between
them.

With the above thoughts in mind, the US puts forward the
following proposal for consideration of the UAR.

(a) that both Israel and the UAR subscribe to a restoration of
the ceasefire for at least a limited period;

(b) that Israel and the UAR (as well as Israel and Jordan)
subscribe to the following statement which would be in the form
of a report from Ambassador Jarring to the Secretary General
U Thant:

The UAR (Jordan) and Israel advise me that they agree:

(a) that having accepted and indicated their willingness to carry out
Resolution 242 in all its parts, they will designate representatives to discussions to be held under my auspices, according to such procedure
and at such places and times as I may recommend, taking into account
as appropriate each side's preference as to method of procedure and
previous experience between the parties;

(b) that the purpose of the aforementioned discussions is to reach
agreement on the establishment of a just and lasting peace between
them based on (1) mutual acknowledgment by the UAR (Jordan) and
Israel of each other's sovereignty, territorial integrity and political independence, and (2) Israeli withdrawal from territories occupied in the
1967 conflict, both in accordance with Resolution 242;

(c) that, to facilitate my task of promoting agreement as set forth
in Resolution 242, the parties will strictly observe, effective July 1 until
at least October 1, the ceasefire resolutions of the Security Council.

We hope that the UAR will find this proposal acceptable; we
are also seeking Israeli acceptance. In the meantime, I am sure you
will share my conviction that everything be done to hold
these proposals in confidence so as not to prejudice the prospects for their acceptance.

I am sending a similar message to Foreign Minister [Abdel
Monem] Rifai [of Jordan].

I look forward to your early reply.

With all best wishes,

Sincerely,

WILLIAM P. ROGERS

(c) Remarks by President Nixon on Acceptance by Both Sides of the United States Cease-Fire Proposal, San Clemente, California, July 31, 1970.[15]

(Complete Text)

Ladies and gentlemen:

As you know, the Secretary of State and I have been meeting for the past two hours and a half on various foreign policy matters, but particularly concentrating on the problems of the Mideast. The Secretary has made a report to me on the latest developments, and I have a prepared statement [16] which will be issued to all of you immediately after this statement.

With regard to the developments in the Mideast, as you know, on June 25th the Secretary announced that the United States was undertaking a major political initiative, and our objective was to encourage the parties to the conflict to stop shooting and to start talking under the auspices of the United Nations Ambassador Jarring [17] in accordance with the pertinent resolutions of the U.N. Security Council.

The Israeli Government is now in the process of drafting its detailed reply to the United States.[18] However, I am pleased to say that we have been informed by the Government of Israel of the cabinet vote to accept the United States proposal, and I am gratified that now all three governments to whom we addressed our initiative have responded positively and accepted the U.S. proposal.[19]

We do not underestimate the difficulties which still lie ahead. The acceptance of the U.S. proposal by the governments principally concerned, important as it is, is only a first step. It will require moderation, flexibility, and a willingness by both sides to accept something less than their maximum positions if progress toward a just and lasting peace between the parties is to be made. But the cease-fire and the negotiations that now seem within reach are an essential beginning.

In this connection I want to reiterate one point, a point that

[15] Text from *Weekly Compilation of Presidential Documents*, August 3, 1970, pp. 1003–1004.

[16] The reference is to an advance text of President Nixon's remarks in their as-delivered form.

[17] Ambassador Jarring began separate discussions with Israel, Jordan, and the U.A.R. at U.N. Headquarters on August 25, 1970; for Secretary-General Thant's report on the reactivation of the Jarring mission see U.N. document S/9902, August 7, 1970.

[18] Unofficial text of the formal Israeli reply, forwarded to the U.S. August 4, 1970, in *New York Times*, August 5, 1970.

[19] Jordan accepted the U.S. proposal on July 26, 1970.

I made last night in my press conference.[20] It is an integral part of our cease-fire proposal that neither side is to use the cease-fire period to improve its military position in the area of the cease-fire lines.[21] All would have to refrain from emplacing new missiles or other installations and from undertaking a military buildup of any kind in such an area.

For our part, we have been engaged since early 1969 in cooperative efforts with the Governments of the Soviet Union, Great Britain, and France to help move the Middle East conflict toward a peaceful settlement.[22] We expect these efforts to continue. We firmly believe, however, that the focus of future efforts must be on the parties directly concerned under the auspices of Ambassador Jarring's mission. We wish him and the parties well in their efforts, and we stand ready to help whenever and wherever we can.

In that connection, in the same area, we have made two appointments to ambassadorial positions today, two of our most distinguished and able Ambassadors. To Jordan, Mr. [L.] Dean Brown, and to Saudi Arabia, Mr. Nicholas [G.] Thacher.

I will say finally, that I believe that all of those who have worked on this initiative within our own Government and particularly those in the State Department, deserve a great deal of credit for the progress that has been made.

As we have indicated, we still have a long way to go before we achieve the results that we hope can be achieved. But in a situation where a year and a half ago there seemed to be no hope, there now appears some hope—some hope that a peaceful settlement can be arrived at.

C. United States Comments on Violations of the Cease-Fire.[23]

(30) Call for Adherence to the Cease-Fire and Standstill Agreement: Department of State Statement, August 19, 1970.[24]

(Complete Text)

We have concluded that there was forward deployment of surface-to-air missiles into and within the zone west of the Suez

---

[20] *Weekly Compilation of Presidential Documents,* August 3, 1970, p. 999.

[21] The 90-day cease-fire and standstill went into effect at the Egyptian-Israeli front along the Suez Canal at 2200 hours GMT on August 7, 1970. For Secretary Rogers' remarks welcoming the cease-fire see *Department of State Bulletin,* August 31, 1970, p. 244.

[22] Cf. *Documents, 1968–69,* pp. 203–205, 210–212.

[23] For the context of this group of documents see *The United States in World Affairs, 1970,* Section 14.

[24] Text from *Department of State Bulletin,* September 7, 1970, p. 278.

Canal around the time the cease-fire went into effect.[25] There is some evidence that this was continued beyond the cease-fire deadline, although our evidence of this is not conclusive.

With respect to additional information which the Israeli Government has brought to our attention concerning possible violations of the cease-fire, we are examining it and are in touch with the parties through diplomatic channels.

We do not now anticipate making further public statements on this matter.

Adherence to the cease-fire and standstill is of great importance to the success of current peace efforts. The main thing now is to concentrate all efforts on getting discussions going under Ambassador Jarring's [U.N. Special Representative Gunnar Jarring] auspices.

The United States believes that these talks should begin promptly.[26]

(31) United States Confirmation of Violations of the Cease-Fire and Standstill Agreement: Department of State Statement, September 3, 1970.[27]

(Complete Text)

Our latest evidence confirms that there have been violations of the cease-fire standstill agreement. We are not going into details. We are taking up this matter with both the U.A.R. and the U.S.S.R. through diplomatic channels. We are continuing to watch the balance closely and, as we have said previously, have no intention of permitting Israel's security to be adversely affected. In the meantime, we believe it is of utmost importance that the talks between the parties under Ambassador Jarring's [U.N. Special Representative Gunnar Jarring] auspices proceed forthwith.[28]

---

25 Cf. note 21 to Document 29 (c).
26 Cf. note 17 to Document 29 (c).
27 Text from *Department of State Bulletin*, September 21, 1970, p. 326.
28 Cf. note 17 to Document 29(c). On September 6, 1970, Israel announced suspension of its participation in the talks but on December 28, 1970 announced its willingness to rejoin the negotiations.

D. Action by the Twenty-Fifth Regular Session of the United Nations General Assembly, September-December 1970.[29]

(32) Extension of the Cease-Fire and Standstill Agreement: Resolution 2628 (XXV), Adopted November 4, 1970.[30]

(*Complete Text*)

The General Assembly,

Seriously concerned that the continuation of the present grave and deteriorating situation in the Middle East constitutes a serious threat to international peace and security,

Reaffirming that no territorial acquisition resulting from the threat or use of force shall be recognized,

Deploring the continued occupation of the Arab territories since 5 June 1967,[31]

Seriously concerned that Security Council resolution 242 (1967) of 22 November 1967,[32] which was unanimously adopted and which provides for a peaceful settlement of the situation in the Middle East, has not yet been implemented,

Having considered the item entitled "The situation in the Middle East",

1. *Reaffirms* that the acquisition of territories by force is inadmissible and that, consequently, territories thus occupied must be restored;

2. *Reaffirms* that the establishment of a just and lasting peace in the Middle East should include the application of both the following principles:

(*a*) Withdrawal of Israeli armed forces from territories occupied in the recent conflict;

(*b*) Termination of all claims or states of belligerency and respect for and acknowledgement of the sovereignty, territorial integrity and political independence of every State in the area and its right to live in peace within secure and recognized boundaries free from threats or acts of force;

3. *Recognizes* that respect for the rights of the Palestinians is an indispensable element in the establishment of a just and lasting peace in the Middle East;

4. *Urges* the speedy implementation of Security Council reso-

[29] For the context of this and the following document see *The United States in World Affairs, 1970,* Section 14.
[30] Text from U.N. General Assembly, *Official Records: 25th Session, Supplement No. 28* (A/8028), p. 5; adopted by a vote of 57–16 with 39 abstentions.
[31] *Documents, 1967,* pp. 125–130.
[32] Same, pp. 169–170.

lution 242 (1967), which provides for the peaceful settlement of the situation in the Middle East, in all its parts;

5. *Calls upon* the parties directly concerned to instruct their representatives to resume contact with the Special Representative of the Secretary-General to the Middle East in order to enable him to carry out, at the earliest possible date, his mandate for the implementation of the Security Council resolution in all its parts;

6. *Recommends* to the parties that they extend the cease-fire for a period of three months [33] in order that they may enter into talks under the auspices of the Special Representative with a view to giving effect to Security Council resolution 242 (1967);

7. *Requests* the Secretary-General to report to the Security Council within a period of two months, and to the General Assembly as appropriate, on the efforts of the Special Representative and on the implementation of Security Council resolution 242 (1967);

8. *Requests* the Security Council to consider, if necessary, making arrangements, under the relevant Articles of the Charter of the United Nations, to ensure the implementation of its resolution.

(33) *Explanation of the United States Vote: Statement by Charles W. Yost, United States Representative to the United Nations, November 4, 1970.*[34]

(Complete Text)

I have asked for the floor in order to explain the United States vote on the draft resolutions set forth in A/L.602 and 604.[35] As the Assembly knows, the United States was not hopeful that this debate in itself at this critical time in the affairs of the Middle East would be helpful. We had feared that many of the acrimonious speeches which we have heard from this podium would be made and that they would damage rather than improve the chances of moving rapidly toward the objective of all of us—a

[33] A 90-day extension of the cease-fire and standstill agreement went into effect on November 5, 1970.

[34] U.S./U.N. Press Release 157, November 4, 1970; text from *Department of State Bulletin,* November 23, 1970, pp. 661–662.

[35] The Latin American draft resolution (A/L.604) was rejected by the General Assembly on November 4, 1970 by a roll call vote of 45 (U.S.) to 49, with 27 abstentions; text in *Department of State Bulletin,* November 23, 1970, p. 663.

peaceful settlement in the Middle East. We have thought that the best course that the Assembly could follow in the debate and in the adoption of resolutions at the end of the debate would be to attempt to concentrate with the greatest firmness and seriousness on what does not divide us but what brings us together.

Now, there are certain matters in connection with this highly controversial problem that do bring us together. We are all agreed that Resolution 242 [36] is the proper basis for a settlement of the Middle Eastern conflict and that it should be carried out promptly in all its parts.

The United States, as you know, put forward an initiative earlier this year [37] which we felt also united all those concerned and indeed, as you know, was accepted by three of the principal parties to the conflict. It embodied a renewed commitment on their part to negotiations under Ambassador Jarring. It involved a recommitment on their part to the salient elements of Resolution 242, that is, the mutual recognition of sovereignty and territorial independence and a commitment on the part of Israel to withdraw in accordance with Resolution 242 from occupied territories; and it embodied a temporary cease-fire. Once again, these were elements which unite us rather than divide us.

Most recently, as you know, the four-power Foreign Ministers met with the Secretary-General at dinner, and at the conclusion of that dinner he issued a statement [38] on their behalf in which he quoted them as agreeing to exert their utmost efforts (1) to enable Ambassador Jarring to resume his mission at the earliest possible date, (2) to search for the possibility through agreement of the parties directly concerned to extend the observance of the cease-fire for a period to be determined, and (3) to find a peaceful solution on the basis of United Nations Security Council Resolution 242. These, again, unite us. These principles and objectives are accepted, I think, by almost all of us here.

Now, how are we at the termination of this debate to further these objectives and not to damage them? You have before you, of course, a United States resolution which we have fully explained and which I shall not comment on further.[39] We have before us the draft resolution contained in A/L.602, put forward

[36] *Documents, 1968–69*, pp. 169–170.

[37] Document 29.

[38] The meeting was held on October 23, 1970; text of Secretary-General Thant's statement in *U.N. Monthly Chronicle*, November 1970, p. 148.

[39] The U.S. draft resolution (U.N. document A/L.603) was not put to a vote; text of the U.S. draft resolution and Ambassador Yost's comments of October 29, 1970, in *Department of State Bulletin*, November 23, 1970, pp. 656–657. Details in *U.N. Monthly Chronicle*, November 1970, pp. 129–136; same, December 1970, pp. 16–24.

by a substantial number of Afro-Asian delegations and eloquently explained and defended by their distinguished representatives. However, I must in all candor note that even with the amendments to this draft resolution which have recently been added, it is clearly a resolution put forward on behalf of one side to the conflict and represents the views of that side. It is therefore inevitably and by its very nature one-sided; and I would therefore argue, despite what I am sure are the excellent intentions of its sponsors, that it divides rather than unites us.

Its adoption would no doubt be considered a victory for one side. But is that what the Assembly really wants? Does the Assembly want to collaborate in victories for one side or the other? Does the Assembly rather not want most of all a resumption of negotiations under Ambassador Jarring and the carrying out of Resolution 242?

We believe that it is quite clear from what has been said in this hall that the adoption of the draft resolution contained in A/L.602 will not facilitate but will create an additional obstacle to the resumption of negotiations and hence to the prompt carrying out of Resolution 242. This draft resolution, moreover, totally ignores the progress made in the area as a result of the acceptance by three of the parties of the U.S. initiative—concrete and significant progress to which I referred a moment ago. Its adoption would therefore, in our view, be a step backward, not a step forward. And the last thing the international community can afford in the Middle East at this time is a step backward. The United States delegation will therefore vote against the draft resolution contained in A/L. 602.

On the other hand, Mr. President, the draft resolution contained in A/L.604, sponsored by a substantial number of American states, is a draft not inspired by or representing either party to the dispute. It has been put foward in a spirit of conciliation with a view to facilitating the earliest possible resumption of negotiations and the carrying out of Resolution 242.

It contains, in the view of my delegation, all of the elements required for this purpose, indeed, all of the elements which most speakers in the debate, including representatives of both sides in the conflict, have said over and over again are necessary in order to achieve our common purposes.

The adoption of this resolution would, therefore, in our view, unite us, rather than divide us. It seems to the U.S. delegation that its adoption would be a constructive conclusion to our debate and would, whether or not we agree with every one of its provisions, promote positively and realistically the resumption of negotiations under Ambassador Jarring and the carrying out

of Resolution 242 in all its parts. The United States would therefore vote in favor of the draft resolution contained in A/L.604.

E. The Fluid and Evolving Situation.

*(34) Address by Assistant Secretary of State Sisco Before the
Commonwealth Club of California, San Francisco, November 6, 1970.*[40]

(*Complete Text*)

Many of us as Americans have referred to the Viet-Nam problem as our most anguishing problem. And if Viet-Nam is our
most anguishing problem, the Middle East is the most dangerous
problem for the United States as we look ahead over the next
decade. And as we talk about the Middle Eastern problem, we
must fully realize that there is more than one Middle Eastern
problem.

In the first instance, there is the Arab-Israeli dispute—a reflection of the very deep suspicions that have long existed in the
area and which are so deeply rooted among the people there
today, young and old. Secondly, there are intra-Arab issues super-
imposed on the Arab-Israeli dispute. The Arab world is characterized by very considerable disunity—moderate governments
versus more extreme governments; established governments
versus revolutionary movements, as reflected by the Palestinian
movement; and guerrilla warfare against established Arab governments. So that it is little wonder that the Middle Eastern
issue is both complex and complicated.

As if this were not enough, there is the fact that this is an area
of potential cooperation or of potential conflict between the major powers, and in particular the United States and the Soviet
Union.

From the point of view of the United States, we have an interest in maintaining friendly relations with all of the countries
in the area because the Middle East is important to us strategic-
ally. It is a key area of communication. We have significant
economic and commercial interests in the area.

One national interest is above all others. The major powers
could be drawn into a confrontation even though neither wants
it. Our overriding national interest and objective therefore is to

40 Text from *Department of State Bulletin*, December 21, 1970, pp. 748–751;
for the context see *The United States in World Affairs, 1970*, Section 14.

try to assure by every means of diplomacy that a peaceful settlement will be achieved, a binding peace that will reduce the inherent risks of major-power confrontation in the Middle East.

THE U.S. PEACE INITIATIVE

Last June the United States put foward a new peace proposal which was designed to get the parties to stop shooting and start talking under the auspices of Ambassador Jarring, the United Nations Representative.[41] The genesis of that peace initiative can be attributed to a 2-hour discussion which I had in April with President Nasser.[42]

As I recall that conversation, I think there was one thing that came out clearly. There was a great deal of emphasis in that conversation on the desire of the U.A.R. for a political solution. I came away with the impression that Egypt was not entirely comfortable, given the amount of Soviet influence in that country. And the principal impression that I came away with was that some new American move toward a political solution would be welcome.

That conversation took place in April. On May 1 President Nasser made a very important speech.[43] He coupled a vitriolic attack on the United States with a direct appeal to President Nixon to make some new move toward a political solution. We read that speech as a second signal. And from those two particular moves we, the President, the Secretary of State, a number of us, developed the American peace proposal of last June.

Now this, the American peace proposal of last June, is a very simple proposition. In the first instance, it called for a limited 90-day cease-fire between Egypt and Israel. I say Egypt and Israel because it was only Egypt and not Jordan that a year before had declared null and void the four Security Council resolutions on the cease-fire.[44] So this proposal called for a 90-day cease-fire.

It also called for the beginning of talks under the auspices of the United Nations Representative based on explicit commitments of the parties. These were very significant commitments.

For the first time Israel committed itself to accepting the United Nations Security Council resolution of November 1967.[45] That was the resolution that contains the principal elements of a Middle Eastern settlement. So for the first time

---

[41] Document 29.
[42] Cf. Document 27.
[43] Cf. *New York Times,* May 2, 1970.
[44] Following the outbreak of the six-day war in June 1967; texts of the Security Council resolutions in *Documents, 1967,* pp. 126, 128, 129–131.
[45] Same, pp. 169–170.

Israel committed itself to that resolution and to carrying it out in all of its parts.

For the first time Israel committed itself to begin discussions indirectly rather than on a direct face-to-face basis, which had long been the Israeli position.

For the first time Israel committed itself to the principle of withdrawal in accordance with the U.N. Security Council resolution.

And in return Egypt and Jordan committed themselves to make a binding peace with Israel based on reciprocal commitments between them. And for the first time Egypt and Jordan explicitly recognized Israel's right to exist within so-called secure and recognized borders.

The U.S. peace proposal was characterized in the media of the Middle East as primarily a procedural proposal designed to get talks started. In actuality, while this proposal was of significance procedurally, it was of far greater significance from a substantive point of view simply because of the commitments that were undertaken by the parties as a basis for talks between them.

Those talks got started, but they were quickly suspended as a result of the violations by both Egypt and the Soviet Union of the cease-fire standstill agreement.[46] Part of the understanding was that during the 90-day period of the cease-fire, both sides would stand still militarily in a zone 50 kilometers west and east of the Suez Canal. In other words, when the parties accepted the American proposal, they accepted the fundamental principle that neither side would try to use the cease-fire period to improve its relative military position in respect to the other.

VIOLATIONS OF THE STANDSTILL

Now, there has been a good deal of discussion as to whether in fact there have been violations of the cease-fire–standstill. Let me make it explicitly clear that our evidence is categoric and incontrovertible.

There were several types of violations.

First, in a number of instances where no positions existed at the time of the cease-fire, weeks later positions had been constructed—new positions.

Second, in a number of instances positions had been partially begun at the time of the cease-fire. Weeks later these positions had been completed.

Third, there were a number of positions already constructed at the time of the cease-fire in which there were no missiles or no

46 Cf. Documents 30–31.

missile-related equipment. Yet weeks later missiles were in these positions, both SAM-2's and SAM-3's, and many of them in an operational capacity.

And fourth, positions and missiles were moved more closely to the Suez Canal itself.

All of these violations were contrary to the basic principle that there should be no military advantage for either side deriving from the cease-fire. Standstill meant standstill.

There were also violations on the Israeli side. There were over-flights that were conducted across the Suez Canal into the 50-kilometer zone west of the canal. There were also other charges made by Egypt with respect to construction on the Israeli side, which we conveyed to the Israelis on behalf of the Egyptians.

What has been the effect of the violations on the military balance? We have never claimed that the violations have had a decisive effect on the military balance. We have made the judgment, however, that the violations placed Israel at a greater disadvantage militarily than at the time of the cease-fire. And so the United States had to take into account not only the violations of the cease-fire–standstill but also the fact that during this period substantial military supplies were going to Egypt from the Soviet Union. During the period of the American peace proposal we made it clear to all concerned that we would approach the question of arms with restraint. And we did pursue a policy of restraint. By September 1970, however, it was clear that it was necessary to take fully into account the violations and ongoing Soviet military supply of Egypt. Concrete steps were taken to give effect to the statements of President Nixon [47] and Secretary Rogers [48] that the United States would not permit the military balance to be upset.

We believe the long-range answer to arms deliveries is an arms limitation agreement between the United States and the Soviet Union.[49] We have in the past 18 months made a number of proposals to this end. However, we have not been successful in getting the Soviet Union to agree to any arms limitation talks on Middle East deliveries of conventional weapons.

SEARCH FOR BASIS FOR RESUMPTION OF TALKS

Now, whatever judgment one might make with respect to the military balance, the fact is that the missile violations have also created a situation where there is even less confidence between the parties than that which was present at the time of the cease-

[47] Document 29 (c).
[48] Document 28.
[49] Documents 10–11.

fire itself. So it is the political-psychological climate that has also
been affected. Will an agreement be honored in the future by the
parties? It is this factor that has created obstacles to the beginning of the talks between the parties. It has also raised some
serious questions as to the Soviet role in the Middle East. No
such violations could take place without Soviet knowledge and
complicity.

In the last 10 days the Middle Eastern question has been discussed before the U.N. General Assembly. And just 48 hours ago
the Assembly adopted a recommendation to the parties that the
cease-fire be extended and that negotiations get started.[50] You
will have noted that in the last 24 hours both Egypt and Israel
have indicated explicitly an intention to abide by the cease-
fire.[51] And we feel in the U.S. Government that there is a reasonable chance that the cease-fire will hold for another period. The
first half of the American peace initiative of last June, the proposal relating to the stopping of the shooting, still continues in
effect. And our job in the days ahead is to make the second half
of the American proposal an operative reality: to get the parties
talking about peace.

We will have to find some formula that will provide the basis
for a resumption of the talks envisaged in the United States proposal of last June. This will take a little doing, since new uncertainties have developed in the area. For example, in Egypt
today a new government is only now beginning to find itself.[52]
Jordan in recent weeks has experienced the agony of a civil war
as well as the agony of outside intervention; [53] the situation
there seems improved. In the area itself, time is not on the side
of either of the established governments, whether they be Arab
or Israeli. This is because the area is in ferment—the Palestinian
movement which is committed to a solution by force is crystal-
lizing into a much more formidable political movement center-
ing on the idea of the need to satisfy the aspirations and the
concerns of the Palestinians by means of some kind of a political
entity.

In this area of turmoil and instability the risks of confrontation between the major powers are great. If a political solution
that stabilizes the area can be achieved, the risk of major-power

50 Document 32.
51 Cf. note 33 to Document 32.
52 The reference is to the government of Muhammad Ahmad Anwar al-Sadat,
who was inaugurated as President on October 17, 1970, for a six-year term
following the death on September 28, 1970 of President Nasser.
53 By Syrian armored and artillery units in northern Jordan; cf. *The United
States in World Affairs, 1970*, Section 15.

involvement would diminish rapidly. We are under no illusions. The differences with respect to negotiating positions between the parties are very great. The gulf is wide, and each of the sides has expressed its negotiating positions in maximum terms.

On the one hand, the Arabs are insisting on total Israeli withdrawal to the lines that existed before the June war. On the other hand, Israel is insisting on major changes in the borders in order to take into account what it considers to be serious security problems as well as the unique history that surrounds the holy city of Jerusalem. Negotiations are apt to be long, drawn out, tortuous, complex, and difficult.

The role of the United States will be to encourage both sides to move toward positions in any negotiation which will meet the legitimate concerns of both sides. Our national interest goes beyond any one state in the area, and it is up to us to try to help move the parties. Our involvement is a major deterrent in the area. And I mean this from the standpoint of Israel as well as from the standpoint of the Arab world. The major-power talks, whether they be bilateral with the Soviet Union or four-power talks at the United Nations,[54] are not a substitute for agreement between the parties. They are not a substitute for negotiations between the parties. The major powers can be the catalyst, but the first and foremost objective is to get the parties to talk to one another on the basis of the United Nations Security Council resolution of November 1967 in hopes that the broad gap between them can be bridged by slow and patient effort. Time is not on the side of either the Israeli establishment or the Arab establishment, but the options for a peaceful settlement remain open. A reasonable settlement is essential because the Middle East is a most dangerous trouble spot. We will do all we can to grasp the opportunities which are present in the fluid and evolving situation in the Middle East.

[54] Cf. note 22 to Document 29(c) and note 38 to Document 33.

F. The Status of Bahrain.

(35) Action by the United Nations Security Council.

  (a) Statement by Ambassador Yost, May 11, 1970.[55]

(*Complete Text*)

The Government of the United States welcomes the unanimous and highly constructive action that this Council has taken today on the question of Bahrain.[56] Our action marks the successful culmination of a diplomatic effort to resolve a dispute that has complicated the life of the Persian Gulf for more than a century. For this, we are indebted to the parties concerned, which have demonstrated the will and vision to act responsibly in an attempt to minimize the danger of future conflict in that important part of the world and to enhance the prospects for fruitful cooperation among the peoples of the gulf in determining its destiny. The readiness of the parties to make the necessary accommodations and to seek a solution by negotiation, inquiry, and other peaceful means should stand as an example for all nations of the successful application of charter principles to international affairs.

We are also gratified by the role played in this matter by our distinguished Secretary General. We salute his willingness to cooperate fully with the parties concerned, as well as his selection of an able and experienced diplomat as his Personal Representative [Vittorio Winspeare Guicciardi, U.N. Under Secretary General and Director General of the U.N. office at Geneva]. In so doing, he has acted in the best traditions of his office and in fulfillment of the purposes of the United Nations relating to the settlement of international disputes and the development of friendly relations among nations. We are happy to see that his efforts have resulted in a solution which merits our unanimous endorsement.

We are also happy to note in Mr. Winspeare's report [57] that all those he consulted in Bahrain wished tranquility, stability, and friendliness in the area, as well as being virtually unanimous in wishing recognition of their identity in a fully independent

55 U.S./U.N. Press Release 62, May 11, 1970; text from *Department of State Bulletin*, June 29, 1970, pp. 814–815. For the context see *The United States in World Affairs, 1970*, Section 16.
56 Document 35 (b).
57 U.N. document S/9772; transmitted to the Security Council by Secretary-General Thant on April 30, 1970.

and sovereign state. This spirit augurs well for the future of Bahrain and the entire area.

Mr. President, the turmoil and turbulence that so often attend events in many parts of our fast-moving world seem too infrequently to allow for timely recourse to the processes of peaceful accommodation. We in this Council have perhaps more reason than most to lament this unfortunate fact, and it therefore obliges us to ensure that when recourse is had to those processes, the Council is not found wanting. Our action today has served this obligation well. It has fulfilled the hopes of both the people of Bahrain and the inhabitants of the entire gulf region. In a wider sense, it can only enhance the image of the United Nations as a force for peace and thus buoy the hopes of nations for the peaceful resolution of other disputes that continue to afflict the world in which we live.

(b) Security Council Resolution 278 (1970), Adopted May 11, 1970.[58]

(Complete Text)

The Security Council,

Noting the communication from the Secretary-General to the Security Council of 28 March 1970,[59]

Noting also the statements made by the representatives of Iran and the United Kingdom of Great Britain and Northern Ireland in their letters to the Secretary-General of 9 and 20 March 1970, respectively,[60]

1. *Endorses* the report of the Personal Representative of the Secretary-General, which has been circulated to the Security Council, under cover of a note from the Secretary-General, on 30 April 1970; [61]

2. *Welcomes* the conclusions and findings of the report, in particular that "the overwhelming majority of the people in Bahrain wish to gain recognition of their identity in a fully independent and sovereign State free to decide for itself its relations with other States".

---

[58] Text from U.N. Security Council, *Official Records: Twenty-fifth Year* (S/INF/25), pp. 7–8; adopted unanimously.

[59] U.N. document S/9726.

[60] Same.

[61] Cf. note 57 to Document 35 (a).

G. The Central Treaty Organization.

(36) *Communiqué of the Seventeenth Session of the CENTO Ministerial Council, Washington, May 14–15, 1970.*[62]

(Complete Text)

The Council of Ministers of the Central Treaty Organization (CENTO) held their Seventeenth Session in Washington on May 14 and 15, 1970. Leaders of the delegations were:—

H.E. Mr. Ardeshir Zahedi (Iran)
H.E. Mr. Agha Hilaly (Pakistan)
H.E. Mr. Ihsan Sabri Çağlayangil (Turkey)
The Rt. Hon. Michael Stewart M.P. (United Kingdom)
The Hon. William P. Rogers (United States of America)

The CENTO Secretary General, Mr. Turgut Menemencioğlu, was present at the meeting.

As host, the Chairman of the meeting, the Honourable William P. Rogers, Secretary of State of the United States of America, read a message from the President of the United States in which the President said, "this is a welcome occasion to reaffirm United States' support for CENTO." [63]

The leaders of the delegations and the CENTO Secretary General in their opening statements expressed their appreciation of the message of the President and of the warm hospitality extended to them by the United States.

In their discussions, held in a cordial and friendly atmosphere, the Council examined the international situation since their meeting last year in Tehran,[64] noting with satisfaction that peace, stability and economic and social progress were maintained in the CENTO Region. They noted with regret, however, that many problems posing a threat to peace in the world still remained unresolved. During these discussions, particular attention was paid to the dangerous situation arising out of the Arab-Israeli dispute in the Middle East. Statements were also made regarding South East Asia and the Persian Gulf, the Cyprus problem, and the disputes concerning Kashmir, Farakkha and the Shatt-Al-Arab. The Council expressed the hope that measures would be taken in all areas of international conflict, in

[62] Text from *Department of State Bulletin,* June 8, 1970, p. 712; for the context see *The United States in World Affairs, 1970,* Section 16.
[63] Secretary Rogers' statement of May 14, 1970 in *Department of State Bulletin,* June 8, 1970, pp. 711–712.
[64] *Documents, 1968–69,* pp. 182–184.

keeping with the principles of international law, equity and justice, to promote peace and security in the world.

The Council reiterated their determination to continue to work for peace and security in the area and to promote further social and economic development in the CENTO region.

In approving the report of the Military Committee, the Council noted the progress made in different fields of cooperation.

The Council reaffirmed its agreement that the economic programme constitutes an important element of the CENTO partnership. They noted with pleasure the high rate of economic growth achieved by the Regional countries. The Council also expressed its appreciation of the ever developing economic cooperation between Iran, Pakistan and Turkey and noted the favourable effects of this development for progress and stability in the Region.

The Council, bearing in mind the important contributions made by CENTO to the strengthening of the economic links between the Regional countries, endorsed the recommendations of the Economic Committee to consider for support regional export-oriented industrial projects which meet the aid criteria of the non-regional governments.

The Council approved the report of the Eighteenth Session of the Economic Committee and noted with satisfaction that the CENTO rail project linking Turkey and Iran will be completed in 1971. The Council further noted that the programme of scientific cooperation had been enlarged and cultural exchanges continued to create still better understanding among the peoples of the Region.

Reviewing the working of the Multilateral Technical Cooperation Fund the Council took note that the projects implemented by the Fund had reached an impressive number. They also noted that the Fund's objective of increasing the technical self-sufficiency of the Regional countries was being well served by the MTCF. They decided to expand the Fund.

The Council welcomed the agreement of the Government of Turkey to continue to make available the services of Mr. Turgut Menemencioğlu as Secretary General of the Organization.

The Council decided to hold their next meeting in Turkey during the week beginning May 10, 1971.

V.
AMERICAN POLICY IN ASIA:
THE WAR IN INDOCHINA

A. The Communist Offensive in Laos.[1]

(37) The Scope of United States Involvement: Statement by President Nixon, Released at Key Biscayne, Florida, March 6, 1970.[2]

(Excerpts)

In light of the increasingly massive presence of North Vietnamese troops and their recent offensives in Laos, I have written letters today to British Prime Minister [Harold] Wilson and Soviet Premier [Aleksei N.] Kosygin asking their help in restoring the 1962 Geneva Agreements for that country.[3]

As Cochairmen of that Conference, the United Kingdom and the Soviet Union have particular responsibilities for seeing that its provisions are honored. My letters note the persistent North Vietnamese violations of the Accords and their current offensives; support the Laotian Prime Minister's own current appeal to the Cochairmen for consultations; urge the Cochairmen to work with other signatories of the Geneva Accords; and pledge full United States cooperation.

Hanoi's most recent military build-up in Laos has been particularly escalatory. They have poured over 13,000 additional troops into Laos during the past few months, raising their total in Laos to over 67,000. Thirty North Vietnamese battalions from regular division units participated in the current campaign in the Plain of Jars with tanks, armored cars, and long-range artil-

---

[1] For the context see *The United States in World Affairs, 1970,* Section 21.
[2] Text from *Weekly Compilation of Presidential Documents,* March 9, 1970, pp. 322–328.
[3] Text in *Documents, 1962,* pp. 282–294.

lery. The indigenous Laotian Communists, the Pathet Lao, are playing an insignificant role.

North Vietnam's military escalation in Laos has intensified public discussion in this country. The purpose of this statement is to set forth the record of what we found in January 1969 and the policy of this administration since that time.

*   *   *

II. THE POLICY OF THIS ADMINISTRATION

Since this administration has been in office, North Vietnamese pressure has continued. Last spring, the North Vietnamese mounted a campaign which threatened the royal capital [Luang Prabang] and moved beyond the areas previously occupied by Communists. A counterattack by the Lao Government forces, intended to relieve this military pressure and cut off supply lines, caught the enemy by surprise and succeeded beyond expectations in pushing them off the strategic central plain in north Laos known as the Plain of Jars.

The North Vietnamese left behind huge stores of arms, ammunition, and other supplies cached on the Plain. During their operations in the Plain of Jars last summer and fall, Lao Government forces captured almost 8,000 tons of Communist equipment, supplies and weapons, including tanks, armored cars, artillery pieces, machine guns, and thousands of individual weapons including about 4,000 tons of ammuntion. The size and nature of these supply caches the Communists had emplaced on the Plain by the summer of 1969 show clearly that many months ago the North Vietnamese were preparing for major offensive actions on Laotian territory against the Royal Lao Government.

During the final months of 1969 and January 1970, Hanoi sent over 13,000 additional troops into Laos and rebuilt their stocks and supply lines. They also introduced tanks and long-range artillery.

During January and February, Prime Minister Souvanna Phouma proposed to the other side that the Plain of Jars be neutralized. The Communists' response was to launch their current offensive which has recaptured the Plain of Jars and is threatening to go beyond the furthest line of past Communist advances.

The Prime Minster is now once again trying to obtain consultations among all the parties to the Geneva Accords, envisaged under Article IV when there is a violation of Lao sovereignty, independence, neutrality, or territorial integrity.

In this situation, our purposes remain straightforward.

We are trying above all to save American and allied lives in South Vietnam which are threatened. By the continual infiltration of North Vietnamese troops and supplies along the Ho Chi Minh Trail, Hanoi has infiltrated over 100,000 men through Laos since this administration took office and over 500,000 altogether. Our air-strikes have destroyed weapons and supplies over the past 4 years which would have taken thousands of American lives.

We are also supporting the independence and neutrality of Laos as set forth in the 1962 Geneva Agreements. Our assistance has always been at the request of the legitimate government of Prime Minister Souvanna Phouma which the North Vietnamese helped establish; it is directly related to North Vietnamese violations of the agreement.

We continue to be hopeful of eventual progress in the negotiations in Paris. But serious doubts are raised as to Hanoi's intentions if it is simultaneously violating the Geneva Agreements on Laos which we reached with them largely on the basis of their own proposals. What we do in Laos has thus as its aim to bring about conditions for progress toward peace in the entire Indo-Chinese Peninsula.

I turn now to the precise nature of our aid to Laos.

In response to press conference questions on September 26, December 8 and January 30, I have indicated: [4]

—That the United States has no ground combat forces in Laos.
—That there were 50,000 North Vietnamese troops in Laos and that "more perhaps are coming."
—That, at the request of the Royal Laotian Government which was set up by the Geneva Accords of 1962, we have provided logistical and other assistance to that government for the purpose of helping it to prevent the Communist conquest of Laos.
—That we have used air power for the purpose of interdicting the flow of North Vietnamese troops and supplies on that part of the Ho Chi Minh Trail which runs through Laos.
—That, at the request of the Royal Laotian Government, we have flown reconnaissance missions in Northern Laos in support of the Laotian Government's efforts to defend itself against North Vietnamese aggression and that we were engaged in "some other activities."

It would, of course, have posed no political problem for me to have disclosed in greater detail those military support activi-

[4] *Weekly Compilation of Presidential Documents,* September 29, 1969, p. 1320; same, December 16, 1969, p. 1725; same, February 2, 1970, p. 96.

ties which had been initiated by two previous administrations and which have been continued by this administration.

I have not considered it in the national interest to do so because of our concern that putting emphasis on American activities in Laos might hinder the efforts of Prime Minister Souvanna Phouma to bring about adherence to the Geneva Agreements by the Communist signatories.

In recent days, however, there has been intense public speculation to the effect that the United States involvement in Laos has substantially increased in violation of the Geneva Accords, that American ground forces are engaged in combat in Laos and that our air activity has had the effect of escalating the conflict.

Because these reports are grossly inaccurate, I have concluded that our national interest will be served by putting the subject into perspective through a precise description of our current activities in Laos.

These are the facts:

—There are no American ground combat troops in Laos.

—We have no plans for introducing ground combat forces into Laos.

—The total number of Americans directly employed by the U.S. Government in Laos is 616. In addition, there are 424 Americans employed on contract to the government or to government contractors. Of these 1040 Americans, the total number, military and civilian, engaged in a military advisory or military training capacity numbers 320. Logistics personnel number 323.

—No American stationed in Laos has ever been killed in ground combat operations.

—U.S. personnel in Laos during the past year has not increased while during the past few months, North Vietnam has sent over 13,000 additional combat ground troops into Laos.

—When requested by the Royal Laotian Government, we have continued to provide military assistance to regular and irregular Laotian forces in the form of equipment, training and logistics. The levels of our assistance have risen in response to the growth of North Vietnamese combat activities.

—We have continued to conduct air operations. Our first priority for such operations is to interdict the continued flow of troops and supplies across Laotian territory on the Ho Chi Minh Trail. As Commander-in-Chief of our Armed Forces, I consider it my responsibility to use our air power to interdict this flow of supplies and men into South Vietnam and thereby avoid a heavy toll of American and allied lives.

—In addition to these air operations on the Ho Chi Minh Trail, we have continued to carry out reconnaissance flights in Northern Laos and to fly combat support missions for Laotian forces when requested to do so by the Royal Laotian Government.

—In every instance our combat air operations have taken place only over those parts of Laos occupied and contested by North Vietnamese and other Communist forces. They have been flown only when requested by the Laotian Government. The level of our air operations has been increased only as the number of North Vietnamese in Laos and the level of their aggression has increased.

Our goal in Laos has been and continues to be to reduce American involvement and not to increase it, to bring peace in accordance with the 1962 Accords and not to prolong the war.

That is the picture of our current aid to Laos. It is limited. It is requested. It is supportive and defensive. It continues the purposes and operations of two previous administrations. It has been necessary to protect American lives in Vietnam and to preserve a precarious but important balance in Laos.

III. The Future

Peace remains the highest priority of this administration. We will continue our search for it in Vietnam. I hope my appeal today to the Geneva Conference Cochairmen will help in Laos. Our policy for that torn country will continue to rest on some basic principles:

—We will cooperate fully with all diplomatic efforts to restore the 1962 Geneva Agreements.

—We will continue to support the legitimate government of Prime Minister Souvanna Phouma and his efforts to deescalate the conflict and reach political understandings.

—Our air interdiction efforts are designed to protect American and allied lives in Vietnam. Our support efforts have the one purpose of helping prevent the recognized Laotian government from being overwhelmed by larger Communist forces dominated by the North Vietnamese.

—We will continue to give the American people the fullest possible information on our involvement, consistent with national security.

I hope that a genuine quest for peace in Indochina can now begin. For Laos, this will require the efforts of the Geneva Conference Cochairmen and the signatory countries.

But most of all it will require realism and reasonableness from Hanoi. For it is the North Vietnamese, not we, who have escalated the fighting. Today there are 67,000 North Vietnamese troops in this small country. There are no American troops there. Hanoi is not threatened by Laos; it runs risks only when it moves its forces across borders.

We desire nothing more in Laos than to see a return to the Geneva Agreements and the withdrawal of North Vietnamese troops, leaving the Lao people to settle their own differences in a peaceful manner.

In the search for peace we stand ready to cooperate in every way with the other countries involved. That search prompted my letters today to the British Prime Minister and the Soviet Premier. That search will continue to guide our policy.

B. The Cambodian Incursion.

(38) *Defensive Action for Peace: Radio-Television Address by President Nixon, April 30, 1970.*[5]

(Complete Text)

Good evening my fellow Americans.

Ten days ago, in my report to the Nation on Vietnam,[6] I announced a decision to withdraw an additional 150,000 Americans from Vietnam over the next year. I said then that I was making that decision despite our concern over increased enemy activity in Laos, in Cambodia, and in South Vietnam.

At that time, I warned that if I concluded that increased enemy activity in any of these areas endangered the lives of Americans remaining in Vietnam, I would not hesitate to take strong and effective measures to deal with that situation.

Despite that warning, North Vietnam has increased its military aggression in all these areas, and particularly in Cambodia.

After full consultation with the National Security Council, Ambassador [Ellsworth] Bunker, General [Creighton W.] Abrams, and my other advisers, I have concluded that the actions of the enemy in the last 10 days clearly endanger the lives of Americans who are in Vietnam now and would constitute an

---

5 Text from *Weekly Compilation of Presidential Documents,* May 5, 1970, pp. 596–601; for the context see *The United States in World Affairs, 1970,* Sections 19 and 20.

6 Document 42.

unacceptable risk to those who will be there after withdrawal of another 150,000.

To protect our men who are in Vietnam and to guarantee the continued success of our withdrawal and Vietnamization programs,[7] I have concluded that the time has come for action.

Tonight, I shall describe the actions of the enemy, the actions I have ordered to deal with that situation, and the reasons for my decision.

Cambodia, a small country of 7 million people, has been a neutral nation since the Geneva Agreement of 1954 [8]—an agreement, incidentally, which was signed by the Government of North Vietnam.

American policy since then has been to scrupulously respect the neutrality of the Cambodian people. We have maintained a skeleton diplomatic mission of fewer than 15 in Cambodia's capital, and that only since last August. For the previous 4 years, from 1965 to 1969,[9] we did not have any diplomatic mission whatever in Cambodia. And for the past 5 years, we have provided no military assistance whatever and no economic assistance to Cambodia.

North Vietnam, however, has not respected that neutrality.

For the past 5 years—as indicated on this map that you see here—North Vietnam has occupied military sanctuaries all along the Cambodian frontier with South Vietnam. Some of these extend up to 20 miles into Cambodia. The sanctuaries are in red and, as you note, they are on both sides of the border. They are used for hit and run attacks on American and South Vietnamese forces in South Vietnam.

These Communist occupied territories contain major base camps, training sites, logistics facilities, weapons and ammunition factories, air strips, and prisoner-of-war compounds.

For 5 years, neither the United States nor South Vietnam has moved against these enemy sanctuaries because we did not wish to violate the territory of a neutral nation. Even after the Vietnamese Communists began to expand these sanctuaries 4 weeks ago, we counseled patience to our South Vietnamese allies and imposed restraints on our own commanders.

In contrast to our policy, the enemy in the past 2 weeks has stepped up his guerrilla actions and he is concentrating his main forces in these sanctuaries that you see on this map where they

---

[7] Cf. *Documents, 1968–69*, pp. 275–291.

[8] Same, *1954*, pp. 283–314.

[9] U.S.–Cambodian relations were reestablished on July 2, 1969 and a U.S. Embassy was opened August 16, 1969 at the chargé d'affaires level and raised to ambassadorial level on September 3, 1970.

are building up to launch massive attacks on our forces and those of South Vietnam.

North Vietnam in the last 2 weeks has stripped away all pretense of respecting the sovereignty or the neutrality of Cambodia. Thousands of their soldiers are invading the country from the sanctuaries; they are encircling the capital of Phnom Penh. Coming from these sanctuaries, as you see here, they have moved into Cambodia and are encircling the capital.

Cambodia, as a result of this, has sent out a call to the United States, to a number of other nations, for assistance. Because if this enemy effort succeeds, Cambodia would become a vast enemy staging area and a springboard for attacks on South Vietnam along 600 miles of frontier—a refuge where enemy troops could return from combat without fear of retaliation.

North Vietnamese men and supplies could then be poured into that country, jeopardizing not only the lives of our own men but the people of South Vietnam as well.

Now confronted with this situation, we have three options.

First, we can do nothing. Well, the ultimate result of that course of action is clear. Unless we indulge in wishful thinking, the lives of Americans remaining in Vietnam after our next withdrawal of 150,000 would be gravely threatened.

Let us go to the map again. Here is South Vietnam. Here is North Vietnam. North Vietnam already occupies this part of Laos. If North Vietnam also occupied this whole band in Cambodia, or the entire country, it would mean that South Vietnam was completely outflanked and the forces of Americans in this area, as well as the South Vietnamese, would be in an untenable military position.

Our second choice is to provide massive military assistance to Cambodia itself. Now unfortunately, while we deeply sympathize with the plight of 7 million Cambodians whose country is being invaded, massive amounts of military assistance could not be rapidly and effectively utilized by the small Cambodian Army against the immediate threat.

With other nations, we shall do our best to provide the small arms and other equipment which the Cambodian Army of 40,-000 needs and can use for its defense. But the aid we will provide will be limited to the purpose of enabling Cambodia to defend its neutrality and not for the purpose of making it an active belligerent on one side or the other.[10]

Our third choice is to go to the heart of the trouble. That

[10] For text on the U.S. note, delivered to Cambodia on August 20, regulating military assistance see *Department of State Bulletin*, October 5, 1970, pp. 387–388.

means cleaning out major North Vietnamese and Vietcong occupied territories, these sanctuaries which serve as bases for attacks on both Cambodia and American and South Vietnamese forces in South Vietnam. Some of these, incidentally, are as close to Saigon as Baltimore is to Washington.

This one, for example [*indicating*], is called the Parrot's Beak. It is only 33 miles from Saigon.

Now faced with these three options, this is the decision I have made.

In cooperation with the armed forces of South Vietnam, attacks are being launched this week to clean out major enemy sanctuaries on the Cambodian-Vietnam border.

A major responsibility for the ground operations is being assumed by South Vietnamese forces. For example, the attacks in several areas, including the Parrot's Beak that I referred to a moment ago, are exclusively South Vietnamese ground operations under South Vietnamese command with the United States providing air and logistical support.

There is one area, however, immediately above Parrot's Beak, where I have concluded that a combined American and South Vietnamese operation is necessary.

Tonight, American and South Vietnamese units will attack the headquarters for the entire Communist military operation in South Vietnam [Communist Central Office for South Vietnam]. This key control center has been occupied by the North Vietnamese and Vietcong for 5 years in blatant violation of Cambodia's neutrality.

This is not an invasion of Cambodia. The areas in which these attacks will be launched are completely occupied and controlled by North Vietnamese forces. Our purpose is not to occupy the areas. Once enemy forces are driven out of these sanctuaries and once their military supplies are destroyed, we will withdraw.

These actions are in no way directed at the security interests of any nation. Any government that chooses to use these actions as a pretext for harming relations with the United States will be doing so on its own responsibility, and on its own initiative, and we will draw the appropriate conclusions.

Now let me give you the reasons for my decision.

A majority of the American people, a majority of you listening to me, are for the withdrawal of our forces from Vietnam. The action I have taken tonight is indispensable for the continuing success of that withdrawal program.

A majority of the American people want to end this war rather than to have it drag on interminably. The action I have taken tonight will serve that purpose.

A majority of the American people want to keep the casualties of our brave men in Vietnam at an absolute minimum. The action I take tonight is essential if we are to accomplish that goal.

We take this action not for the purpose of expanding the war into Cambodia but for the purpose of ending the war in Vietnam and winning the just peace we all desire. We have made and we will continue to make every possible effort to end this war through negotiation at the conference table rather than through more fighting on the battlefield.

Let us look again at the record. We have stopped the bombing of North Vietnam.[11] We have cut air operations by over 20 percent. We have announced withdrawal of over 250,000 of our men. We have offered to withdraw all of our men if they will withdraw theirs. We have offered to negotiate all issues with only one condition—and that is that the future of South Vietnam be determined not by North Vietnam, not by the United States, but by the people of South Vietnam themselves.

The answer of the enemy has been intransigence at the conference table, belligerence in Hanoi, massive military aggression in Laos [12] and Cambodia, and stepped-up attacks in South Vietnam, designed to increase American casualties.

This attitude has become intolerable. We will not react to this threat to American lives merely by plaintive diplomatic protests. If we did, the credibility of the United States would be destroyed in every area of the world where only the power of the United States deters aggression.

Tonight, I again warn the North Vietnamese that if they continue to escalate the fighting when the United States is withdrawing its forces, I shall meet my responsibility as Commander in Chief of our Armed Forces to take the action I consider necessary to defend the security of our American men.

The action that I have announced tonight puts the leaders of North Vietnam on notice that we will be patient in working for peace, we will be conciliatory at the conference table, but we will not be humiliated. We will not be defeated. We will not allow American men by the thousands to be killed by an enemy from privileged sanctuaries.

The time came along ago to end this war through peaceful negotiations. We stand ready for those negotiations. We have made major efforts, many of which must remain secret. I say tonight that all the offers and approaches made previously re-

11 Cf. President Johnson's address, October 31, 1968, in *Documents, 1968–69,* pp. 243–248.
12 Cf. Document 37.

main on the conference table whenever Hanoi is ready to negotiate seriously.

But if the enemy response to our most conciliatory offers for
peaceful negotiation continues to be to increase its attacks and
humiliate and defeat us, we shall react accordingly.

My fellow Americans, we live in an age of anarchy both abroad
and at home. We see mindless attacks on all the great institutions
which have been created by free civilizations in the last 500 years.
Even here in the United States, great universities are being systematically destroyed. Small nations all over the world find themselves under attack from within and from without.

If, when the chips are down, the world's most powerful nation, the United States of America, acts like a pitiful, helpless
giant, the forces of totalitarianism and anarchy will threaten
free nations and free institutions throughout the world.

It is not our power but our will and character that is being
tested tonight. The question all Americans must ask and answer
tonight is this: Does the richest and strongest nation in the history of the world have the character to meet a direct challenge
by a group which rejects every effort to win a just peace, ignores
our warning, tramples on solemn agreements, violates the neutrality of an unarmed people, and uses our prisoners as hostages?

If we fail to meet this challenge, all other nations will be on
notice that despite its overwhelming power the United States,
when a real crisis comes, will be found wanting.

During my campaign for the Presidency, I pledged to bring
Americans home from Vietnam. They are coming home.

I promised to end this war. I shall keep that promise.

I promised to win a just peace. I shall keep that promise.

We shall avoid a wider war. But we are also determined to
put an end to this war.

In this room, Woodrow Wilson made the great decisions which
led to victory in World War I. Franklin D. Roosevelt made the
decisions which led to our victory in World War II. Dwight D.
Eisenhower made decisions which ended the war in Korea [13] and
avoided war in the Middle East.[14] John F. Kennedy, in his finest
hour, made the great decision which removed Soviet nuclear
missiles from Cuba and the Western Hemisphere.[15]

I have noted that there has been a great deal of discussion with
regard to this decision that I have made and I should point out
that I do not contend that it is in the same magnitude as these
decisions that I have just mentioned. But between those decisions

[13] *Documents, 1953,* pp. 289–331
[14] Same, *1958,* pp. 296–371.
[15] Same, *1962,* pp. 367–412.

and this decision there is a difference that is very fundamental. In those decisions, the American people were not assailed by counsels of doubt and defeat from some of the most widely known opinion leaders of the Nation.

I have noted, for example, that a Republican Senator [George D. Aiken of Vermont] has said that this action I have taken means that my party has lost all chance of winning the November elections. And others are saying today that this move against enemy sanctuaries will make me a one-term President.

No one is more aware than I am of the political consequences of the action I have taken. It is tempting to take the easy political path: to blame this war on previous administrations and to bring all of our men home immediately, regardless of the consequences, even though that would mean defeat for the United States; to desert 18 million South Vietnamese people, who have put their trust in us and to expose them to the same slaughter and savagery which the leaders of North Vietnam inflicted on hundreds of thousands of North Vietnamese who chose freedom when the Communists took over North Vietnam in 1954; to get peace at any price now, even though I know that a peace of humiliation for the United States would lead to a bigger war or surrender later.

I have rejected all political considerations in making this decision.

Whether my party gains in November is nothing compared to the lives of 400,000 brave Americans fighting for our country and for the cause of peace and freedom in Vietnam. Whether I may be a one-term President is insignificant compared to whether by our failure to act in this crisis the United States proves itself to be unworthy to lead the forces of freedom in this critical period in world history. I would rather be a one-term President and do what I believe is right than to be a two-term President at the cost of seeing America become a second-rate power and to see this Nation accept the first defeat in its proud 190-year history.

I realize that in this war there are honest and deep differences in this country about whether we should have become involved, that there are differences as to how the war should have been conducted. But the decision I announce tonight transcends those differences.

For the lives of American men are involved. The opportunity for 150,000 Americans to come home in the next 12 months is involved. The future of 18 million people in South Vietnam and 7 million people in Cambodia is involved. The possibility of winning a just peace in Vietnam and in the Pacific is at stake.

It is customary to conclude a speech from the White House by asking support for the President of the United States. Tonight, I depart from that precedent. What I ask is far more important. I ask for your support for our brave men fighting tonight halfway around the world—not for territory—not for glory—but so that their younger brothers and their sons and your sons can have a chance to grow up in a world of peace and freedom and justice.

Thank you and good night.

(39) *Conclusion of the Cambodian Operation: Report by President Nixon Issued at San Clemente, California, June 30, 1970.*[16]

(*Complete Text*)

Together with the South Vietnamese, the Armed Forces of the United States have just completed successfully the destruction of enemy base areas along the Cambodian-South Vietnam frontier.[17] All American troops have withdrawn from Cambodia on the schedule announced at the start of the operation.

The allied sweeps into the North Vietnamese and Vietcong base areas along the Cambodian-South Vietnamese border:

—will save American and allied lives in the future;

—will assure that the withdrawal of American troops from South Vietnam can proceed on schedule;

—will enable our program of Vietnamization to continue on its current timetable;

—should enhance the prospects for a just peace.

At this time, it is important to review the background for the decision, the results of the operation, their larger meaning in terms of the conflict in Indochina—and to look down the road to the future.

It is vital to understand at the outset that Hanoi left the United States no reasonable option but to move militarily against the Cambodian base areas. The purpose and significance of our operations against the Cambodian sanctuaries can only be understood against the backdrop of what we are seeking to accomplish in Vietnam—and the threat that the Communist bases in Cambodia posed to our objectives. Nor can that military action

[16] Text from *Weekly Compilation of Presidential Documents,* July 6, 1970, pp. 842–856; for the context see *The United States in World Affairs, 1970,* Section 20.
[17] Document 38.

of the last two months be divorced from its cause—the threat posed by the constant expansion of North Vietnamese aggression throughout Indochina.

A RECORD OF RESTRAINT

America's purpose in Vietnam and Indochina remains what it has been—a peace in which the peoples of the region can devote themselves to development of their own societies, a peace in which all the peoples of Southeast Asia can determine their own political future without outside interference.

When this Administration took office, the authorized strength of American troops in South Vietnam was 549,500—the high water mark of American military presence in Southeast Asia. The United States had been negotiating at Paris for ten months but nothing had been agreed upon other than the shape of the bargaining table. No comprehensive allied peace proposal existed. There was no approved plan to reduce America's involvement in the war—in the absence of a negotiated settlement.

Since January of 1969, we have taken steps on all fronts to move toward peace. Along with the Government of South Vietnam, we have put forward a number of concrete and reasonable proposals to promote genuine negotiations. These proposals were first outlined by me 13 months ago, on May 14, 1969 [18] and by President Thieu on July 11, 1969.[19] Through both public and private channels, our proposals have been repeated and amplified many times since.

These proposals are designed to secure the removal of all foreign military forces from South Vietnam and to establish conditions in which all political forces can compete freely and fairly in the future of the country. Our principal goal has been to enable the people of South Vietnam to determine their future free of outside interference.

To indicate our good faith, to improve the climate for negotiations, we changed the orders to our commanders in South Vietnam. This has helped to reduce casualties. We have cut tactical air operations in South Vietnam by more than 20 percent. We initiated a troop withdrawal program which, during the course of next spring, will bring American troop strength 265,000 men below the level authorized when this Administration took office.

These are not the actions of a government pursuing a military solution. They are the decisions of a government seeking a just peace at the conference table.

[18] *Documents, 1968–69,* pp. 252–260.
[19] Same, pp. 267–269.

But Hanoi has ignored our unilateral gestures and rejected every offer of serious negotiations. Instead it has insisted that—as a precondition to talks—we pledge unconditionally to withdraw all American forces from South Vietnam and to overthrow the elected government.

These proposals are not a basis for negotiation; they are a demand for surrender. For the United States to accept these conditions would make the negotiations meaningless. Acceptance of such conditions would assure in advance Communist domination of South Vietnam.

With Hanoi's intransigence on the negotiating front, this Administration was faced with essentially three options.

We could have continued the maximum existing level of American involvement in Vietnam. But this was incompatible with the Nixon Doctrine of increasing responsibilities for the Asian countries; [20] and it was unacceptable to the American people.

We could have begun the immediate withdrawal of all our forces. We rejected this course of capitulation which would have only won temporary respite at the price of graver crises later. We also rejected that course as both incompatible with America's commitments and tradition, and disastrous in terms of its long-range consequences for peace in the Pacific and peace in the world.

We selected instead a third option—that of gradually shifting the total combat burden to the South Vietnamese.

Since the beginning of this Administration 17 months ago, it has been our policy to train and equip the South Vietnamese to take over the burden of their own defense from American troops. Even in the absence of progress at the peace table in Paris, and despite continued enemy pressures in South Vietnam, this policy of "Vietnamization" has permitted us to carry out repeated withdrawals of American troops.

As our policy has been tested, more and more Americans have been brought home. By June of 1969, we could announce the pullout of 25,000 American troops.[21] They came home. In September of 1969, we announced the withdrawal of an additional 35,000 American troops.[22] They came home.

In December of 1969, we announced the withdrawal of 50,000 more American troops.[23] They were home by spring of this year. On April 20, I announced the forthcoming withdrawal of an additional 150,000 Americans to be completed during next

[20] Same, pp. 329–334.
[21] Same, pp. 261–263.
[22] Same, pp. 275–276.
[23] Same, pp. 288–291.

spring—50,000 of them will be home or on their way home by the 15th of October.[24]

A POLICY IN TRANSITION

This transfer of primary responsibility for self-defense from American forces to Asian forces reflects our approach to foreign policy. Increasingly, the United States will look to the countries of the region to assume the primary responsibility for their own security—while America moves gradually from a leading to a supporting role.

To be successful this policy requires the striking of a careful balance—whether in South Vietnam or elsewhere in Asia. While the growing strength of our allies, and the growing measure of their regional cooperation allows for a reduction in American presence—they could not survive a sudden and precipitous American withdrawal from our responsibilities. This would lead to a collapse of local strength in the transition period between the old era of principal U.S. involvement to the new era of partnership and emphasis on local and regional cooperation.

Doing too much for an allied people can delay their political maturity, promote a sense of dependency, and diminish that nation's incentive to stand on its own feet. But doing too little for an ally can induce a sense of despair, endanger their right of self-determination and invite their defeat when confronted by an aggressor.

As we have proceeded with Vietnamization it has been with these principles in mind.

Looking at American policy in Vietnam these seventeen months, this Administration—in the generosity of its negotiating offers, in the limitations on its military actions, and in the consistency of its troop withdrawals—has written a record of restraint. The response from the enemy over those same seventeen months has been intransigence in Paris, belligerence from Hanoi and escalation of the war throughout Indochina.

Enemy attacks in Vietnam increased during April.

This past winter Hanoi launched a major offensive against the legitimate government of Laos [25] which they themselves had helped to establish under the 1962 Geneva Accords.[26] For years, in violation of those accords, North Vietnamese troops have occupied Laotian territory and used its eastern regions as a highway for the export of aggression into South Vietnam.

In March and April of this year, Communist troops used

24 Document 42.
25 Cf. Document 37.
26 Cf. note 3 to Document 37.

their long held bases in Cambodia to move against the Government of Cambodia in a way which increased the long-term threat to allied forces in South Vietnam as well as to the future of our Vietnamization and withdrawal programs. These new violations, too, took place against a backdrop of years of Communist disregard of the neutrality and territorial integrity of Cambodia—guaranteed in the 1954 Geneva Agreements to which Hanoi was a signatory.[27]

Background of the April 30 Decision

In assessing the April 30 decision to move against the North Vietnamese and Viet Cong sanctuaries in Cambodia, four basic facts must be remembered.

It was North Vietnam—not we—which brought the Vietnam War into Cambodia.

For five years, North Vietnam has used Cambodian territory as a sanctuary from which to attack allied forces in South Vietnam. For five years, American and allied forces—to preserve the concept of Cambodian neutrality and to confine the conflict in Southeast Asia—refrained from moving against those sanctuaries.

It was the presence of North Vietnamese troops on Cambodian soil that contributed to the downfall of Prince [Norodom] Sihanouk. It was the indignation of the Cambodian people against the presence of Vietnamese Communists in their country that led to riots in Phnom Penh which contributed to Prince Sihanouk's ouster—an ouster that surprised no nation more than the United States. At the end of Sihanouk's rule, the United States was making efforts to improve relations with his government [28] and the Prince was taking steps against the Communist invaders on his national soil.

It was the government appointed by Prince Sihanouk and ratified by the Cambodian National Assembly—not a group of usurpers—which overthrew him with the approval of the National Assembly. The United States had neither connection with, nor knowledge of, these events.

It was the major expansion of enemy activity in Cambodia that ultimately caused allied troops to end five years of restraint and attack the Communist base areas.

The historical record is plain.

Viet Cong and North Vietnamese troops have operated in Eastern Cambodia for years. The primary objective of these Communist forces has been the support of Hanoi's aggression against South Vietnam. Just as it has violated the 1962 Geneva

27 Cf. note 8 to Document 38.
28 Cf. note 9 to Document 38.

Accords on Laos, North Vietnam has consistently ignored its pledge, in signing the 1954 Geneva Accords, to respect Cambodian neutrality and territorial integrity.

In a May 1967 Phnom Penh radio broadcast, Prince Sihanouk's following remarks were reported to the Cambodia people:

> "I must tell you that the Vietnamese communists and the Viet Cong negotiated with us three or four times but that absolutely nothing comes out of the negotiations . . . After I expelled the French and after the French troops left Cambodia, Viet Minh remained in our country in order to conquer it. How can we have confidence in the Viet Minh? . . . If we side with the Viet Minh we will lose our independence."

Late in 1969, Prince Sihanouk ordered Cambodia's underequipped and weak armed forces to exercise some measure of control over North Vietnamese and Viet Cong Communist forces occupying Cambodian territory.

At the same time, the Communist forces were actively preparing in their base areas for new combat in South Vietnam. These areas—on the Cambodian side of the Vietnam-Cambodian border—have for years served as supply depots and base camps for enemy troops infiltrated through Laos into South Vietnam. They have also served as sanctuaries for North Vietnamese and Viet Cong headquarters elements and for combat troops to rest, refit and re-supply on their return from South Vietnam.

Our screening of more than six tons of documents captured in the Cambodian operations has provided conclusive proof of Communist reliance on Cambodia as a logistic and infiltration corridor and as a secure area from which Communist designs on Vietnam as well as in Cambodia itself could be carried out.

On January 6, 1970, Prince Sihanouk departed on vacation in France. His Prime Minister, Lon Nol, and Deputy Prime Minister, [Prince Sisowath] Sirik Matak, were left in charge. In early March, with Sihanouk still in power, there were public demonstrations, first in the Eastern provinces of Cambodia and later in Phnom Penh, against flagrant North Vietnamese violation of Cambodia's territorial integrity.

On March 13, Prince Sihanouk left Paris for Moscow and Peking, avowedly to seek Soviet and Chinese assistance in persuading the Vietnamese Communists to reduce the presence of North Vietnamese and Viet Cong forces in Cambodia.

Then, on March 18, the Cambodian National Assembly by unanimous vote declared that Prince Sihanouk was no longer Chief of State. Cheng Heng was retained as Acting Chief of State. Lon Nol and Sirik Matak kept their positions. Reasons for Sihanouk's ouster included growing objections to his mishandling of the economy and to his by-passing of the Cabinet and National Assembly; but resentment over North Vietnam's flagrant misuse of Cambodian territory certainly contributed. Sihanouk arrived in Peking the same day, and met with the Peking leadership as well as with the North Vietnamese Prime Minister [Pham Van Dong] who had hastened to Peking to greet him. Thereafter Sihanouk has increasingly identified himself with the Communist cause in Indochina.

This government had no advance warning of the ouster of Sihanouk, with whom we had been attempting to improve relations. Our initial response was to seek to preserve the status quo with regard to Cambodia and to try to prevent an expansion of Communist influence. The immunity of the Cambodian sanctuaries had been a serious military handicap for us for many years. But we had refrained from moving against them in order to contain the conflict. We recognized both the problems facing Sihanouk and the fact that he had exercised some measure of control over Communist activities, through regulation of the flow of rice and military supplies into the sanctuaries from coastal ports. We considered that a neutral Cambodia outweighed the military benefits of a move against the base areas.

This is why diplomatically our first reaction to Sihanouk's overthrow was to encourage some form of accommodation in Cambodia. We spoke in this sense to interested governments. And we made clear through many channels that we had no intention of exploiting the Cambodian upheaval for our own ends.

These attempts ran afoul of Hanoi's designs. North Vietnam and the Viet Cong withdrew their representation from Phnom Penh. North Vietnamese and Viet Cong forces began to expand their base areas along the border.

By April 3, they were beginning to launch attacks against Cambodian forces in Svay Rieng Province. Later these attacks were extended to other outposts in Eastern Cambodia, forcing Cambodian troops to evacuate border positions in the Parrot's Beak area by April 10. Communist attacks were also directed against Mekong River traffic.

By April 16, the North Vietnamese and Viet Cong troops began to launch isolated attacks deep into Cambodia including an attack on the capital of Takeo Province south of Phnom Penh.

Despite escalating Communist activity in Cambodia, we continued to exercise restraint. Though the implications of the Communist actions for our efforts in Vietnam were becoming increasingly ominous, Communist intentions in Cambodia were still not absolutely clear. The military moves by the North Vietnamese and Viet Cong in Cambodia could still be interpreted as temporary actions to secure their base camps in light of the uncertainties following Sihanouk's removal.

When I made my April 20 speech announcing the withdrawal of 150,000 troops over the next year, I knew that we might be at a crossroads in Cambodia. I nevertheless made the announcement because it would leave no doubt about our intention to de-escalate the conflict.

I also used the occasion to restate very forthcoming political principles for a negotiated peace. At the same time I described the pattern of North Vietnamese aggression in Indochina, and acknowledged that my withdrawal decision involved some risks when viewed against this enemy escalation. I therefore reiterated my determination to take strong and effective measures if increased enemy action in Laos, Cambodia or South Vietnam jeopardized the security of our remaining forces in Vietnam.

Within days of my April 20 speech, Communist intentions became painfully and unambiguously clear. In the face of our restraint and our warnings, the North Vietnamese continued to expand their territorial control, threatening to link up their base areas. From a series of isolated enclaves, the base areas were rapidly becoming a solid band of self-sustaining territory stretching from Laos to the sea from which any pretense of Cambodian sovereignty was rapidly being excluded.

—On April 20, North Vietnamese forces temporarily captured Saang, only eighteen miles south of Phnom Penh.
—On April 22, Communist forces assaulted the town of Snuol east of Phnom Penh.
—On April 23, they attacked the town of Minot and an important bridge linking the town of Snuol and the capital of Kratie Province on Route 13.
—On April 24, they moved on the resort city of Kep.
—On April 26, they attacked some ships on the Mekong and occupied the town of Angtassom, a few miles west of Takeo.
—They then attacked the city of Chhlong, on the Mekong River north of Phnom Penh, and the port city of Kampot.
—During this same period, they cut almost every major road leading south and east of Phnom Penh.

The prospect suddenly loomed of Cambodia's becoming virtually one large base area for attack anywhere into South Vietnam along the 600 miles of the Cambodian frontier. The enemy in Cambodia would have enjoyed complete freedom of action to move forces and supplies rapidly across the entire length of South Vietnam's flank to attack our forces in South Vietnam with impunity from well-stocked sanctuaries along the border.

We thus faced a rapidly changing military situation from that which existed on April 20.

The possibility of a grave new threat to our troops in South Vietnam was rapidly becoming an actuality.

This pattern of Communist action prior to our decision of April 30 makes it clear the enemy was intent both on expanding and strengthening its military position along the Cambodian border and overthrowing the Cambodian government. The plans were laid, the orders issued, and already being implemented by Communist forces.

Not only the clear evidence of Communist actions—but supporting data screened from more than six tons of subsequently captured Communist documents—leaves no doubt that the Communists' move against the Cambodian Government preceded the U.S. action against the base areas.

Three Options

On April 30, before announcing our response, I outlined the three basic choices we had in the face of the expanding Communist threat.

First, we could do nothing. This would have eroded an important restraint on the loss of American lives. It would have run the risk of Cambodia's becoming one vast enemy staging area, a springboard for attacks on South Vietnam without fear of retaliation. The dangers of having done nothing would not have fully materialized for several months and this government might have been commended for exercising restraint. But, as withdrawals proceeded, our paralysis would have seriously jeopardized our forces in Vietnam and would have led to longer lists of American casualties. The United States could not accept the consequences of inaction in the face of this enemy escalation. The American men remaining in South Vietnam after our withdrawal of 150,000 would have been in severe jeopardy.

Our second choice was to provide massive assistance to Cambodia. This was an unrealistic alternative. The small Cambodian army of 30,000 could not effectively utilize any massive transfusion of military assistance against the immediate enemy threat. We also did not wish to get drawn into the permanent direct defense of Cambodia. This would have been inconsistent with the basic premises of our foreign policy.

After intensive consultations with my top advisers, I chose the third course. With the South Vietnamese we launched joint attacks against the base areas so long occupied by Communist forces.

Our military objectives were to capture or destroy the arms, ammunition and supplies that had been built up in those sanctuaries over a period of years and to disrupt the enemy's communication network. At the least this would frustrate the impact of any Communist success in linking up their base areas if it did not prevent this development altogether.

I concluded that, regardless of the success of Communist assaults on the Cambodian Government, the destruction of the enemy's sanctuaries would:

—remove a grave potential threat to our remaining men in South Vietnam, and so reduce future American casualties.

—give added assurance of the continuance of our troop withdrawal program.

—insure the timetable for our Vietnamization program.

—increase the chances of shortening the war in South Vietnam.

—enhance the prospects of a negotiated peace.

—emphasize to the enemy whether in Southeast Asia or elsewhere that the word of the United States—whether given in a promise or a warning—was still good.

THE MILITARY OPERATIONS

Ten major operations were launched against a dozen of the most significant base areas with 32,000 American troops and 48,-000 South Vietnamese participating at various times. As of today, all Americans, including logistics personnel and advisers, have withdrawn, as have a majority of the South Vietnamese forces.

Our military response to the enemy's escalation was measured in every respect. It was a limited operation for a limited period of time with limited objectives.

We have scrupulously observed the 21-mile limit on penetration of our ground combat forces into Cambodian territory. These self-imposed time and geographic restrictions may have cost us some military advantages, but we knew that we could achieve our primary objectives within these restraints. And these restraints underscored the limited nature of our purpose to the American people.

My June 3 interim report [29] pointed up the success of these operations and the massive amounts of supplies we were seizing and destroying. We have since added substantially to these totals. A full inventory is attached as an appendix to the report. Here are some highlights.

According to latest estimates from the field, we have captured:

—22,892 individual weapons—enough to equip about 74 full-

[29] Text in *Weekly Compilation of Presidential Documents*, June 8, 1970, pp. 721–725.

strength North Vietnamese infantry battalions and 2,509 big crew-served weapons—enough to equip about 25 full-strength North Vietnamese infantry battalions;

—More than 15 million rounds of ammunition or about what the enemy has fired in South Vietnam during the past year;

—14 million pounds of rice, enough to feed all the enemy combat battalions estimated to be in South Vietnam for about four months;

—143,000 rockets, mortars, and recoilless rifle rounds, used against cities and bases. Based on recent experience, the number of mortars, large rockets, and recoilless rifle rounds is equivalent to what the enemy shoots in about 14 months in South Vietnam;

—Over 199,552 anti-aircraft rounds, 5,482 mines, 62,022 grenades, and 83,000 pounds of explosives, including 1,002 satchel charges;

—Over 435 vehicles and destroyed over 11,688 bunkers and other military structures.

And while our objective has been supplies rather than personnel, the enemy has also taken a heavy manpower loss—11,349 men killed and about 2,328 captured and detainees.

These are impressive statistics. But what is the deeper meaning of the piles of enemy supplies and the rubble of enemy installations?

We have eliminated an immediate threat to our forces and to the security of South Vietnam—and produced the prospect of fewer American casualties in the future.

We have inflicted extensive casualties and very heavy losses in material on the enemy—losses which can now be replaced only from the North during a monsoon season and in the face of counteraction by South Vietnamese ground and U.S. air forces.

We have ended the concept of Cambodian sanctuaries, immune from attack, upon which the enemy military had relied for five years.

We have dislocated supply lines and disrupted Hanoi's strategy in the Saigon area and the Mekong Delta. The enemy capacity to mount a major offensive in this vital populated region of the South has been greatly diminished.

We have effectively cut off the enemy from resupply by the sea. In 1969, well over half of the munitions being delivered to the North Vietnamese and Viet Cong in Cambodia came by sea.

We have, for the time being, separated the Communist main force units—regular troops organized in formal units similar to conventional armies—from the guerrillas in the southern part of Vietnam. This should provide a boost to pacification efforts.

We have guaranteed the continuance of our troop withdrawal program. On June 3, I reaffirmed that 150,000 more Americans would return home within a year and announced that 50,000 would leave Vietnam by October 15.

We have bought time for the South Vietnamese to strengthen themselves against the enemy.

We have witnessed visible proof of the success of Vietnamization as the South Vietnamese performed with skill and valor and competence far beyond the expectation of our commanders or American advisers. The morale and self-confidence of the Army of South Vietnam is higher than ever before.

These then are the major accomplishments of the operations against the Cambodian base areas. Americans can take pride in the leadership of General Abrams and in the competence and dedication of our forces.

There is another way to view the success of these operations. What if we had chosen the first option—and done nothing?

The enemy sanctuaries by now would have been expanded and strengthened. The thousands of troops he lost, in killed or captured, would be available to attack American positions and with the enormous resources that we captured or destroyed still in his hands.

Our Vietnamization program would be in serious jeopardy; our withdrawals of troops could only have been carried out in the face of serious threat to our remaining troops in Vietnam.

We would have confronted an adversary emboldened by our timidity, an adversary who had ignored repeated warnings.

The war would be a good deal further from over than it is today.

Had we stood by and let the enemy act with impunity in Cambodia—we would be facing a truly bleak situation.

The allied operations have greatly reduced these risks and enhanced the prospects for the future. However, many difficulties remain and some setbacks are inevitable. We still face substantial problems, but the Cambodian operations will enable us to pursue our goals with greater confidence.

When the decision to go into Cambodia was announced on April 30, we anticipated broad disagreement and dissent within the society. Given the divisions on this issue among the American people, it could not have been otherwise.

But the majority of the Americans supported that decision—and now that the Cambodian operation is over, I believe there is a wide measure of understanding of the necessity for it.

Although there remains disagreement about its long-term significance, about the cost to our society of having taken this action

—there can be little disagreement now over the immediate military success that has been achieved. With American ground operations in Cambodia ended, we shall move forward with our plan to end the war in Vietnam and to secure the just peace on which all Americans are united.

The Future

Now that our ground forces and our logistic and advisory personnel have all been withdrawn, what will be our future policy for Cambodia?

The following will be the guidelines of our policy in Cambodia:

1. There will be no U.S. ground personnel in Cambodia except for the regular staff of our Embassy in Phnom Penh.
2. There will be no U.S. advisers with Cambodian units.
3. We will conduct—with the approval of the Cambodian Government—air interdiction missions against the enemy efforts to move supplies and personnel through Cambodia toward South Vietnam and to re-establish base areas relevant to the war in Vietnam. We do this to protect our forces in South Vietnam.
4. We will turn over material captured in the base areas in Cambodia to the Cambodian Government to help it defend its neutrality and independence.
5. We will provide military assistance to the Cambodian Government in the form of small arms and relatively unsophisticated equipment in types and quantities suitable for their army.[30] To date we have supplied about $5 million of these items principally in the form of small arms, mortars, trucks, aircraft parts, communications equipment and medical supplies.
6. We will encourage other countries of the region to give diplomatic support to the independence and neutrality of Cambodia. We welcome the efforts of the Djakarta group of countries [31] to mobilize world opinion and encourage Asian cooperation to this end.
7. We will encourage and support the efforts of third countries who wish to furnish Cambodia with troops or material. We applaud the efforts of Asian nations to help Cambodia preserve its neutrality and independence.

30 Cf. note 10 to Document 38.
31 The reference is to a conference on Cambodia held by 11 Asian Foreign Ministers in Djakarta, Indonesia on May 16–17; for a Department of State statement supporting the decisions taken by the conference see *Department of State Bulletin,* June 8, 1970, pp. 710–711.

I will let the Asian Governments speak for themselves concerning their future policies. I am confident that two basic principles will govern the actions of those nations helping Cambodia:

—They will be at the request of, and in close concert with the Cambodian Government.

—They will not be at the expense of those nations' own defense—indeed they will contribute to their security which they see bound up with events in Cambodia.

The South Vietnamese plan to help. Of all the countries of Southeast Asia, South Vietnam has most at stake in Cambodia. A North Vietnamese takeover would, of course, have profound consequences for its security. At the same time, the leaders of South Vietnam recognize that the primary focus of their attention must be on the security of their own country. President [Nguyen Van] Thieu has reflected these convictions in his major radio and TV address of June 27. Our understanding of Saigon's intentions is as follows:

1. South Vietnamese forces remain ready to prevent reestablishment of base areas along South Vietnam's frontier.

2. South Vietnamese forces will remain ready to assist in the evacuation of Vietnamese civilians and to respond selectively to appeals from the Cambodian Government should North Vietnamese aggression make this necessary.

3. Most of these operations will be launched from within South Vietnam. There will be no U.S. air or logistics support. There will not be U.S. advisers on these operations.

4. The great majority of South Vietnamese forces are to leave Cambodia.

5. The primary objective of the South Vietnamese remains Vietnamization within their country. Whatever actions are taken in Cambodia, will be consistent with this objective.

In this June 27 speech President Thieu emphasized that his government will concentrate on efforts within South Vietnam. He pledged that his country will always respect the territory, borders, independence and neutrality of Cambodia and will not interfere in its internal politics. His government does not advocate stationing troops permanently in Cambodia or sending the South Vietnamese army to fight the war for the Cambodian army.

Under the foreign policy guidelines first outlined at Guam a year ago,[32] I stressed that a threatened country should first make maximum efforts in its own self-defense. The Cambodian people and soldiers are doing that against the superior force of the North

[32] Cf. reference note 20, above.

Vietnamese and Viet Cong invaders. The majority of the Cambodian people support the present government against the foreign intruders. Cambodian troops have remained loyal and have stood up well in the face of great pressures from a better-armed and experienced foe.

Secondly, our policy stresses there should be regional cooperation where a country is not strong enough to defend herself. Cambodia's neighbors are providing that cooperation by joining with her in a collective effort. Each of them is a target of Communist aggression; each has a stake in Cambodia's neutrality and independence.

Third, the U.S. will assist such self-help and regional actions where our participation can make a difference. Over the long term, we expect the countries of Asia to provide increasingly for their own defense. However, we are now in a transitional phase when nations are shouldering greater responsibilities but when U.S. involvement, while declining, still plays an important role.

In this interim period, we must offset our lower direct involvement with increased military and economic assistance. To meet our foreign policy obligations while reducing our presence will require a redirection—both quantitatively and qualitatively—in our assistance programs.

Prince Sihanouk wrote in December 1969 about the Communist threat to his country and the balance presented by American forces in Southeast Asia. In a generally anti-American article in the official Cambodian Government Party newspaper he stated:

"On the diplomatic and political plane, the fact that the U.S. remains in our region and does not yet leave it allows us maneuverings. . . . to assure on the one hand our more than honorable presence in the concert of nations. . . . this presence (and this is an irony of fate for the anti-imperialists that we are) is an essential condition for the 'respect,' the 'friendship' and even for the aid of our socialist 'friends.' When the U.S. has left these regions, it is certain that the Cambodia of the Sangkum will be the objective of the shellings of the heavy Communist guns: unfriendliness, subversion, aggressions, infiltrations and even occupations."

The Search for Peace

In our search for a lasting peace in Southeast Asia, we are applying the three basic principles of our foreign policy which are set forth in the Foreign Policy Report to Congress last February: [33] partnership, strength and willingness to negotiate.

[33] Document 2.

—The partnership of our Vietnamization Program and of our support for regional defense efforts.

—The strength of our action against the Communist bases in Cambodia and the steadfastness of the American people to see the war through to an honorable conclusion.

—The willingness to negotiate expressed in our generous proposals for a settlement and in our flexibility once Hanoi agrees to serious negotiations.

All three elements are needed to bring peace in Southeast Asia. The willingness to negotiate will prove empty unless buttressed by the willingness to stand by just demands. Otherwise negotiations will be a subterfuge for capitulation. This would only bring a false and transitory peace abroad and recrimination at home.

While we search for genuine negotiation we must continue to demonstrate resolution both abroad and at home and we must support the common defense efforts of threatened Asian nations.

To the leaders in Hanoi, I say the time has come to negotiate. There is nothing to be gained in waiting. There is never an ideal moment when both sides are in perfect equilibrium.

The lesson of the last two months has reinforced the lessons of the last two years—the time has come to negotiate a just peace.

In Cambodia, the futility of expanded aggression has been demonstrated. By its actions in Cambodia, North Vietnam and the Viet Cong provoked the destruction of their sanctuaries and helped to weld together the independent states of Southeast Asia in a collective defense effort, which will receive American support.

The other side cannot impose its will through military means. We have no intention of imposing ours. We have not raised the terms for a settlement as a result of our recent military successes. We will not lower our minimum terms in response to enemy pressure. Our objective remains a negotiated peace with justice for both sides and which gives the people of South Vietnam the opportunity to shape their own future.

With major efforts the North Vietnamese can perhaps rebuild or readjust Cambodia supply areas over a period of months. They can pursue their war against South Vietnam and her neighbors. But what end would a new round of conflict serve? There is no military solution to this conflict. Sooner or later, peace must come. It can come now, through a negotiated settlement that is fair to both sides and humiliates neither. Or it can come months or years from now, with both sides having paid the further price of protracted struggle.

We would hope that Hanoi would ponder seriously its choice,

considering both the promise of an honorable peace and the costs of continued war.

We repeat: all our previous proposals, public and private, remain on the conference table to be explored, including the principles of a just political settlement that I outlined on April 20.

We search for a political solution that reflects the will of the South Vietnamese people, and allows them to determine their future without outside interference.

We recognize that a fair political solution should reflect the existing relationship of political forces.

We pledge to abide by the outcome of the political process agreed upon by the South Vietnamese.

For our part, we shall renew our efforts to bring about genuine negotiations both in Paris and for all of Indochina. As I said in my address last September to the United Nations General Assembly: [34]

"The people of Vietnam, North and South alike, have demonstrated heroism enough to last a century . . . The people of Vietnam, North and South, have endured an unspeakable weight of suffering for a generation. And they deserve a better future."

We call on Hanoi to join us at long last in bringing about that better future.

(40) Limitation on United States Funds for Cambodia: The Cooper-Church Amendment, Passed by the Senate June 30, 1970.[35]

(Complete Text)

"Sec. 47. Limitations on United States Involvement in Cambodia.—In concert with the declared objectives of the President

---

[34] *Documents, 1968–69,* pp. 470–471.

[35] Text from *Congressional Record* (Daily Edition), January 27, 1971, p. S 369; adopted by a vote of 58 to 37. Originally introduced by Senators John Sherman Cooper and Frank Church following President Nixon's decision to send U.S. troops into Cambodia as an amendment to the Foreign Military Sales Act (Public Law 91–672, approved January 12, 1971), the amendment was deleted following a House-Senate conference. A modified version of the amendment was subsequently included in the Special Foreign Assistance Act of 1971 (Public Law 91–652, approved January 5, 1971). For a legislative history of restrictions relating to Cambodia see *Congressional Record* (Daily Edition), January 27, 1971, pp. S 360-S 370.

of the United States to avoid the involvement of the United States in Cambodia after July 1, 1970,[36] and to expedite the withdrawal of American forces from Cambodia, it is hereby provided that unless specifically authorized by law hereafter enacted, no funds authorized or appropriated pursuant to this act, or any other law may be expended after July 1, 1970, for the purpose of—

"(1) retaining United States forces in Cambodia;

"(2) paying the compensation or allowances of, or otherwise supporting, directly or indirectly, any United States personnel in Cambodia who furnish military instruction to Cambodian forces or engage in any combat activity in support of Cambodian forces;

"(3) entering into or carrying out any contract or agreement to provide military instruction in Cambodia or to provide persons to engage in any combat activity in support of Cambodian forces; or

"(4) conducting any combat activity in the air above Cambodia in direct support of Cambodian forces."

C. Winding Down the War in South Vietnam.

(41) Repeal of the Tonkin Gulf Resolution: Public Law 91-672, Approved January 12, 1971.[37]

(Excerpt)

*   *   *

"Sec. 12. The joint resolution entitled "Joint resolution to promote the maintenance of international peace and security in Southeast Asia", approved August 10, 1964 (78 Stat. 384; Public Law 88–408),[38] is terminated effective upon the day that the second session of the Ninety-first Congress is last adjourned." [39]

*   *   *

[36] Documents 38–39.

[37] Excerpt from the Foreign Military Sales Act, Amendments (House Report 15628), passed by the Congress December 31, 1970. Repeal of the Tonkin Gulf resolution was initially introduced April 30, 1970 in the Senate Committee on Foreign Relations as Senate Concurrent Resolution 64, which was adopted by the Committee on May 11, 1970 by a vote of 13 to 1.

[38] Text in *Documents, 1964,* pp. 216–217.

[39] The 91st Congress expired January 3, 1971.

(42) Report on Vietnam: Radio-Television Address by President Nixon, April 20, 1970.[40]

(Complete Text)

Good evening, my fellow Americans:

I have requested this television and radio time tonight to give you a progress report on our plan to bring a just peace to Vietnam.

When I first outlined our program last June, I stated that the rate of American withdrawals from Vietnam would depend on three criteria—progress in the training of the South Vietnamese, progress in the Paris negotiations, and the level of enemy activity.[41]

Tonight I am pleased to report that progress in training and equipping South Vietnamese forces has substantially exceeded our original expectations last June.

Very significant advances have also been made in pacification.

Although we recognize that problems remain, these are encouraging trends.

However, I must report with regret that no progress has taken place on the negotiating front. The enemy still demands that we unilaterally and unconditionally withdraw all American forces, that in the process we overthrow the elected Government of South Vietnam, and that the United States accept a political settlement that would have the practical consequence of the forcible imposition of a Communist government upon the people of South Vietnam.

That would mean humiliation and defeat for the United States. This we cannot and will not accept.

Let me now turn to the third criteria [*sic*] for troop withdrawals —the level of enemy activity. In several areas since December, that level has substantially increased.

In recent months Hanoi has sent thousands more of their soldiers to launch new offensives in neutral Laos in violation of the Geneva Accords of 1962 to which they were signatories.[42]

South of Laos, almost 40,000 Communist troops are now conducting overt aggression against Cambodia, a small neutralist country that the Communists have used for years as a base for

---

[40] Text from *Weekly Compilation of Presidential Documents*, April 27, 1970, pp. 553–557; for the context see *The United States in World Affairs, 1970*, Sections 18 and 19.

[41] *Documents, 1968–69*, pp. 261–263.

[42] Cf. note 3 to Document 37.

attack upon South Vietnam in violation of the Geneva Accords of 1954 to which they were also signatories.[43]

This follows the consistent pattern of North Vietnamese aggression in Indochina. During the ·past 8 years they have sent tens of thousands of troops into all three countries of the peninsula and across every single common border.

Men and supplies continue to pour down the Ho Chi Minh trail; and in the past 2 weeks, the Communists have stepped up their attacks upon allied forces in South Vietnam.

However, despite this new enemy activity, there has been an overall decline in enemy force levels in South Vietnam since December.

As the enemy force levels have declined and as the South Vietnamese have assumed more of the burden of battle, American casualties have declined.

I am glad to be able to report tonight that in the first 3 months of 1970, the number of Americans killed in action dropped to the lowest first quarter level in 5 years.

In June, a year ago, when we began troop withdrawals, we did so on a "cut and try" basis—with no certainty that the program would be successful. In June we announced withdrawal of 25,000 American troops; in September another 35,000 [44] and then in December 50,000 more.[45] These withdrawals have now been completed and as of April 15, a total of 115,500 men have returned home from Vietnam.

We have now reached a point where we can confidently move from a period of "cut and try" to a longer-range program for the replacement of Americans by South Vietnamese troops.

I am, therefore, tonight announcing plans for the withdrawal of an additional 150,000 American troops to be completed during the spring of next year. This will bring a total reduction of 265,500 men in our Armed Forces in Vietnam below the level that existed when we took office 15 months ago.

The timing and pace of these new withdrawals within the overall schedule will be determined by our best judgment of the current military and diplomatic situation.

This far-reaching decision was made after consultation with our commanders in the field and it has the approval of the Government of South Vietnam.

Now, viewed against the enemy's escalation in Laos and Cambodia, and in view of the stepped-up attacks this month in South Vietnam, this decision clearly involves risks.

---

[43] Cf. note 8 to Document 38.
[44] *Documents, 1968–69*, pp. 261–263, 275–276.
[45] Same, pp. 288–291.

But I again remind the leaders of North Vietnam that while we are taking these risks for peace, they will be taking grave risks should they attempt to use the occasion to jeopardize the security of our remaining forces in Vietnam by increased military action in Vietnam, in Cambodia, or in Laos.

I repeat what I said November 3rd [46] and December 15th. If I conclude that increased enemy action jeopardizes our remaining forces in Vietnam, I shall not hesitate to take strong and effective measures to deal with that situation.

My responsibility as Commander in Chief of our Armed Forces is for the safety of our men, and I shall meet that responsibility. The decision I have announced tonight to withdraw 150,000 more men over the next year is based entirely on the progress of our Vietnamization program.

There is a better, shorter path to peace—through negotiations. We shall withdraw more than 150,000 over the next year if we make progress on the negotiating front.

Had the other side responded positively at Paris to our offer of May 14 last year,[47] most American and foreign troops would have left South Vietnam by now.

A political settlement is the heart of the matter. That is what the fighting in Indochina has been about over the past 30 years.

Now, we have noted with interest the recent statement by Soviet Deputy Foreign Minister [Yakov A.] Malik concerning a possible new Geneva Conference on Indochina.

We do not yet know the full implications of this statement. It is in the spirit of the letters I wrote on April 7, to signatories of the 1962 Geneva Accords urging consultations and observance of the Accords. We have consistently said we were willing to explore any reasonable path to peace. We are in the process of exploring this one.

But whatever the fate of this particular move we are ready for a settlement fair to everyone.

Let me briefly review for you the principles that govern our view of a just political settlement.

First, our overriding objective is a political solution that reflects the will of the South Vietnamese people and allows them to determine their future without outside interference.

I again reaffirm this Government's acceptance of eventual, total withdrawal of American troops. In turn, we must see the permanent withdrawal of all North Vietnamese troops and be given reasonable assurances that they will not return.

Second, a fair political solution should reflect the existing relationship of political forces within South Vietnam. We recognize the complexity of shaping machinery that would fairly apportion political power in South Vietnam. We are flexible; we have offered nothing on a take-it-or-leave-it-basis.

And third, we will abide by the outcome of the political process agreed upon. President Thieu and I have repeatedly stated our willingness to accept the free decision of the South Vietnamese people. But we will not agree to the arrogant demand that the elected leaders of the Government of Vietnam be overthrown before real negotiations begin.

Let me briefly review the record of our efforts to end the war in Vietnam through negotiations.

We were told repeatedly in the past that our adversaries would negotiate seriously

—if only we stopped the bombing of North Vietnam;
—if only we began withdrawing our forces from South Vietnam;
—if only we dealt with the National Liberation Front as one of the parties to the negotiations;
—if only we would agree in principle to removal of all of our forces from Vietnam.

We have taken all these steps.

The United States, over a year and a half ago, stopped all bombing of North Vietnam.[48] Long ago we agreed to negotiate with the National Liberation Front as one of the parties. We have already withdrawn 115,500 American troops. Tonight I have announced a decision to reduce American force levels by a quarter of a million men from what they were 15 months ago. We have offered repeatedly to withdraw all of our troops if the North Vietnamese would withdraw theirs. We have taken risks for peace that every fair and objective man can readily recognize.

And still there is no progress at the negotiating table.

It is Hanoi and Hanoi alone that stands today blocking the path to a just peace for all the peoples of Southeast Asia.

When our astronauts returned safely to earth last Friday [April 17],[49] the whole world rejoiced with us. We could have had no more eloquent demonstration of a profound truth—that the greatest force working for peace in the world today is the fact that men and women everywhere, regardless of differences in race, religion, nationality, or political philosophy, value the life of a

[48] Cf. note 11 to Document 38.
[49] The Apollo 13 mission, launched April 11, 1970, made a safe splashdown in the Pacific following an accident which prevented a scheduled moon landing.

human being. We were as one as we thought of those brave men, their wives, their children, their parents.

The death of a single man in war, whether he is an American, a South Vietnamese, a Vietcong, or a North Vietnamese, is a human tragedy. That is why we want to end this war and achieve a just peace. We call upon our adversaries to join us in working at the conference table toward that goal.

No Presidential statement on Vietnam would be complete without an expression of our concern for the fate of the American prisoners of war.[50]

The callous exploitation of the anxieties and anguish of the parents, the wives, the children of these brave men, as negotiating pawns, is an unforgivable breach of the elementary rules of conduct between civilized peoples. We shall continue to make every possible effort to get Hanoi to provide information on the whereabouts of all prisoners; to allow them to communicate with their families; to permit inspection of prisoners-of-war camps; and to provide for the early release of at least the sick and the wounded.

My fellow Americans, 5 years ago American combat troops were first sent to Vietnam. The war since that time has been the longest and one of the most costly and difficult conflicts in our history.

The decision I have announced tonight means that we finally have in sight the just peace we are seeking. We can now say with confidence that pacification is succeeding. We can now say with confidence that the South Vietnamese can develop the capability for their own defense. And we can say with confidence that all American combat forces can and will be withdrawn.

I could not make these statements tonight had it not been for the dedication, the bravery, the sacrifice of hundreds of thousands of young men who have served in Vietnam. Nor could I have made it had it not been for the perseverance of millions of Americans at home.

When men write the history of this Nation, they will record that no people in the annals of time made greater sacrifices in a more selfless cause than the American people sacrificed for the right of 18 million people in a faraway land to avoid the imposition of Communist rule against their will and for the right of those people to determine their own future free of outside interference.

The enemy has failed to win the war in Vietnam because of three basic errors in their strategy.

50 Cf. Document 46.

They thought they could win a military victory. They have failed to do so.

They thought they could win politically in South Vietnam. They have failed to do so.

They thought they could win politically in the United States. This proved to be their most fatal miscalculation.

In this great free country of ours, we debate—we disagree, sometimes violently, but the mistake the totalitarians make over and over again is to conclude that debate in a free country is proof of weakness. We are not a weak people. We are a strong people. America has never been defeated in the proud 190-year history of this country, and we shall not be defeated in Vietnam.

Tonight I want to thank the American people for the support you have given so generously to the cause of a just peace in Vietnam.

It is your steadiness and your stamina that the leaders of North Vietnam are watching tonight. It is these qualities, as much as any proposals, that will bring them to negotiate.

It is America's resolve, as well as America's reasonableness, that will achieve our goal of a just peace in Vietnam and strengthen the foundations of a just and lasting peace in the Pacific and throughout the world.

Thank you and good night.

(43) Communiqué of the Six-Nation Meeting on Vietnam, Saigon, July 5–6, 1970.[51]

(Complete Text)

The Prime Minister and Minister of Foreign Affairs of New Zealand, H. E. Keith Holyoake; The Minister for External Affairs of Australia, H. E. William McMahon; The Minister of Foreign Affairs of the Republic of Korea, H. E. Kyu Hah Choi; The Minister of Foreign Affairs of Thailand, H. E. Thanat Khoman; The Secretary of State of the United States of America, H. E. William P. Rogers, and The Minister of Foreign Affairs of the Republic of Vietnam, H. E. Tran Van Lam, met in Saigon on July 5 and 6, 1970 at the invitation of the Government of the Republic of Vietnam.

The meeting was held to allow the Ministers of the troop-contributing countries to review developments in Vietnam since

51 Department of State Press Release 213, July 10, 1970; text from *Department of State Bulletin*, August 3, 1970, pp. 139–141.

their last consultations [52] and to consider ways in which the allies could continue to work together to bring about an end to the fighting and a peaceful solution to the problems created by North Vietnamese aggression. The Ministers also were enabled to see at first hand examples of the progress being made by the Government of Vietnam in restoring security to and promoting the well-being of its population. The meeting also permitted the Ministers to consider aspects of the security situation in Asia in general.

VIETNAM

The Minister of Foreign Affairs of the Republic of Vietnam reported the progress achieved by the Republic of Vietnam in the economic, social and political fields over the past twelve months. He cited the steady growth of democratic institutions and elected bodies, and the provision made in the law for the operation of political parties and the right to legal opposition. He hoped that various measures being introduced by the Government of the Republic of Vietnam to curb inflation and to increase national production would soon help the country overcome its difficulties and reach its objective of self reliance.

The Minister of Foreign Affairs of the Republic of Vietnam also informed the Ministers of the new land reform program of the Government of the Republic of Vietnam. The Minister expressed the firm conviction that the success of this "Land to the Tillers" program would greatly contribute to the improvement of the rural people's lot, to the strengthening of their confidence in the regime and consequently, to the progress of pacification.

The Minister noted with appreciation the contribution of the United States Government to this program.

The Ministers congratulated the Minister of Foreign Affairs of the Republic of Vietnam on the foregoing matters particularly on its sweeping land reform program. They expressed confidence that the various measures being taken by the Government of the Republic of Vietnam would be effective in alleviating the economic and social problems caused by the war, and in providing a foundation for further long range development of the country. The Ministers assured the Government of the Republic of Vietnam of their desire to render all appropriate assistance and co-operation toward the solution of these problems.

The Ministers acknowledged the steady improvement of the military situation, owing to the rapid development both in strength and in combat effectiveness of the Vietnamese Armed

---

[52] *Documents, 1968–69*, pp. 322–327.

Forces and to the effective support given them by the Allied Forces. They believe that these developments will serve to convince North Vietnam of its futility to dominate South Vietnam by force of arms.

The Ministers noted the encouraging progress of the Republic of Vietnam's self-reliance program and affirmed that it is the success of this program which has made possible the decisions already announced about troop redeployment from Vietnam. The Ministers expressed once again their admiration for the courage and determination displayed by the Government and the people of Vietnam in their struggle for freedom and for the defense of their national territory.

The Ministers followed with great interest the report on the progress of the pacification and rural reconstruction program and on the social change which is taking place in the countryside through this program. They were favorably impressed by the rapid improvement of the security situation and the enthusiastic participation of the rural people in the elections of the hamlet, village and province councils.

They expressed regret that North Vietnam had not shown willingness to negotiate in response to the significant and constructive proposals made by the Republic of Vietnam and the United States at the Paris Talks in an effort to reach a negotiated settlement. They particularly recalled the concrete program proposed by the Governments of Vietnam and of the United States for mutual withdrawals of foreign troops, for a ceasefire under international supervision and for supervised elections in which all political elements could take part. In fact, Vietnam and the United States had indicated readiness to negotiate on all issues except the right to self-determination of the people of South Vietnam. The Ministers also reaffirmed their previous agreement that all the nations which are making available armed forces to help defend the Republic of Vietnam must participate in the settlement of the conflict.

The Ministers expressed special concern about the enemy's inhumanity with regard to prisoners of war. They noted that the Governments of the United States and of Vietnam have sought repeatedly to open productive talks on prisoners of war at the Paris Meetings, but that the other side had rebuffed all such efforts. They expressed their support for the Republic of Vietnam's initiative in undertaking to repatriate sick and wounded prisoners of war to North Vietnam. They condemned North Vietnam's continued refusal to identify all prisoners of war, to allow them all to correspond regularly with their families, and to allow impartial inspection of prisoners of war facilities, as required by the 1949 Geneva Convention on prisoners of war.[53] The Ministers renewed the undertakings of their governments to insure full compliance by their forces with the Geneva Conventions.

The Ministers reiterated their countries' determination to attain a just and lasting peace which would assure the freedom and independence of the Vietnamese people.

Cambodia

The Ministers noted that the North Vietnamese efforts to consolidate their sanctuaries in Cambodia into a large single and militarily immune base area within a short distance of major Vietnamese population centers had posed new threats to the ability of South Vietnam to defend itself. They accordingly expressed satisfaction with the success achieved in the recent allied operations against North Vietnamese forces and supply centers in these sanctuaries.[54] They affirmed that these operations did not represent any intention to expand the Vietnam war but were taken as a measure to defend the Allied Forces and to improve security in Vietnam.

The Ministers expressed their respect and full support for the Cambodian Government's desire for peace and the preservation of its independence, strict neutrality and territorial integrity within its present borders.

They noted with concern the refusal of North Vietnam to comply with the Cambodian Government's request that it withdraw its troops from Cambodia and stop its attack on Cambodian cities and forces. They suggested that free nations examine [what] assistance they could give to Cambodia in response to its requests. They noted that the only threat to Cambodia's neutrality and the only interest in expanding the conflict came from the other side.

The Ministers called upon the members of the 1954 Geneva Agreements Conference[55] to ensure the independence, neutrality and territorial integrity of Cambodia.

The Ministers welcomed the Indonesian initiative in convening the Djakarta Conference on Cambodia[56] and thought that such Asian initiatives to solve Asian problems should be supported and encouraged.

The Ministers took note with satisfaction of the friendly rela-

---

[53] *Geneva Conventions of August 12, 1949, for the Protection of War Victims;* text in United Nations, *Treaty Series,* vol. 75 (1950), No. 972.
[54] Cf. Documents 38–39.
[55] Cf. note 8 to Document 38.
[56] Cf. note 31 to Document 39.

tions between Cambodia and the Republic of Vietnam and Thailand. They also appreciated the good will of the Cambodian Government in its pledge to ensure security to the Vietnamese living in Cambodia and to protect their property.

LAOS

The Ministers noted with deep concern that North Vietnam continued to commit armed attacks against the armed forces of the Royal Government of Laos and to use Laotian territory for infiltrating troops and supplies into the Republic of Vietnam and Cambodia and for instigating insurgency in Thailand.[57] They called for a return to the Geneva Agreements of 1954, and 1962 [58] as the solution to the Laotian issue and urged all who had not yet done so to agree to the consultations called for under Article 4 of the 1962 Agreements.

KOREA

The Minister of Foreign Affairs of the Republic of Korea gave an account of the security situation in the Korean Peninsula, referring to recent acts of provocation and aggression by the North Korean Communists. The Minister drew attention to the indiscriminate and inhumane nature of acts such as the seizure of a Korean passenger airplane and a Korean Navy Broadcasting Vessel, and the recent attempt to set a high-powered bomb at the Memorial Gate of the National Cemetery in Seoul.

The Ministers took note of the militant policy proposed by North Korean Communists, and reiterated their previous agreement that such acts are a matter of grave concern and threaten the peace and security of the Korean Peninsula and the area surrounding it. The Ministers strongly urged that North Korean Communists immediately return the detained crew members and passengers to their homes in the South, together with the seized aircraft and vessel.

The Ministers reaffirmed their support for the Republic of Korea in resisting aggressive acts of the North Korean Communists. The Ministers welcomed the intention of the Government of the Republic of Korea to keep them and other interested governments informed of any future developments through their ambassadors in Seoul.

CONCLUSION

Finally, in view of the current situation in Southeast Asia and Korea, the Ministers reaffirmed their commitment to the Decla-

[57] Cf. Document 37.
[58] Cf. note 3 to Document 37.

ration on Peace and Progress in Asia and the Pacific promul-
gated at the Summit Conference in Manila in October 1966,[59]
and agreed to continue the close cooperation which has existed among the troop-contributing countries.

The Ministers agreed that they would consult about the time
and place of the next meeting.

The Ministers expressed gratitude to the Government and
people of the Republic of Vietnam for their generous hospitality
and warm welcome. They also expressed their appreciation for
the excellent arrangements made for the meeting.

(43A) Protective Retaliation: News Conference Statement by President Nixon, December 10, 1970.[60]

(Excerpt)

*   *   *

Now, there's been, I note, some speculation in the press, and
also some charges from North Vietnam, that there is no understanding that reconnaissance planes are to fly over North Vietnam
since the bombing halt was announced.[61]

I want to be very sure that that understanding is clear. First,
President Johnson said there was such an understanding at the
time of the bombing halt. Secretary [of Defense Clark M.]
Clifford did, and Ambassador [Cyrus R.] Vance did.

But if there is any misunderstanding, I want to indicate the
understanding of this President with regard to the flying of
reconnaissance planes over North Vietnam: I must insist that
there be continued reconnaissance over North Vietnam because, as we are withdrawing our forces, I have to see whether or
not there is any chance of a strike against those forces that remain, and we have to watch for the buildup.

If our planes are fired upon, I will not only order that they
return the fire, but I will order that the missile site be destroyed
and that the military complex around that site which supports it
also be destroyed by bombing. That is my understanding.

Beyond that, there is another understanding with regard to
the bombing of North Vietnam which at a number of these press

[59] Documents, 1966, pp. 292–293.
[60] Text from Weekly Compilation of Presidential Documents, December 14,
1970, pp. 1650–1651; for the context see The United States in World Affairs,
1970, Section 22.
[61] Cf. note 11 to Document 38.

conferences and in my speech on November 3d [62] and in four televised speeches to the Nation last year, I have stated. I restate it again tonight. At a time when we are withdrawing from South Vietnam, it is vitally important that the President of the United States, as Commander in Chief, take the action that is necessary to protect our remaining forces, because the number of our ground combat forces is going down very, very steadily.

Now if, as a result of my conclusion that the North Vietnamese, by their infiltration, threaten our remaining forces, if they thereby develop a capacity and proceed possibly to use that capacity to increase the level of fighting in South Vietnam, then I will order the bombing of military sites in North Vietnam, the passes that lead from North Vietnam into South Vietnam, the military complexes, the military supply lines. That will be the re-action that I shall take.

I trust that that is not necessary. But let there be no misunder-standing with regard to this President's understanding about ei-ther reconnaissance flights or about a step-up of the activities.

*   *   *

D. The Quest for Peace Goes On.[63]

(44) Eight-Point Peace Plan of the Provisional Revolutionary Government of South Vietnam, Presented at Paris by Mrs. Nguyen Thi Binh, September 17, 1970.[64]

(Complete Text)

To respond to the deep desire for peace of broad sectors of the people in South Vietnam, in the United States and in the world, on the instructions of the provisional revolutionary government of the Republic of South Vietnam, I would like to further elabo-rate on a number of points in the 10-point over-all solution [65] as follows:

[1]

The United States Government must put an end to its war of aggression in Vietnam, stop the policy of "Vietnamization" [66]

---

[62] Cf. note 46 to Document 42.

[63] For the context of this group of documents see *The United States in World Affairs, 1970,* Section 21.

[64] Unofficial text from the *New York Times,* September 18, 1970.

[65] *Documents, 1968–69,* pp. 249–252.

[66] Cf. note 7 to Document 39.

of the war, totally withdraw from South Vietnam troops, military personnel, weapons and war materials of the United States as well as troops, military personnel, weapons and war materials of the other foreign countries in the United States camp, without posing any condition whatsoever, and dismantle all United States military bases in South Vietnam.

In case the United States Government declares it will withdraw from South Vietnam all its troops and those of the other foreign countries in the United States camp by June 30, 1971, the people's liberation armed forces will refrain from attacking the withdrawing troops of the United States and those of the other foreign countries in the United States camp; and the parties will engage at once in discussions on:

¶The question of insuring safety for the total withdrawal from South Vietnam of United States troops and those of the other foreign countries in the United States camp.

¶The question of releasing captured military men.

[2]

The question of Vietnamese armed forces in South Vietnam shall be resolved by the Vietnamese parties among themselves.

[3]

The warlike and fascist Thieu-Ky-Khiem administration, an instrument of the United States policy of aggression, is frantically opposing peace, striving to call for the intensification and expansion of the war and for the prolongation of the United States military occupation of South Vietnam, and is enriching itself through the blood of the people.

They are serving the United States imperialist aggressors who massacre their compatriots and devastate their country. They have stepped up the "pacification" campaigns to terrorize the people and hold them in the vise of their regime, set up a barbarous system of jails of the type of the "tiger cages" on Con Son and established a police regime of the utmost cruelty in South Vietnam. They carry out ferocious repression against those who stand for peace, independence, neutrality and democracy, regardless of their social stock, political tendencies and religions; they repress those who are not on their side. They increase forcible press-ganging and endeavor to plunder the property of the South Vietnamese people so as to serve the United States policy of "Vietnamization" of the war.

The restoration of genuine peace in South Vietnam necessitates the formation in Saigon of an Administration without [President Nguyen Van] Thieu [Vice President Nguyen Cao] Ky and [Premier Tran Thien] Khiem, an Administration which stands for peace, independence, neutrality, which improves the people's living conditions, which insures democratic liberties such as freedom of speech, freedom of the press, freedom of assembly, freedom of belief, etc., and releases those who have been jailed for political reasons, and dissolves concentration camps so that the inmates therein may return to and live in their native places. The provisional revolutionary government of the Republic of South Vietnam is prepared to enter into talks with such an Administration on a political settlement of the South Vietnam problem so as to put an end to the war and restore peace in Vietnam.

[4]

The South Vietnamese people will decide themselves the political regime of South Vietnam through really free and democratic general elections, elect a national assembly, work out a constitution of a national and democratic character, and set up a Government reflecting the entire people's aspirations and will for peace, independence, neutrality, democracy and national concord.

The general elections must be held in a really free and democratic way. The modalities of the elections must guarantee genuine freedom and equality during the electoral campaigns and vote proceedings to all citizens, irrespective of their political tendencies, including those who are living abroad. No party shall usurp for itself the right to organize general elections and lay down their modalities. The general elections organized by the United States puppet Administration in Saigon under the bayonets of the United States occupying troops cannot be free and democratic.

A provisional government of broad coalition is indispensable for the organization of really free and democratic general elections and also for insuring the right to self-determination of the South Vietnamese people during the transitory period between the restoration of peace and the holding of general elections.

[5]

The provisional coalition government will include three components:

¶Persons of the provisional revolutionary government of the Republic of South Vietnam.

¶Persons of the Saigon Administration really standing for peace, independence, neutrality and democracy.

¶Persons of various political and religious forces and tendencies standing for peace, independence, neutrality and democracy including those who, for political reasons, have to live abroad.

The provisional coalition government will implement the agreements reached by the parties.

The provisional coalition government will carry out a policy of national concord, insure the democratic freedoms of the people, prohibit all acts of terror, reprisal and discrimination against those who have collaborated with either side, stabilize and improve the living conditions of the people and organize general elections in order to form a coalition government.

The provisional coalition government will pursue a foreign policy of peace and neutrality, practice a policy of good neighborliness with the kingdom of Laos and the kingdom of Cambodia, respect the sovereignty, independence, neutrality and territorial integrity of these two countries; it will establish diplomatic relations with all countries regardless of their political regime, including the United States, in accordance with the five principles of peaceful coexistence.[67]

[6]

Vietnam is one, the Vietnamese people are one. The reunification of Vietnam will be achieved step by step, by peaceful means, on the basis of discussions and agreements between the two zones, without coercion or annexation from either side, without foreign interference. The time for reunification as well as all questions relating to the reunification will be discussed and agreed upon by both zones. Pending the peaceful reunification of the country, the two zones will re-establish normal relations in all fields on the basis of equality and mutual respect, and will respect each other's political regime and internal and external policies.

[7]

The parties will decide together measures aimed at insuring the respect and the correct implementation of the provisions agreed upon.

67 *Documents, 1954,* pp. 278–281.

[8]

After the agreement on and signing of accords aimed at putting an end to the war and restoring peace in Vietnam, the parties will implement the modalities that will have been laid down for a cease-fire in South Vietnam.

To attain a peaceful settlement of the Vietnam problem, the provisional revolutionary government of the Republic of South Vietnam declares its readiness to get henceforth in touch with the forces or persons of various political tendencies and religions in the country and abroad, including members of the present Saigon Administration, except Thieu, Ky and Khiem.

(45) Five-Point Peace Proposal by the United States: Radio-Television Address by President Nixon, October 7, 1970.[68]

(Complete Text)

Good evening, my fellow Americans.

Tonight I would like to talk to you about a major new initiative for peace.

When I authorized operations against the enemy sanctuaries in Cambodia last April,[69] I also directed that an intensive effort be launched to develop new approaches for peace in Indochina.

In Ireland on Sunday [October 4] [70], I met with the chiefs of our delegation [Ambassadors David K. E. Bruce and Philip C. Habib] to the Paris talks. This meeting marked the culmination of a Government-wide effort begun last spring on the negotiation front. After considering the recommendations of all my principal advisers, I am tonight announcing new proposals for peace in Indochina.

This new peace initiative has been discussed with the Governments of South Vietnam, Laos, and Cambodia. All support it. It has been made possible in large part by the remarkable success of the Vietnamization program over the past 18 months. Tonight I want to tell you what these proposals are and what they mean.

First, I propose that all armed forces throughout Indochina cease firing their weapons and remain in the positions they now hold. This would be a "cease-fire-in-place." It would not

---

[68] Text from *Weekly Compilation of Presidential Documents*, October 12, 1970, pp. 1349–1352.
[69] Document 38.
[70] Cf. *Weekly Compilation of Presidential Documents*, October 12, 1970, p. 1332; for President Nixon's statement, October 6, 1970, see same, p. 1342.

in itself be an end to the conflict, but it would accomplish one goal all of us have been working toward: an end to the killing.

I do not minimize the difficulty of maintaining a cease-fire in a guerrilla war where there are no frontlines. But an unconventional war may require an unconventional truce; our side is ready to stand still and cease firing.

I ask that this proposal for a cease-fire-in-place be the subject for immediate negotiation. And my hope is that it will break the logjam in all the negotiations.

This cease-fire proposal is put forth without preconditions. The general principles that should apply are these:

A cease-fire must be effectively supervised by international observers, as well as by the parties themselves. Without effective supervision a cease-fire runs the constant risk of breaking down. All concerned must be confident that the cease-fire will be maintained and that any local breaches of it will be quickly and fairly repaired.

A cease-fire should not be the means by which either side builds up its strength by an increase in outside combat forces in any of the nations of Indochina.

And a cease-fire should cause all kinds of warfare to stop. This covers the full range of actions that have typified this war, including bombing and acts of terror.

A cease-fire should encompass not only the fighting in Vietnam but in all of Indochina. Conflicts in this region are closely related. The United States has never sought to widen the war. What we do seek is to widen the peace.

Finally, a cease-fire should be part of a general move to end the war in Indochina.

A cease-fire-in-place would undoubtedly create a host of problems in its maintenance. But it's always been easier to make war than to make a truce. To build an honorable peace, we must accept the challenge of long and difficult negotiations.

By agreeing to stop the shooting, we can set the stage for agreements on other matters.

A second point of the new initiative for peace is this:

I propose an Indochina Peace Conference. At the Paris talks today, we are talking about Vietnam. But North Vietnamese troops are not only infiltrating, crossing borders and establishing bases in South Vietnam—they are carrying on their aggression in Laos and Cambodia as well.

An international conference is needed to deal with the conflict in all three states of Indochina. The war in Indochina has been proved to be of one piece; it cannot be cured by treating only one of its areas of outbreak.

The essential elements of the Geneva Accords of 1954 [71] and and 1962 [72] remain valid as a basis for settlement of problems between states in the Indochina area. And we shall accept the results of agreements reached between these states.

While we pursue the convening of an Indochina Peace Conference, we will continue the negotiations in Paris. Our proposal for a larger conference can be discussed there as well as through other diplomatic channels.

The Paris talks will remain our primary forum for reaching a negotiated settlement, until such time as a broader international conference produces serious negotiations.

The third part of our peace initiative has to do with the United States forces in South Vietnam.

In the past 20 months, I have reduced our troop ceilings in South Vietnam by 165,000 men. During the spring of next year, these withdrawals will have totaled more than 260,000 men— about one-half the number that were in South Vietnam when I took office.

As the American combat role and presence have decreased, American casualties have also decreased. Our casualties since the completion of the Cambodian operation [73] were the lowest for a comparable period in the last $4\frac{1}{2}$ years.

We are ready now to negotiate an agreed timetable for complete withdrawals as part of an overall settlement.

We are prepared to withdraw all our forces as part of a settlement based on the principles I spelled out previously and the proposals I am making tonight.

Fourth, I ask the other side to join us in a search for a political settlement that truly meets the aspirations of all South Vietnamese.

Three principles govern our approach:
—We seek a political solution that reflects the will of the South Vietnamese people.
—A fair political solution should reflect the existing relationship of political forces in South Vietnam.
—And we will abide by the outcome of the political process agreed upon.

Let there be no mistake about one essential point: The other side is not merely objecting to a few personalities in the South Vietnamese Government. They want to dismantle the organized non-Communist parties and insure the takeover by their party.

[71] Cf. note 8 to Document 38.
[72] Cf. note 3 to Document 37.
[73] Document 39.

They demand the right to exclude whomever they wish from government.

This patently unreasonable demand is totally unacceptable.

As my proposals today indicate, we are prepared to be flexible on many matters. But we stand firm for the right of all the South Vietnamese people to determine for themselves the kind of government they want.

We have no intention of seeking any settlement at the conference table other than one which fairly meets the reasonable concerns of both sides. We know that when the conflict ends, the other side will still be there. And the only kind of settlement that will endure is one that both sides have an interest in preserving.

Finally, I propose the immediate and unconditional release of all prisoners of war held by both sides.

War and imprisonment should be over for all these prisoners. They and their families have already suffered too much.

I propose that all prisoners of war, without exception, without condition, be released now to return to the place of their choice.

And I propose that all journalists and other innocent civilian victims of the conflict be released immediately as well.

The immediate release of all prisoners of war would be a simple act of humanity.

But it could be even more. It could serve to establish good faith, the intent to make progress, and thus improve the prospects for negotiation.

We are prepared to discuss specific procedures to complete the speedy release of all prisoners.

The five proposals that I have made tonight can open the door to an enduring peace in Indochina.

Ambassador Bruce will present these proposals formally to the other side in Paris tomorrow.[74] He will be joined in that presentation by Ambassador [Tran Van] Lam representing South Vietnam.

Let us consider for a moment what the acceptance of these proposals would mean.

Since the end of World War II, there's always been a war going on somewhere in the world. The guns have never stopped firing. By achieving a cease-fire in Indochina, and by holding firmly to the cease-fire in the Middle East,[75] we could hear the

[74] For remarks by Ambassador Bruce, October 8, 1970, to the 87th Plenary Session in Paris see *Department of State Bulletin,* October 26, 1970, p. 468.
[75] Cf. Documents 29–31.

welcome sound of peace throughout the world for the first time in a generation.

We could have some reason to hope that we had reached the beginning of the end of war in this century. We might then be on the threshold of a generation of peace.

The proposals I have made tonight are designed to end the fighting throughout Indochina and to end the impasse in negotiations in Paris. Nobody has anything to gain by delay and only lives to lose.

There are many nations involved in the fighting in Indochina. Tonight, all those nations, except one, announce their readiness to agree to a cease-fire. The time has come for the Government of North Vietnam to join its neighbors in a proposal to quit making war and to start making peace.

As you know, I have just returned from a trip which took me to Italy, Spain, Yugoslavia, England, and Ireland.[76]

Hundreds of thousands of people cheered me as I drove through the cities of those countries.

They were not cheering me as an individual. They were cheering for the country I was proud to represent—the United States of America. For millions of people in the free world, the non-aligned world, and the Communist world, America is the land of freedom, of opportunity, of progress.

I believe there is another reason they welcomed me so warmly in every country I visited, despite their wide differences in political systems and national backgrounds.

In my talks with leaders all over the world, I find that there are those who may not agree with all of our policies. But no world leader to whom I have talked fears that the United States will use its great power to dominate another country or to destroy its independence. We can be proud that this is the cornerstone of America's foreign policy.

There is no goal to which this Nation is more dedicated and to which I am more dedicated than to build a new structure of peace in the world where every nation, including North Vietnam as well as South Vietnam, can be free and independent with no fear of foreign aggression or foreign domination.

I believe every American deeply believes in his heart that the proudest legacy the United States can leave during this period when we are the strongest nation in the world is that our power was used to defend freedom, not to destroy it; to preserve the peace, not to break the peace.

---

[76] Cf. note 23 to Document 21.

It is in that spirit that I make this proposal for a just peace in Vietnam and in Indochina.

I ask that the leaders in Hanoi respond to this proposal in the same spirit. Let us give our children what we have not had in this century, a chance to enjoy a generation of peace.

Thank you. Good night.

E. The Issue of Prisoners of War.

(46) Statement by Ronald L. Ziegler, White House Press Secretary, on the Resolution Adopted by the Third (Social, Humanitarian, and Cultural) Committee of the United Nations General Assembly, December 2, 1970.[77]

(Complete Text)

The Social Committee of the United Nations General Assembly yesterday adopted by a vote of 60 to 16 with 34 abstentions a resolution on prisoners of war.[78] Among other things, it calls upon "all parties to any armed conflict to comply with the terms of the 1949 Geneva Convention," [79] including the humane treatment of prisoners and their regular inspection by a protecting power or a humanitarian organization. It urges the repatriation of seriously sick or wounded persons, as well as those who have undergone a long period of captivity, as called for in the Geneva Convention. The resolution also endorses the efforts of the International Red Cross and calls upon the U.N. Secretary General to exert all efforts to obtain humane treatment for prisoners of war.

The President, on being informed of this resolution, said he is deeply gratified by this United Nations action. He considers it a very legitimate and important expression of world opinion on the issue of prisoners of war. It responds to the concern, which he and all Americans most certainly share, regarding the plight of American prisoners of war in North Vietnam and elsewhere in Southeast Asia.

[77] Text from *Weekly Compilation of Presidential Documents,* December 7, 1970, p. 1618; for the context see *The United States in World Affairs, 1970,* Section 22.

[78] On December 9, 1970, the U.N. General Assembly endorsed the Third Committee's decision in Resolution 2676 (XXV), adopted by a vote of 67–30 with 20 abstentions; text of resolution and related material in *Department of State Bulletin,* January 4, 1971, pp. 11–13.

[79] Cf. note 53 to Document 43.

VI.
AMERICAN POLICY IN ASIA:
EAST ASIA AND THE PACIFIC

A. Multilateral Diplomacy in the Pacific.

(47) The Southeast Asia Treaty Organization: Fifteenth Meeting of the SEATO Council, Manila, July 2–3, 1970.[1]

(a) Statement by Secretary of State Rogers, July 2, 1970.[2]

(Complete Text)

As we begin these important meetings we should remind ourselves of how important a sense of security is to the lives of men and nations. Without it the concept of liberty and prosperity becomes illusory.

The nations represented here demonstrated their understanding of this simple fact when they signed the Southeast Asia Collective Defense Treaty in Manila 15 years ago.[3] That treaty has provided a shield for the remarkable political and economic progress in Southeast Asia during those years.

Since our last ministerial meeting,[4] President Nixon announced a new American policy in Asia. Let me quote his words to make clear what that policy is: [5]

The United States will keep all of its treaty commitments.

We shall provide a shield if a nuclear power threatens the freedom of a nation allied with us or of a nation whose survival we consider vital to our security.

In cases involving other types of aggression, we shall furnish military

[1] For the context see *The United States in World Affairs, 1970,* Section 24.
[2] Department of State Press Release 200, July 2, 1970; text from *Department of State Bulletin,* August 3, 1970, p. 134.
[3] Text in *Documents, 1954,* pp. 319–323.
[4] Same, *1968–69,* pp. 316–322.
[5] Same, pp. 329–334.

and economic assistance when requested. . . . But we shall look to the nation directly threatened to assume the primary responsibility of providing the manpower for its defense.

Now, in Asia, what does this mean? It means that we will remain a Pacific power and a member of the Pacific community. It means that we will support the efforts of our Asian friends to maintain their own sovereignty and security. It does not mean that we will turn our back on our international policies or withdraw into a shell of isolationism.

The Nixon doctrine relates to our relationships with all of Asia. In Indochina it is embodied in the policy of Vietnamization,[5a] under which the primary responsibility for ground combat is passing to our South Vietnamese allies. We are greatly encouraged by their growing self-reliance and by the effectiveness with which they have fought in the Cambodian operation.[6]

While our aim in Cambodia has been to protect our programs in Viet-Nam and to provide the people of South Viet-Nam with the right to determine their own future, we sympathize with Cambodia's resistance to North Vietnamese aggression; and we will continue to supply limited military assistance.[7] We welcome the growing spirit of cooperation between Cambodia and its neighbors—South Viet-Nam, Thailand, and Laos—as a logical and sensible response to a common danger.

However, we concur in the position taken by the Cambodian Government, which does not favor Cambodia's military association with SEATO. Neutrality is the political condition that Cambodia's governments, both past and present, have chosen for themselves. We believe that the neutrality of Cambodia, like that of Laos, will contribute to the stability of the area and to the prospects for peace.

The attention of the world has been focused largely on the military aspects of the war in Indochina. While we will take the military measures we consider necessary, as our Cambodian operation illustrated, our preference has always been, and will remain, a political settlement. The United States will continue to make every effort to achieve peace through negotiation.

We welcome the initiatives which have been taken recently to get such talks going. In particular, we support the current efforts of the 11 Asian nations which met in Djakarta in May,[8] four of which are represented in this room today. Those initia-

5a Cf. note 7 to Document 38.

6 Documents 38–39.

7 Cf. note 10 to Document 38.

8 Cf. note 31 to Document 39.

tives represent an Asian attempt to solve Asian problems. They deserve the support of the international community.

In closing, let me again say that the United States will continue our strong support of SEATO and will continue to believe that our alliance, the alliance represented here, is of great importance to the security of the free world.

(b) Communiqué, July 3, 1970.[9]

(Complete Text)

The Council of the South-East Asia Treaty Organization held its Fifteenth Meeting in Manila from 2 to 3 July 1970, under the chairmanship of His Excellency General Carlos P. Romulo, Secretary of Foreign Affairs of the Republic of the Philippines.

All Member Governments, except France, participated. The Republic of Vietnam, a Protocol State, was represented by an observer.

GENERAL OBSERVATIONS

The Council took note of the significant developments that had taken place in South-east Asia since it last met—the rapidly growing strength and self-reliance of the Republic of Vietnam, the unusually sharp dry season offensive of North Vietnam against Laos, the recently increased aggression against Cambodia by North Vietnam and the Viet Cong and the many efforts by States of South-east Asia and by others to bring about negotiations for a political solution to the problems of Indo-China.

The Council also noted that encouraging economic and social progress had continued during the past year within the Treaty Area. The Council agreed that this progress was facilitated by the growing spirit of regional co-operation among the nations of the area and by their determination to promote the economic and social welfare of their people and to foster individual liberty. The Council believed that much of this economic, political and social advance would not have been possible without the shield which the Manila Treaty has helped to provide since 1954. The Council expressed its resolve to maintain the SEATO deterrent so that this advance could continue.

The Council noted that overt military aggression against South Vietnam, Laos and Cambodia was accompanied by other forms of aggression—subversion, externally-instigated insurgency,

[9] Department of State Press Release 204, July 6, 1970; text from *Department of State Bulletin,* August 3, 1970, pp. 135–137.

infiltration and terrorism—which continued to be a serious threat to peace and security in the area. The Council confirmed its intention to keep this situation under review and expressed its support for the co-operative efforts of States in the area to meet the threat.

The Council noted President Nixon's important formulation of United States policy in Asia, in the terms of the "Nixon Doctrine." The Council considered this to be fully in accord with the spirit and terms of the Manila Treaty.

The Search for Peace

The Council observed that numerous new efforts have been made to bring about consultations and negotiations to achieve a peaceful solution to the conflicts in the Indo-China area and thus permit each State to live in peace and to choose its own way of life. It expressed concern that North Vietnam had not responded constructively to any of these initiatives and expressed the hope that this attitude would change. It noted that negotiations could be undertaken either through a general conference on Indo-China as a whole or through separate negotiations such as those in Paris on Vietnam.

The Council took note, in particular, of the following initiatives aimed at a political settlement, all of which were welcomed by SEATO members:

(a) the repeated affirmations by the United States and the Republic of Vietnam in Paris of the principles of total withdrawal of all non-South Vietnamese troops and of a political solution reflecting the will of all the South Vietnamese people;

(b) the appeal of the Prime Minister of Laos to the Co-Chairmen of the Geneva Conference for consultations in accordance with Article IV of the Declaration on the Neutrality of Laos; [10]

(c) the proposal of the President of the United States in support of the Laotian appeal for consultations among signatory powers as called for under the Geneva Agreements of 1962; [11]

(d) the suggestion by the Government of France for wider negotiations on the problems of Indo-China;

(e) the suggestion by the Prime Minister of New Zealand for an international conference, at which all parties concerned could be represented, to work out the outlines of a regional settlement;

(f) the British Co-Chairman's 1 May proposal to the Soviet Co-Chairman for the reconvening of the Geneva Conference;

[10] *Documents, 1962*, p. 287; cf. Document 37.
[11] *Documents, 1962*, pp. 284–294.

(g) the proposal of the Secretary-General of the United Nations for an international conference on Indo-China;

(h) the call by the Djakarta Conference of Asian and Pacific countries for immediate cessation of hostilities, the withdrawal of all foreign troops from Cambodia, the reactivation of the International Control Commission for Cambodia, and the convening of an international conference on Indo-China.

VIETNAM

The Council reaffirmed its admiration for the courage with which the Government and people of the Republic of Vietnam have defended their freedom and reiterated its concern and sympathy for the suffering so long endured by the Vietnamese people. The Council noted the continuing progress being made by the armed forces of the Republic of Vietnam in improving their capability to counter armed aggression and subversive activity, and warmly welcomed the determined efforts of the Government of the Republic of Vietnam progressively to assume responsibility for the defence of its territory. The Council also heard reports by Members concerning allied troops in South Vietnam and some redeployments within the framework of plans for South Vietnamese forces to assume the ground combat responsibilities within the next year. It welcomed the continuing progress made by the Republic of Vietnam in the political, economic and social fields. The Council agreed that in the absence of a negotiated settlement these developments offered the best chance of bringing about a de-escalation of the war, the achievement of a greater measure of stability, and the maintenance of the Republic of Vietnam's right and capability to determine its own future.

The Council expressed its profound regret that the continued efforts of the Republic of Vietnam and the United States to negotiate a peaceful solution had so far yielded no substantive results. It took note of the flexibility of the proposals put forward by the United States and the Republic of Vietnam and expressed the hope that North Vietnam would show a similar willingness to achieve a peaceful settlement.

The Council took note, however, that North Vietnam's military aggression against South Vietnam was continuing and that it had recently been marked by a new wave of terrorism, murder of civilians, and efforts to disrupt the pacification programme. The Council noted with regret that this aggression is sustained by a heavy flow of weapons and supplies from other Communist regimes.

The Council noted with appreciation the continuing military, economic and humanitarian assistance furnished by member countries during the past year to the Republic of Vietnam. The Council also noted with appreciation the continued assistance rendered by other countries which are not members of SEATO, including substantial military assistance from the Republic of Korea.

LAOS

The Council noted with grave concern that North Vietnam, in open violation of the 1962 Geneva Agreements, continues to maintain military forces in Laos (including large units of its regular Army), to commit armed attacks on the forces of the Royal Government of Laos, to use Lao territory to infiltrate troops and supplies into South Vietnam and Cambodia and to support externally-instigated insurgency in Thailand. The Council viewed as particularly serious the recent heavy attacks against Laos by North Vietnam and its refusal so far to co-operate in consultations to which it is committed under those Agreements. The Council reiterated its call for full implementation by all signatories of the 1962 Geneva Agreements on Laos and expressed support for the efforts of the Royal Lao Government to secure peace and to preserve the sovereignty, independence, neutrality, unity and territorial integrity of Laos.

CAMBODIA

In the light of the magnitude of the changes that had taken place in Cambodia since its last Meeting, the Council reviewed the situation there with special attention. The Council affirmed its support of the sovereignty, independence, neutrality and territorial integrity of Cambodia within its present borders, and declared that it would honour and respect the Cambodian Government's desire to remain neutral. It expressed the conviction that Cambodia's desire for neutrality must be the basis of a settlement and noted that, while North Vietnam professed respect for that neutrality, it had for years violated Cambodian territory and neutrality.

The Council concluded that the recent operations against Vietnamese Communist military facilities in eastern Cambodia had been successful in relieving military pressures against the Republic of Vietnam and would contribute to the realization of the troop replacement programme in Vietnam. The Council condemned North Vietnamese military attacks against Cambodia and expressed understanding of Cambodia's appeal for help in resisting North Vietnam's attempt to dominate it.

While noting that Cambodia had no choice but to resist the

use of force with force, the Council agreed that the cause of peace in South-east Asia could best be furthered by encouraging a political solution based on Cambodia's desire to maintain its sovereignty and neutrality. The Council accordingly applauded the efforts of many nations to bring about a diplomatic solution and withdrawal of all foreign troops. It expressed the hope that a solution to the problems of Cambodia would lead to a more general settlement in South-east Asia. Council Members expressed their readiness to lend all possible assistance to diplomatic efforts to achieve an international solution.

PHILIPPINES

The Council noted with satisfaction the continued efforts of the Government of the Philippines to combat Communist subversion and insurgency, especially in Central Luzon. It also commended the progress achieved by the Philippine Government in the implementation of an integrated socio-economic programme designed to raise the standard of living and eliminate the primary cause of unrest among the people.

THAILAND

The Council noted with appreciation the Royal Thai Government's continued contribution towards the defence of the Republic of Vietnam and its friendly co-operation with Cambodia.

The Council was gratified by the continuing success of the Royal Thai Government and people in their efforts to accelerate economic and social development at all levels of society and by their firm resolve to counter Communist subversion and insurgent activities directed from outside.

COUNTER-SUBVERSION

The Council again affirmed support for SEATO activities designed to aid member countries in the Treaty Area to counter externally-instigated subversion and insurgency. It took note of the steps taken to develop at SEATO Headquarters an Office for Counter-subversion and Counter-insurgency better able to assist Member Governments with advice in this field.

CO-OPERATION IN THE MILITARY FIELD

The Council noted the Report of the Military Advisers and commended the excellent work done by the Military Planning Office in keeping plans up to date and in designing military exercises from which valuable experience was gained.

Five Power Defence Arrangements

The Council welcomed the United Kingdom Government's proposal to maintain a British military presence in the Malaysia-Singapore area as part of a Commonwealth force, subject to the wishes of the countries concerned. It further noted that consultations with those Commonwealth Governments directly involved would take place as soon as possible.[12]

Economic, Cultural and Social Co-operation

The Council reaffirmed the importance of SEATO economic aid activities in helping to create a better life for the peoples of South-east Asia. It also reaffirmed that these activities should be complementary to counter-subversion, counter-insurgency and civic action programmes. The Council further welcomed the fact that member countries are taking advantage of opportunities to provide aid to regional members bilaterally under the SEATO label.

Sixteenth Meeting of the Council

The Council accepted with pleasure the invitation of the United Kingdom Government to hold the Sixteenth Council Meeting in London in 1971.

Pakistan

The Pakistan Delegate wished it to be recorded that he did not participate in the drafting of the Communique.

Expression of Gratitude

The Council expressed its gratitude to the Government and people of the Republic of the Philippines for their generous hospitality and warm welcome, and its appreciation for the excellent arrangements made for the Meeting.

Leaders of Delegations

The leaders of the delegations to the Fifteenth Council Meeting were:

Australia   Right Hon. William McMahon, Minister for External Affairs.

12 Representatives of Australia, Malaysia, New Zealand, Singapore, and the United Kingdom met in London April 15–16, 1971. Text of communiqué, issued at the conclusion of the meeting, and related material in New Zealand, Ministry of Foreign Affairs, *Five Power Defence Arrangements* (Publication No. 410, Wellington, 1971).

New Zealand	Right Hon. Sir Keith Holyoake, G.C.M.G., C.H., M.P., Prime Minister and Minister of Foreign Affairs.
Pakistan	H.E. Mr. Khurram Khan Panni, Ambassador to the Philippines.
Philippines	H.E. General Carlos P. Romulo, Secretary of Foreign Affairs.
Thailand	H.E. Mr. Thanat Khoman, Minister of Foreign Affairs.
United Kingdom	Mr. Anthony Royle, M.P., Parliamentary Under-Secretary of State, Foreign and Commonwealth Office.
United States	Hon. William P. Rogers, Secretary of State.
Republic of Vietnam (Observer)	H.E. Mr. Tran Van Lam, Minister of Foreign Affairs.

(48) The ANZUS Treaty: Communiqué of the Twentieth Meeting of the ANZUS Council, Washington, D.C., September 26, 1970.[13]

(Complete Text)

The ANZUS Council held its Twentieth Meeting in Washington, D.C., on September 26, 1970. The Right Honorable William McMahon, Minister for External Affairs, represented Australia; His Excellency Mr. Frank Corner, Ambassador of New Zealand, represented New Zealand; and the Honorable William Rogers, Secretary of State, represented the United States.

The Representatives discussed general trends and situations in the world of particular concern to them. These included such matters as relations between the major powers and local conflicts involving their interests. They welcomed the promising start of the Strategic Arms Limitation Talks [14] and the conclusion of the renunciation of force agreement between the Federal Republic of Germany and the Union of Soviet Socialist Republics,[15] while noting that concrete progress in improving the situation around Berlin was still necessary, and of vital importance to any future progress.[16] They also indicated concern with

[13] Department of State Press Release 278, September 26, 1970; text from *Department of State Bulletin,* October 19, 1970, pp. 446–448. For the context see *The United States in World Affairs, 1970,* Section 24.
[14] Documents 10–11.
[15] Document 23.
[16] Cf. note 9 to Document 20.

respect to the Middle East situation and expressed the hope that ways could be found to move toward a peaceful settlement.

The Council went on to review developments in the Pacific Area. The Australian and New Zealand representatives took the opportunity to refer to considerations of particular concern to their Governments. The Council discussed the ways in which during the previous year the United States had applied the Nixon Doctrine in Asia, giving specific form to the general principles enunciated by the American President last year at Guam.[17]

Viet-Nam provided one focal point of discussion. The Council agreed that, although North Viet-Nam had expanded its aggression in Indochina, the military security situation in South Viet-Nam had improved and casualties had declined. It noted the improvement in the performance of South Vietnamese troops and in the quality of both their training and their armament, the progress of pacification, and the enlargement of areas in which government control is established. It noted that the steady withdrawal of allied forces, which the Nineteenth ANZUS Council [18] had anticipated would be made possible by the growing capacity of the South Vietnamese to defend themselves, was proceeding satisfactorily: United States force levels had already been reduced considerably and Australia and New Zealand reductions were to begin shortly. It was gratified at the reduction in the intensity of fighting in South Viet-Nam and it expressed the hope that the North Vietnamese would now hasten the advent of peace and stability by entering into serious negotiations at the Paris talks.

The Council expressed concern that repeated Cambodian attempts to secure cessation of the use of Cambodian territory as a haven and supply channel for North Vietnamese/Viet Cong forces had been met, not only by a refusal to withdraw, but by the launching of a North Vietnamese offensive against the Cambodian Government.[19] The Council expressed the hope that all countries would respect Cambodia's neutrality and territorial integrity, which had been violated by Vietnamese Communists, and welcomed the efforts to bring about international cooperation to that end.

The Council also expressed concern that North Viet-Nam had continued and expanded its aggression against the Royal Laotian Government during the past year.[20] It welcomed, however, the contacts that had been taking place between the parties in Laos

17 Cf. note 5 to Document 47.
18 *Documents, 1968–69,* pp. 327–329.
19 Cf. Documents 38–39.
20 Cf. Document 37.

and expressed the hope that they might lead to agreement on genuine respect for the neutrality and territorial integrity of Laos.

The Council recognized the relevance of security arrangements in the Malaysia/Singapore area to the ultimate security and stability of Southeast Asia as a whole. The Representatives discussed the progress made during the past year in the Five-Power arrangements, strongly welcoming the British decision to continue a more active role than previously had seemed possible.[21]

The representatives agreed that the posture of the People's Republic of China is a major factor in the problem of peace and stability in Asia. They expressed their concern at that Government's continuing to promote and assist "revolutionary warfare" in other countries. They expressed the hope that the policies of the PRC would in the future be such as to promote the development of satisfactory relations with its neighbors and with the international community as a whole. They believed that current efforts to maintain and enlarge constructive dialogues with Peking should be continued.

Noting the increasing contribution being made to the economic growth and stability of Asian nations by Japan's cooperation and assistance, the Council observed that Japan would have a major role in the further development of a Pacific area in which all nations would prosper as neighbors. As a leading nation technologically and financially, Japan's policies would have a considerable bearing on the economic progress of the area and on regional stability. The Council expressed its conviction that the three countries should continue to work closely with Japan and others, in particular on the further economic development of the Pacific area.

The Council also discussed developments in Oceania and recognized the changing character of that area as more countries, including Tonga and Fiji in the course of this year, become independent.[22] The Council took note of the continuing work of the South Pacific Commission in the field of economic and social development, and observed that the South Pacific Conference, now an annual event,[23] provides a useful forum for discussion by representatives of the islands and territories of questions of mutual economic and social concern.

---

21 Cf. note 12 to Document 47(b).
22 Tonga and Fiji became independent within the British Commonwealth on June 4, 1970 and October 10, 1970, respectively.
23 The Tenth South Pacific Conference was held September 15–25, 1970 in Suva, Fiji.

The Council also agreed to keep naval activities in the Indian Ocean under close review.

Noting that this present meeting was its Twentieth, the Council looked back upon the nearly two decades since the United States, Australia and New Zealand declared publicly and formally their sense of unity in the ANZUS Treaty.[24] The Council expressed gratification that despite unresolved problems, some of them acute, there has over these two decades been visible movement towards the goal of the ANZUS Treaty—the strengthening of the fabric of peace in the Pacific area. It noted the remarkable economic growth and social development of Asian nations with free economies. The nations of the Western Pacific were increasingly able to assume the primary responsibility and initiative in the affairs of their region. The Council noted with satisfaction the work of existing instruments of regional cooperation and looked with confidence to their further strengthening. In this context, it reaffirmed the continuing importance of ANZUS to the three partners in their efforts to press toward their common goal of strengthening security and advancing prosperity in the Pacific to the end that all peoples and all governments can live in peace with one another in the Pacific Region.

(49) The United States Contribution to the Asian Development Bank: Message from President Nixon to the Congress, February 25, 1970.[25]

(*Complete Text*)

To the Congress of the United States:

In 1966, the United States—with strong bipartisan approval of the Congress—joined with other nations in the establishment of the Asian Development Bank.[26] Since then this Bank has shown its ability to marshal funds from Asia, Europe and this continent for the purpose of economic development. In the short span of three years, it has effectively put these resources to work. It has demonstrated an ability to make a major contribution to Asian

[24] Signed September 1, 1951 at San Francisco; entered into force April 29, 1952. Text in *Documents, 1951,* pp. 263–266.

[25] House Document 91–260, 91st Congress, 2nd session; text from *Weekly Compilation of Presidential Documents,* March 2, 1970, pp. 264–268.

[26] The Articles of Agreement Establishing the Asian Development Bank entered into force August 22, 1966; text of President Johnson's message to Congress recommending approval of U.S. participation in *Documents, 1966,* pp. 260–263.

economic development. It gives evidence of a unique capability for acting as a catalyst for regional cooperation. And it can assist individal Asian countries find solutions to their problems on a multilateral basis.

Now it is time for the United States to reaffirm its support of the Asian Development Bank.

Experience has shown that effective Bank support of certain projects and programs essential to economic growth and development in Asia must involve some financing on easier repayment terms. The economic capabilities of some of the countries of Asia have not yet reached a level of development adequate to service needed loans on conventional terms. The Bank cannot furnish this needed financing out of its ordinary resources and the limited amount of special funds now available to it.

To measure up to its potential for assisting in the economic growth of Asia, the Bank must have adequate facilities and resources to provide concessional as well as conventional financing. I believe that the United States should now join with other donors in providing the Special Funds that will enable the Bank to meet a wider range of Asia's development needs.

———

The proposal I am submitting to the Congress would authorize the United States to pledge a contribution of $100 million to the Bank's Special Funds over a three-year period. It would authorize the appropriation of $25 million in the present fiscal year, and $35 million and $40 million, respectively, in the next two fiscal years.

This proposal is designed to assure that the United States contribution will have maximum impact on Asian development problems, that the Bank's Special Funds will constitute a truly multilateral financing facility, and that the United States contribution will take account of our own balance of payments position. To assure that other advanced countries provide their fair share of these funds, the United States contribution would not exceed that contributed by other donors as a group, nor would it constitute the largest single contribution to the Bank's Special Funds. The terms governing the use of the United States contribution are clearly set forth in the bill I am transmitting to the Congress.

———

This support by our country will enable the Asian Development Bank to more effectively perform its critical role in promoting Asian economic progress. The Bank is in a unique position to do this because:

—It is first and foremost *a bank,* applying sound economic and financial principles to the job of development.

—It is *Asia's own creation,* largely conceived, established, financed and operated by Asians to meet Asian problems.

—It embodies equitable arrangements for *sharing the burden* of providing development finance.

—It brings to bear on Asia's challenging development problems *the cooperative efforts of 33 nations,* with balanced representation among Asian and non-Asian members, and among developed and developing countries.

—Its progress to date gives promise that it will become the important focal point for Asian development efforts envisaged by its founders.

———

Other developed country members already have responded to the Bank's need for Special Funds resources.

Japan has earmarked $100 million of which $40 million has already been paid. Canada is contributing $25 million in five equal annual installments, while Denmark and The Netherlands have also contributed a total of $3.1 million.

The Governors of the Bank have supplemented these contributions by setting aside for Special Funds purposes $14.5 million of the Bank's own paid-in convertible currency capital resources, as permitted by the Bank's charter.

A United States contribution at this time will give additional needed strength to this essential supplement to the Bank's Ordinary Capital resources, and will encourage other developed countries to contribute to the Special Funds facility.

———

This proposal has been developed after careful study of the pressing development needs of Asia, of the ability of the Asian Development Bank to use Special Funds resources to help meet those needs, and of our own fiscal and balance of payments problems. I believe that it represents a sound and realistic balancing of those factors, and that it will serve the national interests of the United States in a number of ways.

—It will further demonstrate the strong United States interest in the economic development of Asia.

—It is responsive to the developmental needs of Asia and to Asian initiatives already taken to meet them.

—It will strengthen the Bank as a multilateral regional institution capable of dealing with current and future development problems in Asia.

—It will encourage other advanced nations to provide their fair share of concessional aid to Asia—a region heretofore predominantly dependent on United States aid.

—It takes account of our fiscal and financial problems and contains the necessary balance of payments safeguards.

—It constitutes another example of effective utilization of the multilateral approach to economic development.

I urge the Congress to give this proposal its whole-hearted and prompt approval.[27]

RICHARD NIXON

The White House
February 25, 1970

B. The United States and the People's Republic of China.

(50) Resumption of Ambassadorial-Level Meetings in Warsaw: Department of State Statement, January 8, 1970.[28]

(Complete Text)

The Governments of the United States and the People's Republic of China have agreed to hold the 135th ambassadorial-level meeting in Warsaw January 20, 1970. The United States will be represented by Ambassador Walter J. Stoessel, Jr. The Chinese side will be represented by Chargé d'Affaires Lei Yang.

The meeting will be held at the Embassy of the People's Republic of China, with holdings of subsequent meetings alternating between the United States and the People's Republic of China Embassies.

(51) Cancellation of the Warsaw Meeting: Department of State Statement, May 18, 1970.[29]

We regret the action of the Communist Chinese in canceling the May 20 meeting, at which we had hoped that some progress might be made in reducing tensions between us.

27 The 91st Congress adjourned without taking action on President Nixon's request; cf. statement by President Nixon, December 30, 1970, in *Weekly Compilation of Presidential Documents*, January 4, 1971, p. 10.
28 Text from *Department of State Bulletin*, January 26, 1970, p. 83. For the context of this and the following document see *The United States in World Affairs, 1970*, Section 23.
29 Text from *Department of State Bulletin*, June 8, 1970, p. 713.

We cannot of course in any way accept the charges made by the Chinese in their announcement. These charges completely distort the intention and effect of our recent actions in Southeast Asia as has been made abundantly clear in many public statements by the administration.[30]

We nevertheless stand ready to meet again and to engage in constructive discussion when a mutually convenient time can be found.

C. The United States and Japan.[31]

(52) Extension of the United States-Japanese Treaty of Mutual Cooperation and Security.

(a) United States Statement, Washington, June 22, 1970.[32]

(Complete Text)

Secretary Rogers noted, in his meeting this afternoon with Foreign Minister [Kiichi] Aichi, that tomorrow, June 23, is the 10th anniversary of the U.S.–Japan Treaty of Mutual Cooperation and Security.[33]

The Secretary expressed the conviction that this treaty has served both countries well and lies at the heart of the cooperative relationship which has developed between the United States and Japan and which is vital to the future well-being of both peoples.

Secretary Rogers reaffirmed, on behalf of the United States, the understanding reached last November by President Nixon and Prime Minister [Eisaku] Sato [34] that the two Governments intend to maintain the treaty, whose role they valued highly in maintaining the peace and security of the Far East including Japan.

On the basis of this firm foundation, the Secretary said, he was confident that the decade of the 1970's would see the further strengthening of the ties between the two countries and of their commitment to peace and prosperity for all mankind.

---

30 Documents 38–39.
31 For the context of this group of documents see *The United States in World Affairs, 1970*, Section 25.
32 Department of State Press Release 187, June 12, 1970; text from *Department of State Bulletin,* July 13, 1970, p. 33.
33 Signed at Washington, January 19, 1960; text and related material in *Documents, 1960*, pp. 416–431.
34 Same, *1968–69*, pp. 336–341.

The Secretary said he was happy to note that the Government of Japan shared these views, as indicated in its statement of June 22.

(b) Japanese Statement, Tokyo, June 22, 1970.[35]

(Complete Text)

At the lapse of the initial period of 10 years of the Treaty of Mutual Cooperation and Security between Japan and the United States of America, the government confirms its intention to firmly maintain the treaty in the interest of the maintenance of the security of Japan.

Back in 1952 our country chose resolutely to conclude the peace treaty with the majority of the allied powers [36] and at the same time concluded the security treaty with the United States [37] in order to ensure our national security and reconstruction under the precarious situation then prevailing in the Far East. Subsequently, we concluded with the United States in 1960 the present Treaty of Mutual Cooperation and Security, by revising the former security treaty and placing the Japanese-American relationship on the basis of equal partnership.

That the nation has enjoyed peace in the turbulence of the world today and that it has achieved an unprecedented economic prosperity and improvement in the people's living bear out the wisdom of the national choice thus made on the course of external policy. The government is convinced that unswerving pursuit of this policy in the 1970's is supported extensively by the people.

The will and spirit of the people to defend their homeland is the basic foundation of national security. However, no nation in today's world can expect to maintain its security by itself. The best conceivable way to secure national existence and development, it is believed, is to build up our self-defense power in consonance with national capabilities and to ensure the peace and security of the Far East including Japan by the Japanese-American security system.

The government is determined to make every effort, with cor-

---

35 Text from *Department of State Bulletin*, July 13, 1970, pp. 33–34.

36 Signed at San Francisco September 8, 1951 and entered into force April 28, 1952; text in *Documents, 1951*, pp. 470–479. For text of President Harry S. Truman's Proclamation on entry into force of the treaty see same, *1952*, pp. 288–299.

37 Signed at San Francisco September 8, 1951 and entered into force April 28, 1952; text in *Documents, 1951*, pp. 266–268.

rect appraisal of hard realities and with vigilance on the evolution of the times, toward the relaxation of international tension and the establishment of permanent peace.

The government calls upon the nation for further understanding and cooperation.

(53) Economic and Political Issues: Joint Statement by Secretary of State Rogers, Secretary of Commerce Maurice Stans, Foreign Minister Kiichi Aichi, and Trade Minister Kiichi Miyazawa, Washington, June 24, 1970.[38]

(Complete Text)

The Secretaries of State and Commerce and the Foreign and Trade Ministers of Japan met and reviewed the discussions of the past several days [39] which covered a number of items of mutual concern between the United States and Japan. They noted that in some respects considerable progress had been made which served to reaffirm the important and close ties that bind the United States and Japan, particularly in the political and economic fields.

On the subject of textiles, they regretted that it had not been possible to reach an understanding on the pending problem of textile imports into the United States. They recognized, however, that this problem was of broad significance and expressed the desire that discussions continue at an appropriate time in an effort to resolve the problem. Although they expressed their disappointment that the problem of textiles could not be resolved at this time, they stressed the overall success of U.S.–Japan economic relations which have enabled each country to become the largest overseas market of the other. They expressed their understanding that the two countries had become increasingly interdependent, particularly in the economic field, and that policies and actions of either country have a correspondingly large impact on the other.

With regard to the Treaty of Mutual Cooperation and Security, they noted with gratification that the two governments had decided to continue the treaty which has just completed ten years of successful operation. They drew particular attention to the statements issued on this subject on June 22 by the two governments.[40]

38 Text from *Department of State Bulletin,* July 13, 1970, p. 34.
39 The U.S.-Japanese talks began on June 22, 1970.
40 Document 52.

With regard to Okinawa, they noted that negotiations for the return of Okinawa to Japanese administrative control, as envisaged in the Communique of November 1969, had commenced in Tokyo.[41] They were confident that these negotiations would proceed smoothly to a conclusion which would enable reversion to be accomplished in 1972.

They also reviewed the situation in Southeast Asia. Foreign Minister Aichi described the efforts of Japan together with representatives of Indonesia and Malaysia to carry out the decision of the recent Djakarta Conference urging withdrawal of all foreign forces from Cambodia.[42] It was agreed that these efforts were important to both Governments as well as other nations of Asia.

In conclusion the Foreign Ministers agreed that the joint efforts of the U.S. and Japan to strengthen their close relations and to cooperate in making the maximum contribution to peace and stability in Asia should be intensified. Secretary Rogers said he looked forward to discussing these matters during his visit to Tokyo July 7 to July 9.[43]

D. United States Policy Prospects in the Far East.

(54) Asia in the Decade of the Seventies: Address by U. Alexis Johnson, Under Secretary of State for Political Affairs, Before the Cleveland Council on World Affairs, Cleveland, Ohio, February 28, 1970.[44]

(Excerpt)

*   *   *

I am glad to talk about East Asia as a whole because we sometimes tend to get so preoccupied with the problems of Viet-Nam that we tend to lose sight of the broader perspective of which it is only a part.

Our basic objective in East Asia, as elsewhere in the world, is the establishment of a peaceful community of nations, each free to choose its own way of government and its own way of life, to develop its resources to the maximum, and to have peaceful and productive relations with its neighbors.

[41] *Documents, 1968–69,* pp. 336–341.
[42] Cf. note 31 to Document 39.
[43] Cf. *Department of State Bulletin,* August 3, 1970, pp. 144–149.
[44] Text from *Department of State Bulletin,* March 23, 1970, pp. 381–387.

When this is stated it often sounds like a pious platitude. But it is far more than that. For it is only as we move toward that kind of world that we will be able in our own country to sleep more easily at night and devote more of our resources to productive purposes.

We recognize that to develop this kind of community of nations there must be security. This having been said, and while United States interests remain essentially the same and our commitments firm, we must recognize that there is undeniably a change in the mood of the American people. They will be cautious about undertaking new commitments. They are becoming somewhat impatient with carrying what many consider to be a disproportionate share of the burden of military security and economic assistance abroad. They are asking more and more frequently what other countries are doing to help themselves and each other and to share these burdens. It is a good and proper question. The American people sense that changing conditions bring changing problems and accordingly require changing answers.

SUBSTANTIAL AND DRAMATIC ECONOMIC PROGRESS

What is it that has changed? Economic progress is visible almost everywhere in free Asia, is at least substantial, and, as I have mentioned, in some cases dramatic.

Governments are increasingly capable and willing to assume responsibility not only for their own people but in regional matters in collaboration with their neighbors. They are beginning to help each other.

The most notable case of progress and confidence is, of course, Japan, whose 100 million people have a substantially higher total national product than do the 750 million people of mainland China. As the third greatest industrial producer in the world, Japan has taken her rightful place as one of the great trading and developed nations of the world. Except for Canada, Japan buys more from us and sells to us more than any other country in the world. Japan has taken a major lead in regional economic cooperation. Her contribution to the Asian Development Bank matches that of the United States.[45] In recent years Japan has greatly enlarged her economic assistance in East Asia and, in fact, the amount of Japanese economic resources to developing countries exceeded $1 billion in 1968. The Japanese Government has just announced that it expects the amount to be $1.4 billion in 1970.

45 Cf. Document 49.

The Republic of Korea, in a brief 17 years, has risen from the ruins of a devastating war and has developed one of the highest growth rates in the world, and astonishes its visitors by the vitality and confidence of its economic progress.

In the Republic of China on Taiwan, we have seen equally dramatic progress in economic growth. Not only has per capita income doubled in the last 10 years, but the Republic of China is also helping others to help themselves with technical aid programs in over 20 countries in Southeast Asia, Africa, and Latin America.

Thailand, a country of crucial importance to the area, has a long tradition of independence and self-reliance. It is making impressive economic progress, combating insurgency within its own borders, contributing troops to the struggle in South Viet-Nam, and providing leadership in regional cooperation and organization in Southeast Asia. The United States welcomes and supports these efforts. We have some military forces stationed in Thailand with full Thai agreement as part of our common efforts in Viet-Nam. We have kept and will continue to keep our commitment to Thailand under the SEATO treaty.[46]

Australia and New Zealand, both also prospering economically, have troops fighting by our side in Viet-Nam. In addition, they have announced that they intend to maintain troops in Malaysia and Singapore after the British withdrawal from that area in 1971, in fuller recognition of their role as Asian powers.[47] This constructive and statesmanlike action will contribute greatly to stability and confidence in the region.

Perhaps the most dramatic recent single element in the actual and potential transformation of Southeast Asia has been the change in Indonesia. While the developments there to which I have already referred arose from internal factors,[48] I am sure that there are few who would disagree that it is very unlikely this change would have taken place if there had not been the background of a firm free-world posture elsewhere in Southeast Asia.

Our former dependency, the Philippines, is independently developing its own economic and political institutions. The President, during his trip to Manila last year,[49] expressed our desire to establish a new relationship with the Philippines,

[46] Cf. note 3 to Document 47 (a).
[47] Cf. note 12 to Document 47 (b).
[48] The reference is to the overthrow of President Sukarno September 30, 1965; cf. *The United States in World Affairs, 1965*, pp. 241–243.
[49] July 26–27, 1969; cf. *Weekly Compilation of Presidential Documents*, August 4, 1969, pp. 1034–1040.

based upon mutual trust, respect, confidence, and cooperation. For their part, the Philippine leaders wish to reduce their country's dependence upon the United States.

Political stability and economic development in Laos are confounded by the presence on Lao soil of over 50,000 North Vietnamese troops with the purpose of facilitating the flow of men and supplies to South Viet-Nam and fighting a war in north Laos to put pressure on Souvanna Phouma's Royal Laotian Government. We are also conscious of the potential Communist threat through Laos to the security of Thailand. U.S. policy is directed at supporting an independent and neutral Laos and the full implementation of the Geneva agreements of 1962.[50] American military and economic assistance is provided the Lao Government at its request in an effort to counter North Vietnamese aggression and preserve a neutral Laos within the framework of the Geneva agreements. We have no combat troops in Laos. We continue to support political and diplomatic initiatives undertaken by the Lao Government to keep Laos identified as an area of multilateral concern rather than one of direct confrontation between the United States and major Communist powers.[51]

Laos, Cambodia, Viet-Nam, and Thailand, despite numerous rivalries and difficulties, have been quietly working together for a considerable period on a plan for the development of the valley of the Mekong River for the benefit of the whole region.

As you know, we reestablished diplomatic relations with Cambodia last year.[52]

One of the most interesting, and in the long run perhaps one of the most potentially significant, developments has been the beginnings, albeit tentative, of collaboration between the countries of the region in purely Asian terms. The Asian and Pacific Council (ASPAC) and the Association of Southeast Asian Nations (ASEAN) are groupings of exclusively Asian countries developed at Asian initiative to collaborate on Asian problems. They are still in their formative stages and have confined themselves to general political and cultural and some economic collaboration. They have already provided useful forums for quiet and constructive discussion of potentially difficult problems.

NEW DIRECTIONS IN U.S. POLICY

It is against this background of changing circumstances—for the most part changes representing increased capacities,

[50] *Documents, 1962,* pp. 284–294.

[51] Cf. Document 37.

[52] Cf. note 9 to Document 38.

strength, confidence, and determination in the area itself—that last year at Guam President Nixon outlined new directions in our policy toward Asia.[53] Welcoming, and encouraged by, these developments in Asia, the President said that he felt the time had now come for the United States to assume less of a predominant and more of a supporting role in the area. He said that from now on we will look to the nation directly threatened to assume the primary responsibility for providing manpower for its defense, especially for internal defense. While we are prepared to furnish military aid and training, we would not be prepared to assume such defense as a primary or exclusively American undertaking.

The President reiterated this policy in his report on foreign policy issued last week.[54] At the same time the President was careful to point out that this was no policy of isolation from or indifference to events in Asia. As he again said in that report, we remain involved in Asia, we are a Pacific power, and we have learned that peace for us is much less likely if there is no peace in Asia. It was on these grounds in the 1950's that we undertook security commitments with a number of Asian countries; and as he has repeatedly said, we will keep those commitments. As he also said, we are prepared to provide the necessary shield if a nuclear power threatens the freedom of a nation allied with us or of a nation whose survival we consider vital to our security and the security of the region as a whole.

In his state of the Union message,[55] the President further pointed out that:

> The nations of each part of the world should assume the primary responsibility for their own well-being; and they themselves should determine the terms of that well-being. . . .
>
> To insist that other nations play a role is not a retreat from responsibility; it is a sharing of responsibility.

In trying to project our own role and interest in Asia into this next decade, I think it useful to remind ourselves that the President's mention of our concern with developments in Asia and the Pacific is not something new but goes back into our earliest history as a nation. The second consulate established by the Continental Congress was in Canton, China. Our Navy established an Asiatic squadron in the middle of the last century, and ships of that squadron were employed by Commodore Perry in the initiative we took to force Japan to abandon its isolation. We estab-

[53] *Documents, 1968–69,* pp. 329–334.
[54] Document 2.
[55] Document 1.

lished ourselves on Midway in 1867 and on Samoa in 1878. Just
2 years after the ending of the Civil War, we purchased Alaska
from Russia. In 1898 we sent a fleet and expeditionary force to
bring the Philippines under American rule and also acquired
Guam. In the same year we also annexed Hawaii. We sent troops
to Peking in 1900, and American garrisons were stationed in
Shanghai, Tientsin, and Peking; a naval patrol was maintained
on the Yangtze River until the outbreak of World War II. President Roosevelt intervened to bring an end to the Russo-Japa-
nese War in 1905. We maintained an expeditionary force in
Siberia from 1918 to 1920. For us, World War II started—as well
as ended—in the Pacific. In connection with all the discussion
now of the importance—or lack of importance—of Viet-Nam, I
think it interesting to recall that it was the Japanese movement
into what is now South Viet-Nam that in many ways marked the
final breaking point in the chain of events leading up to our war
with Japan.

I do not want to labor the point any further but have cited
these examples to remind ourselves that American interest in and
concern with Asian affairs is nothing new and that even during
the long period we tried to isolate ourselves from much of the
rest of the world, particularly from Europe, we never had a similar policy in the Pacific. Thus, in looking to the 1970's, I do
not feel that our friends in Asia should be concerned that the
United States is beginning to move toward divorcing itself from
an interest in Asia. In fact, our interest in the Pacific Basin is
now greater than it has ever been in our history and undoubtedly will continue to grow. However, the ways in which we give
expression to this interest will change as circumstances change.

Realistic Expectations

Given this background, what can we hope for and realistically
expect in Asia itself in the 1970's? First, as I indicated, we cannot
expect that any magic formula is going to produce peace, tranquility, and prosperity throughout the area. It will remain an
area of ferment, an area of change, but I also believe generally
an area of progress—progress both in those things of concern to
the area and those things of concern to us. This involves in particular what is going to happen with respect to Japan, in most
ways the overwhelmingly most powerful country in the area;
what is going to happen with respect to China, overwhelmingly
the most populous country in the world; and Indonesia, the second most populous country in East Asia. It also involves the
relationships—economic, political, and security—that develop
among all of the countries of the area.

First, with respect to Japan, a country virtually without any natural resources except the genius of its people, its future is going to depend very heavily on whether the free-world economic system remains healthy. This, of course, involves the question of whether the world's financial system can develop so as to accommodate the burgeoning of the world's trade without recurring crises and whether sources of raw materials and markets are going to remain open so that trade can develop rather than falling back on the outworn shibboleths and practices of national autarky and protectionism. Needless to say, the policies that Japan itself pursues with regard to its own economy is going to have a major influence on this situation. If the free-world economy remains healthy, it is estimated that by the end of the 1970's Japan will have again more than doubled this national product and will have reached a per capita income of about $4,200, or equal to ours as of today. Just in terms of our own economic interests, this probably means at least a doubling of our present level of trade, which is presently about $7 billion in both directions.

The glass is much darker with respect to mainland China. The spectacular achievements of the Chinese peoples in Taiwan, Hong Kong, and Singapore well demonstrate what that great people can do, accommodating themselves to the modern world, if given a reasonably rational political and economic environment in which to work. The question with respect to mainland China is whether the situation there will develop in such a way as to bring about such a system for its own people as well as a system which is willing to live and let live in the international community. There is no certainty as to what will happen in this regard, especially in such a historically short timespan as the next decade. However, all of us who profess to have some knowledge of the great Chinese people I am sure believe that their good sense and pragmatism eventually will assert themselves. The question is when and how. In the meanwhile, my own view is that what is done from the outside is not going greatly to influence the convulsions through which that country is now going; however, we should seek to maintain the dialogue with the leaders of Communist China which we initiated in 1954 and remain responsive to any indications of less hostile attitudes from Peking. It was in this spirit that we recently began to talk once again with the Chinese in Warsaw [56] and have eased some restrictions on trade with Communist China.[57]

---

[56] Cf. Documents 50–51.
[57] Announced July 21, 1969; cf. *Department of State Bulletin,* August 18, 1969, p. 126.

I would hope and expect that with continued support and assistance from the outside Indonesia would continue to move toward overcoming its monumental problems. In terms of natural resources, Indonesia is one of the three or four most blessed countries in the world; its people are intelligent and gifted; and I am confident that it can have a bright future.

Given conditions of security and confidence, to which our contributions, while perhaps at least relatively less, will continue to be of major importance, I am satisfied that Thailand, Malaysia, and Singapore will continue to make progress. The Philippines is going through a time of some stress, but very properly they are working at their problems in their own way.

At such time as peace is established in Viet-Nam, I am confident that country can achieve a record that will be even more impressive than that that has been made by South Korea. There is no people in Southeast Asia that is more energetic, intelligent, and adaptable than the people of Viet-Nam. And the natural resources of South Viet-Nam far surpass those of Korea. It is basically a food-surplus area and, given conditions of reasonable security and stability, will be able quickly to achieve a large degree of economic self-sufficiency.

Growth of Regional Cooperation

Finally, I turn to the region as a whole. From the standpoint of our interests, the ideal is a community of the free states of Asia cooperating together for their common interests in political, economic, and security fields with which we are associated only to the degree that those states desire our association. This is the goal set by President Nixon. I have already mentioned the growth of economic cooperation among the states of the area— manifested in such ways as the founding of the Asian Development Bank,[58] which was genuinely at the initiative of the countries of the area rather than from any direction from the United States; the Southeast Asian Economic Development Conference and the Southeast Asian Agricultural Development Conference, which have been at the initiative of Japan and with which we have no formal association; the Mekong River Development Committee, which was created by ECAFE [Economic Commission for Asia and the Far East].

In the political field the 10-nation ASPAC, again with which we have no formal association, is showing increasing vigor and accomplishment. There is also the political association of ASEAN, and in the educational field the Southeast Asian Ministers of Education Organization. I could go on, but I think that I have made the point that in the economic and political fields real progress is being made in regional cooperation and development. I would expect Japan to take an increasing role in these developments, especially contributing an ever-increasing amount in the broad field of economic aid and cooperation. During his visit to Washington last November, this was also the goal set for Japan by Prime Minister Sato.[59]

In the security field, we already have the fact that other countries of the area—Korea, Thailand, Australia, and New Zealand —are contributing to what they feel is the common cause in South Viet-Nam.[60] Obviously, cooperation in the security field will come somewhat slower and with greater difficulty than it has already come in the political and economic fields. However, that it will come I have no question, although it is not possible at this time to predict the forms and the way that it will take.

There are some who look to Japan as the nation in this area with the potential to make the greatest security contribution. There are, no doubt, some Japanese who may think this way, but the large majority of the Japanese people now reject an overseas military role for Japan. Japan's policy is one for its leaders and people to make. As the President said last week, we shall not ask Japan to assume responsibilities inconsistent with the deeply felt concerns of its people.[61] Under present circumstances Japan's most effective contribution may well be to take care of the local defense of its territory, including Okinawa when it assumes responsibility there, and continue to provide increasing economic cooperation with the other nations in Asia. Both we and Japan well recognize that security in the area is not just a matter of military power but also very importantly the political, social, and economic health of the countries of the area. To this Japan's contribution can be of great importance.

Thus, this is the next decade as I see it in East Asia. It will not be an area from which we will want to divorce ourselves, but rather an area which, in both absolute and relative terms, will be increasingly important to us. It will not be an area devoid of difficulties and crises which may at times involve our responsibilities and interests, but it will, I am convinced, be an area with which we can and must continue to associate ourselves in ways that take account of the evolution of conditions and events in both the area and our own country.

59 Cf. note 34 to Document 52(a).
60 Cf. Document 43.
61 Cf. note 54, above.

VII.
THE UNITED STATES
AND AFRICA

A. United States Policy Formulation.

(55) Report by Secretary of State Rogers Following a Visit to Ten African Countries, February 7–23, 1970.[1]

(a) Letter from Secretary of State Rogers to President Nixon Submitting the African Policy Statement, March 26, 1970.[2]

(Complete Text)

Dear Mr. President:

We have prepared and are submitting for your approval the attached statement on our policies in Africa.[3] This is the first full statement of this kind by the United States Government in recent years. It represents, as you know, the results of numerous discussions with African leaders, a reflection of your own observations and interests regarding the continent, and conclusions arising from my own recent tour of Africa.[4] It reflects with greater detail the principles of our African policy set forth in the Report on Foreign Policy in the 1970's.[5]

The report emphasizes elements of our relationship to Africa both economic and political which will be of special importance in the coming months.

We believe the actions and objectives set forth in this paper

[1] For the context see *The United States in World Affairs, 1970,* Section 32.
[2] Department of State Press Release 105, March 27, 1970; text from *Department of State Bulletin,* April 20, p. 513.
[3] Document 55 (b).
[4] For statements and remarks made by Secretary Rogers during his African visit see *Department of State Bulletin,* March 23, 1970, pp. 365–380.
[5] Document 2.

represent a positive program within current budgetary and legislative guidelines. We have not suggested precise levels for the economic programs in view of the current studies of the worldwide foreign assistance policy.[6] We feel it important, however, that our programs be certainly not less than the present level. We intend, within that level, to demonstrate herein how our current capabilities can respond more fully to Africa's stated needs.

In the ensuing weeks we shall be discussing aspects of the program with members of the Congress. We shall be developing other aspects in direct consultation with African governments, governments of other countries participating in African development and significant regional and international institutions.

As time goes on, we shall be building on this foundation, expanding where we can to increase the total effectiveness of our relationship with this significant continent. I believe you will find in our approach the basis for the positive expression of U.S. interest in Africa which you have so strongly encouraged.

Respectfully yours,

WILLIAM P. ROGERS

The President
The White House

Enclosure:
African Policy Statement

(b) The United States and Africa: Policy Statement, Released March 28, 1970.[7]

(Excerpts)

*　　*　　*

B. WHAT WE SEEK

We seek a relationship of constructive cooperation with the nations of Africa—a cooperative and equal relationship with all who wish it. We are prepared to have diplomatic relations under conditions of mutual respect with all the nations of the continent. We want no military allies, no spheres of influence, no big power competition in Africa. Our policy is a policy related to

---

[6] Cf. Document 95.
[7] Text from *Department of State Bulletin,* April 20, 1970, pp. 514–521.

African countries and not a policy based upon our relations with non-African countries.

As early as 1957, when he returned from a mission to Africa on behalf of President Eisenhower, the then Vice President Nixon recommended that the U.S. assign a higher priority to our relations with an Africa, which he recognized to be of growing importance to the United States. Specifically he said: [8]

> The United States must come to know these leaders better, to understand their hopes and aspirations, and to support them in their plans and programs for strengthening their own nations and contributing to world peace and stability. To this end, we must encourage the greatest possible interchange of persons and ideas with the leaders and peoples of these countries. We must assure the strongest possible diplomatic and consular representation to those countries and stand ready to consult these countries on all matters affecting their interests and ours.

Personal relationships between members of the Administration and African leaders have been widely expanded. President Nixon met leaders from 10 African countries during the past year. I met a number of African leaders during 1969 and in the fall met and discussed common issues with 26 African Foreign Ministers at the United Nations General Assembly. The meetings included and contributed to closer understanding even with states with which we have no current diplomatic relations; in the case of Mauritania the discussion with the Foreign Minister [Hamdi Ould Mouknass] in New York was the first step toward a resumption of relations which has now taken place.[9] In February I became the first Secretary of State to tour Africa.[10] I visited 10 African countries. I also spoke with leaders of the Organization of African Unity, the UN Economic Commission for Africa and other regional bodies. I met in Kinshasa [capital of the Democratic Republic of the Congo] with the American chiefs of mission and principal officers from the African countries in which we are represented.

It is through open and honest exchanges such as these that we can better understand the needs and aspirations of the peoples and governments of Africa and they can learn of the objectives and problems we Americans face at this time and place in history.

Some of my countrymen used to long for the luxury of isolation behind the protection of two great oceans. But the time for that has passed. The continental size of the United States, its

[8] *Documents, 1957,* p. 293.
[9] During the winter of 1969–1970. Relations were broken off June 7, 1967 at the time of the Arab-Israeli war of June 1967.
[10] Cf. note 4 to Document 55 (a).

vast productive power, its technological capabilities, its inter-dependence with other parts of this planet impel us into active participation in world affairs.

But in this participation we do not seek any kind of domina-tion. We seek with all nations the closest relationship which is mutually acceptable and beneficial, but seek it with full respect for diversity among nations.

*   *   *

E. ECONOMIC ASSISTANCE POLICY

An American economic assistance program in Africa is in United States national interests. We wish to see African coun-tries develop and take their rightful place in cooperative inter-national efforts to resolve worldwide problems. The drive and determination to develop must come from the African countries themselves. But at this point in their development, when per capita annual incomes average about $135, most of these coun-tries need substantial external assistance to achieve rates of prog-ress responsive to the minimum aspirations of their more than 300 million people for a better life. Our principal concern, therefore, is how most effectively to make capital assistance and technical knowledge from the developed nations available to these developing nations.

Ever since the wave of independence swept through Africa in the late '50's and early '60's, Western European nations and multidonor organizations have provided 60 to 70 percent of economic assistance to Africa. Because of their strong traditional and historic links to Africa, we hope the European nations will continue to provide the bulk of foreign assistance to Africa. But the United States also has deep and special ties to Africa. We should do our fair share in support of the independence and growth of African nations.

F. U.S. ASSISTANCE

The total U.S. share has, in fact, averaged about $350 million a year for the past several years. This is about 20 percent of all external assistance to Africa. We intend to maintain a substantial contribution, hopefully with a larger share in economic develop-ment programs.

Our bilateral assistance program has included resources from A.I.D. [Agency for International Development], PL–480, the Export-Import Bank and the Peace Corps. In the form of loans, grants and personnel, it has reached some thirty-five African countries. It has assisted national development programs, as well as regional projects. We have worked through regional organizations, and jointly with other donors. The United States will continue to provide assistance to those nations which have been given emphasis in the past. At the same time, mindful of needs throughout the continent, we have decided to make our approach to African assistance more flexible than it has recently been:

—We will to the extent permitted by legislation also provide limited assistance in other African countries to projects which contribute significantly to increased production and revenues.

—We will continue to emphasize aid to regional programs and projects, giving special attention to innovative ways to make our efforts effective.

—We wish to do more to strengthen African economic institutions including the UN Economic Commission for Africa, the African Development Bank, the OAU's Scientific, Technical, and Research Commission and subregional organizations.

—-We will utilize food aid to advance economic development objectives and to help tide nations over emergency food shortages.

—We will more and more orient the program of the Peace Corps to meet the technical, educational and social development needs of African nations.

—We will concentrate our economic assistance in the coming years in the fields of agriculture, education, health including demographic and family planning, transportation and communications.

—We are actively studying the requirement that U.S. loans to Africa be used almost exclusively for the purchase of American goods and services.

We intend to provide more assistance to Africa through international institutions and multidonor arrangements. We contribute 40 percent of the budget of the UN Development Program; 40 percent of its program is now being directed to Africa. We also contribute 40 percent of the budget of the International Development Association; in the past year its loans to Africa have risen substantially to 20 percent of all its loans, and the prospect is that this proportion will continue to rise.

We are seeking a substantial increase in the absolute amount of United States contributions to these institutions. The United States is now engaged in discussions with other members of IDA, under the leadership of the World Bank [International Bank for

Reconstruction and Development], which we hope will lead to larger contributions by all donor members of IDA. We have proposed to Congress an increased contribution to UNDP.

In addition to our participation in international organizations, we are working more closely with other donors in World Bank and IMF [International Monetary Fund] sponsored consultative groups for several African countries, and in projects involving several donors. With limited total aid resources, we believe these mechanisms greatly increase the effectiveness of foreign aid.

We also look forward to joining with other non-African donors in support of the African Development Bank. This young institution, which has the financial backing of thirty-one African governments, has prospects for promoting significant pan-African cooperation in economic progress. It has already raised $67 million from its members in fully convertible currencies. It needs, however, a source of funds that could be loaned to its members on concessional terms. We are participating in discussions with other non-African donors which we hope will lead to the creation of special funds for this purpose. In the meantime, we are assisting the Bank directly in its efforts to develop and carry out urgently needed projects in its member countries.

An important portion of our assistance to Africa supports regional projects and regional institutions. In Addis Ababa, in the United Nations Economic Commission for Africa, one sees one of the most successful forms of international economic cooperation. Any serious appraisal of the development prospects in Africa makes clear the need for much greater regional cooperation. Many African nations are small; their national boundaries frequently split natural economic regions. Most national markets are too small to support industry using modern technology. Africans have already demonstrated their recognition of the need for regional cooperation by establishing regional educational, technical and research institutes, economic communities, common markets, common financial arrangements and even common currencies. We hope to remain in the forefront of cooperative efforts to foster regional cooperation in Africa.

Our Food for Peace programs have been a major means of economic assistance in many African countries, through credit sales, food-for-work, donations and emergency relief efforts. In the past few years, 40 percent of our aid to Africa has taken these forms. We will maintain this assistance wherever food aid can make an important contribution to economic development or help meet serious emergencies.

The Peace Corps conducts programs in twenty-three African

countries. This, too, will be continued as long as African governments find the Peace Corps' efforts useful to them. The Peace Corps is seeking to intensify its recruitment of experienced and highly qualified personnel in order to emphasize technically oriented positions needed in development efforts. The Peace Corps is also moving ahead to make qualified volunteers available to international organizations working in the development field.

In our programs for youth, we shall intensify our efforts to establish personal relationships between African and American young political leaders, technicians, students and businessmen.

We shall expand inter-African scholarships and third-country training programs for youth within Africa, while maintaining traditional exchanges with the United States.

We shall encourage more of our own country's diverse public and private groups to learn about and from Africans.

G. Joint Public-Private Technical Cooperation

We shall encourage the greater utilization of American citizens from the private sector to meet developmental needs in Africa. The International Executive Service Corps, an American private organization which recruits American businessmen for short-term service in developing nations has pointed the way. This technique has already proven its usefulness in a number of countries as a means of offering American management experience to budding private industry and to government in African countries. We desire to see what can be done further to encourage this approach.

I have also called for a study of how the United States Government can establish a clearing house for requests from the more advanced developing nations for the provision of technical and professional services to meet scientific, technological and industrial requirements. Such a clearing house should be able to draw on both public and private personnel, and should have sufficient funds available where necessary to "top-off" salaries offered by these developing nations to foreign experts, so that the total earnings of the American specialists would continue to match their current value in the United States.

In these and other fashions we should like to share some of the positive aspects of our science, technology and management experience, as well as some of the lessons we have been learning from our own development. I have in mind not only our achievements in communications, industry and science, but some of the grave by-products of these accomplishments, such as over-urbanization and pollution.

The U.S. Government recognizes the great potential of African labor to play a constructive role in the sound economic development of free and independent African nations. We have, therefore, consistently sought friendly understanding of the labor movements of African countries. We hope we can continue to make some significant contributions.

It is our policy to continue to support and encourage African governments in the development and execution of comprehensive labor manpower programs. And while recognizing African preferences for a distinctive African approach to trade union matters, we encourage close fraternal relations between the leaders and members of the African trade unions and Western national and international labor organizations.

H. PRIVATE INVESTMENT

There has been a steady growth in U.S. private investment in Africa since most of the African nations achieved their independence. By the end of 1968 the value of U.S. private investment in OAU member states was almost $2 billion. Between 1963 and 1968, U.S. private investment in Africa grew at an average annual rate of about fourteen percent.

We believe that private investment can and should play a growing role, above and beyond public assistance, in African development. Africans themselves desire to participate in such investment. In many countries, in the face of limited capital resources, it is the government rather than the private sector which has the financial wherewithal to join with foreign private investors. Thus, "joint ventures" frequently involve a combination of foreign private and African governmental capital. We are prepared to encourage American investors to cooperate in such endeavors under adequate investment protection.

Our investment policy should be creative and flexible. It should be deeply concerned with the social environment in which it operates. When investing abroad, modern American businessmen offer training, profit-sharing and other opportunities. At the same time, as businessmen, they expect stability for the enterprises in which they join and a reasonable return on their investments. While the United States Government has guaranty programs available to many American investors, these are insurance and not the basis on which businessmen make investment. Thus, they pay great heed to African government programs to foster a favorable investment climate. Therefore, an investment code, assurances from the African governments and reasonable entry, work and tax arrangements, can make the difference between an American's willingness or unwillingness to work out an investment.

Mineral and petroleum development account for nearly three-fourths of current U.S. private investment in Africa. The industry is exceptionally able to seek out new sources and new opportunities to meet growing demands.

The same is not the case, however, for investments in manufacturing, agro-business and commerce. Thus, we are already conducting certain programs to stimulate American private efforts in these fields.

—We have an increasingly successful, albeit modest, effort at getting American investors to look at integrated, large-unit agricultural schemes in Africa. In the past three years, American companies have made 27 preliminary studies, leading to ten in-depth studies and four investment commitments. Several more are currently being negotiated.

—We are also seeking to interest medium size American investors to look at opportunities to help contribute to African markets, i.e., flour milling, bus transportation; and for meeting specialized markets which Africa could fill, such as plywood, shrimp fishing and food processing.

Success in these and other programs depends on the already-mentioned favorable investment climate, on enterprises tailored to realistic market size, and ultimately on getting the prospective American investor to go to Africa to see for himself what the conditions are and what his opportunity costs are.

The new Overseas Private Investment Corporation [OPIC] is authorized [11] to provide guaranties, some equity, local currency loans and sound investment project advice to form the basis for a more efficient, flexible and aggressive approach to the promotion of U.S. investment in developing nations. It will be an important element in stimulating further American private investment in Africa.

I. Increased and Improved Trade Relations

I was deeply impressed on my recent trip by the great dependence of so many African countries on exports of one or two agricultural or mineral commodities. Sudden changes in world market prices for these commodities can cause violent fluctua-

[11] By the Foreign Assistance Act of 1969 (Public Law 91–175, approved December 30, 1969). For text of President Nixon's signature statement, December 31, 1969, see *Weekly Compilation of Presidential Documents,* January 5, 1970, pp. 8–9.

tions in export earnings and can disrupt development programs. In recognition of this instability the United States over the years has participated in international efforts to stabilize prices and incomes of primary products. We were one of the initial signatories of the International Coffee Agreement. The President is now recommending to the Congress renewal of the legislative authority for our continued adherence to this agreement.[12] By the same token, we are continuing to participate in the discussions within UNCTAD [United Nations Conference on Trade and Development] working toward an international agreement on cocoa.

But the problem of prices affects other commodities as well. We have joined international efforts, such as those recently conducted at African initiative in the World Bank and IMF, to see whether new and additional measures can be taken to stabilize prices and incomes.

Several months ago the President set forth proposals for generalized tariff preferences for all developing nations, so that they could more readily find markets for their manufactured and semi-manufactured products in the developed nations, including the United States. To this end, we are actively seeking agreement with other developed nations on some generalized preference scheme.

We are mindful of the special relationship which exists between some African and some European countries. Our purpose, however, is to give all developing nations much improved access for exports of their manufactures to the markets of all developed nations on an equal basis. We are also urging the elimination of discriminatory tariffs—sometimes called "reverse preferences"—which put our goods at a competitive disadvantage in many African markets. We hope that European nations see no linkage between eliminating the preferences they currently receive in some twenty African nations and their levels of aid to those countries.

In the meantime, we have been most encouraged to learn of the important first step taken by the member nations [Cameroon, the Central African Republic, Chad; and Gabon] of the Central African Customs and Economic Union (UDEAC), to reduce their general tariffs on most imported goods by fifty per-

12 Public Law 91–694, approved January 12, 1971, authorized continued participation in the International Coffee Agreement through July 30, 1971. Cf. texts of President Nixon's Fifth Annual Report transmitted to the Congress May 11, 1970 in *Department of State Bulletin*, June 8, 1970, pp. 719–725 and Sixth Annual Report transmitted to the Congress April 1, 1971 in same, May 3, 1971, pp. 584–590.

cent. They thus move closer to a nondiscriminatory tariff position.

This measure offers the prospect of greater American trade with these countries.

J. The Problem of Southern Africa

One of the most critical political problems of continental concern relates to southern Africa. The problems of southern Africa are extremely stubborn. Passions are strong on both sides. We see no easy solutions.

Yet the modern world demands a community of nations based on respect for fundamental human rights. These are not only moral and legal principles; they are powerful and ultimately irresistible political and historical forces. We take our stand on the side of those forces of fundamental human rights in southern Africa as we do at home and elsewhere.

In Southern Rhodesia, we have closed our consulate.[13] Our representatives in Salisbury were accredited to the Queen of England. When the Queen's authority was no longer recognized by the regime we withdrew our consulate. We have also determined not to recognize the white-minority regime in Salisbury and will continue to support UN economic sanctions.

To alleviate the difficulties of certain refugees in the United States, particularly of those from southern Africa, with respect to travel abroad, the United States expects in the near future to issue travel documentation as provided under the Protocol to the 1951 Geneva Convention on the Status of Refugees.[14]

In the matter of Namibia (South West Africa),[15] The United States has respected the international status of that territory since 1920. It has sought in the United Nations, before the International Court of Justice and in direct exchanges with South Africa, to defend that status. We have sought equally to defend the rights of the inhabitants, which that status was established to protect. We are now participating in UN deliberations on this matter. Any further actions which the U.S. may take, in the UN or elsewhere, will continue to be consistent with our historic support of the law.

Our relations with the Republic of South Africa have been a matter of particular attention. We do not believe cutting our ties with this rich, troubled land would advance the cause we pursue or help the majority of the people of that country. We continue to make known to them and the world our strong views on

13 Cf. note 28 to Document 59.
14 Opened for signature July 28, 1951; cf. *Docmuents, 1951*, pp. 383–384.
15 Documents 62–63.

apartheid. We are maintaining our arms embargo.[16] We oppose their continued administration of Namibia (South West Africa) and their implementation of apartheid and other repressive legislation there. We will continue to make clear that our limited governmental activities in South Africa do not represent any acceptance or condoning of its discriminatory system.

As for the Portuguese Territories,[17] we shall continue to believe that their peoples should have the right of self-determination. We will encourage peaceful progress toward that goal. The declared Portuguese policy of racial toleration is an important factor in this equation. We think this holds genuine hope for the future. Believing that resort to force and violence is in no one's interest, we imposed an embargo in 1961 against the shipment of arms for use in the Portuguese territories. We have maintained this embargo and will continue to do so.

The smaller independent states south of the Zambesi also deserve attention. They are seeking to create multiracial societies free of the predominant influence of the minority-dominated states adjoining and surrounding them. They cannot exist without a realistic relationship with their neighbors. At the same time it is in the interest of all those who wish to see these states develop and prosper to provide alternative sources of assistance and means of access to these states. This the United States, in cooperation with other donors, will seek to do. At the same time, the United States will seek to be responsive to requests from these states for a higher level of U.S. diplomatic representation.

In all these ways, as well as in positions taken in the United Nations and through diplomatic channels, we shall work to bring about a change of direction in parts of Africa where racial oppression and residual colonialism still prevail.

At the same time, we cannot accept the fatalistic view that only violence can ultimately resolve these issues. Rather we believe that solution lies in the constructive interplay of political, economic and social forces which will inevitably lead to changes.

CONCLUSION

As the President said in his Report to the Congress on Foreign Policy: [18] "We want the Africans to build a better life for themselves and their children. We want to see an Africa free of poverty and disease, and free too of economic or political dependence on any outside power. And we want Africans to build this

[16] Cf. Document 61.
[17] Cf. Documents 64–65.
[18] Document 2.

future as they think best, because in that way both our help and their efforts will be most relevant to their needs."

B. Relations with the Organization of African Unity.

(56) Message from Secretary of State Rogers to President Ahmadou Ahidjo of Cameroon, President of the O.A.U., on the Seventh Anniversary of the Organization, May 25, 1970.[19]

(Complete Text)

MAY 25, 1970

His Excellency
El Hadj AHMADOU AHIDJO
President, Organization of African Unity

On the Seventh Anniversary of the founding of the Organization of African Unity I extend on behalf of the American Government and people congratulations and a reaffirmation of our firm support and friendship to the peoples of the Organization's member states and their leaders.

As you know, I recently enjoyed a firsthand view of a large portion of your continent.[20] Consequently I am aware of the progress the OAU and its member states are making—often in the face of great difficulties. Such progress testifies to the independence and strength of the African spirit. It augurs a future which will fulfill the aspirations of the people. The Organization of African Unity is playing a strategic role in preserving and nurturing that spirit.

For our part, be assured of our faithful effort to assist in achieving your goals of regional cooperation, economic development and the advancement of human dignity on the African continent. It gives me personal pleasure to make this reaffirmation to you and to the Organization of African Unity on this occasion.

WILLIAM P. ROGERS

[19] Text from *Department of State Bulletin*, June 15, 1970, p. 752; for the context see *The United States in World Affairs, 1970*, Section 31.
[20] Cf. note 4 to Document 55.

C. Civil War in Nigeria.

(57)   The Surrender of Biafra: News Briefing by Under Secretary of State Elliot L. Richardson, January 13, 1970.[21]

(Excerpt)

*   *   *

I want to take this opportunity just to say a few words to you about the situation in Nigeria and the Biafran enclave and the measures that are being taken to cope with the humanitarian aspect of the situation and also to try to assure that those individuals who had been engaged in hostilities against the Federal Military Government are themselves treated with clemency and magnanimity.

First, though, I think it is important to emphasize the feeling that we in the Department of State who have been working on various aspects of this problem for these many months must have, as well as I am sure other Americans do, about the fact that at long last—whatever may have been our sympathies toward the participants in this tragic struggle—at least now there is the opportunity to bring relief to all the victims in this situation.

The frustrating aspect of it, while the fighting was on, was that we knew there were people in need and yet the avenues of relief were many times blocked by one obstacle or another. Fortunately, through the efforts and energy of many people—including most particularly for the United States our Special Relief Coordinator, Ambassador Clyde [C.] Ferguson [,Jr.]—a great deal was done. But we knew that it was never really enough; and so, in addition, through the efforts of many people, coordinated in this Department by Mr. William Brubeck, who headed a special task force in the Bureau of African Affairs, we have also tried to make the resources and assistance and support of the United States available to support efforts to bring about an end to the fighting.

We have had to recognize that too conspicuous an initiative by the United States in this respect might be counterproductive, and so we have generally followed a course of encouraging the initiatives of others and making available our help to them,

21 Text from *Department of State Bulletin,* February 2, 1970, pp. 120–121; for the context of this and the following document see *The United States in World Affairs, 1970,* Introduction to Chapter 8.

making it known to them that we stood ready to assist in whatever way we could.

And so, on the relief side, Ambassador Ferguson and, on the side of seeking to bring about an end to the fighting, Mr. Brubeck have been our own frontline representatives.

We feel that from the standpoint of a constructive role for the United States, this has been on the whole a successful course. In the end, obviously, our role was not instrumental in bringing about an end to the fighting. And yet, now that it has come about, much of the work and planning that has been done on the relief and humanitarian side can be brought to bear.

Our contingency studies, preparing for the possibility of military victory, go back to early December. During that period, Ambassador Ferguson worked on the revival of the possibility of utilizing the Cross River route and daylight airlift. He went to Nigeria to conduct a detailed first-hand study of the situation. Various plans were made, including the plans that are now being brought to bear to provide expedited and expanded transportation facilities. We can go further into this if there are any questions on the subject.

Before, however, turning to questions, I do have several points to mention that bring you up to date on things that we are doing as of today.

As I think you know, Assistant Secretary [for African Affairs David D.] Newsom saw General Gowon [Maj. Gen. Yakubu Gowon, head of the Federal Military Government] today.[22] We have not yet had a report of this. When we do, we will have a better idea of what we can usefully do to help the Nigerian Government in meeting its current problems, such as the C–130 aircraft and helicopters which the President has offered and assistance in expanding the international observer force.

Ambassador Ferguson is consulting with the Prime Minister [Harold Wilson] in London on coordination of all relief efforts, following several days of similar consultation with the relief agencies in Geneva.

In response to the request of UNICEF [United Nations Children's Fund], we have asked AID to consult with them urgently to provide any necessary assistance in moving 48 trucks for them from the United States to Nigeria by airlift, if required. In addition, we have located four prepackaged hospital units which we are prepared to move to Nigeria as rapidly as possible if the Nigerians can use them.

22 Cf. Document 58.

Ambassador Ferguson has already allocated to the Red Cross $2 million for direct support to the Nigerian Red Cross of the $10 million committed by the President for relief on Monday [January 12]. Those funds will be immediately available.

*   *   *

(58) *Relief and Rehabilitation Efforts: Statement by David D. Newsom, Assistant Secretary for African Affairs, Before the Subcommittee on Refugees and Escapees of the Senate Committee on the Judiciary, January 21, 1970.*[23]

(Complete Text)

With the end of the civil war in Nigeria [23a] the United States has two immediate concerns:

—We wish to be fully prepared to assist in meeting needs for relief and rehabilitation in Nigeria.

—We wish in doing this to build our longer term relations with Africa's most populous country on a positive basis.

I have just returned from Nigeria, where I met with General Gowon [Maj. Gen. Yakubu Gowon, head of the Federal Military Government of Nigeria] on January 13. I conveyed to him the interest and concern of President Nixon in assisting the Nigerian Government to the fullest extent in the arrangements of relief and rehabilitation. This expression of interest continued the pattern of humanitarian concern which has characterized our policy throughout this tragic episode.

General Gowon expressed appreciation for the President's offer. He stressed that he wished to be certain that requests for relief were based on genuine need and were coordinated. As a result of the coordination taking place in Nigeria, we have most recently been asked to supply 50 jeeps, 50 trucks, and three packaged disaster hospitals. These are being shipped. We anticipate further requests as needs develop.

I returned from Nigeria with a strong impression of the desire of the Nigerian leaders to demonstrate their ability to heal the wounds of the civil war. Several Nigerians stressed to me the importance Nigeria attaches to being directly associated with relief efforts in the former Biafran enclave. There is both pride

23 Text from *Department of State Bulletin*, February 16, 1970, pp. 185–186.
23a Cf. Document 57.

of person involved and pride of race. All reports received suggest that the Nigerians are carrying out their commitment to honorable and humane treatment of both civilian and military elements of the secessionist area.

The war left a mark of resentment against some agencies which helped provide relief to Biafra. Despite this the Nigerians are utilizing relief workers of many different agencies and nationalities previously in the enclave. The former head of the Biafran Red Cross has been appointed as a deputy to the head of the Nigerian Red Cross and has already gone to work at Enugu.

Information on current conditions in the enclave is still fragmentary. The first outside observers who were able to visit the war-ravaged area last week, Hendrick Beer, Secretary General of the League of Red Cross Societies, and Lord Hunt, Prime Minister Wilson's Relief Coordinator, have both reported they found the overall picture encouraging. They, and other observers, however, noted pockets of severe need, both for food and medical care. Observers have reported favorably on the present relief operation under the general direction of the Nigerian Red Cross and have found that reports of large numbers of refugees having taken to the bush seem so far to have been exaggerated. Refugees are reported moving back to their villages in great numbers. They appear to be in fair condition, with the elderly and wounded in greatest need of care. Federal troops were reported by all observers to have been assisting the Nigerian Red Cross in relief work with no observed excesses on the part of the troops.

Nevertheless, neither we nor, we feel, the Nigerians are complacent about the situation, even though conditions are better than many had predicted. The untrained eye does not necessarily see acute hunger. Some projections of the incidence of malnutrition among the population suggest a major problem. We have asked our people in Lagos to lay the results of such surveys before Nigerian authorities while at the same time indicating our readiness to be of help. Ambassador Ferguson is with me to provide additional information on our relief effort as may be required.[24]

Finally, one comes back from Lagos with a feeling that the relationships of the United States and other governments with Nigeria during this period will have broader significance. The Nigerians feel that the ability of an important black African nation to manage its affairs is at stake. There is an acute sensitivity about advice and actions which do not acknowledge Ni-

24 Text of Ambassador Ferguson's statement in *Department of State Bulletin*, February 16, 1970, pp. 186–188.

geria's sovereignty. In consideration of the importance we attach to our relations with Nigeria and other nations of the Organization of African Unity, we are maintaining the closest of consultations on these matters of concern. Through this policy we feel we will have the best chance to render assistance where needed and to place our relations with this significant nation on a sound footing.

D. The Question of Southern Rhodesia (Zimbabwe).

(59) *United States Veto of the Five-Power Draft Security Council Resolution: Statement by Ambassador Yost to the Security Council, March 17, 1970.*[25]

(*Complete Text*)

Mr. President, only the most serious of considerations would cause us to take the step of casting our negative vote on a resolution of such importance.[26]

The United States has stanchly supported the economic sanctions which had been imposed on Rhodesia. We were prepared to look with favor on the suggestions put forward earlier in the debate by the distinguished Ambassador of Finland [Max Jakobson] [27] for taking further action in common. We shall still continue, of course, to explore all possibilities in this sense.

However, we are not able to support the resolution which, by implication, calls upon the United Kingdom to use force. We have repeatedly stated the view that force is not the answer to this problem. For this reason we oppose a resolution condemning the United Kingdom for failure to use it.

We closed our consulate in Southern Rhodesia,[28] thus leaving our citizens in that country with no direct protection. We did so in the belief that it remained possible for our citizens at least to be in contact with their own country and with consulates elsewhere in Africa. We cannot now agree not only to cut off all their

---

25 U.S./U.N. Press Release 36, March 17, 1970; text from *Department of State Bulletin*, April 13, 1970, p. 506. For the context of this and the following document see *The United States in World Affairs, 1970*, Sections 31 and 40.

26 U.N. document S/9696/Corr. 1 and 2; text in *Department of State Bulletin*, April 13, 1970, pp. 508–509.

27 Cf. *U.N. Monthly Chronicle*, April 1970, pp. 16–17.

28 The U.S. closed its consulate in Salisbury on March 17, 1970; cf. statement by Secretary Rogers, March 2, 1970, in *Department of State Bulletin*, March 30, 1970, p. 412.

communications with the rest of the world but even to cut off all means by which they might leave Southern Rhodesia. Paragraph 6,[29] in our view, would amount to barring American citizens in Rhodesia from contact with the outside world, and this we cannot support. Besides the grave effect this action would have on United States citizens, many of whom are there for the sole purpose of alleviating suffering among the black majority of the population, we do not think that such an action is in the interests of the oppressed majority in Rhodesia, nor indeed that it would have any decisive effect on the illegal minority regime [of Prime Minister Ian D. Smith].

It is with very great reluctance, therefore, that we take this step. We have felt, and continue to feel, that a little greater effort to find common ground might have obviated this necessity. Let us not now abandon the search for common ground but resolve to try all the harder to grapple together with the problem of Rhodesia, which so deeply concerns us all and which, sooner or later, must and will be resolved in the interest of the oppressed majority.

(60) United Nations Security Council Resolution 277 (1970), Adopted March 18, 1970.[30]

(Complete Text)

The Security Council,

Reaffirming its resolutions 216 (1965) of 12 November 1965, 217 (1965) of 20 November 1965,[31] 221 (1966) of 9 April 1966, 232 (1966) of 16 December 1966 [32] and 253 (1968) of 29 May 1968,[33]

Reaffirming that, to the extent not superseded in the present resolution, the measures provided for in resolutions 217 (1965), 232 (1966), and 253 (1968), as well as those initiated by Member States in implementation of those resolutions, shall continue in effect,

---

29 Calling for immediate severance of all economic "and other relations with the illegal racist minority régime in Southern Rhodesia, including railway, maritime, air transport, postal, telegraphic and wireless communications and other means of communication."

30 Text from U.N. Security Council, *Official Records: Twenty-Fifth Year* (S/INF/25), pp. 5–6; adopted by a vote of 14–0 with 1 abstention.

31 Cf. *The United States in World Affairs, 1965*, p. 335.

32 *Documents, 1966*, pp. 320–322.

33 The content of this resolution is summarized in same, *1968–69*, pp. 370–372.

Taking into account the reports[34] of the Committee established in pursuance of Security Council resolution 253 (1968),

Noting with grave concern that:

(*a*) The measures so far taken have failed to bring the rebellion in Southern Rhodesia to an end,

(*b*) Some States, contrary to resolutions 232 (1966) and 253 (1968) of the Security Council and to their obligations under Article 25 of the Charter of the United Nations,[35] have failed to prevent trade with the illegal régime of Southern Rhodesia,

(*c*) The Governments of the Republic of South Africa and Portugal have continued to give assistance to the illegal régime of Southern Rhodesia, thus diminishing the effects of the measures decided upon by the Security Council,

(*d*) The situation in Southern Rhodesia continues to deteriorate as a result of the introduction by the illegal régime of new measures, including the purported assumption of republican status, aimed at repressing the African people in violation of General Assembly resolution 1514 (XV) of 14 December 1960,[36]

Recognizing the legitimacy of the struggle of the people of Southern Rhodesia to secure the enjoyment of their rights as set forth in the Charter and in conformity with the objectives of General Assembly resolution 1514 (XV),

Reaffirming that the present situation in Southern Rhodesia constitutes a threat to international peace and security,

Acting under Chapter VII of the Charter,[37]

1. *Condemns* the illegal proclamation of republican status of the Territory by the illegal régime in Southern Rhodesia;

2. *Decides* that Member States shall refrain from recognizing this illegal régime or from rendering any assistance to it;

3. *Calls upon* Member States to take appropriate measures, at the national level, to ensure that any act performed by officials and institutions of the illegal régime in Southern Rhodesia shall not be accorded any recognition, official or otherwise, including judicial notice, by the competent organs of their State;

4. *Reaffirms* the primary responsibility of the Government of the United Kingdom of Great Britain and Northern Ireland to enable the people of Zimbabwe to exercise their right to self-determination and independence, in accordance with the Charter of the United Nations and in conformity with General Assembly

---

[34] U.N. documents S/8954 and S/9252 and Add. 1.

[35] Concerning agreement by U.N. members "to accept and carry out the decisions of the Security Council in accordance with the present Charter."

[36] *Documents, 1960*, pp. 575–577.

[37] Dealing with "Action with Respect to Threats to the Peace, Breaches of the Peace, and Acts of Aggression."

resolution 1514 (XV), and urges that Government to discharge fully its responsibility;

5. *Condemns* all measures of political repression, including arrests, detentions, trials and executions, which violate fundamental freedoms and rights of the people of Southern Rhodesia;

6. *Condemns* the policies of the Governments of South Africa and Portugal, which continue to maintain political, economic, military, and other relations with the illegal régime in Southern Rhodesia in violation of the relevant resolutions of the United Nations;

7. *Demands* the immediate withdrawal of South African police and armed personnel from the Territory of Southern Rhodesia;

8. *Calls upon* Member States to take more stringent measures in order to prevent any circumvention by their nationals, organizations, companies and other institutions of their nationality, of the decisions taken by the Security Council in resolutions 232 (1966) and 253 (1968), all provisions of which shall fully remain in force;

9. *Decides,* in accordance with Article 41 of the Charter [38] and in furthering the objective of ending the rebellion, that Member States shall:

(*a*) Immediately sever all diplomatic, consular, trade, military and other relations that they may have with the illegal régime in Southern Rhodesia, and terminate any representation that they may maintain in the Territory;

(*b*) Immediately interrupt any existing means of transportation to and from Southern Rhodesia;

10. *Requests* the government of the United Kingdom, as the administering Power, to rescind or withdraw any existing agreements on the basis of which foreign consular, trade and other representation may at present be maintained in or with Southern Rhodesia;

11. *Requests* Member States to take all possible further action under Article 41 of the Charter to deal with the situation in Southern Rhodesia, not excluding any of the measures provided in that Article;

12. *Calls upon* Member States to take appropriate action to suspend any membership or associate membership that the illegal régime of Southern Rhodesia has in the specialized agencies of the United Nations;

13. *Urges* member States of any international or regional organizations to suspend the membership of the illegal régime of

[38] Concerning measures not involving the use of armed force which may be invoked by the Security Council to give effect to its decisions.

Southern Rhodesia from their respective organizations and to refuse any request for membership from that régime;

14. *Urges* Member States to increase moral and material assistance to the people of Southern Rhodesia in their legitimate struggle to achieve freedom and independence;

15. *Requests* the specialized agencies and other international organizations concerned, in consultation with the Organization of African Unity, to give aid and assistance to refugees from Southern Rhodesia and those who are suffering from oppression by the illegal régime of Southern Rhodesia;

16. *Requests* Member States, the United Nations, the specialized agencies and other international organizations in the United Nations system to make an urgent effort to increase their assistance to Zambia as a matter of priority with a view to helping it solve such special economic problems as it may be confronted with arising from the carrying out of the decisions of the Security Council on this question;

17. *Calls upon* Member States, in particular those with primary responsibility under the Charter for the maintenance of international peace and security, to assist effectively in the implementation of the measures called for by the present resolution;

18. *Urges,* having regard to the principle stated in Article 2 of the Charter, States not Members of the United Nations to act in accordance with the provisions of the present resolution;

19. *Calls upon* Member States to report to the Secretary-General by 1 June 1970 on the measures taken to implement the present resolution; [39]

20. *Requests* the Secretary-General to report to the Security Council on the progress of the implementation of the present resolution, the first report to be submitted no later than 1 July 1970; [40]

21. *Decides* that the Committee of the Security Council established in pursuance of resolution 253 (1968), in accordance with rule 28 of the provisional rules of procedure of the Council, shall be entrusted with the responsibility of:

(*a*) Examining such reports on the implementation of the present resolution as will be submitted by the Secretary-General;

(*b*) Seeking from Member States such further information regarding the effective implementation of the provisions laid down in the present resolution as it may consider necessary for the proper discharge of its duty to report to the Security Council;

[39] U.N. document S/9844 and Add. 1–3.
[40] U.N. document S/9853.

(*c*) Studying ways and means by which Member States could carry out more effectively the decisions of the Security Council regarding sanctions against the illegal régime of Southern Rhodesia and making recommendations to the Council;

22. *Requests* the United Kingdom, as the administering Power, to continue to give maximum assistance to the Committee and to provide the Committee with any information it may receive in order that the measures envisaged in the present resolution as well as resolutions 232 (1966) and 253 (1968) may be rendered fully effective;

23. *Calls upon* Member States, as well as the specialized agencies, to supply such information as may be sought by the Committee in pursuance of the present resolution;

24. *Decides* to maintain this item on its agenda for further action as appropriate in the light of developments.[41]

E. *Apartheid* in the Republic of South Africa.

(61) *Action by the United Nations Security Council, July 23, 1970.*

(a) *Strengthening of the Arms Embargo: Resolution 282 (1970).*[42]

(*Complete Text*)

The Security Council,

Having considered the question of race conflict in South Africa resulting from the policies of *apartheid* of the Government of the Republic of South Africa, as submitted by forty Member States,[43]

Reiterating its condemnation of the evil and abhorrent policies of *apartheid* and the measures being taken by the Govern-

[41] The Security Council met again in November 1970 at the request of Burundi, Nepal, Sierra Leone, Syria, and Zambia and unanimously adopted a resolution (S/RES/288 (1970), November 17, 1970) reaffirming its condemnation of Southern Rhodesia's illegal declaration of independence and calling on the United Kingdom "to take urgent and effective measures to bring to an end the illegal rebellion . . . and enable the people to exercise their right to self-determination. . . ." Details in *U.N. Monthly Chronicle,* December 1970, pp. 3–10.

[42] Text from U.N. Security Council, *Official Records: Twenty-Fifth Year* (S/INF/25), p. 12; adopted by a vote of 12–0 with 3 abstentions. For the context see *The United States in World Affairs, 1970,* Section 31.

[43] U.N. document S/9867.

ment of South Africa to enforce and extend those policies beyond
its borders,

Recognizing the legitimacy of the struggle of the oppressed
people of South Africa in pursuance of their human and political
rights as set forth in the Charter of the United Nations and the
Universal Declaration of Human Rights,[44]

Gravely concerned by the persistent refusal of the Government of South Africa to abandon its racist policies and to abide
by the resolutions of the Security Council and the General Assembly on this question and others relating to southern Africa,

Gravely concerned by the situation arising from violations of
the arms embargo called for in its resolutions 181 (1963) of 7
August 1963,[45] 182 (1963) of 4 December 1963 [46] and 191 (1964)
of 18 June 1964,[47]

Convinced of the need to strengthen the arms embargo called
for in the above resolutions,

Convinced further that the situation resulting from the continued application of the policies of *apartheid* and the constant
build-up of the South African military and police forces, made
possible by the continued acquisition of arms, military vehicles
and other equipment and of spare parts for military equipment
from a number of Member States and by local manufacture of
arms and ammunition under licences granted by some Member
States, constitutes a potential threat to international peace and
security,

Recognizing that the extensive arms build-up of the military
forces of South Africa poses a real threat to the security and sovereignty of independent African States opposed to the racial
policies of the Government of South Africa, in particular the
neighboring States,

1. *Reiterates* its total opposition to the policies of *apartheid*
of the Government of the Republic of South Africa;

2. *Reaffirms* its resolutions 181 (1963), 182 (1963) and 191
(1964);

3. *Condemns* the violations of the arms embargo called for in
resolutions 181 (1963), 182 (1963) and 191 (1964);

4. *Calls upon* all States to strengthen the arms embargo

(a) By implementing fully the arms embargo against South
Africa unconditionally and without reservations whatsoever;

(b) By withholding the supply of all vehicles and equipment

[44] *Documents, 1948,* pp. 430–435.
[45] Same, *1963,* pp. 355–356.
[46] Same, pp. 357–359.
[47] Same, *1964,* pp. 370–372.

for use of the armed forces and paramilitary organizations of South Africa;

(c) By ceasing the supply of spare parts for all vehicles and military equipment used by the armed forces and paramilitary organizations of South Africa;

(d) By revoking all licences and military patents granted to the South African Government or to South African companies for the manufacture of arms and ammunition, aircraft and naval craft or other military vehicles and by refraining from further granting such licences and patents;

(e) By prohibiting investment in, or technical assistance for, the manufacture of arms and ammunition, aircraft, naval craft, or other military vehicles;

(f) By ceasing provision of military training for members of the South African armed forces and all other forms of military co-operation with South Africa;

(g) By undertaking the appropriate action to give effect to the above measures;

5. *Requests* the Secretary-General to follow closely the implementation of the present resolution and report to the Security Council from time to time;

6. *Calls upon* all States to observe strictly the arms embargo against South Africa and to assist effectively in the implementation of the present resolution.

(b) **Explanation of the United States Abstention: Statement by William B. Buffum, Deputy United States Representative to the United Nations.**[48]

(*Complete Text*)

The United States abhors and totally rejects the doctrine of apartheid. The United States considers that apartheid and repressive measures adopted in South Africa for its implementation are in violation of South Africa's undertakings under the United Nations Charter. We oppose apartheid also since it is the antithesis of a cardinal principle of our basic belief that all men are created equal.

We are struggling to make this deep conviction of ours a reality, both at home and abroad. We are determined to eliminate

48 U.S./U.N. Press Release 100, July 23, 1970; text from *Department of State Bulletin*, August 17, 1970, pp. 203–205.

racial discrimination within our own borders. We are equally resolved to oppose vigorously all forms of racial discrimination elsewhere. President Nixon categorically so affirmed in discussing southern Africa in his February 18, 1970, report to our Congress on United States foreign policy for the 1970's.[49] He said:

Clearly there is no question of the United States condoning, or acquiescing in, the racial policies of the white-ruled regimes. For moral as well as historical reasons, the United States stands firmly for the pinciples of racial equality and self-determination.

Accordingly, we have strongly and repeatedly urged the Government of South Africa to change its racial policies, and we have warned that Government of the dangers inherent in the continued pursuit of its policies.

The United States does not believe it is in the interests of a long-term solution in this area to send arms and lethal equipment to South Africa. The United States has itself scrupulously avoided any contribution of lethal weapons to South Africa and continues to believe that it is in the interest of the total international community to do likewise. Mr. President [Guillermo Sevilla-Sacasa of Nicaragua], as early as 1962—before there was a Security Council embargo—the United States voluntarily prohibited the sale to South Africa of arms which could be used to enforce apartheid.[50] In August 1963—again on our own and before there was a Security Council embargo—we informed the Council that, effective the end of that calendar year, we would not sell any military equipment to South Africa,[51] subject only to our honoring existing contracts and our right to interpret our policy in the future in the light of requirements for assuring the maintenance of international peace and security. The United States solemnly and formally affirmed these obligations we had freely undertaken in voting in favor of the Security Council's resolutions of 1963 and 1964 which established an arms embargo against South Africa.[52]

We have faithfully carried out these obligations. We intend to continue to carry them out. Our own embargo on the sale of arms to South Africa was reaffirmed as late as March of this year. Let me reaffirm once again before the Security Council that the United States supports the Council's resolutions on the sale of arms to South Africa and that our Government would not be able

[49] Document 2.
[50] Cf. statement by Ambassador Adlai E. Stevenson, August 2, 1963, in *Documents, 1963*, p. 352.
[51] Same.
[52] Cf. notes 45–46 to Document 61 (a).

to associate itself with any measures which might result in an increase in the flow of arms to South Africa.

Mr. President, some of the preceding speakers have referred to arms supplied to South Africa by the United States over the last few years. I again affirm that deliveries currently being made consist entirely of some spare parts and stemmed from contracts entered into prior to the effective date of the United States embargo, specifically, December 31, 1963. I would also point out that deliveries of major items of military equipment under these contracts have long since been completed. It is a basic tenet of United States trade policy that valid contracts should be honored.

Mr. President, the United States is able to support the basic intent of the draft resolution [53] before us and many of its specific provisions. In particular, we fully endorse the expression of total opposition to the policy of apartheid and the reaffirmation of Resolutions 181, 182, and 191. We supported them, we have fully and faithfully abided by them, and would wish that all states had done likewise.

However, while the present text is a welcome improvement over the draft originally circulated,[54] we cannot support it in its entirety. It is clear that the more sweeping provisions contained in this draft resolution—provisions which go beyond the limits to which my Government can commit itself—cannot command the wide support in the Council that would make them effective. On the contrary, we would in all seriousness ask whether they may not carry with them the danger of weakening instead of strengthening the measure of compliance required to give practical effect to resolutions of this Council. We are concerned that their embodiment in this resolution may serve only to divide the Council, fail to fulfill their intended purpose, and thus operate to the detriment of both the people of South Africa and the United Nations.

We will therefore abstain when the Council votes on this text. We particularly regret the necessity for this decision in view of our longstanding record of support for and observance of earlier Council resolutions on this subject. We would have been happy to support a resolution which had unanimous support in the Council. We believe that such a conclusion to the recent debate would have contributed effectively to the achievement of our common objective. We have been and remain eager to assure that there is no misunderstanding, particularly in South Africa,

53 Document 61(a).
54 U.N. document S/9882.

that this Council remains unanimous in its condemnation of the policies of apartheid.

F. The Question of South West Africa (Namibia).

(62) Strengthening of Economic Sanctions: United Nations Security Council Resolution 283 (1970), Adopted July 29, 1970.[55]

(Complete Text)

The Security Council,

Reaffirming once more the inalienable right of the people of Namibia to freedom and independence recognized in General Assembly resolution 1514 (XV) of 14 December 1960,[56]

Reaffirming Security Council resolutions 264 (1969) of 20 March 1969[57] and 276 (1970) of 30 January 1970[58] in which the Council recognized the decision of the General Assembly to terminate the Mandate for South West Africa and assume direct responsibility for the Territory until its independence and in which the continued presence of the South African authorities in Namibia, as well as all acts taken by that Government on behalf of or concerning Namibia after the termination of the Mandate, were declared illegal and invalid,

Recalling its resolution 269 (1969) of 12 August 1969,[59]

Noting with great concern the continued flagrant refusal of the Government of South Africa to comply with the decisions of the Security Council demanding the immediate withdrawal of South Africa from the Territory,

Deeply concerned that the enforcement of South African laws and juridical procedures in the Territory have continued in violation of the international status of the Territory,

Reaffirming its resolution 282 (1970) of 23 July 1970[60] on the

[55] Text from U.N. Security Council, *Official Records: Twenty-Fifth Year* (S/INF/25), pp. 2–3; adopted by a vote of 13–0, with 2 abstentions. For the context of this and the following document see *The United States in World Affairs, 1970,* Section 32.

[56] Cf. note 36 to Document 60.

[57] Cf. Ambassador Yost's statement of March 20, 1969 in *Documents, 1968–69,* pp. 383–386.

[58] Establishing a Subcommittee of Experts; details in *U.N. Monthly Chronicle,* February 1970, pp. 3–13.

[59] Cf. Ambassador Yost's statement of August 11, 1969 in *Documents, 1968–69,* pp. 386–391.

[60] Document 61 (a).

arms embargo against the Government of South Africa and the significance of that resolution with regard to the Territory and people of Namibia,

Recalling the decision taken by the Security Council on 30 January 1970 to establish, in accordance with rule 28 of its provisional rules of procedure, an *Ad Hoc* Sub-Committee of the Council to study, in consultation with the Secretary-General, ways and means by which the relevant resolutions of the Council, including resolution 276 (1970), could be effectively implemented in accordance with the appropriate provisions of the Charter of the United Nations, in the light of the flagrant refusal of South Africa to withdraw from Namibia, and to submit its recommendations to the Council,

Having examined the report submitted by the *Ad Hoc* Sub-Committee [61] and the recommendations contained in that report,

Bearing in mind the special responsibility of the United Nations with regard to the Territory of Namibia and its people,

1. *Requests* all States to refrain from any relations—diplomatic, consular or otherwise—with South Africa implying recognition of the authority of the Government of South Africa over the Territory of Namibia;

2. *Calls upon* all States maintaining diplomatic or consular relations with South Africa to issue a formal declaration to the Government of South Africa to the effect that they do not recognize any authority of South Africa with regard to Namibia and that they consider South Africa's continued presence in Namibia illegal;

3. *Calls upon* all States maintaining such relations to terminate existing diplomatic and consular representation as far as they extend to Namibia, and to withdraw any diplomatic or consular mission or representative residing in the Territory;

4. *Calls upon* all States to ensure that companies and other commercial and industrial enterprises owned by, or under direct control of, the State cease all dealings with respect to commercial or industrial enterprises or concessions in Namibia;

5. *Calls upon* all States to withhold from their nationals or companies of their nationality not under direct governmental control, government loans, credit guarantees and other forms of financial support that would be used to facilitate trade or commerce with Namibia;

6. *Calls upon* all States to ensure that companies and other commercial enterprises owned by, or under direct control of, the

---

[61] U.N. document S/9863.

State cease all further investment activities, including concessions in Namibia;

7. *Calls upon* all States to discourage their nationals or companies of their nationality not under direct governmental control from investing or obtaining concessions in Namibia, and to this end to withhold protection of such investment against claims of a future lawful government of Namibia;

8. *Requests* all States to undertake without delay a detailed study and review of all bilateral treaties between themselves and South Africa in so far as these treaties contain provisions by which they apply to the Territory of Namibia;

9. *Requests* the Secretary-General to undertake without delay a detailed study and review of all multilateral treaties to which South Africa is a party and which, either by direct reference or on the basis of relevant provisions of international law, might be considered to apply to the Territory of Namibia;

10. *Requests* the United Nations Council for Namibia to make available to the Security Council the results of its study and proposals with regard to the issuance of passports and visas for Namibians, and to undertake a study and make proposals with regard to special passport and visa regulations to be adopted by States concerning travel of their citizens to Namibia;

11. *Calls upon* all States to discourage the promotion of tourism and emigration to Namibia;

12. *Requests* the General Assembly, at its twenty-fifth session, to set up a United Nations fund for Namibia[62] to provide assistance to Namibians who have suffered from persecution and to finance a comprehensive educational and training programme for Namibians, with particular regard to their future administrative responsibilities in the Territory;

13. *Requests* all States to report to the Secretary-General on measures they have taken in order to give effect to the provisions set forth in the present resolution;

14. *Decides* to re-establish, in accordance with rule 28 of its provisional rules of procedure, the *Ad Hoc* Sub-Committee on Namibia and to request the Sub-Committee to study further effective recommendations on ways and means by which the relevant resolutions of the Council can be effectively implemented in accordance with the appropriate provisions of the Charter of the United Nations, in the light of the flagrant refusal of South Africa to withdraw from Namibia;

15. *Requests* the Sub-Committee to study the replies submitted by Governments to the Secretary-General in pursuance

62 Reseolution 2679 (XXV), adopted December 9, 1970 by a vote of 104–2, with 8 abstentions.

of paragraph 13 of the present resolution and to report to the Council as appropriate;

16. *Requests* the Secretary-General to give every assistance to the Sub-Committee in the performance of its tasks;

17. *Decides* to remain actively seized of this matter.

(63) Advisory Opinion by the International Court of Justice: United Nations Security Council Resolution 284 (1970), Adopted July 29, 1970.[63]

(Complete Text)

The Security Council,

Reaffirming the special responsibility of the United Nations with regard to the Territory and the people of Namibia,

Recalling its resolution 276 (1970) of 30 January 1970 on the question of Namibia,[64]

Taking note of the report and recommendations [65] submitted by the *Ad Hoc* Sub-Committee established in pursuance of Security Council resolution 276 (1970),

Taking further note of the recommendation of the *Ad Hoc* Sub-Committee on the possibility of requesting an advisory opinion from the International Court of Justice,

Considering that an advisory opinion from the International Court of Justice would be useful for the Security Council in its further consideration of the question of Namibia and in furtherance of the objectives the Council is seeking,

1. *Decides* to submit, in accordance with Article 96, paragraph 1, of the Charter of the United Nations, the following question to the International Court of Justice, with the request for an advisory opinion which shall be transmitted to the Security Council at an early date:

"What are the legal consequences for States of the continued presence of South Africa in Namibia, notwithstanding Security Council resolution 276 (1970)?"; [66]

[63] Text from U.N. Security Council, *Official Records: Twenty-Fifth Year* (S/INF/25), p. 4; adopted by a vote of 12–0, with 3 abstentions.
[64] Cf note 58 to Document 62.
[65] Cf. note 61 to Document 62.
[66] The International Court of Justice handed down its advisory opinion on June 21, 1971; text in *International Legal Materials: Current Documents* (The American Society of International Law, Washington, D.C.), July 1971, pp. 677–722. The operative clauses of the advisory opinion read as follows:
"(1) that, the continued presence of South Africa in Namibia being

2. *Requests* the Secretary-General to transmit the present resolution to the International Court of Justice, in accordance with Article 65 of the Statute of the Court, accompanied by all documents likely to throw light upon the question.

G. The Invasion of the Republic of Guinea.[67]

(64) *Withdrawal of Invading Forces: United Nations Security Council Resolution 289 (1970), Adopted November 23, 1970.*[68]

(Complete Text)

The Security Council,

Having heard the statement made by the Permanent Representative of the Republic of Guinea,

Having taken note of the request made by the President [Sékou Touré] of the Republic of Guinea,[69]

1. *Demands* the immediate cessation of the armed attack against the Republic of Guinea;

2. *Demands* the immediate withdrawal of all external armed forces and mercenaries, together with the military equipment used in the armed attack against the territory of the Republic of Guinea;

3. *Decides* to send a special mission to the Republic of Guinea to report on the situation immediately;

4. *Decides* that this special mission be formed after consulta-

---

illegal, South Africa is under obligation to withdraw its administration from Namibia immediately and thus put an end to its occupaton of the Territory;

" (2) that States Members of the United Nations are under obligation to recognize the illegality of South Africa's presence in Namibia and the invalidity of its acts on behalf of or concerning Namibia, and to refrain from any acts and in particular any dealings with the Government of South Africa implying recognition of the legality of, or lending support or assistance to, such presence and administration;

" (3) that it is incumbent upon States which are not Members of the United Nations to give assistance, within the scope of subparagraph (2) above, in the action which has been taken by the United Nations with regard to Namibia."

[67] For the context of this group of documents see *The United States in World Affairs, 1970*, Section 31.

[68] Text from U.N. Security Council, *Official Records: Twenty-Fifth Year* (S/INF/25), p. 13; adopted unanimously.

[69] U.N. document S/9988.

tion between the President of the Security Council [George J. Tomeh of Syria] and the Secretary-General;

5. *Decides* to maintain the matter on its agenda.

(65) Condemnation of Portugal: United Nations Security Council Resolution 290 (1970), Adopted December 8, 1970.[70]

(Complete Text)

The Security Council,

Having considered with appreciation the report [71] of the Security Council Special Mission to the Republic of Guinea established under resolution 289 (1970) of 23 November 1970,[72]

Having heard further statements by the Permanent Representative of the Republic of Guinea,

Gravely concerned that the invasion of the territory of the Republic of Guinea on 22 and 23 November 1970 from Guinea (Bissau) was carried out by naval and military units of the Portuguese armed forces, and by the armed attack against the Republic of Guinea on 27 and 28 November 1970,

Gravely concerned that such armed attacks directed against independent African States pose a serious threat to the peace and security of independent African States,

Mindful of its responsibility to take effective collective measures for the prevention and removal of threats to international peace and security,

Recalling its resolutions 218 (1965) of 23 November 1965 and 275 (1969) of 22 December 1969 which condemned Portugal and affirmed that the situation resulting from the policies of Portugal both as regards the African population of its colonies and the neighbouring States adversely affects the peace and stability of the African continent,

Reaffirming the inalienable right of the people of Angola, Mozambique and Guinea (Bissau) to freedom and independence in accordance with the Charter of the United Nations and the provisions of General Assembly resolution 1514 (XV) of 14 December 1960,[73]

---

[70] Text from U.N. Security Council, *Official Records: Twenty-Fifth Year* (S/INF/25), pp. 13–14; adopted by a vote of 11–0, with 4 abstentions. For text of a statement by Ambassador Yost in explanation of the U.S. abstention see *Department of State Bulletin,* January 18, 1971, pp. 98–99.

[71] U.N. document S/10009 and Add. 1.

[72] Document 64.

[73] *Documents, 1960,* pp. 575–577.

Grieved at the loss of life and extensive damage caused by the armed attack and invasion of the Republic of Guinea,

1. *Endorses* the conclusions of the report of the Special Mission to the Republic of Guinea;

2. *Strongly condemns* the Government of Portugal for its invasion of the Republic of Guinea;

3. *Demands* that full compensation by the Government of Portugal be paid to the Republic of Guinea for the extensive damage to life and property caused by the armed attack and invasion and requests the Secretary-General to assist the Government of the Republic of Guinea in the assessment of the extent of the damage involved;

4. *Appeals* to all States to render moral and material assistance to the Republic of Guinea to strengthen and defend its independence and territorial integrity;

5. *Declares* that the presence of Portuguese colonialism on the African continent is a serious threat to the peace and security of independent African States;

6. *Urges* all States to refrain from providing the Government of Portugal with any military and material assistance enabling it to continue its repressive actions against the peoples of the Territories under its domination and against independent African States;

7. *Calls upon* the Government of Portugal to apply without further delay to the peoples of the Territories under its domination the principles of self-determination and independence in accordance with the relevant resolutions of the Security Council and General Assembly resolution 1514 (XV);

8. *Solemnly warns* the Government of Portugal that in the event of any repetition of armed attacks against independent African States, the Security Council shall immediately consider appropriate effective steps or measures in accordance with the relevant provisions of the Charter of the United Nations;

9. *Calls upon* the Government of Portugal to comply fully with all the resolutions of the Security Council, in particular the present resolution, in accordance with its obligations under Article 25 of the Charter; [74]

10. *Requests* all States, in particular Portugal's allies, to exert their influence on the Government of Portugal to ensure compliance with the provisions of the present resolution;

11. *Requests* the President of the Security Council [Yakov Malik of the U.S.S.R.] and the Secretary-General to follow closely the implementation of the present resolution;

12. *Decides* to remain actively seized of the matter.

[74] Cf. note 35 to Document 60.

VIII.
INTER-AMERICAN AFFAIRS

A. The Organization of American States.

(66) *First Special Session of the General Assembly of the Organization of American States, Washington, June 25-July 8, 1970.*[1]

(a) *Address by Secretary of State Rogers, Chairman of the United States Delegation, June 26, 1970.*[2]

(Complete Text)

On behalf of President Nixon and the people of the United States, I would like to express the warm welcome of our country to the Ministers and other officials attending this first meeting of the General Assembly of the Organization of American States under its revised charter.[3] I regret that I will have to leave on Sunday [June 29] for a previously scheduled visit to the Far East [4] and that because of the changes in dates of this meeting I will be able to be with you only for 2 days. There is no doubt in my mind that the days ahead will be fruitful in organizing the work of our new institutions—and I want to take this opportunity to offer any assistance that you may need while here in Washington.

---

[1] For the context see *The United States in World Affairs, 1970,* Section 29.
[2] Department of State Press Release 195, June 26, 1970; text from *Department of State Bulletin,* July 27, 1970, pp. 115–119.
[3] Protocol of Amendment to the Charter of the Organization of American States (Protocol of Buenos Aires), signed at Buenos Aires, February 27, 1967 and entered into force February 27, 1970; official text in Department of State, *Treaties and Other International Acts Series,* No. 6847. Summary of amendments and related material in *Documents, 1968–69,* pp. 399–405.
[4] For documentation on Secretary Rogers' two-week trip to the Philippines, South Vietnam, Japan, and the United Kingdom see *Department of State Bulletin,* August 3, 1970, pp. 133–149.

I should also like to take this opportunity, Mr. President [Fernando Amiano Tio, of the Dominican Republic], to extend my congratulations and very good wishes to you on your election as the President of this first General Assembly.

We in the United States are mindful that the roots of this body extend back to Simón Bolívar's first Congress of American States in 1826 and even before that to the war of liberation which Bolívar led and which had so many ties to our own war of independence. Our task is to apply the principles developed over our long history to making the inter-American system more responsive to the changing needs of the present time.

We have not attained all the goals of the charter, to be sure, though it is worth noting that, on the question of peace, our hemisphere in recent decades has a record unrivaled by that of any other major area. In our quest to provide for the betterment of all, we have many problems. We face, in differing degrees, issues of social unrest, poverty, decaying urban centers, et cetera—in addition to trade and other economic problems.

Added to our other heavy international commitments, these grave domestic problems place new burdens on the people of the United States. Nevertheless, the United States is fully aware of the need for common action to deal with the problems besetting all the peoples of our hemisphere.

To begin with, let me underscore that the United States does not, and will not, consider the interests of Latin America as secondary or of low priority. In no other area of the world are our basic long-range interests more deeply involved than in Latin America. Neither our other international interests nor our domestic concerns will reduce or tarnish the firmness of our commitment to the hemisphere.

It was in that conviction that President Nixon set out the principles of our new approach to Latin America.[5] Let me refer to them again:

—First, a firm commitment to the inter-American system—as exemplified by the Organization of American States.

—Second, respect for national identity and national dignity.

—Third, a firm commitment to continued U.S. assistance for hemisphere development.

—Fourth, a belief that the principal future pattern of this assistance must be U.S. support for Latin American initiatives and that this can best be achieved on a multilateral basis within the inter-American system.

—Fifth, a dedication to improving the quality of life in the

Western Hemisphere—to making people the center of our concerns.

In the 8 months which have followed since President Nixon spoke, our aim has been to implement those principles with specific actions. I would like to describe some of the things we have done.

ECONOMIC DEVELOPMENT AND TRADE

In economic development and trade, encouraging progress has already been made, which underlines our resolve to work together to realize the goals of the Alliance for Progress.[6]

Our first commitment, in the area of economic development, has been to strengthen the multilateral institutions of the region. As one step we have decided to submit our policies for economic development in the hemisphere for review by the Inter-American Committee on the Alliance for Progress (CIAP). We expect to make our first submission in the late summer or early fall of this year.

We are taking steps to give greater financial support to the Inter-American Development Bank, which has just completed its 10th year as a dynamic force for development. The U.S. share of the replenishment fund is $1.8 billion; the President is now asking Congress to approve the necessary implementing legislation.[7] This new fund will permit the bank to increase its lending in the hemisphere by 50 percent in the next 3 to 4 years.

Our trade policies are being adjusted to take into account, and encourage, the economic change in Latin America from an almost total dependence upon imports of manufactured products to a search for markets abroad for products you now manufacture. We want to see Latin American exports become more competitive. In the Special Committee on Consultation and Negotiations [CECON],[8] for example, we are working with you to identify obstacles impeding access to the U.S. market of over 800 Latin American products.

During the year we have also made efforts to reach agreement with other developed countries on a generalized system of prefer-

[6] The principles of the Alliance for Progress were embodied in the Charter of Punta del Este (Uruguay), signed August 17, 1961; text in *Documents, 1961*, pp. 416–432.

[7] International Financial Institutions Bill (Public Law 91–599, approved December 30, 1970). Cf. President Nixon's signature statement, December 30, 1970 in *Weekly Compilation of Presidential Documents*, January 4, 1971, p. 10.

[8] Cf. note 23 to Document 67.

ences for the exports of manufactured and semimanufactured products of the less developed nations.

In our assistance programs we are giving priority to support of local private investment and to promotion of Latin American exports both to the more industrialized countries and within Latin America itself. And we have implemented our policy of "untying" AID loans to allow purchases anywhere in the hemisphere.

In addition, we have undertaken to join with you in developing procedures within the inter-American system for advance consultation on trade policy initiatives by any of us that might prejudice the trade interests of other OAS members.

We believe the course of our partnership is the right one. It is adapted to meet the changes taking place in your countries and in mine. It maintains my Government's commitment to assist in the development of the hemisphere, yet takes fully into account the force of nationalism and the policy of each of your nations to bear the principal responsibility for your own destiny. It acknowledges that none of us—neither you in Latin America nor we in the United States—possess[es] all of the answers to our problems. And it emphasizes that these answers must be sought and found by all of us working together, each sharing in the providing as well as the receiving.

Here again the Inter-American Committee on the Alliance for Progress can contribute, not only by guiding and coordinating our efforts but also by stimulating member countries to choose economic and social development goals which have the greatest impact on the most people.

Structure of the OAS

The increased emphasis we wanted to give to nonpolitical matters in the revised charter is reflected in the elevation of the Economic and Social Council and the Council for Education, Science, and Culture to a level of equality with the Permanent Council of the OAS. At the same time the establishment of three Councils of equal level will put a greater management responsibility upon the general Secretariat of the Organization, which must serve all three.

These welcome changes emphasize the need to strengthen the structure of this Organization and of its Secretariat. We believe the Secretary General [Galo Plaza Lasso of Ecuador]—no less than the General Assembly to which he is ultimately responsible —must play an increasingly important unifying role. Thus, in order to make the most productive use of the resources of the

OAS, it will be all the more necessary to maintain a centralized OAS administration.

In this connection we must also make certain that the member governments receive a continuing appraisal of how programs are being carried out and goals are being met. We should seek adequate mechanisms to provide member governments with adequate inspection, appraisal, and evaluation.

Traditional Concerns and New Problems

I have briefly outlined our views on the promotion of trade and development in the hemisphere and on the structure of the OAS. I would like to touch on four other problems. Two involve traditional concerns: peacekeeping and the need to respond to emergency situations. Two are in different ways products of modern society: pollution of the environment and the issues raised by new forms of political terrorism.

Last year, when conflict broke out between Honduras and El Salvador, the OAS scored a notable achievement in peacemaking. The special OAS committee dispatched to the scene secured a cease-fire within 5 days. Since then the continuing involvement of the OAS has helped preserve the peace and advance the prospect of settlement. We can also take satisfaction from the new frontier pacification plan formulated by the OAS and agreed to with the participation of the Central American Foreign Ministers. These successes underscore that the inter-American system does have the capability of acting in the field of peace and security.

However, the successes should not obscure the need to settle disputes peacefully before they reach the stage of conflict. Upon approval of the statutes of the Inter-American Committee on Peaceful Settlement, together with the new role of the Permanent Council, we will set into motion improved machinery for the pacific settlement of disputes. I know that I express the view of all of us when I say I hope that this machinery will be utilized in as broad and constructive a way as possible.

In the Central American conflict the OAS not only helped in the role of peacemaking but also in the humanitarian tasks of protecting civilians and relieving suffering. More recently the tragedy caused by the earthquake in Peru [May 31]—to which the Peruvian people have reacted so bravely—has called for another humanitarian response. As elsewhere in the hemisphere this tragedy has produced great compassion and concern in the United States. I hope you will excuse this personal reference when I say that I am proud of the way the people of the United

States have responded with relief assistance and food supplies.[9] We, and I know all the countries represented here, extend our condolences to the people of Peru for the vast loss of life and suffering they have undergone.

In the Peruvian tragedy as well as in Central America, the Inter-American Emergency Aid Fund, created in 1965 at the initiative of our distinguished colleague the Foreign Minister of Mexico, has been helpful. In suggesting the establishment of this fund, Dr. [Antonio] Carrillo Flores proposed that it be used to assist victims of emergency situations, whether earthquakes, floods, or social disturbances.

These experiences suggest the need for reviewing the OAS capability in emergency situations. In particular there is a need for rapid and accurate assessment of requirements and for effective coordination of humanitarian assistance. Today an earthquake is involved. Tomorrow it may be a disturbance of another kind giving rise to the need to help. For example, when emergency evacuation of foreign nationals is necessary, perhaps the OAS could take a leadership role as has been done by other organizations elsewhere in the world.

Another new direction for OAS action might relate to the pollution, of the environment, which threatens us all. The United Nations has already directed its attention to this problem.[10] And the North Atlantic Treaty Organization last year formed a committee to coordinate joint pilot projects in environmental problems undertaken for the benefit of all its member countries.[11]

If the OAS considered initiating such a role, the undertaking would correspond to the greater emphasis we are giving under the revised charter to the field of science and technology.

TERRORISM AND KIDNAPING

The fourth issue which demands our immediate attention is on the agenda of this Assembly—the problem of terrorism, and particularly kidnaping and extortion.

We live in an era of increasing violence as a mode of dissent. None of our countries is immune to it. In dealing with the problem we must be most careful to distinguish between criminal acts of terrorism and legitimate expressions of discontent.

Bearing this in mind, I hope this Assembly can deal effectively

[9] Cf. *Weekly Compilation of Presidential Documents,* June 15, 1970, p. 756; same, June 29, 1970, pp. 810–811; same, July 6, 1970, pp. 860–861.
[10] Cf. U.N. General Assembly Resolution 2398 (XXIII), December 3, 1968; text in *Documents, 1968–69,* pp. 460–462.
[11] Cf. *NATO Letter,* February 1970, pp. 15–18.

with terrorism and kidnaping, especially in their international aspects. We support the proposal to brand them as common crimes and to treat them accordingly, both domestically and internationally. I hope the Assembly will address itself particularly to terrorism directed against representatives of foreign states. Such acts clearly and distinctly violate the principles governing the conduct of relations between states. We would suggest that the Assembly initiate steps to prepare a new international agreement defining these acts as international crimes and establishing appropriate measures to deal with them.

Terrorism and kidnaping on this continent affect states from other areas as well. As we all know too well, these crimes have already involved kidnapings of representatives of friendly nations outside the hemisphere. The inspiration for armed struggle and violence in our hemisphere also does not stem solely from forces within our countries. Therefore, I think it would be appropriate to appeal to all facets of world opinion to use their influence to help bring an end to such acts.

Mr. President, in the final analysis our efforts to solve the problems of our hemisphere will be measured by the extent to which what we do helps our people achieve the economic and social justice they desire and deserve. We must constantly look behind the programs, the reports, and the statistics for results— and ask ourselves if conditions of life are improving and if the pace of that improvement is fast enough.

The progress each of us wants should be the result of an effort that reflects, as our charter [12] puts it, "the desire of the American peoples to live together in peace." It is this desire that has motivated one of the most significant recent steps taken in the Americas—a step, it should be emphasized, taken as a result of a Latin American initiative. I refer to the Treaty for the Prohibition of Nuclear Weapons in Latin America.[13]

It was because the United States fully supports the hopes of the Latin American peoples to create a nuclear-free zone in their countries that we signed protocol II.[14]

Since that signing in 1968, the United States has been conducting the necessary technical reviews preparatory to ratification. I am now pleased to announce that this review has been completed and that President Nixon intends in the very near

12 Charter of the Organization of American States, signed at Bogotá, Colombia April 30, 1948; text in *Documents, 1948,* pp. 484–502.
13 Treaty for the Prohibition of Nuclear Weapons in Latin America (Treaty of Tlatelolco), opened for signature in Mexico City, February 14, 1967; text in *Documents on Disarmament, 1967,* pp. 69–83.
14 Text and related material in *Documents, 1968–69,* pp. 392–399.

future to submit protocol II to the United States Senate for its
advice and consent to ratification.[15]

Mr. President, to achieve the results for mankind that we seek
we need to work harmoniously in a partnership in which all
members cooperate—and none dominates. My delegation holds
the firm conviction that this can be done and that we can move
dramatically toward a major goal outlined in the OAS Charter:
"the consolidation on this continent, within the framework of
democratic institutions, of a system of individual liberty and
social justice based on respect for the essential rights of man." [16]

(b) Resolution on Acts of Terrorism and Kidnapping Adopted by the O.A.S. General Assembly June 30, 1970.[17]

(Complete Text)

GENERAL ACTION AND POLICY OF THE ORGANIZATION
WITH REGARD TO ACTS OF TERRORISM AND, ESPECIALLY,
THE KIDNAPPING OF PERSONS AND EXTORTION IN
CONNECTION WITH THAT CRIME

Whereas:

Acts of terrorism, and especially kidnapping of persons and
extortion connected with that crime, are occurring with increasing frequency and seriousness in this hemisphere;

Such acts have been characterized by the Permanent Council of
the Organization, in its resolution of May 15, 1970,[18] as such
cruel and irrational crimes that they attack the very spirit of
mercy of the American peoples and constitute common crimes,
whose seriousness makes them crimes against humanity;

The governments of the member states of the Organization
unanimously repudiate such acts, which constitute serious violations of the fundamental rights and freedoms of man; and those
governments are firmly determined to prevent the repetition of
such acts;

The political and ideological pretexts utilized as justification for
these crimes in no way mitigate their cruelty and irrationality
or the ignoble nature of the means employed, and in no way

---

[15] Document 70.
[16] *Documents, 1948,* p. 485.
[17] O.A.S. document AG/RES. 4 (I-E/70); adopted unanimously. Text from
Department of State Bulletin, July 27, 1970, p. 119.
[18] O.A.S. document CP/RES. 5 (7/70).

remove their character as acts in violation of essential human rights;

The member states of the Organization, in the exercise of their sovereignty and their territorial jurisdiction, have invariably reaffirmed the rights of the individual and the principles of universal morality;

The process of economic development and the social progress of the hemisphere, in which our governments are engaged not only directly but also through inter-American cooperation, are disturbed by the crimes in question;

Kidnapping and extortion connected with that crime, as well as offenses against the lives of representatives of foreign states and of other persons, are heinous crimes that have aroused world opinion and that shatter the very bases of friendly national and international relations; and

The proliferation of such crimes in the hemisphere creates a situation that requires prompt and effective measures on the part of the Organization and of its member states,

THE GENERAL ASSEMBLY

Resolves:

1. To condemn strongly, as crimes against humanity, acts of terrorism and especially the kidnapping of persons and extortion in connection with that crime.

2. Also to condemn such acts, when perpetrated against representatives of foreign states, as violations not only of human rights but also of the norms that govern international relations.

3. To declare that these acts constitute serious common crimes characterized by flagrant violation of the most elemental principles of the security of the individual and community as well as offenses against the freedom and dignity of the individual, the safeguarding of which should be a guiding criterion of every society.

4. To recommend to the member states that have not yet done so the adoption of such measures as they may deem suitable, in the exercise of their sovereignty, to prevent, and when appropriate to punish, crimes of this kind, defining them in their legislation.

5. To request the governments of the member states to facilitate, in accordance with their laws, an exchange of information that will help in the prevention and punishment of crimes of this kind.

6. To charge the Inter-American Juridical Committee with preparing an opinion on the procedures and measures necessary to make effective the purposes of this resolution. To this end,

the Committee shall hold a special meeting, which shall begin within sixty days of the closing date of this session of the General Assembly. The Committee shall conclude the work entrusted to it within sixty days of the date on which it meets for that purpose.

7. Also to charge the Inter-American Juridical Committee with preparing, within the period set in the preceding paragraph, one or more draft inter-American instruments on kidnapping, extortion, and assaults against persons, in cases in which these acts may have repercussions on international relations.

8. To request the Inter-American Juridical Committee to report on its work to the Permanent Council of the Organization, which may, on an urgent basis, convoke a special session of the General Assembly or order the holding of an inter-American specialized conference to consider the opinion and the draft or drafts prepared by the Committee.

THE GENERAL ASSEMBLY

Expresses:

Its adherence to the principles set forth in the American Declaration of the Rights and Duties of Man [19] and in the economic and social standards of the Charter of the Organization of American States.

B. Economic and Social Problems.

(67) Eighth Special Meeting of the Inter-American Economic and Social Council, Caracas, Venezuela, February 3–6, 1970.[20]

> *(a) Message from President Nixon, Read to the Council by Charles A. Meyer, Assistant Secretary of State for Inter-American Affairs, February 4, 1970.*[21]

(Complete Text)

Dear Mr. Chairman [*Sir Eric E. Williams, Prime Minister of Trinidad and Tobago*]:

[19] Adopted at Bogotá, Colombia on May 2, 1948; text in *Documents, 1948,* pp. 528–532.
[20] For the context see *The United States in World Affairs, 1970,* Section 27.
[21] Text from *Weekly Compilation of Presidential Documents,* February 9, 1970, pp. 130–131.

I send to you and to the other distinguished representatives of the Americas my cordial greetings and my very best wishes for the success of the work which you begin this evening.

The great concerns that this Eighth Special Meeting of the Inter-American Economic and Social Council address lie at the heart of the more mature and more effective relationship among us that we all seek. Yet those concerns—some of them complex, many of them technical, all of them difficult—are only expressions of a still more fundamental concern: the people of the Americas and the quality of their lives.

Today the leaders of the Americas share a historic opportunity —the chance to bring our peoples the benefits of modern science and technology and to give to them and to their children fuller and more productive lives. There is no task which deserves greater effort and attention than the one of securing peace, development and progress for our own hemisphere. There is no subject with which I have been more concerned.

During the first year of my Administration, I have devoted a great deal of attention and thought to how the United States can effectively contribute its share of this common responsibility, and to how to redefine and reinvigorate our relationship so as to meet the needs and realities of the 1970's.

As you know, my Administration undertook a very careful and systematic study of the problems of the region and of the premises that should underlie our policies. In my address to the Inter-American Press Association last October,[22] I expressed the results of that study in the form of the organizing concepts around which I believe United States policy toward this region should be built. In that speech I proposed that we forge a vigorous new partnership based upon shared responsibility, increased communication and interchange, and respect for each other's national identity and national dignity. In that speech I said that our goal for the 70's should be a decade of Action for Progress in the Americas.

I reaffirm that goal tonight.

To translate our words into actions and to find ways in which the United States can take effective action to carry out its share of the common responsibility toward our peoples—these are now major tasks of my Government. We have made a beginning, but only a beginning. We have a long way to go.

Some of the measures which I have already instituted in the fields of trade, development assistance, science and technology have already been described by the United States delegation to the meetings of the Special Committee of this Council which

22 *Documents, 1968–69,* pp. 429–438.

were held in Washington last November [23] and here in Caracas last week. All of you know, for example, of the major effort we are pushing to achieve a liberal system of worldwide generalized trade preferences; of the liberalization of the untying provisions of our assistance loans which I have authorized to give the hemisphere special treatment; of the major steps we are prepared to take to support your efforts to broaden scientific and technological exchange.

I want to take this occasion to report to you tonight an additional action which I have taken to give further substance to my commitment that the United States will do its part.

I have just presented to the Congress my recommendations for the budget for the United States Government for Fiscal Year 1971.[24] In constructing that budget, I tried to give special attention to the needs of the hemisphere and to include a number of new elements to carry out the concept of partnership.

I have included in the budget a contingency account of $540 million to provide for expanded multilateral assistance through the international financial institutions. A very substantial part of these funds is to be available to respond to new proposals for replenishment of the funds of the Inter-American Development Bank.[25]

In the 1971 budget I have also requested $556 million in AID funds for the hemisphere. This is the largest of the regional AID programs and reflects an increase of about 20% over the 1970 appropriation levels. Included in this total is over $100 million in support of the kinds of programs that have been discussed here. For the most significant of these, we have estimated the following amounts in the budget.

—$30 million for assistance in developing securities markets and securities commissions;

—$20 million for the promotion of tourism, including establishment of essential infrastructure;

—$20 million to support science and technology efforts;

—$15 million to support trade expansion.

In addition to the foregoing, I have decided to advance the request for funds to fill the United States subscription of $206 million to the callable capital of the Inter-American Development ment Bank which had originally been planned for 1971. Accord-

[23] For a U.S. statement made before a meeting of the Special Committee on Consultations and Negotiations, November 18, 1969, see *Department of State Bulletin*, December 29, 1969, pp. 631–634.

[24] Document 4.

[25] Cf. note 7 to Document 66.

ingly, I will shortly submit to the Congress a request for a supplement to the 1970 budget to cover this item.

Obviously, we still face very serious problems and very large obstacles to progress; there are often practical and serious limits and constraints which inhibit our efforts to meet the aspirations that surge out of our societies. I know, for example, that in the field of trade policy there are highly complex, highly technical and often conflicting factors which sometimes make agreement difficult. I cannot guarantee that we will always be able to meet your aspirations. But the point I want to stress is that my Administration will continue vigorously and persistently to try to overcome obstacles to satisfactory agreements, and to do all it practically can to assure that our trade policies support the region's development.

Since we are a community of widely diverse peoples, it will not be easy to forge a new partnership. Our perceptions of self interest and of reality are often different. Our emotional reactions are different. As I said last October, partnership, mutuality of interests, do not flow naturally. We must work at them. The United States for its part will do so energetically and sincerely.

I take this occasion, Mr. Chairman, to pledge to the peoples of America that my Administration will strive to demonstrate in action our commitment to progress and to the enhancement of the dignity of life in this Hemisphere. I pledge to you that I will continue personally to direct the attack of the United States on the problems that all of us confront as we proceed together on this difficult but inescapable task—to give to our peoples and to their children peace, prosperity, justice and dignity.

RICHARD NIXON

(b) **Statement by Assistant Secretary of State Meyer, February 5, 1970.**[26]

(*Excerpt*)

*　　*　　*

With your permission, Mr. Chairman, I should like to mention for the record some of the steps taken and proposals made by the United States in these last few months. For convenience, I shall address the three major categories on which we have all

[26] Department of State Press Release 32, February 5, 1970; text from *Department of State Bulletin,* March 2, 1970, pp. 256–259.

been working: first, trade; second, development assistance; third, science and technology.

In the field of trade:

—President Nixon has broken new ground in committing the United States Government to press for a liberal, worldwide system of generalized preferences for all developing countries. The benefits of such a system would be great, and the United States is working hard to bring it about. In response to Latin American requests we are also studying measures specifically designed to help the economically relatively less developed countries under a generalized preference system.

—The United States has agreed to take a number of other steps to stimulate exports from hemisphere countries. My Government has pledged: increased assistance to the export promotion activities of the Latin American countries including those being undertaken by the Inter-American Export Promotion Center; a proposal to eliminate duties on products of special interest to Latin America that are not produced in substantial quantities in the United States; Export-Import Bank technical assistance for developing export credit facilities; a commitment to seek an increase in the duty-free allowance for certain liquors for U.S. tourists returning from other hemisphere countries; and an affirmation for Latin America of our "standstill" policy on new trade restrictions, which was personally directed by President Nixon.

In the field of development assistance:

—President Nixon has proposed that multilateral mechanisms within the inter-American system be given increased responsibility for operations and decisions. The scope and nature of the mechanisms will, of course, be shaped in the dialogue of partners in the months to come. To this end, my delegation has announced an offer by the United States to provide an initial grant of $3 million to CIAP [Inter-American Committee on the Alliance for Progress] and/or IDB to strengthen technical staff and establish field missions which our Latin colleagues decided should go most appropriately to CIAP. The U.S. delegation has also offered to provide $15 million to a fund that would enable CIAP and/or IDB to play a greater role in identifying and preparing project proposals.

—The United States has agreed to submit to CIAP, for its review, U.S. economic and financial programs as they affect the other nations of the hemisphere.

—The United States has offered its cooperation in a study of the debt service problem by the appropriate international lending institutions. Moreover, the United States stands ready to join in an approach to the other creditor nations. Over 65 percent of the payments of the Latin American countries due in the next 5 years is owed to the European countries and Japan, and only 30 percent to the United States. The cooperation of all major donors is clearly required to make this effort a success.

—In June, the President authorized the elimination of the "additionality" requirement in connection with procurement financed by U.S. program-loan dollars. Effective November 1, the President announced the untying of AID loan dollars to permit procurement not only in the United States but anywhere in Latin America.[27] In response to Latin American concerns, President Nixon recently authorized the retroactive application of the untying decision to loans made before November 1, when the borrower so requests and where the procurement process has not yet been initiated.

—In another response to Latin American concern, President Nixon directed that, with regard to procurement made in Latin America under AID loans, a 50–50 test of origin will apply instead of the 90–10 test of origin, which will continue to apply for U.S. products financed under such loans.

—The President has approved complete removal of special letter of credit procedures applicable to dollars used for local cost procurement by AID and the Fund for Special Operations of the Inter-American Development Bank.

—In November, the United States announced its intention to expand technical assistance in establishing national and regional capital markets and in easing access to American capital markets. To help implement this offer, the United States has now taken a number of specific initiatives, including a specific offer to provide up to $5 million to CIAP as a special fund to help finance country studies on the establishment of capital markets.

—The United States has announced its willingness to expand its program of financial support to the local private sector in Latin America.

—In support of economic integration in Latin America, the United States has reiterated its offers for financial assistance to the Andean Group, the Caribbean Free Trade Association, the Central American Common Market, and to the eventual Latin American Common Market when the necessary preliminary steps have been taken.

—In the area of physical integration, President Nixon has

<hr>

27 Cf. *Documents, 1968–69*, p. 434.

sent a message to the U.S. Congress urging appropriation of funds for the completion of the Pan-American Highway through the Darien Gap in Panama and Colombia.

—We will support the inter-American sponsorship of the Year of the Americas in the early 1970's. The Year of the Americas should serve as a focus of accelerated development of Latin American tourist potential and the occasion for special Americas-oriented cultural, educational, and informational programs in which private and governmental institutions would take part.

—The United States no longer imposes limitations on the exports of similar commodities in the negotiation and implementation of P.L. 480 sales agreements with Latin America. These "offset" provisions had been a long-time contentious issue in our concessional sales of agricultural commodities.

In the field of science and technology:

—The International Committee of the Federal Council for Science and Technology has recently established a Latin American subcommittee to work out specific ways in which U.S. scientific and technological skills can be applied to Latin American development. This subcommittee is also looking for ways to apply the scientific knowledge gained from the exploration of space to the solution of development problems in the hemisphere.

—Provisions are being worked out to make available U.S. Government-owned patents useful to the development of the hemisphere.

—The President's Office of Science and Technology, in cooperation with AID, is developing a program for the training and orientation of Latin American specialists in the field of scientific and technical information.

—We have indicated our support for regional programs of scientific and technological development and for encouragement of Latin American cooperation on a bilateral and regional basis in scientific teaching and research. We propose to work closely in these areas with the Executive Committee of the Inter-American Cultural Council and the Inter-American Committee on Science and Technology, and we look forward to participating in an OAS-sponsored conference to be held next year on the application of science and technology to Latin America.

Mr. Chairman, this partial list of United States initiatives and commitments does not, of course, reflect the new actions and proposals announced by President Nixon in his message to you. The record I have cited here must be viewed in the perspective of that message.

In all that I have said, I do not suggest that we have met or solved every great problem. The problems that we face together are not susceptible to easy solution. Nor do I suggest that we have acted in every area in which you have asked us to act. We all should recognize that each of our societies must deal with practical constraints. But as President Nixon has pointed out, my Government is determined to do all it can to remove such constraints.

We won't achieve perfection instantaneously; we won't achieve it without continuing the dialogue we have started, without continuing the search for answers that are satisfactory to all of us. And even then perfection will not be within our grasp. Our hope is a better, a fuller, and a freer life.

We have learned much about each other in the Alliance we have undertaken together. With regard to our ministerial meetings in this IA–ECOSOC, all those present from Port-of-Spain to Caracas have agreed that the form of the meetings must change—no longer just words—but what? In this case and on this date and here in Caracas I urge that the most important responsibility of this ministerial meeting is to define or agree to define the future functions of this vital inter-American mechanism within the framework of our new OAS Charter.[28] Our organization must be flexible but well organized. We must know who is doing what and where. This certainly is a ministerial responsibility.

The future is immensely challenging. A young generation of dedicated Latin Americans is prepared to carry forward and to give form to the image of development in this challenging future. It is better prepared than any of our generation. We have much to learn from youth, and the inter-American system can serve as a forum for its concerns and aspirations.

I am persuaded that the course we have embarked upon is the right one. It acknowledges that we do not have all or even very many of the answers to the great problems of development and that these answers must be sought and found by all of us working together. Above all, it foresees that together we are and will be engaged in a process, a process in which the forms and techniques of cooperation will evolve as we gain experience.

*　　*　　*

[28] Cf. note 3 to Document 66.

(68) *Eleventh Annual Meeting of the Board of Governors of the Inter-American Development Bank, Punta del Este, Uruguay, April 20–24, 1970: Statement by Secretary of the Treasury David M. Kennedy, U.S. Governor of the Bank, April 23, 1970.*[29]

(Excerpt)

*   *   *

INCREASE IN RESOURCES

The main task of this meeting is to make adequate provision for obtaining the capital resources needed by the Bank in the first half of its second decade of lending. I have been authorized by President Nixon to announce that the United States is prepared to join Latin American efforts in accomplishing this task. In the context of a proposal with full Latin American support, we would be prepared to approach the U.S. Congress promptly for increases in both our Ordinary Capital subscription and our contribution to the Fund for Special Operations.[30] Specifically, the United States would be prepared to seek legislative authority for

—an increase in its paid-in Ordinary Capital subscription of $150 million combined with a $674 million increase in its callable Ordinary Capital subscription, both as our established share of a $2 billion overall increase in the Bank's Ordinary Capital resources.

—a substantial contribution to the Fund for Special Operations as part of an overall increase in Fund resources which would reflect the progress Latin economies have made these past 10 years, as well as their commitment to the role of multilateral institutions in development.

Resources should be sought in a magnitude which will cover requirements foreseen for the Bank in a 3- to 5-year period. They should permit the Bank to provide half again as much financing per year as the approximately $600 million which the Bank committed to loans in 1969. Moreover, they should ensure funding for new types and directions of activities that are now under preliminary consideration in the Bank.

But provision for the future requires more than money alone.

[29] Text from *Department of State Bulletin*, May 11, 1970, pp. 658–661; for the context see *The United States in World Affairs, 1970*, Section 27.
[30] Cf. note 7 to Document 66.

It requires adaptation to reflect new realities in the seventies. It requires new relationships beyond the hemisphere to reflect Latin America's growing integration into the world economy and the world's growing commitment to multilateral development financing.

I have three major areas in mind where beneficial changes could be made. First, the present practice of extending Fund for Special Operations loans on a local-currency repayable basis involves the potential problem of excess accumulations of such currencies in the Bank's accounts. A shift to a policy of repayment in the currencies lent, combined with an appropriate easing of repayment terms as necessary, would avoid the problem. This would permit the Fund ultimately to become a revolving source of hard-currency financing. I understand that a move in this direction already has widespread support.

Second, our concern for achieving more balanced growth in the hemisphere suggests that the financial needs of the least developed members should have first claim on the Bank's concessional-loan resources. The opposite side of the same coin is that the region's more advanced countries should place relatively greater reliance on Ordinary Capital financing. This could be considered a cooperative contribution on the part of the stronger countries toward self-help in the hemispheric sense. It would also complement the willingness of the larger members to allow a greater usefulness of their local-currency subscriptions to the Fund for Special Operations. In this latter connection an expansion of the group of countries allowing this broader use would be widely applauded.

Finally, I believe that multiple benefits would accrue not only to the Bank but to Latin American development in general if other developed countries—regional and nonregional—could be brought within the Bank's membership. Additional Ordinary Capital resources would become available, and access to capital markets would be easier. Membership would also elicit additional concessional-loan resources more effectively. In the light of experience elsewhere, I am confident that these benefits can be obtained without changing the essentially regional character of the Bank. Indeed, it is my confidence in the permanent Latin character of our Bank which permits this judgment. Serious efforts to move in this desirable direction have important and broadening support, and steps are needed now to move toward the removal of existing barriers. This is the time to begin. I strongly urge that the Board of Governors take the necessary steps which will lead to opening our doors to Canada and others.

The provision of the resources called for and the adoption of the policy changes recommended entail real burdens and real sacrifices for all of us. Nevertheless—and with full consideration of the intense competing demands for budgetary resources—I offer full assurance of President Nixon's readiness to support these financial and policy measures. I believe such support constitutes solid evidence of our commitment to Latin America and to hemispheric development.

*   *   *

(69) Establishment of the Inter-American Social Development Institute: Statement by President Nixon, August 19, 1970.[31]

(Complete Text)

In accordance with Section 401 of the Foreign Assistance Act of 1969,[32] I submitted Monday [August 17] to the Senate for confirmation a Board of Directors for the Inter-American Social Development Institute.[33]

I have also directed that $10 million of economic assistance funds be transferred to the Institute to finance its initial operations.

The Institute will provide grant support for innovative, experimental programs undertaken primarily by private non-profit organizations. It is designed as a pilot project to bring the dynamism of U.S. and Latin American private groups to bear on development problems through people-to-people programs, and to help broaden the participation of individuals in the processes of development.

The Institute will be limited in size and scope of operations to help keep it on a path of creative innovation. It will be separate from existing government agencies and it will not have personnel permanently assigned abroad. It is my hope that the Institute will develop a fresh approach to support new and experimental efforts by private organizations to contribute to social and institutional development, particularly in the areas of education and agriculture. The Board of Directors will, of course, establish detailed operating guidelines for the Institute.

The Director of the Office of Management and Budget

[31] Text from Weekly Compilation of Presidential Documents, August 24, 1970, p. 108.
[32] Public Law 91–175, approved December 30, 1969. For President Nixon's statement on signing the measure see Weekly Compilation of Presidential Documents, January 5, 1970, pp. 9–10.
[33] Same, August 24, 1970, p. 1079.

[George P. Shultz] will assist the Board of Directors in forming the Institute. He will also conduct by June 1971 a review of the Institute's operations and funding requirements, including its relationship to any new organizational arrangements for foreign aid programs which may be proposed.

C. Treaty for the Prohibition of Nuclear Weapons in Latin America (Treaty of Tlatelolco), Signed February 14, 1967.[34]

(70) *Additional Protocol II to the Treaty for the Prohibition of Nuclear Weapons: Message from President Nixon to the Senate Requesting Its Advice and Consent to Ratification, August 13, 1970.*[35]

(Complete Text)

To the Senate of the United States:

I transmit herewith Additional Protocol II[36] to the Treaty for the Prohibition of Nuclear Weapons in Latin America, with a view to receiving the advice and consent of the Senate to its ratification. The Additional Protocol was signed on behalf of the United States on April 1, 1968.[37]

For the information of the Senate, I transmit also the report by the Secretary of State[38] with respect to the Protocol and a copy of the Treaty to which it relates.

The Treaty for the Prohibition of Nuclear Weapons in Latin America, done at Mexico City February 14, 1967, is the first successful attempt to create a nuclear-free zone in a populated region of the world. The Treaty is limited to states located in the Latin American region and is already in force among 16 Latin American nations.

Additional Protocol II is designed for nuclear-weapon states, which are not eligible to sign the Treaty itself. It calls upon them to respect the denuclearized status of Latin America, not to contribute to violation of the Treaty, and not to use or threaten to use nuclear weapons against the Treaty parties.

---

[34] Cf. note 13 to Document 66 (a).

[35] Text from *Weekly Compilation of Presidential Documents*, August 17, 1970, pp. 1063–1064; for the context see *The United States in World Affairs, 1970*, Section 28.

[36] Department of State, *Treaties and Other International Acts Series*, No. 7137; text in *Documents, 1968–69*, pp. 392–394.

[37] Cf. Vice-President Hubert H. Humphrey's remarks at the signing ceremony in same, 398–399.

[38] Text of Secretary Rogers' report of July 16, 1970 in *Department of State Bulletin*, September 14, 1970, pp. 306–308.

It is in the best interests of the United States to assume these obligations toward the Latin American countries bound by the Treaty. By creating this nuclear-free zone the nations of Latin America have made an important contribution to peace and security in the Western Hemisphere. Ratification by the United States of Additional Protocol II would not only indicate our support for the Latin American nuclear-free zone but would reinforce our other arms control efforts such as the Non-Proliferation Treaty.[39]

I recommend that the Senate give early and favorable consideration to Additional Protocol II and give its advice and consent to ratification,[40] subject to the statement which accompanies the report of the Secretary of State. That statement, which is similar to the one made by the United States at the time of signature,[41] expresses our understanding concerning territories and territorial claims, transit and transport privileges, non-use of nuclear weapons, and the definition of "nuclear weapon." The statement also reaffirms our willingness to make available nuclear explosion services for peaceful purposes on a nondiscriminatory basis under appropriate international arrangements.

RICHARD NIXON

The White House
    August 13, 1970

D. The United States and Mexico.

(71) Meeting of President Nixon and President Gustavo Díaz Ordaz, Puerto Vallarta, Jalisco, Mexico, August 20–21, 1970: Joint Statement, August 21, 1970.[42]

(Complete Text)

President Gustavo Diaz Ordaz and President Richard Nixon welcomed the opportunity to renew their personal friendship

39 *Documents, 1968–69,* pp. 62–68.
40 The Senate gave its advice and consent to ratification, with understandings and declarations, on April 19, 1971; Protocol II entered into force for the U.S. May 12, 1971.
41 *Documents, 1968–69,* pp. 396–398; text of proposed U.S. statement in *Department of State Bulletin,* September 14, 1970, p. 309.
42 Text from *Weekly Compilation of Presidential Documents,* August 24, 1970, pp. 1094–1095.

and the informal conversations begun at their meeting at Amistad Dam in September 1969.[43] The two Presidents reviewed overall relations between the two countries and discussed specifically (1) a comprehensive boundary settlement between the two countries, (2) the problem of salinity in the waters of the lower Colorado River which are delivered to Mexico, and (3) cooperation in combatting illicit traffic in narcotics.

The two Presidents agreed on the principles which were proposed to them by their respective Secretaries for Foreign Relations to be incorporated in a treaty settling all boundary differences between the United States and Mexico and establishing procedures for averting such differences in the future. Their agreement includes the disposition of all territory that had currently been in dispute and particularly the Presidio/Ojinaga dispute pending since 1907. It also provides for the re-establishment of the middle of the Rio Grande (Rio Bravo) as the boundary between the United States and Mexico, wherever it has lost this character, for measures to resolve any boundary questions that might arise as a result of future deviations of the Rio Grande and Colorado River from their present course and for the establishment of fixed maritime boundaries in the Gulf of Mexico and the Pacific Ocean.

Further details on the agreement are being released jointly today by the Secretary for Foreign Relations and the Secretary of State.[44] The two Presidents emphasized their belief that agreement on these principles is an historic achievement and, that once formalized and ratified according to constitutional procedures, the resultant treaty will be one of the most significant agreements between their two governments in this century.

The two Presidents also discussed the salinity problem that has existed on the lower Colorado River for several years. President Nixon noted that the United States, looking toward a new agreement, has proposed certain new measures that would result in significant improvements in the waters received by Mexico. President Diaz Ordaz said that the Mexican Government regards this proposal as constructive and will study it carefully. The two Presidents instructed their representatives on the International Boundary and Water Commission to examine these proposals in

---

[43] September 8, 1969; documentation in *Weekly Compilation of Presidential Documents,* September 13, 1969, pp. 1238–1242.
[44] Text of White House announcement and statement of principles, August 21, 1970, in *Department of State Bulletin,* September 14, 1970, pp. 296–300. The boundary treaty was signed in Mexico City on November 23, 1970; for text of Department of State announcement see same, December 21, 1970, pp. 765–766.

detail and to make appropriate recommendations. They also agreed to reiterate the policy which the two governments have followed during recent years to consult before undertaking works which could cause natural problems similar to that mentioned in this paragraph.

President Diaz Ordaz and President Nixon reaffirmed their determination to suppress the illicit international traffic in marijuana, narcotics and dangerous drugs which has endangered the well-being of both countries. They expressed satisfaction at the vigorous efforts against the illicit use of narcotics on both sides of the border and the high spirit of cooperation which prevails between the two governments. President Nixon congratulated the Mexican Government on the success of its campaign to prevent production and illicit trafficking in narcotics. Both Presidents instructed their Attorneys General [John N. Mitchell and Lic. Julio Sanchez Vargas], who met simultaneously with them, and other appropriate authorities of their governments, to maintain the closest cooperation in this field.[45]

The two Presidents also discussed the broad subject of trade between the two countries and agreed that they would seek ways to encourage a continued growth in their bilateral trade. President Nixon assured President Diaz Ordaz of his desire to encourage trade between the two countries.

The two Presidents expressed their gratification over additional recent examples of the close cooperation between the two countries, in particular the signing of (1) a Civil Air Agreement,[46] (2) a Weather Agreement,[47] and (3) a Treaty for the Recovery and Return of Stolen Archeological, Historical and Cultural Properties and for the promotion of cultural exchanges between the two countries.[48]

During their conversations, the two Presidents reiterated their desire to continue efforts to better the understanding between their two peoples and to contribute to the mutual respect and

[45] Text of declaration on the problem of illicit narcotics traffic in same, September 14, 1970, p. 300.

[46] Entered into force July 1, 1970 by exchange of notes signed in Mexico City and Tlatelolco; text in Department of State, *Treaties and Other International Acts Series*, No. 6917.

[47] Entered into force August 1, 1970 by exchange of notes signed at Mexico City and Tlatelolco July 31, 1970; text in Department of State, *Treaties and Other International Acts Series*, No. 6941.

[48] Department of State announcement, July 17, 1970, and text of treaty signed on the same day at Mexico City in *Department of State Bulletin*, August 17, 1970, pp. 206–207. The U.S. Senate gave its advice and consent to ratification on February 10, 1971 and the treaty entered into force on March 24, 1971 (Department of State, *Treaties and Other International Acts Series*, No. 7088).

close friendship which have made the relationship between their two countries an example to all nations. They agreed that their respective Foreign Secretaries and Ambassadors should continue the discussion of matters of common interest. President Diaz Ordaz expressed to President Nixon his satisfaction with their meeting and the value he placed on their exchange of views. President Nixon congratulated President Diaz Ordaz on the many significant accomplishments of his administration, and expressed his great affection for Mexico and his deep gratitude for the warmth of the reception given him and Mrs. Nixon by the Government and the people of Mexico.

E. The United States and Canada.

(72) United States Opposition to the Extension by Canada of High Seas Jurisdiction: Department of State Statement, April 15, 1970.[49]

(Complete Text)

Last week the Canadian Government introduced in the House of Commons two bills dealing with pollution in the Arctic, fisheries, and the limits of the territorial sea.[50] The enactment and implementation of these measures would affect the exercise by the United States and other countries of the right to freedom of the seas in large areas of the high seas and would adversely affect our efforts to reach international agreement on the use of the seas.

The bills seek to establish pollution zones in Arctic waters up to 100 miles from every point of Canadian coastal territory above the 60th parallel. Within these zones, Canada would assert the right to control all shipping, to prescribe standards of vessel construction, navigation, and operation, and to prohibit, if Canada deemed it necessary, the free passage of vessels in those waters. Additionally, the legislation seeks to authorize the establishment of exclusive Canadian fisheries in areas of the high seas beyond 12 miles, such as the Gulf of St. Lawrence and the Bay of Fundy, and of a 12-mile territorial sea off Canada's coasts.

International law provides no basis for these proposed unilat-

---

[49] Department of State Press Release 121, April 15, 1970; text from *Department of State Bulletin*, May 11, 1970, pp. 610–611. For the context see *The United States in World Affairs, 1970,* Section 41.
[50] On April 1, 1970; cf. *External Affairs* (Canada), May 1970, pp. 130–131.

eral extensions of jurisdiction on the high seas, and the United States can neither accept nor acquiesce in the assertion of such jurisdiction.

We are concerned that this action by Canada, if not opposed by us, would be taken as precedent in other parts of the world for other unilateral infringements of the freedom of the seas. If Canada had the right to claim and exercise exclusive pollution and resources jurisdiction on the high seas, other countries could assert the right to exercise jurisdiction for other purposes, some reasonable and some not, but all equally invalid according to international law. Merchant shipping would be severely restricted, and naval mobility would be seriously jeopardized. The potential for serious international dispute and conflict is obvious.

The United States has long sought international solutions rather than national approaches to problems involving the high seas. We are working for appropriate action within the United Nations framework looking toward the conclusion of a new international treaty dealing with the limit of the territorial sea,[51] guaranteeing freedom of transit through and over international straits, and defining preferential fishing rights for coastal states on the high seas.

We are also seeking new international means for controlling pollution on the high seas. Last fall 47 countries, including the United States and Canada, participated in the preparation of two international conventions [52] establishing the right of a coastal state to take certain limited antipollution measures against vessels on the high seas and also imposing strict liability upon the owners of vessels responsible for pollution.

These conventions, which the United States has recently signed, were concluded under U.N. auspices at Brussels. Other international approaches to control of pollution are underway at NATO and the U.N. Moreover, the United States is acutely aware of the peculiar ecological nature of the Arctic region and the potential dangers of oil pollution in that area. The Arctic is a region important to all nations in its unique environment and its increasing significance as a world trade route and as a source

51 Cf. Documents 81–82.

52 The International Convention Relating to Intervention on the High Seas in Cases of Oil Pollution Casualties and the International Convention on Civil Liability for Oil Pollution Damage, done at Brussels at the International Legal Conference on Marine Pollution Damage held November 10-28, 1969. The United States and 18 other nations signed the two conventions on November 29, 1969. For President Nixon's message to the Senate asking for its advice and consent to ratification of the two conventions see *Department of State Bulletin,* June 15, 1970, pp. 756–757; text of Secretary Rogers' report to the President in same, pp. 757–759.

of natural resources. We believe the Arctic beyond national jurisdiction should be subject to internationally agreed rules protecting its assets, both living and nonliving, and have noted with pleasure the Canadian Prime Minister's [Pierre Elliott Trudeau] public statement that Canada would be prepared to enter into multilateral efforts to develop agreed rules of environmental protection. To this end, we intend shortly to ask other interested states to join in an international conference designed to establish rules for the Arctic beyond national jurisdiction by international agreement. We would be pleased if Canada were to join us in organizing such a conference.

We regret that the Canadian Government, while not excluding these cooperative international approaches to our mutual problems involving the oceans, now proposes to take unilateral action to assert its own jurisdiction and establish its own rules pending the conclusion of international agreements satisfactory to it. For the reasons indicated earlier, the United States cannot accept these unilateral jurisdictional assertions, and we have urged the Canadian Government to defer making them effective while cooperating in efforts promptly to reach internationally agreed solutions.

If, however, the Canadian Government is unwilling to await international agreement, we have urged that in the interest of avoiding a continuing dispute and undermining our efforts to achieve international agreement we submit our differences regarding pollution and exclusive fisheries jurisdiction beyond 12 miles to the International Court of Justice, the forum where disputes of this nature should rightfully be settled. Canada's action last week excluded such disputes from its acceptance of the International Court's compulsory jurisdiction. However, such action only prevents Canada from being forced into the Court. It does not preclude Canada from voluntarily joining with us in submitting these disputes to the Court or an appropriate chamber of the Court.

With respect to the 12-mile limit on the territorial sea, we have publicly indicated our willingness to accept such limit, but only as part of an agreed international treaty also providing for freedom of passage through and over international straits.

The history of U.S.–Canadian relations is unique in world affairs for its closeness and cooperation. We are confident that, in this spirit, our two countries will continue to resolve our differences amicably and with mutual understanding.

[*For a further exposition of American views defining the limits of the territorial sea, see Documents 81–82, below.*]

IX.
THE UNITED NATIONS AND
INTERNATIONAL COOPERATION

A. The Twenty-Fifth Anniversary of the United Nations: Commemorative Session, New York, N.Y., October 14–24, 1970.

(73) A Generation of Peace: Address by President Nixon, to the Twenty-Fifth Anniversary Session of the General Assembly, New York, N.Y., October 23, 1970.[1]

(Complete Text)

Mr. President [Edvard Hambro of Norway], Mr. Secretary General, distinguished Chiefs of State and Heads of Government, Your Excellencies the Foreign Ministers, and Delegates here assembled:

I am honored to greet the members of the United Nations on behalf of the United States as we celebrate this organization's 25th anniversary. On this historic occasion I wish to pay a special tribute to the founders of the United Nations—to Secretary General U Thant and to all others who have played indispensable roles in its success.

In considering an anniversary and in celebrating one, there is a temptation to recount the accomplishments of the past, to gloss over the difficulties of the present, and to speak in optimistic or even extravagant terms about our hopes for the future.

This is too important a time and too important an occasion for such an approach. The fate of more than $3\frac{1}{2}$ billion people today rests on the realism and candor with which we approach the great issues of war and peace, of security and progress, in this world that together we call home.

[1] Text from *Weekly Compilation of Presidential Documents*, October 26, 1970, pp. 1434–1440; for the context see *The United States in World Affairs, 1970*, Section 42.

So I would like to speak with you today not ritualistically but realistically; not of impossible dreams but of possible deeds.

The United Nations was born amid a great upwelling of hope that at last the better nature of man would triumph. There was hope that Woodrow Wilson's dream of half a century ago—that the world's governments would join "in a permanent league in which they are pledged to use their united power to maintain peace by maintaining right and justice"—would at last be realized.

Some of those early hopes have been realized. Some have not.

The U.N. has achieved many successes in settling or averting conflicts.

The U.N. has achieved many successes in promoting economic development and in fostering other areas of international cooperation, thanks to the work of dedicated men and women all over the world.

These are matters that all the members of the United Nations can point to with very great pride.

But we also know that the world today is not what the founders of the U.N. hoped it would be 25 years ago. Cooperation among nations leaves much to be desired. The goal of the peaceful settlement of disputes is too often breached. The great central issue of our time—the question of whether the world as a whole is to live at peace—has not been resolved.

This central issue turns in large part on the relations among the great nuclear powers. Their strength imposes on them special responsibilities of restraint and wisdom. The issue of war and peace cannot be solved unless we in the United States and the Soviet Union demonstrate both the will and the capacity to put our relationship on a basis consistent with the aspirations of mankind.

Commenting here today on U.S.–Soviet relationships, I see no point in responding in kind to traditional cold war rhetoric. The facts of the recent past speak for themselves. An effort to score debating points is not the way to advance the cause of peace.

In fact, one of the paramount problems of our time is that we must transcend the old patterns of power politics in which nations sought to exploit every volatile situation for their own advantage, or to squeeze the maximum advantage for themselves out of every negotiation.

In today's world, and especially where the nuclear powers are involved, such policies invite the risk of confrontations and could spell disaster for all. The changes in the world since World War II have made more compelling than ever the central idea behind the United Nations: that individual nations must be ready at last to take a farsighted and a generous view. The profoundest national interest of our time—for every nation—is not immediate gain but the preservation of peace.

One of the reasons the world had such high hopes for the United Nations at the time of its founding was that the United States and the Soviet Union had fought together as allies in World War II. We cooperated in bringing the U.N. into being. There were hopes that this cooperation would continue.

It did not continue, and much of the world's—and the U.N.'s —most grievous troubles since have stemmed from that fact of history.

It is not my intention to point fingers of blame, but simply to discuss the facts of international life as they are.

We all must recognize that the United States and the Soviet Union have very profound and fundamental differences.

It would not be realistic, therefore, to suggest that our differences can be eliminated merely by better personal relationships between the heads of our governments. Such a view would slight the seriousness of our disagreements.

Genuine progress in our relations calls for specifics, not merely atmospherics. A true detente is built by a series of actions, not by a superficial shift in the apparent mood.

It would not be realistic to suggest that all we need to improve our relations is "better mutual understanding."

Understanding is necessary. But we do understand one another well enough to know that our differences are real, and that in many respects we will continue to be competitors. Our task is to keep that competition peaceful, to make it creative.

Neither would it be realistic to deny that power has a role in our relations. Power is a fact of international life. Our mutual obligation is to discipline that power, to seek together with other nations to ensure that it is used to maintain peace, not to threaten the peace.

I state these obstacles to peace because they are the challenge that must be overcome.

Despite the deep differences between ourselves and the Soviet Union, there are four great factors that provide a basis for a common interest in working together to contain and to reduce those differences.

The first of these factors is at once the most important and the most obvious. Neither of us wants a nuclear exchange that would cost the lives of tens of millions of people. Thus, we have a powerful common interest in avoiding a nuclear confrontation.

The second of these factors is the enormous cost of arms. Certainly we both should welcome the opportunity to reduce the burden, to use our resources for building rather than destroying.

The third factor is that we both are major industrial powers, which at present have very little trade or commercial contact with one another. It would clearly be in the economic self-interest of each of us if world conditions would permit us to increase trade and contact between us.

The fourth factor is the global challenge of economic and social development. The pressing economic and social needs around the world can give our competition a creative direction.

Thus, in these four matters, we have substantial mutual incentives to find ways of working together despite our continuing difference of views on other matters.

It was in this spirit that I announced, on taking office, that the policy of the United States would be to move from an era of confrontation to one of negotiation.[2]

This is a spirit that we hope will dominate the talks between our two countries on the limitation of strategic arms.[3]

There is no greater contribution which the United States and the Soviet Union together could make than to limit the world's capacity for self-destruction.

This would reduce the danger of war. And it would enable us to devote more of our resources—abroad as well as at home—to assisting in the constructive works of economic development and in peaceful progress: in Africa, for example, where so many nations have gained independence and dignity during the life of the United Nations; in Asia, with its rich diversity of cultures and peoples; and in Latin America, where the United States has special bonds of friendship and cooperation.

Despite our many differences, the United States and the Soviet Union have managed ever since World War II to avoid direct conflicts. But history shows—as the tragic experience of World War I indicates—that great powers can be drawn into conflict without their intending it by wars between smaller nations.

The Middle East is a place today where local rivalries are intense, where the vital interests of the United States and the Soviet Union are both involved. Quite obviously, the primary responsibility for achieving a peaceful settlement in the Middle East rests on the nations there themselves. But in this region in particular, it is imperative that the two major powers conduct themselves so as to strengthen the forces of peace rather than to strengthen the forces of war.

It is essential that we and the Soviet Union join in efforts to-

2 Cf. *Documents, 1968–69*, p. 41.
3 Documents 10–11.

ward avoiding war in the Middle East, and also toward developing a climate in which the nations of the Middle East will learn to live and let live. It is essential not only in the interest of the people of the Middle East themselves, but also because the alternative could be a confrontation with disastrous consequences for the Middle East, for our nations and for the whole world.

Therefore, we urge the continuation of the cease-fire [4] and the creation of confidence in which peace efforts can go forward.

In the world today we are at a crossroads. We can follow the old way, playing the traditional game of international relations, but at ever-increasing risk. Everyone will lose. No one will gain. Or we can take a new road.

I invite the leaders of the Soviet Union to join us in taking that new road—to join in a peaceful competition, not in the accumulation of arms but in the dissemination of progress; not in the building of missiles but in waging a winning war against hunger and disease and human misery in our own countries and around the globe.

Let us compete in elevating the human spirit, in fostering respect for law among nations, in promoting the works of peace. In this kind of competition, no one loses and everyone gains.

Here at the United Nations, there are many matters of major and immediate global concern on which nations even when they are competitors have a mutual interest in working together as part of the community of nations.

In approaching these matters each of us represented here, in our national interest as leaders and in our self-interest as human beings, must take into consideration a broader element: "The World Interest."

It is in the world interest to avoid drifting into a widening division between have and have-not nations.

Last month I proposed a major transformation of the American foreign aid program.[5] A major thrust of my proposals is to place larger shares of American assistance under international agencies, in particular the World Bank, the U.N. Development Program, the Regional Development Banks. We seek to promote greater multilateral cooperation and the pooling of contributions through impartial international bodies. We are also encouraging developing countries to participate more fully in the determination of their needs. Within the inter-American system, for example, new mechanisms have been established for a continuing and frank dialogue.[6]

[4] Documents 29–33.
[5] Document 97.
[6] Cf. Documents 67–69.

In the spirit of the U.N.'s second development decade,[7] we shall strive to do our full and fair share in helping others to help themselves—through government assistance, through encouraging efforts by private industry, through fostering a spirit of international volunteer service.

It is in the world interest for the United States and the United Nations, all nations, not to be paralyzed in its most important function, that of keeping the peace.

Disagreements between the major powers in the past have contributed to this paralysis. The United States will do everything it can to help develop and strengthen the practical means that will enable the United Nations to move decisively to keep the peace. This means strengthening both its capacity for peacemaking, settling disputes before they lead to armed conflict, and its capacity for peacekeeping, containing and ending conflicts that have broken out.

It is in the world interest that we cooperate, all of us, in preserving and restoring our natural environment.

Pollution knows no national or ideological boundaries. For example, it has made Lake Erie barely able to support life, it is despoiling Lake Baikal, and it puts Lake Tanganyika in future jeopardy. The U.N. is uniquely equipped to play a central role in an international effort to curtail its ravages.

It is in the world interest for the resources of the sea to be used for the benefit of all—and not to become a source of international conflict, pollution, and unbridled commercial rivalry.

Technology is ready to tap the vast, largely virgin resources of the oceans. At this moment, we have the opportunity to set up rules and institutions to ensure that these resources are developed for the benefit of all mankind and that the resources derived from them are shared equitably. But this moment is fleeting. If we fail to seize it, storm and strife could become the future of the oceans.

This summer the United States submitted a draft United Nations convention on this matter [8] which I hope will receive early and favorable attention.

It is in the world interest to ensure that the quantity of life does not impair the quality of life.

As the U.N. enters its second development decade, it has both the responsibility and the means to help nations control the population explosion which so impedes meaningful economic growth. The United States will continue to support the rapid

---

7 Documents 77–78.
8 Document 80.

development of U.N. services to assist the population and family planning programs of member nations.

It is in the world interest that the narcotics traffic be curbed.

Drugs pollute the minds and bodies of our young people, bringing misery, violence, and human and economic waste. This scourge of drugs can be eliminated through international co-operation. I urge all governments to support the recent recommendations of the U.N. Commission on Narcotic Drugs, to take the first step toward giving them substance by establishing a United Nations Fund for Drug Control.[9] And I urge all governments to support a strengthened narcotics treaty that would govern all production by restricting it solely to medical and scientific purposes. The United States has already circulated such a proposal for consideration at the next session of the U.N. Narcotics Commission.

It is in the world interest to put a decisive end to sky piracy and the kidnaping and murder of diplomats.

In this assembly last year, I called for international action to put an end to air piracy.[10] This problem has grown even more acute. Recent events have dramatically underscored its gravity and also underscored the fact that no nation is immune from it. The United States has taken a number of steps on its own initiative.[11] But this issue requires effective international actions, including measures to permit the suspension of airline services to countries where such piracy is condoned.[11a]

The increase of kidnapings of accredited diplomats is a closely related matter that should urgently concern every member of this Assembly.

Finally, it is in the world interest to ensure that the human rights of prisoners-of-war are not violated.

In an address earlier this month proposing a cease-fire in Indochina,[12] I called for the immediate and unconditional release by both sides of prisoners-of-war and innocent victims of the conflict. This is not a political or a military issue. It is a humanitarian issue. The United Nations should register its concern

[9] The U.N. Commission on Narcotic Drugs held its second special session in Geneva September 28-October 2, 1970; background and details in *U.N. Monthly Chronicle,* October 1970, pp. 26–27; same, November 1970, p. 151. On December 15, the General Assembly adopted Resolution 2719 (XXV), by a vote of 106–0, with 8 abstentions, requesting immediate implementation of the Commission's recommendations; details in *U.N. Monthly Chronicle,* January 1971, p. 72.

[10] *Documents, 1968–69,* p. 473.

[11] Document 83.

[11a] Cf. Documents 84–85.

[12] Document 45.

about the treatment of prisoners-of-war and press all adversaries in this conflict, indeed in every conflict, to honor the Geneva Convention.[13]

I have mentioned some of the problems on which the United Nations can—if its members have the will—make substantial progress. There are many others. I urge this body, and the U.N. system, to move ahead rapidly with effective action. And as we move ahead, the United States will do its full share.

The United States came to its present position of world power without either seeking the power or wanting the responsibility. We shall meet that responsibility as well as we can.

We shall not be so pious or so hypocritical as to pretend that we have not made mistakes, or that we have no national interests of our own which we intend to protect.

But we can with complete honesty say that we maintain our strength to keep the peace, not to threaten the peace. The power of the United States will be used to defend freedom, never to destroy freedom.

What we seek is not a Pax Americana, not an American Century, but rather a structure of stability and progress that will enable each nation, large and small, to chart its own course, to make its own way without outside interference, without intimidation, without domination by ourselves or any other nation. The United States fully understands and respects the policy of nonalignment, and we welcome joint efforts, such as the recent meeting in Lusaka,[14] to further international cooperation.

We seek good relations with all the people of the world. We respect the right of each people to choose its own way.

We do hold certain principles to be universal:

—that each nation has a sovereign right to its own independence and to recognition of its own dignity.

—that each individual has a human right to that same recognition of his dignity.

—that we all share a common obligation to demonstrate the mutual respect for the rights and feelings of one another that is the mark of a civil society and also of a true community of nations.

As the United Nations begins its next quarter century, it does so richer in experience, sobered in its understanding of what it

13 Cf. Document 46 and note 53 to Document 43.
14 The Third Conference of Nonaligned Countries met in Lusaka, Zambia September 8–10, 1970; text of the Lusaka Declaration on Peace, Independence, Development, Co-operation and Democratisation of International Relations in *International Legal Materials: Current Documents* (The American Society of International Law, Washington, D.C.), January 1971, pp. 215–219.

can do and what it cannot, what should be expected and what should not.

In the spirit of this 25th anniversary, the United States will go the extra mile in doing our part toward making the U.N. succeed. We look forward to working together—working together with all nations represented here in going beyond the mere containment of crises to building a structure of peace that promotes justice as well as assuring stability that will last because all have a stake in its lasting.

I remember very vividly today my visit to India in 1953 when I met for the first time one of the world's greatest statesmen, Prime Minister Nehru. I asked him, as he considered that great country, with its enormous problems, what was its greatest need? He replied: "The greatest need for India, and for any newly independent country, is for 25 years of peace—a generation of peace."

In Africa, in Asia, in Latin America, in Western Europe, in Eastern Europe—in all the 74 nations I have now visited, one thing I have found is that whatever their differences in race or religion or political systems, whatever their customs, whatever their condition, the people of the world want peace.

So let the guns fall silent and stay silent.

In Southeast Asia, let us agree to a cease-fire and negotiate a peace.

In the Middle East, let us hold to the cease-fire and build a peace.

Through arms control agreements, let us invest our resources in the development that nourishes peace.

Across this planet let us attack the ills that threaten peace.

In the untapped oceans of water and space, let us harvest in peace.

In our personal relations and in our international relations, let us display the mutual respect that fosters peace.

Above all, let us, as leaders of the world, reflect in our actions what our own people feel. Let us do what our own people need. Let us consider the world interest—the people's interest—in all that we do.

Since the birth of the United Nations—for the first time in this century—the world's people have lived through 25 years without a world war.

Let us resolve together that the second quarter century of the United Nations shall offer the world what its people yearn for, and what they deserve: a world without any war, a full generation of peace.

(74) Declaration on the Occasion of the Twenty-Fifth Anniversary of the United Nations: General Assembly Resolution 2627 (XXV), Adopted October 24, 1970.[15]

(*Complete Text*)

The General Assembly
Adopts the following Declaration:

DECLARATION ON THE OCCASION OF THE TWENTY-FIFTH ANNIVERSARY OF THE UNITED NATIONS

We, the representatives of the States Members of the United Nations, assembled at United Nations Headquarters on 24 October 1970 on the occasion of the twenty-fifth anniversary of the coming into force of the Charter of the United Nations, now solemnly declare that:

1. In furtherance of the anniversary objectives of peace, justice and progress, we reaffirm our dedication to the Charter of the United Nations and our will to carry out the obligations contained in the Charter.

2. The United Nations, despite its limitations, has, in its role as a centre for harmonizing the actions of nations in attaining the purposes mentioned in Article 1 of the Charter, made an important contribution to the maintenance of international peace and security, to developing friendly relations based on respect for the principle of equal rights and self-determination of peoples and to achieving international co-operation in economic, social, cultural and humanitarian fields. We reaffirm our deep conviction that the United Nations can provide a most effective means to strengthen the freedom and independence of nations.

3. In pursuance of the purposes of the Charter, we reaffirm our determination to respect the principles of international law concerning friendly relations and co-operation among States. We will exert our utmost efforts to develop such relations among all States, irrespective of their political, economic and social systems, on the basis of strict observance of the principles of the Charter, and in particular the principle of sovereign equality of States, the principle that States shall refrain in their international relations from the threat or use of force against the terri-

15 Text from U.N. General Assembly, *Official Records: 25th Session, Supplement No. 28* (A/8028), pp. 3–5; adopted without a vote.

torial integrity or political independence of any State, the principle that they shall settle their international disputes by peaceful means, the duty not to intervene in matters within the domestic jurisdiction of any State, the duty of States to co-operate with one another in accordance with the Charter, and the principle that States shall fulfil in good faith the obligations assumed by them in accordance with the Charter. The progressive development and codification of international law, in which important progress was made during the first twenty-five years of the United Nations, should be advanced in order to promote the rule of law among nations. In this connexion we particularly welcome the adoption today of the Declaration on Principles of International Law concerning Friendly Relations and Co-operation among States in accordance with the Charter of the United Nations.[16]

4. Despite the achievements of the United Nations, a grave situation of insecurity still confronts the Organization and armed conflicts occur in various parts of the world, while at the same time the arms race and arms expenditure continue and a large part of humanity is suffering from economic under-development. We reaffirm our determination to take concrete steps to fulfil the central task of the United Nations—the preservation of international peace and security—since the solution to many other crucial problems, notably those of disarmament and economic development, is inseparably linked thereto, and to reach agreement on more effective procedures for carrying out United Nations peace-keeping consistent with the Charter. We invite all Member States to resort more often to the peaceful settlement of international disputes and conflicts by the means provided for in the Charter, notably through negotiation, inquiry, mediation, conciliation, arbitration and judicial settlement, making use as appropriate of the relevant organs of the United Nations, as well as through resort to regional agencies or arrangements or other peaceful means of their own choice.

5. On the threshold of the Disarmament Decade, we welcome the important international agreements which have already been achieved in the limitation of armaments, especially nuclear arms. Conscious of the long and difficult search for ways to halt and reverse the arms race and of the grave threat to international peace posed by the continuing development of sophisticated weapons, we look forward to the early conclusion of further agreements of this kind and to moving forward from arms limitation to a reduction of armaments and to disarmament every-

---

[16] Resolution 2625 (XXV); adopted without a vote.

where, particularly in the nuclear field, with the participation of all nuclear Powers. We call upon all Governments to renew their determination to make concrete progress towards the elimination of the arms race and the achievement of the final goal—general and complete disarmament under effective international control.

6. We acclaim the role of the United Nations in the past twenty-five years in the process of the liberation of peoples of colonial, Trust and other Non-Self-Governing Territories. As a result of this welcome development, the number of sovereign States in the Organization has been greatly increased and colonial empires have virtually disappeared. Despite these achievements, many Territories and peoples continue to be denied their right to self-determination and independence, particularly in Namibia,[17] Southern Rhodesia,[18] Angola, Mozambique and Guinea (Bissau),[19] in deliberate and deplorable defiance of the United Nations and world opinion by certain recalcitrant States and by the illegal régime of Southern Rhodesia. We affirm the inalienable right of all colonial peoples to self-determination, freedom and independence and condemn all actions which deprive any people of these rights. In recognizing the legitimacy of the struggle of colonial peoples for their freedom by all appropriate means at their disposal, we call upon all Governments to comply in this respect with the provisions of the Charter, taking into account the Declaration on the Granting of Independence to Colonial Countries and Peoples adopted by the United Nations in 1960.[20] We reemphasize that these countries and peoples are entitled, in their just struggle, to seek and to receive all necessary moral and material help in accordance with the purposes and principles of the Charter.

7. We strongly condemn the evil policy of *apartheid,* which is a crime against the conscience and dignity of mankind and, like nazism, is contrary to the principles of the Charter. We reaffirm our determination to spare no effort, including support to those who struggle against it, in accordance with the letter and spirit of the Charter, to secure the elimination of *apartheid* in South Africa.[21] We also condemn all forms of oppression and tyranny wherever they occur and racism and the practice of racial discrimination in all its manifestations.

8. The United Nations has endeavoured in its first twenty-five years to further the Charter objectives of promoting respect for,

---

[17] Cf. Documents 62–63.
[18] Cf. Document 59.
[19] Cf. Documents 64–65.
[20] *Documents, 1960,* pp. 575–577.
[21] Cf. Document 61.

and observance of, human rights and fundamental freedoms for all. The international conventions and declarations concluded under its auspices give expression to the moral conscience of mankind and represent humanitarian standards for all members of the international community. The Universal Declaration of Human Rights,[22] the International Covenants on Human Rights,[23] the International Convention on the Elimination of All Forms of Racial Discrimination [24] and the Convention on the Prevention and Punishment of the Crime of Genocide [25] constitute a landmark in international co-operation and in the recognition and protection of the rights of every individual without any distinction. Although some progress has been achieved, serious violations of human rights are still being committed against individuals and groups in several regions of the world. We pledge ourselves to a continued and determined struggle against all violations of the rights and fundamental freedoms of human beings, by eliminating the basic causes of such violations, by promoting universal respect for the dignity of all people without regard to race, colour, sex, language or religion, and in particular through greater use of the facilities provided by the United Nations in accordance with the Charter.

9. During the past twenty-five years, efforts have been made, by adopting specific measures and by fashioning and employing new institutions, to give concrete substance to the fundamental objectives enshrined in the Charter, to create conditions of stability and well-being and to ensure a minimum standard of living consistent with human dignity. We are convinced that such economic and social development is essential to peace, international security and justice. The nations of the world have, therefore, resolved to seek a better and more effective system of international co-operation whereby the prevailing disparities may be banished and prosperity secured for all. International efforts for economic and technical co-operation must be on a scale commensurate with that of the problem itself. In this context, the activities of the United Nations system designed to secure the economic and social progress of all countries, in particular the developing countries, which have grown significantly in the past twenty-five years, should be further strengthened and increased. Partial, sporadic and half-hearted measures will not suffice. On

---

22 General Assembly Resolution 217 A (III), December 10, 1948; text in *Documents, 1948*, pp. 430–435.
23 Cf. Same, *1966*, p. 370.
24 Same, pp. 398–412.
25 Cf. Document 86.

the occasion of this anniversary, we have proclaimed the 1970s to be the Second United Nations Development Decade, which coincides with and is linked to the Disarmament Decade, and have adopted the International Development Strategy for the Second United Nations Development Decade.[26] We urge all Governments to give their full support to its most complete and effective implementation in order to realize the fundamental objectives of the Charter.

10. The new frontiers of science and technology demand greater international co-operation. We reaffirm our intention to make full use, *inter alia,* through the United Nations, of the unprecedented opportunities created by advances in science and technology for the benefit of peoples everywhere in such fields as outer space, the peaceful uses of the sea-bed beyond national jurisdiction [27] and the improvement of the quality of the environment, so that the developed and developing countries can share equitably scientific and technical advances, thus contributing to the acceleration of economic development throughout the world.

11. The great increase in the membership of the Organization since 1945 [28] testifies to its vitality; however, universality in terms of membership in the Organization has not yet been achieved. We express the hope that in the near future all other peace-loving States which accept and, in the judgement of the Organization, are able and willing to carry out the obligations of the Charter will become Members. It is furthermore desirable to find ways and means to strengthen the Organization's effectiveness in dealing with the growing volume and complexity of its work in all areas of its activities, and notably those relating to the strengthening of international peace and security, including a more rational division and co-ordination of work among the various agencies and organizations of the United Nations system.[29]

12. Mankind is confronted today by a critical and urgent choice: either increased peaceful co-operation and progress or disunity and conflict, even annihilation. We, the representatives of the States Members of the United Nations, solemnly observing the twenty-fifth anniversary of the United Nations, reaffirm our determination to do our utmost to ensure a lasting peace on earth and to observe the purposes and principles embodied in

[26] Document 78.
[27] Cf. Documents 79–80.
[28] From 51 to 127 members.
[29] Cf. Documents 75–76.

the Charter, and express full confidence that the actions of the United Nations will be conducive to the advancement of mankind along the road to peace, justice and progress.

B. Toward a More Effective United Nations.

(75)   Statement by Secretary of State Rogers Before the Subcommittee on International Organizations and Movements of the House Committee on Foreign Affairs, August 6, 1970.[30]

(Complete Text)

Mr. Chairman [Representative Cornelius E. Gallagher]:

I welcome this opportunity to appear before your subcommittee to discuss the United Nations. As you have stated, Mr. Chairman, its 25th anniversary [31] is an occasion "to ascertain where the United Nations fits in the overall framework of U.S. foreign policy for the decade of the 1970's." We all know that U.S. participation in the U.N. must be grounded on policies that protect our national interest and that are convincing to the Congress and to the American public if they are to be successful.

Last fall the President reaffirmed to the U.N. General Assembly our fundamental national interest in maintaining that "structure of international stability on which peace depends and which makes orderly progress possible." [32] He urged the U.N. not only to pursue its efforts at peacekeeping but to concentrate as well on activities which contribute to peace building. For example, he stressed protecting the environment, sharing the benefits of space technology, fostering economic development and population control, and securing the safety of international air travel.

As I have stated in previous congressional appearances, this administration will, to the extent feasible, look to multilateral institutions—and particularly to the U.N.—to deal with threats to security and to promote peaceful settlement of conflicts.

Though considerably short of our hopes, the U.N.'s accomplishments in keeping the peace are substantial; i.e., by turning back aggression in Korea, by preventing and containing violence in Cyprus, the Congo, Kashmir, and over many years in

[30] Department of State Press Release 232, August 6, 1970; text from *Department of State Bulletin*, August 24, 1970, pp. 220–224. For the context see *The United States in World Affairs, 1970*, Section 40.
[31] Cf. Documents 73–74.
[32] *Documents, 1968–69*, p. 469.

the Middle East. In addition, the U.N. has successfully fostered arms control agreements, raised living standards in developing areas, drafted rules of law to regulate the behavior of nations in outer space and the oceans, and facilitated the orderly process of decolonization. Certainly in implementing the provisions of the charter with respect to economic development, human rights, and self-determination, there has been much more progress than might have been expected at the inception of the United Nations.

Yet, with all of its achievements, the U.N. has fallen short of the world's hopes and needs. It must be acknowledged that with respect to problems of war and peace confidence in the U.N. has waned. Some of its difficulties are the aftermath of its early successes, particularly in speeding the transition to independence for hundreds of millions of people in scores of new nations. Others are the result of unrealistic expectations that attended its creation.

This anniversary year is a time for stocktaking, and we are undertaking a candid appraisal of the U.N.'s strengths and short-comings. Along with other nations, we are searching for measures to make the U.N. more responsive and effective. We are enlisting the talents and energies of leading citizens and experts in this exercise. The President on July 9 appointed a Commission for the Observance of the 25th Anniversary, under the chairmanship of Ambassador Henry Cabot Lodge.[33] Broadly representative, its membership is drawn from across the nation and includes eight Members of Congress, including the chairman of this committee. The first working meeting was held yesterday.

The Executive order establishing the Commission [34] provides that it is to undertake a searching reappraisal of the potential of the U.N. to promote international peace and stability in conditions of justice and progress, to consider measures to improve the effectiveness of the U.N. and of U.S. participation therein, and to recommend new proposals to assist the President in his determination of U.S. policy toward the U.N.

Mr. Chairman, without anticipating the recommendations the Commission may make,[35] I should like to indicate very broadly four key areas in which we believe that steps could be taken to

---

[33] Text of the White House announcement in *Weekly Compilation of Presidential Documents*, July 13, 1970, pp. 922–923.

[34] Text of Executive Order 11546, July 9, 1970, in same, p. 923.

[35] The Commission's report was submitted April 26, 1971; excerpt of the summary of recommendations and preface, together with Ambassador Lodge's letter of transmittal, in *Department of State Bulletin*, August 2, 1971, pp. 128–136. Text of President Nixon's letter in same, p. 127.

make the U.N. a more effective instrument to meet changing
world needs.

PEACEKEEPING AND SETTLEMENT OF DISPUTES

First, there is a clear need to strengthen the U.N.'s capacity
to deal with political crises, to take emergency peacekeeping action, and to promote the peaceful settlement of disputes.

The U.N. is not yet able to undertake peacekeeping operations in a systematic way, nor to finance them properly. The financial picture in particular is disturbing, in that no agreement
has been reached on overcoming the U.N. deficit caused by the
refusal of the Soviets and French to pay certain peacekeeping
expenses in the early 1960's. We believe that every effort must
be made to wipe out this deficit, and we are pleased that the
Secretary General has initiated discussions to that end.

Clearly there are limits to what can be expected of the U.N.
in the field of peacekeeping, but we believe the time is ripe for
a new effort to arrive at a more reliable understanding on ground
rules and procedures for the conduct of peacekeeping operations.
We have been discussing this matter directly with the Soviet
Union and in a special U.N. committee.[36] We are searching for
an understanding whereby, without prejudice to the General
Assembly's residual authority, the Security Council would authorize and define the mandate of peacekeeping operations and
the Secretary General would implement the mandate in consultation with member governments most concerned. One question
at issue is the degree of flexibility to be left to the Secretary General to adapt operations to the circumstances of each case. We
have stressed the need for flexibility in this regard since we do
not think it practical to subject all operational decisions to the
risk of a veto. I can report that our discussions with the Soviet
Union on this subject have been businesslike and that they are
continuing.

We believe that an agreement along these lines is the key to
other steps needed to improve advance arrangements for making available observers, military contingents, and logistical support when needed. Various proposals for standby forces and for
more reliable financing have been advanced at your hearings
and in recent studies. We are studying these carefully and will
look for opportunities to make progress on them.

We are also concerned with the peaceful settlement of disputes.
This includes enhancing the capacity of the U.N. for alleviating

[36] The U.N. Special Committee on Peace-keeping Operations. Background and
details in *U.N. Monthly Chronicle,* December 1970, pp. 52–55; same, January
1971, p. 52.

tension, for conciliation, and for early warning of impending conflict. We are therefore making a special effort to revitalize provisions of the charter relating to timely action by the General Assembly and the Security Council in recommending methods of adjustment of international disputes, and for engaging the Secretary General in their early stages.

The involvement of the United Nations in the Arab-Israeli dispute illustrates both the organization's strengths and weaknesses in keeping the peace and promoting the peaceful settlement of disputes. We are encouraged by recent developments as a result of our recent initiative on the Middle East.[37]

THE INTERNATIONAL COURT OF JUSTICE

The second area is in finding ways to strengthen the International Court of Justice. The Court did not have a single case on its docket until a week ago, and a revival of the Court's functions is long overdue. As I noted in an address to the American Society of International Law last April,[38] there are numerous ways in which the role of the Court might be enhanced. Among these are: greater use of chambers of the Court, meetings of the chambers outside The Hague; establishing regional chambers, particularly in the developing world; and giving regional organizations access to the Court.

We are engaged in consultations with a number of governments to find a basis for appropriate action at the coming General Assembly on the role of the Court.[39] The major problem, of course, is the failure of states to submit disputes to the Court. For our part we are examining various disputes to which we are a party to determine whether the Court might be brought into play. In this connection we were pleased to join in support of a Security Council resolution on July 29 requesting an advisory opinion from the Court on the legal consequences for states of the continued presence of South Africa in South-West Africa.[40]

PROCEDURAL AND INSTITUTIONAL REFORMS

The third area we are examining is how the United Nations system can improve its performance as an operating institution. Raising the performance level means attention to budgetary

[37] Document 29.
[38] *Department of State Bulletin,* May 11, 1970, pp. 623–627.
[39] On December 15, 1970, the General Assembly unanimously adopted Resolution 2723 (XXV) calling for suggestions on widening the role of the International Court of Justice; text of resolution and related material in *Department of State Bulletin,* January 25, 1971, pp. 116–124.
[40] Document 63.

and financial problems and to parliamentary and administrative procedures. Along with many of the larger contributors to the U.N. budget, we have become increasingly concerned about rising costs and about the need to insure adequate accountability on the part of the U.N. and specialized agencies for the uses made of our contributions.

It is clear that the U.N. must organize itself to assure better coordination of priorities, better budget planning, and in general a more efficient use of resources. The need to improve the organization's effectiveness underlies this administration's request for a contribution of $20 million toward the cost of expanding U.N. Headquarters in New York. This will prevent a further fragmentation of central headquarters, which could lead to lower efficiency and increased operating costs. I strongly hope that the necessary authorization and appropriation can be voted by the Congress before the opening of the General Assembly on September 15.[41]

As many of the witnesses before this committee have stressed, basic structural changes in the U.N. Charter probably are not feasible at this time. Yet certain procedural reforms could help expedite U.N. action. Selecting members for the main councils with more attention to their ability to contribute to constructive action as the charter requires, streamlining parliamentary procedures, and avoiding emotional excesses and impractical recommendations are among the steps required for better performance.

In particular, the U.N. system will have to adopt certain institutional reforms to put it in a position to handle larger resources for economic development programs in an efficient manner. A recent study by Sir Robert Jackson [42] of Australia underscored what needs to be done to improve the managerial capacity of the U.N. Development Program. It stressed the need to accord more authority and to provide better management tools to the UNDP so that it can serve as the overall coordinator of the entire U.N. system's effort in economic development and provide direction to the efforts of the various specialized agencies that operate in this field. We have strongly supported these reforms, and I am pleased to report that good progress has been made in achieving a wide consensus among member governments in support of those reforms we consider essential. We shall now watch carefully to see that they are implemented promptly by the Administrator [Paul G. Hoffman of the U.S.] of the U.N. Development Program and the agencies concerned.

41 Public Law 91–622, approved December 31, 1970.
42 R. G. A. Jackson, *A Study of the Capacity of the United Nations Development System* (U.N. Publication DP/5; 2 vols., Geneva, 1969).

Dissemination of Benefits of New Technology

The fourth area we are examining is the possibility of greater use of the U.N. system for technological cooperation aimed at the orderly development of resources and the widest dissemination of the benefits of new technology. For the near future a principal value of the U.N. may well be its ability to draft rules and provide a mechanism for facilitating international cooperation in dealing with new technology. We want to strengthen its capacities in this field, with urgent priority to the international task of protecting man's environment, to the dangers of excessive population growth, and to the need to halt the epidemic of abuse of dangerous drugs.

With respect to the seabeds we have taken a major initiative and are pressing for early action. On May 23, 1970, the President called for a treaty under which nations would renounce all national claims over the natural resources of the seabed beyond the point where the high seas reach a depth of 200 meters and would agree to regard these resources as the common heritage of mankind.[43] Under this proposal an international regime would provide for the collection of substantial mineral royalties to be used for international community purposes, particularly economic assistance to developing countries. On August 3 the United States submitted as a working paper for discussion a Draft United Nations Convention on the International Seabed Area.[44]

The problem of safeguarding the environment is of paramount international concern; and at our initiative, it is now under consideration in numerous international forums, including NATO, the OECD [Organization for Economic Cooperation and Development], and the Economic Commission for Europe. As you are aware, intensive preparations are being made in the U.N. for a conference in Stockholm in 1972 [45] which, for the first time, will focus attention on environmental problems on a global scale. We are cooperating with many Government agencies and private institutions in these preparations. We are also working in the U.N., and by other means, to carry out the President's pledge to share with other nations the benefits from our exploration of outer space.

These, Mr. Chairman, are the four areas in which we have been working to enhance the U.N.'s effectiveness. In mentioning them I do not mean to minimize other tasks. We shall continue to support realistic and constructive U.N. efforts to facilitate

43 Document 79.
44 Document 80.
45 Cf. *Documents 1968–69*, pp. 460–462.

peaceful decolonization and self-determination. Our recent actions in support of U.N. goals with regard to the questions of southern Africa are proof of our continuing opposition to policies of apartheid and the denial of the right of self-determination in that part of Africa. In the area of human rights, we shall press for the early establishment of the office of a U.N. Commissioner for Human Rights.[46] Finally, as you know, the administration has requested the Senate to give its advice and consent to ratification of the Genocide Convention.[47]

We are acting on this broad range of issues because of our conviction that the U.N. is not only a diplomatic forum for harmonizing the actions of nations, vital as that is. It is also an action agency with important assignments for the 1970's.

The U.N. has developed in many ways little foreseen by its founders. Its purposes remain as stated in the charter, but its operations have changed and greatly expanded. Horizons are both more limited—as a result of present constraints on the U.N.'s ability to take collective action for peace—and wider, as development needs and the new technology put an even higher premium on international cooperation.

We must be alert to recognize the interrelationship between international peace and security and these new areas of international concern and cooperation. Individual steps in both fields —dealing with the whole complex of conditions that generate national and international tension and dissatisfaction—are the components out of which we must try to build security in the future.

Finally, there are those who say that the U.N. is experiencing a lack of confidence. That may be, but there is no question of its relevance to us and to the world of today and tomorrow. The only realistic choice we have then is to make it more effective; to renew its confidence; to help it gain greater public support.

---

[46] On December 14, 1970. The General Assembly decided to defer until its 26th session consideration of this issue.
[47] Document 86.

(76) Statement by Samuel De Palma, Assistant Secretary of State for International Organization Affairs, to the Fifth (Administrative and Budgetary) Committee of the United Nations General Assembly, October 21, 1970.[48]

(*Excerpt*)

*   *   *

Sound Financing

Turning now to the four specific questions I posed earlier, there is, first of all, the question of the financial status of this organization. Clearly, the financial situation is critical. We are grateful to the Secretary General for so courageously and graphically presenting the realities of this situation to us.[49] He has told us that the circumstances which confront us urgently call for renewed attempts by the Secretariat and the member states to restore the solvency of the organization. He has been telling us of the worsening situation for some years now, and the fact that many member governments have ignored his warnings almost completely is a matter of deep concern to us. We find encouragement in his statement that in the light of his consultations and contacts over recent months, there is a good prospect that an imaginative initiative may meet with a positive response from all quarters.

On September 30, 1970, speaking in the plenary session, the chairman of the United States delegation to the General Assembly [Charles W. Yost] commented as follows concerning this matter: [50]

The persistence of the United Nations financial deficit undermines confidence in the organization, threatens its capabilities in many fields, and casts a cloud over its future. The United States welcomes the Secretary General's recent call for "a concerted effort to restore the financial solvency of the Organization." We hope that he will himself take a lead in such an effort, in which we shall certainly play our part.

Budgetary Policies and Practices

The second major question calling for our careful consideration is that of budgetary policies and practices—and particularly

[48] U.S./U.N. Press Release 145; text from *Department of State Bulletin*, December 7, 1970, pp. 701–709. For the context see *The United States in World Affairs, 1970*, Section 41.

[49] Statement of October 5, 1970; cf. *U.N. Monthly Chronicle*, November 1970, pp. 152–153.

[50] *Department of State Bulletin*, October 19, 1970, p. 444.

the manner in which these are reflected in the budget estimates for 1971.

We think that the Secretary General has wisely recognized, as we all must recognize, that in the light of the United Nations deficit, the financial burden upon members and the unfinished state of the manpower utilization survey, a prospective budget level for 1971 of $200 million was simply too high. We congratulate him for his initiative in reexamining the total potential requirement for 1971 and for his courage and realism in proposing a substantial reduction. We consider this a proper response to the need for a sound fiscal policy. We have always believed that, as is the case with governments, international organizations which face urgent priority needs and certain unavoidable expenditures must put to one side lower priority needs and less essential expenditures and, to the extent possible, meet new demands by the use of existing resources. We will support the Secretary General's proposed reduction and will respond affirmatively to his call for restraint on the part of governments.

We will look forward with great interest to the Secretary General's more detailed presentation, indicating the various administrative and financial particulars of his proposed measures for reducing the projected budget by $7 million.

We are pleased that the Secretary General is relying so heavily on the work of the Administrative Management Service.[51] We await his detailed report to this committee later in the present session on the work of that Service during its first year of operation. It seems evident to us that the Service has already usefully assisted the Secretary General in the complicated area of manpower planning. We note the Secretary General's observation that many of the Administrative Management Service recommendations are of a long-term nature, so that the full impact of the survey will be felt within the Secretariat over a longer time frame. We agree that, once completed, the survey should provide the Secretary General with a better perspective from which to view the manpower requirements of the organization as a whole and to make such adjustments as would resolve each of the major problems identified. We think it is a prudent decision, therefore, to maintain for all offices and departments, through 1971, the level of personnel approved for 1970, whether on an established or provisional basis.

The United States delegation suggests that there is one area of expenditure, not mentioned by the Secretary General, which could produce substantial savings while improving the overall

51 Set up by the Secretary-General in 1969, the Administrative Management Service consists mainly of experienced staff.

performance of our organization. I refer to the plethora of conferences and documentation.

I doubt if there is a single member state whose delegation is not overwhelmed by the heavy schedule of conferences and the outpouring of documents, made worse by their tardiness. Let us face the fact that the image of this organization is one of so many decisionmaking bodies meeting so frequently and publishing so much material that no one can keep up with those meetings and documents, let alone implement the decisions which are taken. We recognize that the responsibility for certain very sizable often low-priority and relatively unproductive expenditures involved in this area rests far more with governments than with the Secretariat. Indeed, we would wish to compliment the Office of Conference Services for its efforts to reduce conference and documentation costs.

But clearly this is an area in which Draconian measures are called for. We have already reached the stage where we are drowning our real accomplishments under a flood of words and burying our best achievements under an avalanche of paper. We are informed that the present annual cost of documentation is about $20 million. The United States delegation therefore proposes that this committee find ways to reduce the appropriations for documentation for 1971 by up to $1 million below the estimates presented. For example, much as we agree with the great importance of the Stockholm Conference on the Environment, we seriously question the need for an allocation of $700,000 for documentation for this conference. We invite the representatives of the Secretary General to discuss with the Advisory Committee on Administrative and Budgetary Questions [52] and with this committee ways in which such a reduction could be applied with least detriment to or delay in carrying out essential parts of the United Nations work program.

In addition to a substantial reduction in documentation, this committee should also seek a significant decrease in the number of conferences held each year and a more strict limitation upon the holding of conferences at locations where the costs are greater than at Headquarters. Surely we owe this response to the Secretary General's call for restraint on the part of governments.

Beyond these suggestions for committee action, Mr. Chairman [Max H. Wershof of Canada], we will reserve for the detailed examination of the budget sections any further comments concerning the areas in which we believe economies can be made based on more careful choice of priorities.

[52] A twelve-member expert body which examines budget estimates for the General Assembly.

COORDINATION OF SPECIALIZED AGENCY BUDGETS

Mr. Chairman, I would like to deal now with the matter of budgetary policies and practices as they relate not only to the United Nations but also to the specialized agencies as a group. The United States delegation believes that the time has come when each organization in the United Nations family must begin to see itself more as a member of the United Nations system and less as an independent entity. It is also time for this General Assembly to exercise a greater coordinating role over the budgets of all the organizations in the system. The budget of the United Nations cannot be considered in isolation from the budgets of the specialized agencies. Nor can any of the specialized agencies look at their budgets and programs without regard to the budgets and programs of the other specialized agencies or the United Nations.

I would point out that the Charter of the United Nations and the relationship agreements that the United Nations entered into with the specialized agencies years ago do, in fact, contemplate a coordinated approach to budgetary matters. Article 17 of the United Nations Charter provides that the General Assembly shall examine the administrative budgets of the specialized agencies with a view to making recommendations to the agencies concerned. The relationship agreements also provide for close budgetary and financial relationships between the United Nations and the agencies in order that the administrative operations of the United Nations and of the agencies can be carried out in the most efficient and economical manner possible and so that the maximum measure of coordination and uniformity with respect to these operations shall be served. Under the agreements, the General Assembly is expected to examine the budgets of the agencies and is authorized to comment on any item contained therein.

If such arrangements were considered desirable when the United Nations system was first being developed, they are all the more important now, considering the vast growth in expenditures and activities of the United Nations organizations. Unfortunately, however, the General Assembly's review of these budgets of the specialized agencies has been all too cursory. We urge that the General Assembly give greater priority to its annual agenda item dealing with administrative and budgetary coordination of the United Nations organizations.

The need for the action I am suggesting is made more urgent by the rapid growth which has occurred in the assessed budgets of these organizations. It should be noted that in the period from

1965 to 1970 the assessed budgets of the United Nations and the specialized agencies have risen from a total of about $245 million to a total of about $400 million, an increase of about 63 percent. Governments are now being asked to contribute to assessed budgets of international organizations sums of money of a magnitude which require all those budgets to be scrutinized with the greatest of care.

I must add that we have been particularly concerned about the manner in which these increases have occurred. We are told that the increases in certain budget items are "mandatory" and accordingly there is no alternative to an overall budgetary increase. We do not accept this as a valid approach to the problem. In our view, when certain aspects of the budget are subject to upward pressures resulting from such factors as wage and price increases, a serious effort must first be made to absorb resulting increases within the existing budget level. Surely, there are in all budgets some expenditures of a low-priority nature which can be eliminated or at least reduced to compensate for what are called mandatory increases in other items. National governments are compelled to follow this practice. There is no reason why international organizations cannot do likewise.

Further, we are concerned at the approach to the second element in the increase in the assessed budgets of international organizations; namely, program increases. First of all, there appears to exist a philosophy that the next budget of every agency should reflect a program increase. We do not accept this as a valid budgetary philosophy. Surely, there are times when it is more important to look to the more effective implementation of existing programs than to launch new initiatives which divert the attention of the organization from important programs recently established. In view of the rapid budgetary growth of the United Nations system in the past decade, we believe that that time has come. Secondly, it should be realized that amounts which appear in assessed budgets as program increases are made up basically of expenditures for new staff, new consultants, new experts, more travel, more conferences and documentation, etc. Experience demonstrates that frequently new programs can be initiated with existing staff resources, existing expenditures for consultants and experts, existing travel funds, and existing provisions for conference and documentation expenses. There are always existing programs of a lower priority than those about to be launched, and these can be eliminated or reduced, thus freeing resources which were being devoted to them.

Mr. Chairman, my Government believes that the Advisory Committee on Administrative and Budgetary Questions must be put in a position to give greater attention to these problems in its annual examination of the assessed budgets of the United Nations and the specialized agencies. As we stated last year, we believe that the Advisory Committee must expand its program of work so that it can devote significantly more time to the problem of insuring better budgetary practices as well as better administrative and management practices on the part of all organizations in the United Nations system.

IMPROVED ADMINISTRATION AND MANAGEMENT

I wish to turn now, Mr. Chairman, to the third question which the United States delegation believes should be carefully considered by the Fifth Committee this year; namely, the question of introducing sophisticated and up-to-date administrative and management techniques to insure proper planning, execution, and evaluation of our various operations and programs. In the view of my delegation, important efforts in this direction are underway but much more remains to be done.

One such effort is the work of the Administrative Management Service, which, as soon as it completes the manpower utilization survey, should be able to give greater attention to the various management problems existing in the organization.

Another effort in the direction of better management now underway is that directed at establishing a computer center for all members of the United Nations family of organizations. This is a major effort in the management field which can bring very valuable results if it is properly directed and implemented. We have been concerned by the reluctance of certain agencies to participate fully in the project as yet. We have also been concerned that it has taken such a long period of time to provide governments with precise information about the manner in which the center is to operate and about the costs which will be involved. The Secretary General has now placed this information before us in document A/C.5/1305, and we look forward to the Advisory Committee's report on this matter.

PROGRAM BUDGETING

A third significant effort is that in the direction of program budgeting, which can become an important aid to proper management. The United States delegation welcomes this development, to which additional impetus has been given by the [Maurice] Bertrand report.[53] At the same time, we endorse the words of caution in the Advisory Committee's report on this mat-

[53] U.N. document A/7822/Annex.

ter,[54] for we believe that program budgeting can become a valuable tool only if we establish the necessary preconditions and organizational framework.

There is at the present time no effective procedure in our organization under which the financial aspects of programs are considered as an integral part of the decisionmaking process in the development of substantive programs. Nor is there an effective procedure for the assignment of relative priorities to our manifold endeavors. This question of priorities is a key issue which vitally affects the future of this organization. This was clearly stated by the Secretary General in his foreword to the 1971 budget estimates, and the United States agrees with his statement of the problem. You will recall that in his foreword he said that:

> . . . the single most important factor which determines the order of magnitude of the Organization's budget is the cumulative effect of the programmes and other specific activities which are decided upon in different contexts. . . . There is a distinct case . . . for the establishment of real priorities with reference to the more important issues of the times. This is an all-important challenge which the membership and the Secretariat must meet together in the near future if the prestige and effectiveness of the United Nations is to be maintained.

The United States also shares the dissatisfaction over present procedures expressed by the chairman [Jan P. Bannier, Netherlands] of the Advisory Committee on Administrative and Budgetary Questions in his address to this committee on October 5.[55] Mr. Bannier recalled that the Fifth Committee seldom considers the substantive aspect of activities, how necessary they are, how urgent, whether they can be carried out more efficiently by other bodies of the United Nations or, we would add, by national governments. Mr. Bannier also noted with dissatisfaction that financial implications are not taken seriously in program-formulating bodies, that such bodies do not ask the question that is fundamental to sound programing—namely, are the proposed programs worthwhile in relation to the cost and in relation to alternative programs that could be carried out for the same cost? My Government fully agrees with Mr. Bannier's conclusion that if this organization is to be able to respond to future demands and at the same time avoid an unjustified growth of its budget, the program-formulating organs will have to adopt a much more critical approach to the various proposals that are put before them and approve only those that are really urgent. As he points out, this

---

[54] U.N. document A/8033.
[55] Cf. *U.N. Monthly Chronicle,* November 1970, pp. 153–154.

will require a more comprehensive analysis and better planning and programing than has been made available to member states so far.

Mr. Chairman, I want to stress at this point that while the Advisory Committee on Administrative and Budgetary Questions must necessarily work within the framework of priorities as presented to it and is not in a position to question substantive aspects of activities encompassed in the proposed budget, the Fifth Committee, composed as it is of government representatives of all member states, can and should examine priorities and other substantive aspects in much greater detail in the future. In other words, we have the greatest confidence in the work of the Advisory Committee, and we shall give its recommendations our fullest support. But that does not relieve the Fifth Committee of its responsibility to examine, indeed to reexamine, both proposed and on-going activities in the light of an overall assessment of priorities. We look forward to the Secretary General's proposals concerning program budgeting, which we hope will provide some guidelines for dealing with the problems mentioned, and we expect to have more to say on this subject when the report is before us.

Evaluation of Programs and Activities

Mr. Chairman, there is another aspect of the management problem which concerns all members having an interest in the proper administration of the programs of the United Nations and the specialized agencies. This is the problem of evaluating the effectiveness of these programs. As someone has said, there exists a credibility gap between the announced aims and claims of success with respect to these programs and the meager information available to governments about the actual results and real value of these same programs.

Now, it may well be that governments have not analyzed with sufficient care the information already available to them, and it is also possible that the programs in question do not all lend themselves to the kind of evaluation that governments have expected. Nevertheless, it is certain, as pointed out by Sir Robert Jackson's Capacity Study,[56] that much more needs to be done in the evaluation of United Nations and specialized agency programs—and it must be done quickly if those programs are to have continued government support.

Mr. Chairman, my Government attaches the greatest importance to this problem of evaluation of United Nations activities.

[56] Cf. note 42 to Document 75.

It is for this reason that we have supported the work of the Joint Inspection Unit and have urged that reports of external auditors be expanded to include observations on administrative and management matters as well as on fiscal questions. But we believe that additional measures are required.

There is now available to this committee a report of the Secretary General (A/7938), submitted in response to a request of the General Assembly, which sets forth the terms of reference, annual expenditures, and estimated outlay of manpower of bodies established for purposes of administrative and budgetary control, investigation, and coordination. In considering this report, Committee V should keep in mind the need to strengthen the U.N.'s evaluation machinery. We hope it will study how the work of various bodies in this area can be better coordinated and integrated. In particular we would suggest that it consider the possibility of setting up a mechanism—a central mechanism—which would meet the need for effective, independent evaluation of activities of the entire United Nations system. Mr. Chairman, this problem will not go away. It deeply affects confidence in the entire United Nations system and requires the earliest possible attention.

We will be afforded an opportunity to consider ways of developing better management procedures and policies when we consider the several interrelated questions to be discussed under the agenda item on the implementation of the recommendations of the *Ad Hoc* Committee of Experts to Examine the Finances of the United Nations and the Specialized Agencies. We will have before us the matter of program budgeting with the related question of the establishment of priorities. We will have an opportunity to deal with the 2-year budget cycle. We will have to consider future evaluation machinery, the relationship between the United Nations and the specialized agencies with respect to administrative and budgetary questions, and the role of the Advisory Committee. These are all extremely complex matters, the resolution of which will call for the most expert and competent judgment and understanding. As was recently noted by the distinguished Representative from Brazil, we are indebted for such progress as we have made on these complex affairs to the work of the *Ad Hoc* Committee of Experts to Examine the Finances of the United Nations and the Specialized Agencies.

The time has come to move to the next stage of our effort to strengthen, to bring a greater order to, and where appropriate, to streamline our policies and procedures. To this end, we might consider whether we should reactivate the *Ad Hoc* Committee of

Experts [57] and charge it with studying and recommending the measures to be undertaken by the United Nations and the specialized agencies as appropriate for dealing with the problems I have mentioned. We would, of course, have to establish very specific terms of reference for the committee, and my delegation will have suggestions to make at the appropriate time.

*   *   *

C. The Second United Nations Development Decade.[58]

(77) Statement by Senator Jacob K. Javits, United States Representative to the United Nations General Assembly, Before the Second (Economic and Financial) Committee, October 16, 1970.[59]

(Excerpt)

*   *   *

Accustomed as we are to the art of accommodation, which is the essence of our political democracy at home, and mindful of the more difficult art of welding together the unique needs and interests of now 127 nations, we yet marvel, despite all our difficulties, that we have arrived at this final point of a comprehensive strategy. We know a document this comprehensive [60] cannot satisfy wholly any government. We appreciate the serious efforts of adjustment and compromise almost every government has made. We regret some have been able to participate only marginally, while others have felt too many have done too little, or too late to give maximum impact to this central effort of the 25th anniversary session. But we do hope it will be possible now with a minimum of controversy and a maximum of agreement to join the international community in consummating this effort with a Second Development Decade strategy document worthy of the united conscience of free men everywhere.

---

[57] Opposition by the developing countries forced postponement of this issue until the 26th Regular Session. For actions taken by the 25th General Assembly on administrative and budgetary questions see *U.N. Monthly Chronicle*, January 1971, pp. 83–95.

[58] For the context of this group of documents see *The United States in World Affairs, 1970*, Sections 39 and 41.

[59] U.S./U.N. Press Release 141, October 16, 1970; text from *Department of State Bulletin*, November 16, 1970, pp. 607–609.

[60] Document 78.

Had it proven possible for us adequately to accommodate all my Government's deepest convictions about development, it would be unnecessary to register any observations at this late stage. But such observations, like the observations of other countries, are important for the record and germane to all subsequent undertakings of the Decade. Our own observations on this document express my Government's own assessment of what it can and should do to insure the success of this global effort.

I ask that the following be included in the annex to the report of Committee II as a formal statement of the delegation of the United States:

The United States supports the concept of the strategy and has participated actively in the negotiations that have preceded our consideration of the document before us. The United States, while emphasizing its support for the strategy, must make clear its interpretation of certain paragraphs and the reasons why it cannot accept certain others.

1. Regarding paragraph 5, the United States does believe that improvement in the general international situation would have a positive effect on the development process. It believes, however, that any catalogue of the general political and security matters herein recorded more properly belong in other documents developed by other and more appropriate committees and agencies of the United Nations.

2. Concerning paragraphs 12 and 19, the United States regards the strategy as providing a framework for international cooperation. It will cooperate with other governments to give effect to the strategy in the broadest spirit of international solidarity and, as far as its resources may permit and its laws may provide, accepts the policy measures set forth in the strategy as a guide to a concerted program of action. The United States Government cannot accept the operative language in paragraph 19 and the analogous language in paragraph 12, which it feels imply a legal commitment where one in fact does not exist.

3. The United States can accept paragraph 21 since it appears to be recognized that the conduct of studies and perhaps intergovernmental consultations may be all that is practicable by the date cited and that there will be no need for further international action in some cases.

4. We believe Resolution 73 (X) of the Trade and Development Board fulfills the request in the first sentence of paragraph 24 for guidelines on commodity pricing policy. In our view this resolution correctly states that one of the aims of pricing policy is to obtain stable prices at levels remunerative to producers and

equitable to consumers with a view to improving the rate of growth of foreign exchange earnings derived from these products, and their predictability. The United States cannot accept the last-minute substitution of "increasing" for "improving" in the second sentence.

5. The United States regards paragraph 25 as subject to the same qualifications as earlier comparable undertakings accepted by the United States in the General Agreement on Tariffs and Trade, in United Nations Conference on Trade and Development Resolution A.II.I of the first session, and in the Inter-American Economic and Social Council. In these it is explicitly recognized there may be exceptional circumstances which make it impossible to give effect to the recommendation.

6. Concerning paragraph 35, the United States Government proposes to provide adjustment assistance only in situations where industries, firms, or workers are, or are threatened to be, adversely affected by increased imports.

7. Regarding paragraph 42, the United States faces staggering domestic needs which have given rise to a national debate, still unresolved, on how to apply limited public and private resources to seemingly limitless requirements. The combination of these internal requirements and of the enormous burdens carried by us externally, plus the frustrations, as well as the successes, of nation-building in the developing world have brought a profound reexamination of aid policy in the United States and the best means for conducting it in the future. We are thus unable now to say when the United States may meet the 1-percent aid objective, or even whether our efforts toward this objective will be successful. At the same time it is important to bear in mind that while the flow of official resources requires congressional action in our country, the flow of private resources is expandable without such action and is, of course, likely to be responsive to mutually beneficial investment policies in the developing countries. We are prepared to make our best efforts to increase both official and private flows, and we hope we can be successful in moving closer to the aid objective. It is in this spirit that we are willing to join in international reaffirmation of the aid target.

8. The United States Government agrees that developed countries should endeavor to provide a substantial part of financial resources transfers by way of net official development assistance and should make their best efforts to increase the volume of such official development assistance. It is not, however, in a position to accept specific targets or dates in this respect as provided in paragraphs 43 and 63.

9. While we cannot accept the language of paragraph 52, we

recognize that satisfactory operation of the international monetary system is a matter of importance to the developing countries. The overriding concern regarding the facility for Special Drawing Rights [60a] is to establish this facility firmly as an effective and valued reserve asset. At the same time there have been suggestions for a modification of the Special Drawing Rights facility, with respect to the possibility of establishing a link between the issuance of Special Drawing Rights and the financing of economic development. The Managing Director [Pierre-Paul Schweitzer of France] of the International Monetary Fund has stated that the Executive Directors of the Fund would want to give careful consideration to the Fund's program of work in this field. This consideration will be followed closely and with interest.

10. The United States does not interpret paragraph 74 as in any way prejudicing the sanctity of freely concluded contractual arrangements or the obligations of states under international law to pay prompt, adequate, and effective compensation in the event of the termination of these arrangements as the result of nationalization programs.

11. The strategy is necessarily a highly condensed summary of conclusions reached over a considerable period of time. In the interests of brevity and uniformity, some substantively significant distinctions, such as that between "should" and "will" as used in the policy measures, have become indistinct. In our view, the implementation of the policy measures, and the interpretation of the document, should take into account the agreements, resolutions, and decisions reached in the relevant intergovernmental bodies of the United Nations system.

In conclusion, Mr. Chairman, I would like to emphasize once again the support of my Government for the concept of the Decade and our appreciation for the spirit in which member governments of all the United Nations organizations and agencies have worked so long and hard to produce this strategy. It will initiate a major new chapter in international cooperation and is an auspicious and fitting beginning to the second quarter century of the life of the United Nations.

[60a] Cf. note 17 to Document 2.

(78) International Development Strategy for the Second United Nations Development Decade: General Assembly Resolution 2626 (XXV), Adopted October 24, 1970.[61]

(*Excerpts*)

The General Assembly

1. *Proclaims* the Second United Nations Development Decade starting from 1 January 1971;

2. *Adopts* the following International Development Strategy for the Decade:

A. PREAMBLE

(1) On the threshold of the 1970s, Governments dedicate themselves anew to the fundamental objectives enshrined in the Charter of the United Nations twenty-five years ago to create conditions of stability and well-being and to ensure a minimum standard of living consistent with human dignity through economic and social progress and development.

(2) The launching in 1961 of the First United Nations Development Decade [62] marked a major world-wide endeavour to give concrete substance to this solemn pledge. Since then attempts have continued to be made to adopt specific measures and to fashion and employ new institutions of international co-operation for this purpose.

(3) However, the level of living of countless millions of people in the developing part of the world is still pitifully low. These people are often still undernourished, uneducated, unemployed and wanting in many other basic amenities of life. While a part of the world lives in great comfort and even affluence, much of the larger part suffers from abject poverty, and in fact the disparity is continuing to widen. This lamentable situation has contributed to the aggravation of world tension.

(4) The current frustrations and disappointments must not be allowed to cloud the vision or stand in the way of the development objectives being really ambitious. Youth everywhere is in ferment, and the 1970s must mark a step forward in securing the well-being and happiness not only of the present generation but also of the generations to come.

(5) The success of international development activities will depend in large measure on improvement in the general international situation, particularly on concrete progress towards general

61 Text from U.N. General Assembly, *Official Records: 25th Session, Supplement No. 28* (A/8028), pp. 39–49; adopted without a vote.
62 *Documents, 1961*, pp. 535–539.

and complete disarmament under effective international control, on the elimination of colonialism, racial discrimination, *apartheid* and occupation of territories of any State and on the promotion of equal political, economic, social and cultural rights for all members of society. Progress towards general and complete disarmament should release substantial additional resources which could be utilized for the purpose of economic and social development, in particular that of developing countries. There should, therefore, be a close link between the Second United Nations Development Decade and the Disarmament Decade.[63]

(6) In the conviction that development is the essential path to peace and justice, Governments reaffirm their common and unswerving resolve to seek a better and more effective system of international co-operation whereby the prevailing disparities in the world may be banished and prosperity secured for all.

(7) The ultimate objective of development must be to bring about sustained improvement in the well-being of the individual and bestow benefits on all. If undue privileges, extremes of wealth and social injustices persist, then development fails in its essential purpose. This calls for a global development strategy based on joint and concentrated action by developing and developed countries in all spheres of economic and social life: in industry and agriculture, in trade and finance, in employment and education, in health and housing, in science and technology.

(8) The international community must rise to the challenge of the present age of unprecedented opportunities offered by science and technology in order that the scientific and technological advances may be equitably shared by developed and developing countries, thus contributing to accelerated economic development throughout the world.

(9) International co-operation for development must be on a scale commensurate with that of the problem itself. Partial, sporadic and half-hearted gestures, howsoever well intentioned, will not suffice.

(10) Economic and social progress is the common and shared responsibility of the entire international community. It is also a process in which the benefits derived by the developing countries from the developed countries are shared by the world as a whole. Every country has the right and duty to develop its human and natural resources, but the full benefit of its efforts can be realized only with concomitant and effective international action.

(11) The primary responsibility for the development of developing countries rests upon themselves, as stressed in the Char-

[63] Designated by General Assembly Resolution 2602 E (XXIV), December 16, 1969.

ter of Algiers; [64] but however great their own efforts, these will not be sufficient to enable them to achieve the desired development goals as expeditiously as they must unless they are assisted through increased financial resources and more favourable economic and commercial policies on the part of developed countries.

(12) Governments designate the 1970s as the Second United Nations Development Decade and pledge themselves, individually and collectively, to pursue policies designed to create a more just and rational world economic and social order in which equality of opportunities should be as much a prerogative of nations as of individuals within a nation. They subscribe to the goals and objectives of the Decade and resolve to take the measures to translate them into reality. These aims and measures are set out in the following paragraphs.

B. GOALS AND OBJECTIVES

(13) The average annual rate of growth in the gross product of the developing countries as a whole during the Second United Nations Development Decade should be at least 6 per cent, with the possibility of attaining a higher rate in the second half of the Decade to be specified on the basis of a comprehensive mid-term review. This target and those derived from it are a broad indication of the scope of convergent efforts to be made during the Decade at the national and international levels; it should be the responsibility of each developing country to set its own target for growth in the light of its own circumstances.

(14) The average annual rate of growth of gross product per head in developing countries as a whole during the Decade should be about 3.5 per cent with the possibility of accelerating it during the second half of the Decade in order at least to make a modest beginning towards narrowing the gap in living standards between developed and developing countries. An average annual growth rate of 3.5 per cent per head will represent a doubling of average income per head in the course of two decades. In countries with very low incomes per head, efforts should be made to double such incomes within a shorter period.

[64] The "Charter of Algiers of the Economic Rights of the Third World" was drawn up by a 71-nation conference of developing countries held in Algiers in October 1967. The Charter was formally recognized by the second U.N. Conference on Trade and Development (UNCTAD II) held in New Delhi February 1-March 29, 1968; cf. UNCTAD Resolution 24 (II), March 26, 1968 in *Proceedings of the United Nations Conference on Trade and Development, Second Session* (U.N. Publication, Sales No.: E.68.II.D. 14), p. 431.

(15) The target for growth in average income per head is calculated on the basis of an average annual increase of 2.5 per cent in the population of developing countries, which is less than the average rate at present forecast for the 1970s. In this context, each developing country should formulate its own demographic objectives within the framework of its national development plan.

(16) An average annual rate of growth of at least 6 per cent in the gross product of developing countries during the Decade will imply an average annual expansion of:

(a) 4 per cent in agricultural output;
(b) 8 per cent in manufacturing output.

(17) For attaining the over-all growth target of at least 6 per cent *per annum,* there should be an average annual expansion of:

(a) 0.5 per cent in the ratio of gross domestic saving to the gross product so that this ratio rises to around 20 per cent by 1980;
(b) Somewhat less than 7 per cent in imports and somewhat higher than 7 per cent in exports.

(18) As the ultimate purpose of development is to provide increasing opportunities to all people for a better life, it is essential to bring about a more equitable distribution of income and wealth for promoting both social justice and efficiency of production, to raise substantially the level of employment, to achieve a greater degree of income security, to expand and improve facilities for education, health, nutrition, housing and social welfare, and to safeguard the environment. Thus, qualitative and structural changes in the society must go hand in hand with rapid economic growth, and existing disparities—regional, sectoral and social—should be substantially reduced. These objectives are both determining factors and end-results of development; they should therefore be viewed as integrated parts of the same dynamic process and would require a unified approach:

(a) Each developing country should formulate its national employment objectives so as to absorb an increasing proportion of its working population in modern-type activities and to reduce significantly unemployment and underemployment;
(b) Particular attention should be paid to achieving enrolment of all children of primary school age, improvement in the quality of education at all levels, a substantial reduction in illit-

eracy, the reorientation of educational programmes to serve development needs and, as appropriate, the establishment and expansion of scientific and technological institutions;

(c) Each developing country should formulate a coherent health programme for the prevention and treatment of diseases and for raising general levels of health and sanitation;

(d) Levels of nutrition should be improved in terms of the average caloric intake and the protein content, with special emphasis being placed on the needs of vulnerable groups of population;

(e) Housing facilities should be expanded and improved, especially for the low-income groups and with a view to remedying the ills of unplanned urban growth and lagging rural areas;

(f) The well-being of children should be fostered;

(g) The full participation of youth in the development process should be ensured;

(h) The full integration of women in the total development effort should be encouraged.

C. POLICY MEASURES

(19) The above goals and objectives call for a continuing effort by all peoples and Governments to promote economic and social progress in developing countries by the formulation and implementation of a coherent set of policy measures. Animated by a spirit of constructive partnership and co-operation, based on the interdependence of their interests and designed to promote a rational system of international division of labour, and reflecting their political will and collective determination to achieve these goals and objectives, Governments, individually and jointly, solemnly resolve to adopt and implement the policy measures set out below.

(20) The policy measures should be viewed in a dynamic context, involving continuing review to ensure their effective implementation and adaptation in the light of new developments, including the far-reaching impact of rapid advance in technology, and to seek new areas of agreement and the widening of the existing ones. Organizations of the United Nations system will appropriately assist in the implementation of these measures and in the search for new avenues of international co-operation for development.

*   *   *

3. FINANCIAL RESOURCES FOR DEVELOPMENT

(42) Each economically advanced country should endeavour to provide by 1972 annually to developing countries financial

resource tranfers of a minimum net amount of 1 per cent of its gross national product at market prices in terms of actual disbursements, having regard to the special position of those countries which are net importers of capital. Those developed countries which have already met this target will endeavour to ensure that their net resource transfers are maintained and envisage, if possible, an increase in them. Those developed countries which are unable to achieve this target by 1972 will endeavour to attain it not later than 1975.

(43) In recognition of the special importance of the role which can be fulfilled only by official development assistance, a major part of financial resource transfers to the developing countries should be provided in the form of official development assistance. Each economically advanced country will progressively increase its official development assistance to the developing countries and will exert its best efforts to reach a minimum net amount of 0.7 per cent of its gross national product at market prices by the middle of the Decade.

(44) Developed countries members of the Development Assistance Committee of the Organisation for Economic Co-operation and Development will exert their best efforts to reach as soon as possible, and in any case before 31 December 1971, the norms set out in the Supplement to the 1965 Recommendation on Financial Terms and Conditions adopted by the Development Assistance Committee on 12 February 1969,[65] designed to soften and harmonize the terms and conditions of assistance to developing countries. Developed countries will consider measures aimed at the further softening of the terms and will endeavour to arrive at a more precise assessment of the circumstances of the individual developing countries and at a greater harmonization of terms given by individual developed countries to individual developing countries. Developed countries will consider, in the further evolution of their assistance policy and with a view to attaining concrete and substantive results by the end of the Decade, the specific suggestions contained in decision 29 (II) of 28 March 1968,[66] adopted by the United Nations Conference on Trade and Development at its second session, and made in other international forums for further softening of the terms and conditions of aid.

(45) In the light of the relevant decision of the Conference at

[65] Organization for Economic Cooperation and Development, *Development Assistance, 1969 Review*, Annex III.
[66] *Proceedings of the United Nations Conference on Trade and Development, Second Session*, vol. 1 and Corr. 1 and 3 and Add. 1 and 2, *Report and Annexes* (U.N. Publication, Sales No.: E.68.II.D.14), p. 40.

its second session, financial assistance will, in principle, be untied. While it may not be possible to untie assistance in all cases, developed countries will rapidly and progressively take what measures they can in this respect both to reduce the extent of tying of assistance and to mitigate any harmful effects. Where loans are tied essentially to particular sources, developed countries will make, to the greatest extent possible, such loans available for utilization by the recipient countries for the purchase of goods and services from other developing countries.

(46) Financial and technical assistance should be aimed exclusively at promoting the economic and social progress of developing countries and should not in any way be used by the developed countries to the detriment of the national sovereignty of recipient countries.

(47) Developed countries will provide, to the greatest extent possible, an increased flow of aid on a long-term and continuing basis and by simplifying the procedure of the granting and effective and expeditious disbursement of aid.

(48) Arrangements for forecasting and, if possible, forestalling debt crises will be improved. Developed countries will help in preventing such crises by providing assistance on appropriate terms and conditions, and developing countries by undertaking sound policies of debt management. Where difficulties do arise, the countries concerned will stand ready to deal reasonably with them within the framework of an appropriate forum in co-operation with the international institutions concerned, drawing upon the full range of the available methods including, as may be required, measures such as arrangements for rescheduling and refinancing of existing debts on appropriate terms and conditions.

(49) The volume of resources made available through multilateral institutions for financial and technical assistance will be increased to the fullest extent possible and techniques will be evolved to enable them to fulfill their role in the most effective manner.

(50) Developing countries will adopt appropriate measures for inviting, stimulating and making effective use of foreign private capital, taking into account the areas in which such capital should be sought and bearing in mind the importance for its attraction of conditions conducive to sustained investment. Developed countries, on their part, will consider adopting further measures to encourage the flow of private capital to developing countries. Foreign private investment in developing countries should be undertaken in a manner consistent with the development objectives and priorities established in their national plans.

Foreign private investors in developing countries should endeavour to provide for an increase in the local share in management and administration, employment and training of local labour, including personnel at the managerial and technical levels, participation of local capital and reinvestment of profits. Efforts will be made to foster better understanding of the rights and obligations of both host and capital-exporting countries, as well as of individual investors.

(51) In the context of the search for appropriate means for dealing with the problem of disruption of development arising from adverse movements in the export proceeds of developing countries, the International Bank for Reconstruction and Development has been requested to pursue its efforts at working out a scheme of supplementary financing. The Bank is invited to give further consideration to the adoption of supplementary financial measures at the earliest practicable opportunity.

(52) As soon as adequate experience is available on the working of the scheme of Special Drawing Rights,[66a] serious consideration will be given to the possibility of the establishment of a link between the allocation of new reserve assets under the scheme and the provision of additional development finance for the benefit of all developing countries. The question will, in any case, be examined before the allocation of Special Drawing Rights in 1972.

*   *   *

D. **Question of the Reservation Exclusively for Peaceful Purposes of the Sea-Bed and the Ocean Floor and the Subsoil Thereof, Underlying the High Seas Beyond the Limits of Present National Jurisdiction, and the Use of Their Resources in the Interests of Mankind.**[67]

(79) United States Policy: Statement by President Nixon, May 23, 1970.[68]

(Complete Text)

The nations of the world are now facing decisions of momentous importance to man's use of the oceans for decades ahead. At

66a Cf. note 17 to Document 2.
67 For the context of this group of documents see *The United States in World Affairs, 1970*, Section 41.
68 Text from *Weekly Compilation of Presidential Documents*, May 25, 1970, pp. 677–678.

issue is whether the oceans will be used rationally and equitably and for the benefit of mankind or whether they will become an arena of unrestrained exploitation and conflicting jurisdictional claims in which even the most advantaged states will be losers.

The issue arises now—and with urgency—because nations have grown increasingly conscious of the wealth to be exploited from the seabeds and throughout the waters above, and because they are also becoming apprehensive of the ecological hazards of unregulated use of the oceans and seabeds. The stark fact is that the law of the sea is inadequate to meet the needs of modern technology and the concerns of the international community. If it is not modernized multilaterally, unilateral action and international conflict are inevitable.

This is the time, then, for all nations to set about resolving the basic issues of the future regime for the oceans—and to resolve it in a way that redounds to the general benefit in the era of intensive exploitation that lies ahead. The United States as a major maritime power and a leader in ocean technology to unlock the riches of the ocean has a special responsibility to move this effort forward.

Therefore, I am today proposing that all nations adopt as soon as possible a treaty under which they would renounce all national claims over the natural resources of the seabed beyond the point where the high seas reach a depth of 200 meters (218.8 yards) and would agree to regard these resources as the common heritage of mankind.

The treaty should establish an international regime for the exploitation of seabed resources beyond this limit. The regime should include the collection of substantial mineral royalties to be used for international community purposes, particularly economic assistance to developing countries. The regime should also establish general rules to prevent unreasonable interference with other uses of the ocean, to protect the ocean from pollution, to assure the integrity of the investment necessary for such exploitation, and to provide for peaceful and compulsory settlement of disputes.

I propose two types of machinery for authorizing exploitation of seabed resources beyond a depth of 200 meters.

First, I propose that coastal nations act as trustees for the international community in an international trusteeship zone comprised of the continental margins beyond a depth of 200 meters off their coasts. In return, each coastal state would receive a share of the international revenues from the zone in which it acts as trustee and could impose additional taxes if it deemed this desirable.

As a second step, agreed international machinery would authorize and regulate exploration and use of seabed resources beyond the continental margins.

The United States will introduce specific proposals at the next meeting of the United Nations Seabeds Committee to carry out these objectives.[69]

Although I hope agreement on such steps can be reached quickly, the negotiation of such a complex treaty may take some time. I do not, however, believe it is either necessary or desirable to try to halt exploration and exploitation of the seabeds beyond a depth of 200 meters during the negotiating process.

Accordingly, I call on other nations to join the United States in an interim policy. I suggest that all permits for exploration and exploitation of the seabeds beyond 200 meters be issued subject to the international regime to be agreed upon. The regime should accordingly include due protection for the integrity of investments made in the interim period. A substantial portion of the revenues derived by a state from exploitation beyond 200 meters during this interim period should be turned over to an appropriate international development agency for assistance to developing countries. I plan to seek appropriate congressional action to make such funds available as soon as a sufficient number of other states also indicate their willingness to do so.

I will propose necessary changes in the domestic import and tax laws and regulations of the United States to assure that our own laws and regulations do not discriminate against U.S. nationals operating in the trusteeship zone off our coast or under the authority of the international machinery to be established.

It is equally important to assure unfettered and harmonious use of the oceans as an avenue of commerce and transportation, and as a source of food. For this reason the United States is currently engaged with other states in an effort to obtain a new law of the sea treaty. This treaty would establish a 12-mile limit for territorial seas and provide for free transit through international straits. It would also accommodate the problems of developing countries and other nations regarding the conservation and use of the living resources of the high seas.

I believe that these proposals are essential to the interests of all nations, rich and poor, coastal and landlocked, regardless of their political systems. If they result in international agreements, we can save over two-thirds of the earth's surface from national conflict and rivalry, protect it from pollution, and put it to use for the benefit of all. This would be a fitting achievement for this 25th anniversary year of the United Nations.

[69] Document 80.

(80) Summary of the Draft Convention on the International Seabed Area: United States Working Paper Submitted to the United Nations Committee on the Peaceful Uses of the Seabed, Geneva, August 3, 1970.[70]

(Complete Text)

On May 23, 1970, President Nixon announced a new oceans policy for the United States [71] and stated that the United States would make specific proposals at the U.N. Seabeds Committee in August with regard to the proposed regime for the seabeds beyond national jurisdiction which he set forth in broad outline in his announcement. The submission of a Draft United Nations Convention on the International Seabed Area to the Seabeds Committee [72] as a working paper for discussion within that committee, as well as with other governments and within the United States, implements the President's announcement. The draft convention and its appendices raise a number of questions with respect to which further detailed study is clearly necessary and do not necessarily represent the definitive views of the United States Government.

The basic structure of the convention reflects the President's proposals that states should by international agreement renounce their sovereign rights in the seabed under the high seas beyond a water depth of 200 meters; establish an international regime for the area beyond with certain basic principles and general rules applicable throughout this area; authorize coastal states as Trustees for the international community to carry out the major administrative role in licensing the exploration and exploitation of natural resources from the limit of coastal state national jurisdiction to the edge of the continental margin and to share in the international revenues from the Trusteeship Area which they administered; and establish international machinery to perform similar functions in the area beyond the continental margin.

BASIC PRINCIPLES

Among the basic principles which would become applicable to the entire International Seabed Area (including the Inter-

[70] Text from *Department of State Bulletin*, August 24, 1970, pp. 213–215.
[71] Document 79.
[72] U.N. document A/AC.138/25 submitted August 3, 1960 to the second session of the U.N. Seabeds Committee held in Geneva August 3–28, 1970; cf. *U.N. Monthly Chronicle*, April 1970, pp. 40–43. The first session of the Seabeds Committee was held in New York March 2–26, 1970; cf. same, August-September 1970, pp. 40–43.

national Trusteeship Area) under the convention would be the following:

The International Seabed Area would be the common heritage of mankind, and no state could exercise sovereignty or sovereign rights over this area or its resources or, except as provided in the convention, acquire any right or interest therein.

The International Seabed Area would be open to use by all states without discrimination, except as otherwise provided in the convention, and would be reserved exclusively for peaceful purposes.

Provision would be made for the collection of revenues from mineral production in the Area to be used for international community purposes including economic advancement of developing countries and for promotion of the safe, efficient, and economic exploitation of the mineral resources of the seabed.

Exploration and exploitation of the natural resources of the Area must not result in unjustified interference with other activities in the marine environment, and all activities in the Area must be conducted with adequate safeguards against pollution and for the protection of human life and the marine environment.

A contracting party would be responsible for insuring that those authorized by it (as Trustee in the Trusteeship Area) or sponsored by it (in the area beyond) complied with the convention. Contracting parties would also be responsible for any damage caused by those authorized or sponsored by them.

The general rules would be as follows:

MINERAL RESOURCES

All exploration and exploitation of the mineral deposits in the Area would be licensed by the appropriate Trustee in the Trusteeship Area and by the International Seabed Resource Authority in the area beyond, subject to general provisions relating to the terms of licenses included in appendices forming part of the convention, a number of which allow greater discretion to the Trustee State in the case of the Trusteeship Area. The contracting parties would have primary responsibility for inspecting activities licensed or sponsored by them. The International Seabed Resource Authority would also have authority to inspect and determine if a licensed operation violates the convention. Licenses would be revoked only for cause and in accordance with the convention. Expropriation of investments made, or unjustifiable interference with operations conducted pursuant to a license, would be prohibited.

LIVING RESOURCES OF THE SEABED

All contracting parties would have the right to explore and exploit these resources (e.g., king crab) subject to necessary conservation measures and the right of the Trustee in the Trusteeship Area to decide whether and by whom such resources should be exploited.

PROTECTION OF THE MARINE ENVIRONMENT, LIFE, AND PROPERTY

The International Seabed Resource Authority would be authorized to prescribe rules to protect against pollution of the marine environment and injury to persons and resources resulting from exploration and exploitation and to prevent unjustifiable interference with other activities in the marine environment.

SCIENTIFIC RESEARCH

Each party would agree to encourage, and to obviate interference with, scientific research and to promote international cooperation in scientific research.

INTERNATIONAL TRUSTEESHIP AREA

The provisions of the convention relating to the International Trusteeship Area would define the outer limit of this area as a line beyond the base of the continental slope where the downward inclination of the seabed reaches a specified gradient. Such gradient would be determined by technical experts, who would take into account, among other factors, ease of determination, the need to avoid dual administration of single resource deposits, and the avoidance of including excessively large areas in the Trusteeship Area. Other provisions would limit the Trustee's rights to those set forth in the convention. These rights of the Trustee State would include the issuing, suspending, and revoking of mineral exploration and exploitation licenses subject to the rules set forth in the convention and its appendices, full discretion to decide whether a license should be issued and to whom a license should be issued, exercise of criminal and civil jurisdiction over its licensees, and retention of a portion (a figure between $33\frac{1}{3}$ percent and 50 percent is suggested for consideration) of the fees and payments required under the convention for activities in the Area. The Trustee State would also be able to collect and retain additional license and rental fees to defray its administrative expenses and to collect other additional payments, retaining the same portion as indicated above of such other additional payments.

International Seabed Resource Authority

The principal organs of the proposed International Seabed Resource Authority would be an Assembly of all contracting parties; a Council of 24 members, including the six most industrially advanced contracting states, at least 12 developing countries, and at least two land-locked or shelf-locked states; and a Tribunal of from five to nine judges elected by the Council.

The Assembly, which would meet at least once every 3 years, would elect members of the Council, approve budgets proposed by the Council, approve proposals of the Council for changes in allocation of net income within the limits prescribed in an appendix to the convention, and make recommendations.

The Council, which would make decisions only with the approval of a majority of both the six most industrially advanced contracting states and of the 18 other contracting states, would appoint the commissions provided for in the convention, submit to the Assembly budgets and proposals for changes in the allocation of net income within the limits prescribed in an appendix, and could issue emergency orders at the request of a contracting party to prevent serious harm to the marine environment.

The Tribunal would decide all disputes and advise on all questions relating to the interpretation and application of the convention. It would have compulsory jurisdiction in respect of any complaint brought by a contracting party against another contracting party for failure to fulfill its obligations under the convention, or whenever the Operations Commission, on its own initiative or at the request of any licensee, considered that a contracting party or licensee had failed to fulfill its obligations under the convention. If the Tribunal found the contracting party or licensee in default, such party or licensee would be obligated to take the measures required to implement the Tribunal's judgment. The Tribunal would have the power to impose fines of not more than $1,000 for each day of an offense as well as to award damages to the other party concerned. Where the Tribunal determined that a licensee had committed a gross and persistent violation of the provisions of the convention and within a reasonable time had not brought its operations into compliance, the Council could either revoke the license or request the Trustee Party to do so. Where a contracting party failed to perform the obligations incumbent on it under a judgment of the Tribunal, the Council, on application of the other party to the case, could decide upon measures to give effect to the judgment, including, when appropriate, temporary suspension of the rights of the defaulting party under the convention (the extent of such suspension to be related to the extent and seriousness of the violation). In addition, any contracting party, and any person directly affected, could bring before the Tribunal the question of the legality of any measure taken by the Council, or one of its commissions, on the ground of violation of the convention, lack of jurisdiction, infringement of important procedural rules, unreasonableness, or misuse of powers; and the Tribunal could declare such measure null and void.

The convention also provides for the establishment of three commissions, each of from five to nine members. The Rules and Recommended Practices Commission would consider and recommend to the Council adoption of annexes as described below. The Operations Commission would issue licenses for mineral exploration and exploitation in the area beyond the International Trusteeship Area and supervise the operations of licensees in cooperation with the Trustee or sponsoring party, but not itself engage in exploration or exploitation. The International Seabed Boundary Review Commission would review the delineation of boundaries submitted by the contracting parties for approval in accordance with the convention, negotiate differences among the parties and if the differences were not resolved initiate appropriate proceedings before the Tribunal, and render advice to contracting parties on boundary questions.

The members of the Rules and Recommended Practices Commission and the International Seabed Boundary Review Commission would not be full-time employees of the Authority.

The Secretariat of the Authority would consist of a Secretary General appointed by the Council and a staff appointed by the Secretary General under the general guidelines established by the Council.

Any amendment of the convention or the appendices would require the approval of the Council and a two-thirds vote of the Assembly and would come into force only when ratified by two-thirds of the contracting parties, including each of the six most industrially advanced contracting states.

Appendices, which are integral parts of the convention, are included in the draft convention by way of example only, as they require extensive consideration of the questions involved by technically qualified experts.

The illustrative appendices included in the draft convention relate to (a) terms and procedures applying to all licenses in the International Seabed Area; (b) terms and procedures applying to licenses in the International Seabed Area beyond the International Trusteeship Area; (c) terms and procedures for licenses in the International Trusteeship Area; (d) division of revenue; and (e) designation of members of the Council representing the six most industrially advanced states.

Appendix A, applicable to the entire International Seabed Area, would provide for non-exclusive *exploration* licenses not restricted as to area authorizing geophysical and geochemical measurements and bottom sampling and exclusive *exploitation* licenses including the right to undertake deep drilling which would expire at the end of 15 years if no commercial production were achieved. Deep drilling for purposes other than exploration or exploitation of seabed minerals would be authorized under a permit issued at no charge by the Authority, provided the proposed drilling would not pose an uncontrollable hazard to human safety and the environment. Appendix A also provides for certification by the Trustee or sponsoring party of the operator's technical and financial competence. Minimum and maximum limits on required license fees (the applicable fee to be specified in an annex to the convention with authorization to the Trustee or sponsoring party to impose additional fees within specified limits to help cover its administrative costs) are set out. Provision is also made for the categories of minerals and areas covered by licenses and relinquishment of part of the licensed area when production commences. Maximum and minimum required rental fees prior to and after attaining commercial production (the applicable fee to be specified in an annex to the convention) and minimum annual work requirements are provided for. Submission of work plans and data under exploitation licenses prior to commercial production and submission of production plans and reports are required. Rules are set forth with regard to unit operations. Appendix A further contains minimum and maximum required payments on production, the applicable amount to be specified in an annex to the convention (such payments to be percentages of the gross value at the site of oil and gas or minerals, to be proportional to production, and to be in the nature of payments ordinarily made to governments under similar conditions). The levels of payments on production and work requirements would be graduated to take account of probable risk and cost to the investor, including such factors as water depth, climate, volume, or production, vicinity to existing production, or other factors affecting the economic rent that can reasonably be anticipated from mineral production in a given area. Finally, the operator and the authorizing or sponsoring party, as appropriate, would be liable for damage to other users of the environment, and operators would be required to subscribe to an insurance plan or provide other means of guaranteeing responsibility.

Appendix B, applicable to the area beyond the International Trusteeship Area, would permit contracting parties to obtain exploration and exploitation licenses from the Authority if they designate a specific agency to act as operator on their behalf and to authorize persons they sponsor to apply for licenses. It would require the sponsoring party to certify as to the technical and financial competence of the operator and would require the Authority to grant licenses on proper application unless another application for the same block had been received at the monthly intervals at which applications were opened. If more than one application had been received, the license would be awarded in accordance with competitive bidding among the applicants. There would also be provision for award of a license by competitive bidding in the event of termination, forfeiture, or revocation of an exploitation license or sale of a block contiguous to a block on which production had begun or of a block from which hydrocarbons or other fluids were being drained. Appendix B would authorize transfer of an exploitation license with the approval of the sponsoring party and the Authority and the payment of a transfer fee. It would provide limits on the duration of exploitation licenses and would set out minimum and maximum work requirements, the applicable amount of such work requirements to be stipulated in an annex to the convention.

Appendix C, applicable solely to the International Trusteeship Area, would reaffirm the Trustee's exclusive right, in its discretion, to approve or disapprove applications for exploration and exploitation licenses and to use any system for this purpose. It would establish the term of the exploitation license and conditions, if any, under which it might be renewed, provided that continuance after the first 15 years is contingent upon achieving commercial production. Finally, appendix C would impose proration and set work requirements above the minimums specified in appendix A.

Appendix D would provide that the net income, after administrative expenses of the Authority, would be devoted to the economic advancement of developing states parties to the convention and would be divided among a list of stipulated international and regional development organizations, the list to indicate the percentages assigned to each organization.

Appendix E would stipulate the formula for determining the six most industrially advanced contracting parties for purposes of designation to the Council.

Annexes to the convention would be prepared by the Rules and Recommended Practices Commission, submitted for comments to the contracting parties and to the Council for adoption and would come into force unless more than one-third of the contracting parties disapproved within 3 months. In addition to fixing the level, basis, and accounting procedures for determining international fees and other forms of payment within the ranges specified in appendix A and establishing work requirements for the area beyond the Trusteeship Area within the ranges specified in appendix B, annexes could establish criteria for defining the technical and financial competence of applicants for licenses and would assure that all exploration and exploitation activities and deep drilling would be conducted with strict and adequate safeguards for the protection of human life and safety, the marine environment, and living marine organisms. Annexes would be drawn up to prevent or reduce to acceptable limits interference arising from exploration and exploitation activities with other uses and users of the marine environment, assure safe design and construction of fixed exploration and exploitation installations and equipment, and other related matters. Any contracting party believing that a provision of an annex could not be reasonably applied to it because of special circumstances might seek a waiver from the Operations Commission.

The convention would provide for due protection of the integrity of investments in the International Seabed Area made prior to the coming into force of the convention. Authorizations by a contracting party to exploit mineral resources of the International Seabed Area granted prior to July 1, 1970, would be continued without change after the coming into force of the convention, with the contracting parties being obligated to pay the production requirements provided under the convention. New activities under such authorizations would be subject to the regulatory requirements of the convention relating to pollution and unjustifiable interference with other uses of the marine environment. With respect to authorizations granted after July 1, 1970, the authorizing contracting party would be bound either to issue a new license in its capacity as Trustee or, in the area beyond, to sponsor the licensee's application for a new license from the International Seabed Resource Authority. A new license issued by a Trustee would include the same terms and conditions as the previous authorization, and the Trustee would be responsible for compliance with the increased obligations resulting from the application of the convention. Moreover, any contracting party authorizing activities after July 1, 1970, would be required to compensate the licensee for any investment losses resulting from the application of the convention.

E. Defining the Limits of the Territorial Sea.[73]

(81)   United States Views: Department of State Statement, February 25, 1970.[74]

(Complete Text)

The United States Government has recently been discussing the question of the proper limit for territorial seas with many nations.[75] Widespread disagreement on the proper breadth of the territorial sea makes it urgent that the community of nations attempt once again to fix a limit. The United States supports the 12-mile limit as the most widely accepted one, but only if a treaty can be negotiated which will achieve widespread international acceptance and will provide for freedom of navigation through and over international straits.[76] At the same time the United States will attempt to accommodate the interests of coastal states in the fishery resources off their coasts.

The United States Government hopes this initiative will be successful. Until that objective is realized, the United States will continue to adhere to the position that it is not obliged to recognize territorial seas which exceed 3 miles.

(82)   Proposed Conference on the Law of the Sea: Note from Secretary of State Rogers to U Thant, Secretary-General of the United Nations, June 12, 1970.[77]

(Complete Text)

The Secretary of State of the United States of America presents his compliments to the Secretary-General of the United Nations and has the honor to refer to the Secretary-General's note LE 113 (304) of 29 January 1970 regarding resolution 2574A (XXIV) adopted by the General Assembly at its 1833rd Plenary meeting on 15 December 1969.[78]

---

[73] For the context of this group of documents see *The United States in World Affairs, 1970,* Section 41.

[74] Department of State Press Release 64, February 25, 1970; text from *Department of State Bulletin,* March 16, 1970, p. 343.

[75] Cf. Document 72.

[76] Cf. Documents 79–80.

[77] U.S./U.N. Press Release 81, June 12, 1970; text from *Department of State Bulletin,* August 13, 1970, pp. 38–39.

[78] *Documents, 1968–69,* pp. 483–485.

The United States Government strongly supports the efforts of the United Nations to provide for the codification and progressive development of international law. These efforts of the United Nations with respect to the international law of the sea provide an excellent example of its accomplishments regarding a subject of great importance to all nations. The work of the United Nations in this field began over twenty years ago, and resulted in the 1958 and 1960 United Nations conferences on the Law of the Sea.[79] The 1958 conference completed the four United Nations Conventions on the Law of the Sea which contain basic rules regarding the rights and duties of states in the use of the seas. It would appear to be unnecessary and unwise to repeat the work which the United Nations has already completed and which is reflected in these Conventions.

The United States Government is pleased to note that the United Nations has continued its work in this field in recent years. In particular, the General Assembly has established a Committee on the Peaceful Uses of the Seabed and the Ocean Floor beyond the Limits of National Jurisdiction,[80] which is charged with considering the problems posed by the development of seabeds technology.

There are certain outstanding issues regarding the Law of the Sea which were either unresolved by the 1958 and 1960 United Nations conferences or have matured since that time, that should be addressed and resolved by new treaties. Specifically, these include the basic questions of the breadth of the territorial sea and the regime for the exploration and exploitation of the natural resources of the seabeds beyond the limits of national jurisdiction.

A resolution of the territorial sea issue in itself directly raises questions of concern to many states regarding other applicable rules of law, particularly questions regarding international straits and coastal fisheries beyond the territorial sea. Similarly, the establishment of an international regime and international machinery for the exploitation of seabed resources beyond the limits of national jurisdiction requires agreement on a clear, precise and internationally accepted definition of the areas involved. A precise seaward limit of the continental shelf was not established by the 1958 United Nations conference.

In connection with the foregoing issues, it must be borne in

[79] Cf. same, *1958*, pp. 555–561; for background see *The United States in World Affairs, 1958*, pp. 411–413. The four conventions were approved by the U.S. Senate on May 26, 1960; for background see same, *1960*, pp. 359–360.
[80] Resolution 2467 A (XXIII), adopted December 21, 1968; cf. *Documents, 1968–69*, p. 481 at note 94.

mind that the international community has become increasingly aware of the need to protect the environment. The United States Government firmly supports the efforts of the United Nations and its Specialized Agencies to deal with this pressing problem on an international basis. It is convinced that the protection of the environment, and particularly the prevention of pollution, must occupy a major role in the further development of the international law of the sea.

The United States Government believes that the outstanding issues regarding the law of the sea could appropriately be addressed and resolved at a future Law of the Sea conference or conferences. In this connection, it should be noted that the considerations and questions bearing upon the breadth of the territorial sea are in many respects different from those bearing upon a seabeds regime and boundary. All of the outstanding issues are important and require appropriate concentration of effort and attention. The United States Government believes that the procedures for the resolution of these issues should be structured so as to assure that each issue receives appropriate attention in a manner which will facilitate its examination and enhance the opportunity for agreement.

There are doubtlessly a variety of means available for assuring an orderly and successful resolution of these issues. While the United States Government is most interested in learning the views of the other members of the United Nations on this matter, it wishes to point out to the Secretary-General the procedure it has considered during informal discussions with other states, based on the concept that the issues be addressed in manageable packages. The questions of the breadth of the territorial sea, international straits, and coastal fisheries were carefully and thoroughly reviewed at the earlier United Nations conferences. The resolution of these directly inter-related questions has been discussed informally by many members of the United Nations recently. The General Assembly might accordingly decide that these issues should be addressed and resolved as soon as practicable. The establishment of a regime for the exploitation of seabed resources beyond the limits of national jurisdiction involves certain new and challenging legal and institutional problems. The General Assembly might accordingly instruct the Committee on the Peaceful Uses of the Seabed and the Ocean Floor simultaneously to accelerate the preparation of such a regime, which along with the question of the boundary for the seabeds beyond the limits of national jurisdiction, might also be addressed and agreed upon as soon as practicable. The problem of protecting the ocean environment arises in the context of many issues, and should be carefully examined in connection with each issue. At the same time, the United Nations and its Specialized Agencies might proceed with their work in this field, certain aspects of which could more appropriately be dealt with separately from the more general problems of the Law of the Sea.

The United States Government wishes to emphasize its view that timely agreement on these substantive issues should be the central objective of the procedures adopted, and believes that all suggestions which will enhance the possibility for timely agreement should be given the most careful consideration.[81]

F. The Problem of Aerial Hijacking.[82]

(83) *Action by the United States: Statement by President Nixon, September 11, 1970.*[83]

(Complete Text)

The menace of air piracy must be met—immediately and effectively. I am therefore announcing the following actions to deal with this problem:

1. To protect United States citizens and others on U.S. flag carriers, we will place specially trained, armed United States Government personnel on flights of U.S. commercial airliners. A substantial number of such personnel are already available and they will begin their duties immediately. To the extent necessary they will be supplemented by specially trained members of the Armed Forces who will serve until an adequate force of civilian guards has been assembled and trained. We will also make antisabotage training available to airlines personnel.

2. I have directed the Department of Transportation to have American flag carriers extend the use of electronic surveillance equipment and other surveillance techniques to all gateway airports and other appropriate airports in the United States and —wherever possible—in other countries. The Federal Govern-

81 The General Assembly decided to convene a Conference on the Law of the Sea in 1973 to deal with a broad range of issues related to those set forth in the present document; cf. Resolution 2750 C (XXV), adopted December 17, 1970 by a vote of 108–7 with 6 abstentions.

82 For the context of this group of documents see *The United States in World Affairs, 1970*, Section 41.

83 Text from *Weekly Compilation of Presidential Documents*, September 14, 1970, pp. 1193–1194.

ment will provide enforcement officers to work with this equipment, to conduct searches when appropriate, and to make necessary arrests. Such equipment and techniques have already helped to reduce the problem of air piracy in many areas.

3. I have directed the Departments of Transportation, Treasury, and Defense, the Central Intelligence Agency, the Federal Bureau of Investigation, the Office of Science and Technology, and other agencies to accelerate their present efforts to develop security measures, including new methods for detecting weapons and explosive devices. At the same time, the Departments of Defense and Transportation will work with all U.S. airlines in determining whether certain metal detectors and x-ray devices now available to the military could provide immediate improvement in airport surveillance efforts. To facilitate passenger surveillance, appropriate agencies of the Federal Government will intensify their efforts to assemble and evaluate all useful intelligence concerning this matter and to disseminate such information to airlines and law enforcement personnel.

4. I am directing the State Department and other appropriate agencies to consult fully with foreign governments and foreign carriers concerning the full range of techniques which they use to foil hijackers. Some foreign airlines—though they are particularly susceptible to hijacking—have been successful in deterring hijackers and in coping with piracy attempts. We want to learn all we can from their experience.

5. It is imperative that all countries accept the multilateral convention providing for the extradition or punishment of hijackers which will be considered at the International Conference which will be held under the auspices of the International Civil Aviation Organization.[84] I affirm the support of the United States both for this Convention and for the Tokyo Convention,[85] which provides for the prompt return of hijacked aircraft, passengers, and crew. I call upon other governments to become parties to these conventions.

I further call upon the international community to take joint action to suspend airline services with those countries which refuse to punish or extradite hijackers involved in international blackmail. For this purpose and in order to consider other ways and means of meeting this new international menace, I have directed the Secretary of State to ask the President of the

---

[84] Document 85.

[85] Convention on Offenses and Certain Other Acts Committed on Board Aircraft, signed at Tokyo September 14, 1963 and entered into force December 4, 1969; Department of State, *Treaties and Other International Acts Series*, No. 6768.

Council of the International Civil Aviation Organization [Assad Kotaite of Lebanon] immediately to convene that Council in an emergency meeting.[86]

6. It is the policy of the United States Government to hold the countries in which hijacked planes are landed responsible for taking appropriate steps to protect the lives and the property of U.S. citizens.

7. An additional indication of our deep concern with the hijacking menace is the request which the United States and the United Kingdom [87] made earlier this week for an urgent meeting of the United Nations Security Council to consider this problem. I am gratified by the unanimous action of the Security Council in calling upon the parties concerned immediately to release all hijacked passengers and crews.[88] I am pleased, too, that the Security Council has asked all nations to take all possible legal steps to protect against further hijackings or other interference in international civil aviation.

———

These are not the only steps we will take in the coming months to meet the threat of airplane hijacking. But they do provide a decisive program for the immediate future. The Secretary of Transportation [John A. Volpe] will direct this program and take responsibility for preparing further proposals. In this capacity he will work closely with the Secretary of State, the Secretary of the Treasury, the Attorney General [John N. Mitchell], and the Secretary of Defense.

Piracy is not a new challenge for the community of nations. Most countries, including the United States, found effective means of dealing with piracy on the high seas a century and a half ago. We can—and we will—deal effectively with piracy in the skies today.

---

[86] Text of U.S. letter to the President of the Council of the International Civil Aviation Organization in *Department of State Bulletin*, September 28, 1970, p. 343. An emergency meeting of the Council was held in Montreal September 18-October 1, 1970; for text of resolution adopted by the Council and related material see *Department of State Bulletin*, October 19, pp. 449–453.

[87] U.N. documents S/9931 and S/9932, September 9, 1970.

[88] Resolution 286 (1970), September 9, 1970; adopted without vote.

(84) Action by the United Nations General Assembly: Resolution 2645 (XXV), Adopted November 25, 1970.[89]

(Complete Text)

The General Assembly,

Recognizing that international civil aviation is a vital link in the promotion and preservation of friendly relations among States and that its safe and orderly functioning is in the interest of all peoples,

Gravely concerned over acts of aerial hijacking or other wrongful interference with civil air travel,

Recognizing that such acts jeopardize the lives and safety of the passengers and crew and constitute a violation of their human rights,

Aware that international civil aviation can only function properly in conditions guaranteeing the safety of its operations and the due exercise of the freedom of air travel,

Endorsing the solemn declaration [90] of the extraordinary session of the Assembly of the International Civil Aviation Organization held at Montreal from 16 to 30 June 1970,

Bearing in mind General Assembly resolution 2551 (XXIV) of 12 December 1969 and Security Council resolution 286 (1970) of 9 September 1970 adopted by consensus at the 1552nd meeting of the Council,[91]

1. *Condemns,* without exception whatsoever, all acts of aerial hijacking or other interference with civil air travel, whether originally national or international, through the threat or use of force, and all acts of violence which may be directed against passengers, crew and aircraft engaged in, and air navigation facilities and aeronautical communications used by, civil air transport;

2. *Calls upon* States to take all appropriate measures to deter, prevent or suppress such acts within their jurisdiction, at every stage of the execution of those acts, and to provide for the prosecution and punishment of persons who perpetrate such acts, in a manner commensurate with the gravity of those crimes, or, without prejudice to the rights and obligations of States

[89] Text from U.N. General Assembly, *Official Records: 25th Session, Supplement No. 28* (A/8028), pp. 126–127; adopted by a vote of 105–0 with 8 abstentions.

[90] International Civil Aviation Organization, *Resolutions Adopted by the Assembly, Seventeenth Session (Extraordinary)* (Montreal, 1970), Resolution A17–1; reprinted in *Department of State Bulletin,* September 14, 1970, p. 303.

[91] Cf. note 88 to Document 83.

under existing international instruments relating to the matter, for the extradition of such persons for the purpose of their prosecution and punishment;

3. *Declares* that the exploitation of unlawful seizure of aircraft for the purpose of taking hostages is to be condemned;

4. *Declares further* that the unlawful detention of passengers and crew in transit or otherwise engaged in civil air travel is to be condemned as another form of wrongful interference with free and uninterrupted air travel;

5. *Urges* States to the territory of which a hijacked aircraft is diverted to provide for the care and safety of its passengers and crew and to enable them to continue their journey as soon as practicable, and to return the aircraft and its cargo to the persons lawfully entitled to possession;

6. *Invites* States to ratify or accede to the Convention on Offences and Certain Other Acts Committed on Board Aircraft signed at Tokyo on 14 September 1963,[92] in conformity with the Convention;

7. *Requests* concerted action on the part of States, in accordance with the Charter of the United Nations, towards suppressing all acts which jeopardize the safe and orderly development of international civil air transport;

8. *Calls upon* States to take joint and separate action, in accordance with the Charter, in co-operation with the United Nations and the International Civil Aviation Organization to ensure that passengers, crew and aircraft engaged in civil aviation are not used as a means of extorting advantage of any kind;

9. *Urges* full support for the current efforts of the International Civil Aviation Organization towards the development and co-ordination, in accordance with its competence, of effective measures in respect of interference with civil air travel;

10. *Calls upon* States to make every possible effort to achieve a successful result at the diplomatic conference to convene at The Hague in December 1970 for the purpose of the adoption of a convention on the unlawful seizure of aircraft, so that an effective convention may be brought into force at an early date.[93]

---

92 Cf. note 85 to Document 83.
93 Document 85.

(85) International Conference on Air Law, The Hague, December 1–16, 1970.

(a) Convention for the Suppression of Unlawful Seizure of Aircraft, Approved December 16, 1970.[94]

(Complete Text)

The States Parties to This Convention

Considering that unlawful acts of seizure or exercise of control of aircraft in flight jeopardize the safety of persons and property, seriously affect the operation of air services, and undermine the confidence of the peoples of the world in the safety of civil aviation;

Considering that the occurrence of such acts is a matter of grave concern;

Considering that, for the purpose of deterring such acts, there is an urgent need to provide appropriate measures for punishment of offenders;

Have agreed as follows:

Article 1

Any person who on board an aircraft in flight:

(a) unlawfully, by force or threat thereof, or by any other form of intimidation, seizes, or exercises control of that aircraft, or attempts to perform any such act, or

(b) is an accomplice of a person who performs or attempts to perform any such act,

commits an offence (hereinafter referred to as "the offence").

Article 2

Each Contracting State undertakes to make the offence punishable by severe penalties.

Article 3

1. For the purpose of this Convention, an aircraft is considered to be in flight at any time from the moment when all its external doors are closed following embarkation until the moment when any such door is opened for disembarkation. In the case of a forced landing, the flight shall be deemed to continue until the competent authorities take over the responsibility for the aircraft and for persons and property on board.

---

[94] Department of State Press Release 354, December 17, 1970; text from *Department of State Bulletin*, January 11, 1971, pp. 53–55.

2. This Convention shall not apply to aircraft used in military, customs or police services.

3. This Convention shall apply only if the place of take-off or the place of actual landing of the aircraft on board which the offence is committed is situated outside the territory of the State of registration of that aircraft; it shall be immaterial whether the aircraft is engaged in an international or domestic flight.

4. In the cases mentioned in Article 5, this Convention shall not apply if the place of take-off and the place of actual landing of the aircraft on board which the offence is committed are situated within the territory of the same State where that State is one of these referred to in that Article.

5. Notwithstanding paragraphs 3 and 4 of this Article, Articles 6, 7, 8 and 10 shall apply whatever the place of takeoff or the place of actual landing of the aircraft, if the offender or the alleged offender is found in the territory of a State other than the State of registration of that aircraft.

ARTICLE 4

1. Each Contracting State shall likewise take such measures as may be necessary to establish its jurisdiction over the offence and any other act of violence against passengers or crew committed by the alleged offender in connection with the offence, in the following cases:

(a) when the offence is committed on board an aircraft registered in that State;

(b) when the aircraft on board which the offence is committed lands in its territory with the alleged offender still on board;

(c) when the offence is committed on board an aircraft leased without crew to a lessee who has his principal place of business or, if the lessee has no such place of business, his permanent residence, in that State.

2. Each Contracting State shall likewise take such measures as may be necessary to establish its jurisdiction over the offence in the case where the alleged offender is present in its territory and it does not extradite him pursuant to Article 8 to any of the States mentioned in paragraph 1 of this Article.

3. This Convention does not exclude any criminal jurisdiction exercised in accordance with national law.

ARTICLE 5

The Contracting States which establish joint air transport operating organizations or international operating agencies, which operate aircraft which are subject to joint or international registration shall, by appropriate means, designate for each aircraft the State among them which shall exercise the jurisdiction and have the attributes of the State of registration for the purpose of this Convention and shall give notice thereof to the International Civil Aviation Organization which shall communicate the notice to all States parties to this Convention.

ARTICLE 6

1. Upon being satisfied that the circumstances so warrant, any Contracting State in the territory of which the offender or the alleged offender is present, shall take him into custody or take other measures to ensure his presence. The custody and other measures shall be as provided in the law of that State but may only be continued for such time as is necessary to enable any criminal or extradition proceedings to be instituted.

2. Such State shall immediately make a preliminary enquiry into the facts.

3. Any person in custody pursuant to paragraph 1 of this Article shall be assisted in communicating immediately with the nearest appropriate representative of the State of which he is a national.

4. When a State, pursuant to this Article, has taken a person into custody, it shall immediately notify the State of registration of the aircraft, the State mentioned in Article 4, paragraph 1(c), the State of nationality of the detained person and, if it considers it advisable, any other interested States of the fact that such person is in custody and of the circumstances which warrant his detention. The State which makes the preliminary enquiry contemplated in paragraph 2 of this Article shall promptly report its findings to the said States and shall indicate whether it intends to exercise jurisdiction.

ARTICLE 7

The Contracting State in the territory of which the alleged offender is found shall, if it does not extradite him, be obliged, without exception whatsoever, and whether or not the offence was committed in its territory, to submit the case to its competent authorities for the purpose of prosecution. Those authorities shall take their decision in the same manner as in the case of any ordinary offence of a serious nature under the law of that State.

ARTICLE 8

1. The offence shall be deemed to be included as an extraditable offence in any extradition treaty existing between Contract-

ing States. Contracting States undertake to include the offence as an extraditable offence in every extradition treaty to be concluded between them.

2. If a Contracting State which makes extradition conditional on the existence of a treaty receives a request for extradition from another Contracting State with which it has no extradition treaty, it may at its option consider this Convention as the legal basis for extradition in respect of the offence. Extradition shall be subject to the other conditions provided by the law of the requested State.

3. Contracting States which do not make extradition conditional on the existence of a treaty shall recognize the offence as an extraditable offence between themselves subject to the conditions provided by the law of the requested State.

4. The offence shall be treated, for the purpose of extradition between Contracting States, as if it had been committed not only in the place in which it occurred but also in the territories of the States required to establish their jurisdiction in accordance with Article 4, paragraph 1.

ARTICLE 9

1. When any of the acts mentioned in Article 1(a) has occurred or is about to occur, Contracting States shall take all appropriate measures to restore control of the aircraft to its lawful commander or to preserve his control of the aircraft.

2. In the cases contemplated by the preceding paragraph, any Contracting State in which the aircraft or its passengers or crew are present shall facilitate the continuation of the journey of the passengers and crew as soon as practicable, and shall without delay return the aircraft and its cargo to the persons lawfully entitled to possession.

ARTICLE 10

1. Contracting States shall afford one another the greatest measure of assistance in connection with criminal proceedings brought in respect of the offence and other acts mentioned in Article 4. The law of the State requested shall apply in all cases.

2. The provisions of paragraph 1 of this Article shall not affect obligations under any other treaty, bilateral or multilateral, which governs or will govern, in whole or in part, mutual assistance in criminal matters.

ARTICLE 11

Each Contracting State shall in accordance with its national law report to the Council of the International Civil Aviation

Organization as promptly as possible any relevant information in its possession concerning:

(a) the circumstances of the offence;

(b) the action taken pursuant to Article 9;

(c) the measures taken in relation to the offender or the alleged offender, and, in particular, the results of any extradition proceedings or other legal proceedings.

ARTICLE 12

1. Any dispute between two or more Contracting States concerning the interpretation or application of this Convention which cannot be settled through negotiation, shall, at the request of one of them, be submitted to arbitration. If within six months from the date of the request for arbitration the Parties are unable to agree on the organization of the arbitration, any one of those Parties may refer the dispute to the International Court of Justice by request in conformity with the statute of that court.

2. Each State may at the time of signature or ratification of this Convention or accession thereto, declare that it does not consider itself bound by the preceding paragraph. The other Contracting States shall not be bound by the preceding paragraph with respect to any Contracting States having made such a reservation.

3. Any Contracting State having made a reservation in accordance with the preceding paragraph may at any time withdraw this reservation by notification to the Depositary Governments.

ARTICLE 13

1. This Convention shall be open for signature at The Hague on 16 December 1970, by States participating in the International Conference on Air Law held at The Hague from 1 to 16 December 1970 (hereinafter referred to as The Hague Conference). After 31 December 1970, the Convention shall be open to all States for signature in Moscow, London and Washington. Any State which does not sign this Convention before its entry into force in accordance with paragraph 3 of this Article may accede to it at any time.

2. This Convention shall be subject to ratification by the signatory States. Instruments of ratification and instruments of accession shall be deposited with the Governments of the Union of Soviet Socialist Republics, the United Kingdom of Great Britain and Northern Ireland, and the United States of America, which are hereby designated the Depositary Governments.

3. This Convention shall enter into force thirty days following

the date of the deposit of instruments of ratification by ten States signatory to this Convention which participated in The Hague Conference.[95]

4. For other States, this Convention shall enter into force on the date of entry into force of this Convention in accordance with paragraph 3 of this Article, or thirty days following the date of deposit of their instruments of ratification or accession, whichever is later.

5. The Depositary Governments shall promptly inform all signatory and acceding States of the date of each signature, the date of deposit of each instrument of ratification or accession, the date of entry into force of this Convention and other notices.

6. As soon as this Convention comes into force, it shall be registered by the Depositary Governments pursuant to Article 102 of the Charter of the United Nations and pursuant to Article 83 of the Convention on International Civil Aviation (Chicago, 1944).[96]

ARTICLE 14

1. Any Contracting State may denounce this Convention by written notification to the Depositary Governments.

2. Denunciation shall take effect six months following the date on which notification is received by the Depositary Governments.

IN WITNESS WHEREOF the undersigned Plenipotentiaries, being duly authorized thereto by their Governments, have signed this Convention.

DONE at The Hague, this sixteenth day of December, one thousand nine hundred and seventy, in three originals, each being drawn up in four authentic texts in the English, French, Russian and Spanish languages.

(b) Statement by John B. Rhinelander, Deputy Legal Adviser and Acting Chief of the United States Delegate, December 16, 1970.[97]

(Complete Text)

The delegation of the United States of America wants to express its gratitude to the Government of the Kingdom of the

---

[95] Entered into force October 14, 1971; Department of State, *Treaties and Other International Acts Series*, No. 7192.

[96] Signed December 7, 1944; text in *Documents, 1944–1945*, pp. 585–607.

[97] Text from *Department of State Bulletin*, January 11, 1971, pp. 51–52.

Netherlands for the invitation to hold this important, and very successful, diplomatic conference at The Hague.

We would also like to express our appreciation to the President of the conference, Professor Riphagen [W. Riphagen, of the Netherlands], who served us all, well and wisely, and to Dr. [P. K.] Roy and other members of the Secretariat, who had the unenviable responsibility of making sure, under great pressure, that the mechanics of this large gathering did not fail.

We would like to note with great satisfaction the very large number of countries ably represented here and the fact that on final reading the text of the Convention for the Suppression of Unlawful Seizure of Aircraft was adopted without dissenting vote.

We have approved a convention which, as many delegates noted earlier, will be called the "hijacking convention," regardless of its official name and the fact that many treaties are frequently identified by the name of the city where finally adopted.

This conference had before it the task of preparing an effective, widely acceptable international convention, a convention designed to insure that all hijackers, wherever found, will be severely punished for an act which endangers the safety and lives of all passengers and crew aboard and risks possible damage to or destruction of the aircraft.

Our starting point was the draft convention prepared by the Legal Committee. Our task was to improve it to insure that our objective would be achieved.

Our delegation believes this diplomatic conference has achieved its objective and that this result will be insured when states have ratified or acceded to the convention and it has become widely accepted.

I will mention only briefly the provisions we believe are vitally important.

First, the convention provides that if a state does not extradite a hijacker, it will submit the case, without exception whatsoever, to its competent authorities for the purpose of prosecution. This obligation is emphatic and applies whatever the motivation of the hijacker.

Second, the convention provides hijacking will be subject to severe penalties in all states. We think this is important and in keeping with the grave nature of the act. The convention throughout recognizes hijacking as a serious crime, an important step forward in the development of conventional international law.

Third, the convention provides for universal criminal jurisdiction over hijackers, wherever found, by obligating contracting states to establish necessary criminal jurisdiction enabling each state to prosecute a hijacker if that state does not extradite him. This provision—akin to the response of states in prior years to the threat of piracy—is one of the most important features in the entire convention and was added at this conference. For the first time, the hijackers will be subject to punishment regardless of where the hijacking took place.

Finally, the convention will facilitate extradition of hijackers between contracting states. This feature of the convention represents an important supplement to bilateral and multilateral extradition treaties and national laws and policies dealing with extradition.

In brief, this convention deprives hijackers of asylum from prosecution. A hijacker will either be extradited for purposes of prosecution or prosecuted where found.

I will not refer to all the other features of the convention at this time but simply note two more amendments adopted at this conference which we believe important. The first is paragraph 2 of article 9, which deals with the obligations of states with respect to a hijacked aircraft, its passengers, crew, and cargo, presently contained in article 11 of the Tokyo Convention.[98] The second is article 11 of the present convention, which provides for reporting obligations by states to the ICAO Council, as recommended by the Seventeenth (Extraordinary) Assembly last June.[99] We believe the importance of these provisions, which serve to establish a new international norm, will become apparent with the passage of time.

With respect to the final clauses, my Government has strongly supported the Vienna formula in the past and will do so in the future. Our support for an all-states formula in this convention should not be regarded as a precedent.

My delegation believes this convention marks an important international reaction to lawless acts which, regardless of motivation, must be punished. Accordingly, I have been authorized to sign the convention this afternoon on behalf of the United States of America. My delegation hopes that many others participating at this conference will also sign and that those who are not able to sign here at The Hague will sign early next year in Washington, London, and Moscow.

In closing, my delegation hopes that states will ratify or accede

[98] Cf. note 85 to Document 83.
[99] Cf. Document 84 at note 90.

to this important convention as soon as possible. We believe that the goal of those gathered here at The Hague should be to bring this convention into effect at the earliest possible moment.

That is the next task of governments represented at this conference. Our successful efforts here will not be fully realized until that is accomplished.

G. Convention on the Prevention and Punishment of the Crime of Genocide, First Transmitted to the Senate on June 16, 1949.

(86) *Report of Secretary of State Rogers to President Nixon Recommending Ratification, February 5, 1970.*[100]

(Complete Text)

DEPARTMENT OF STATE,
Washington, February 5, 1970

THE PRESIDENT: I respectfully recommend that you request the Senate of the United States to give its advice and consent [101] to United States ratification of the Convention on the Prevention and Punishment of the Crime of Genocide. The text of the Convention is enclosed.[102] I believe that ratification is in the interests of the United States and that there is no constitutional obstacle to ratification. I am pleased to report that the Attorney General agrees that there are no constitutional obstacles to United States ratification.

The Convention was adopted unanimously by the General Assembly of the United Nations on December 9, 1948,[103] and signed by the United States two days later. It was submitted to the Senate by President [Harry S.] Truman on June 16, 1949 (Executive O, 81st Congress, 1st Session). Hearings were held in 1950 by a Subcommittee of the Foreign Relations Committee which reported it favorably to the full Committee. Neither the Committee nor the Senate as a whole has yet taken action on the Convention.

[100] Text from *Department of State Bulletin*, March 16, 1970, pp. 351–352.
[101] Text of President Nixon's message to the Senate, February 19, 1970, in *Weekly Compilation of Presidential Documents*, February 23, 1970, p. 244.
[102] *Documents, 1948*, pp. 435–438; also reprinted in *Department of State Bulletin*, March 16, 1970, pp. 352–353.
[103] Text in U.S. Senate Document 123, 81st Congress, 1st Session, *A Decade of American Foreign Policy: Basic Documents, 1941–49* (Washington: G.P.O., 1970), pp. 966–969.

The Convention entered into force on January 12, 1951. So far seventy-four countries have become parties. It is anomalous that the United States, which firmly opposes the crime of genocide and which played a leading role in bringing about the recognition of genocide as a crime against international law, is not among the parties to the Convention.

Genocide has been perpetrated many times throughout history. Although man has always expressed his horror at this crime, little was done to prevent or punish it before the 1930's. World War II witnessed the most drastic series of genocidal acts ever committed. The revulsion of civilized society manifested itself in a United Nations General Assembly resolution of December 11, 1946,[104] declaring genocide to be a crime under international law and recommending international cooperation in its prevention and punishment. This resolution was the impetus for the drafting of the Convention on the Prevention and Punishment of the Crime of Genocide.

The Convention provides in Article II that any of the following five acts, if accompanied by the intent to destroy, in whole or in part, a national, ethnical, racial, or religious group, constitutes the crime of genocide.

(a) Killing members of the group;

(b) Causing serious bodily or mental harm to members of the group;

(c) Deliberately inflicting on the group conditions of life calculated to bring about its physical destruction in whole or in part;

(d) Imposing measures intended to prevent births within the group; and

(e) Forcibly transferring children of the group to another group.

In addition to genocide itself, the Convention provides that conspiracy, attempt and direct and public incitement to commit genocide, and complicity in genocide shall be punishable.

In requesting Senate advice and consent to ratification, I recommend that you suggest an understanding to make clear that the United States Government understands and construes the words "mental harm" appearing in Article II(b) of this Convention to mean permanent impairment of mental faculties.

The contracting parties undertake to enact legislation necessary to give effect to the provisions of the Convention "in accordance with their respective constitutions." It is clear, therefore,

---

[104] Resolution 96 (I).

that the Convention was not expected to be self-executing. I do not recommend, however, that the Executive Branch propose any specific implementing legislation at this time. The Departments of State and Justice will be prepared to discuss this question should the Congress request our views.

Persons charged with genocide would be tried by a competent tribunal of the state in whose territory the act was committed. Parties to the Convention are bound to grant extradition, in accordance with their laws and treaties, of persons charged with crimes falling under the Convention. Genocide is not to be considered a political crime for the purposes of extradition.

Disputes regarding the interpretation, application or fulfillment of the Convention shall be submitted to the International Court of Justice. In addition, any contracting party may call on competent organs of the United Nations to take such action under the United Nations Charter as they consider appropriate toward the prevention and suppression of acts of genocide or any of the related accessorial acts.

I am convinced that the American people together with all the peoples of the world will hail United States ratification of this Convention as a concrete example of our dedication to safeguarding human rights and basic freedoms.

Respectfully submitted,

WILLIAM P. ROGERS

H. Review of the Twenty-Fifth Regular Session of the United Nations General Assembly, September 15–December 17, 1970.

(87) Year-End Roundup Issued by the United States Mission to the United Nations, December 17, 1970.[105]

(Excerpts)

INTRODUCTION

Twenty-fifth Anniversary of the United Nations

The 25th anniversary commemorative session, held from October [14] through October 24 as part of the 25th General Assembly, included addresses by representatives of 87 member states, the Secretary General, and Assembly President Hambro.

[105] U.S./U.N. Press Release 200, December 17, 1970; text from *Department of State Bulletin,* February 8, 1971, pp. 173–186; For the context see *The United States in World Affairs, 1970,* Section 40.

The commemorative session culminated on October 24, the 25th anniversary of the charter's entry into force, with the adoption by acclamation of three declarations:

—Declaration on Principles of International Law concerning Friendly Relations and Co-operation among States in accordance with the Charter of the United Nations; [106]
—An International Development Strategy for the Second United Nations Development Decade; [107]
—Declaration on the Occasion of the Twenty-fifth Anniversary of the United Nations.[108]

The Friendly Relations Declaration has been widely acclaimed as an important statement of international law, elaborating and clarifying seven of the most basic principles of international law contained in the United Nations Charter.

The development strategy is a comprehensive statement of essentials for national and international action during the Second Development Decade, 1971–80. Despite reservations by the United States [109] and other countries on various points, the document is a major step toward a systematic and more rational approach to economic and social development.

The 25th anniversary declaration embodies the Assembly's consensus on common purposes, reflecting basic aims of the charter with particular emphasis on development, disarmament, and the abolition of racism and colonialism.

President Nixon, who made a major address on October 23,[110] was one of 45 heads of state and heads of government to speak either at the commemorative session or at other times during the 25th Assembly. Participating also were three vice presidents, three deputy heads of government, 91 foreign ministers, and 12 other ministers of Cabinet rank.

*   *   *

Security Council
First Periodic Council Meeting
Secretary Rogers represented the United States in the first periodic meeting of the Security Council, convened under article 28, paragraph 2, of the charter. The meeting took place *in*

[106] General Assembly Resolution 2625 (XXV).
[107] Document 78.
[108] Document 74.
[109] Cf. Document 77.
[110] Document 73.

camera on October 21, and the foreign ministers of all but four of the 15 Security Council members were present.[111] The members of the Security Council were unanimous in agreeing that the holding of each periodic meetings constituted an important step toward strengthening the Council's ability to act effectively for the maintenance of international peace and security.

*   *   *

Admission of Fiji

Fiji was admitted as the 127th member of the United Nations by the General Assembly on October 13 [112] on the unanimous recommendation by the Security Council.[113]

During the discussion of Fiji's application for membership in the Security Council, the United States proposed that the application be referred to the Council's admissions committee, as provided for in rule 59 of the provisional rules of procedure of the Security Council.

The United States held that return to such a procedure, which has not been observed in recent years, would better enable the Council to determine whether an applicant is willing and able to bear the burdens and obligations of membership. The United States stated that Fiji clearly met the qualifications for membership and therefore felt that the time was particularly appropriate to reestablish use of the admissions committee.

The United States also made clear that it considered that provisions in rule 59 calling for an application to be submitted to the General Assembly at least 35 days before a regular session and 14 before a special session did not apply to applications received during a session of the General Assembly. Nevertheless, opposition led by the U.S.S.R. and Zambia defeated the U.S. proposal. Although the U.S. effort was defeated this time, we believe that in the future the proposal to use the admissions committee will be more favorably received. Both the United Kingdom and France have stated that they believe the rule should be followed in the future, and we hope that such procedure will prevail at the time of consideration of any new application for membership in the U.N. by any state.

111 Burundi, Sierra Leone, Syria and Zambia were represented by their Permanent Representatives to the U.N. For text of communiqué issued at the close of the meeting by Secretary-General Thant see *U.N. Monthly Chronicle,* November 1970, p. 124.
112 Resolution 2622 (XXV).
113 Resolution 287 (1970), October 10, 1970.

Guinea Complaint [114]

* * *

Question of Cyprus

On December 10 the Security Council met to consider the question of Cyprus and the renewal of the Council's mandate to maintain the United Nations Peacekeeping Force in Cyprus (UNFICYP). After hearing statements by representatives of Cyprus, Turkey, and Greece, the Security Council voted unanimously to extend UNFICYP's mandate for another 6 months, to June 15, 1971.[115]

In a statement in explanation of vote,[116] Ambassador [Christopher H.] Phillips expressed his appreciation of the skill and efficiency of UNFICYP. He went on, however, to express his disappointment that the intercommunal talks on Cyprus had lost their momentum and both sides had stiffened their positions. Ambassador Phillips said that the purpose of this extension of UNFICYP's mandate, like previous extensions, was not intended to give UNFICYP a permanent status and reminded members that peacekeeping was not a substitute for peacemaking.

GENERAL ASSEMBLY

Middle East [117]

The Middle East was the dominant political concern of the 25th General Assembly. The general problem of a peaceful settlement was debated in plenary, while the Special Political Committee dealt with the problems of the Palestinians and the U.N. Relief and Works Agency for Palestine Refugees in the Near East (UNRWA), which is in serious financial straits. The question of human rights in the occupied territories was considered in both the Special Political Committee and the Third Committee.

* * *

Chinese Representation

The General Assembly again reaffirmed its 1961 decision [118] that any proposal to change the representation of China in the

114 For the substance of this section see Documents 64–65.

115 Resolution 291 (1970), December 10, 1970.

116 Text in *Department of State Bulletin,* January 11, 1971, pp. 70–71.

117 For the substance of this section see Documents 29–33.

118 Resolution 1668 (XVI), adopted December 15, 1961 by a vote of 61–34 with 7 abstentions; text in *Documents, 1961,* pp. 502–503.

United Nations is an important question requiring a two-thirds vote for adoption. This resolution was adopted 66 in favor (U.S.), 52 against, with 7 abstentions.[119]

A resolution,[120] sponsored by Albania and 17 other countries, to expel the Republic of China and to seat representatives of the People's Republic of China in the United Nations obtained a simple majority (51 in favor, 49 against (U.S.), with 25 abstentions) but failed to obtain the required two-thirds votes for passage.

While the Albanian resolution gained a majority for the first time, there is nevertheless a growing and strong sentiment in the Assembly that the People's Republic of China should not be admitted at the price of expelling the Republic of China, which effectively governs 14 million people and has always faithfully carried out its obligations under the charter.

This feeling was perhaps strengthened by the realization by many countries after the vote on the Albanian resolution that had it not been for the two-thirds rule, the Republic of China would have been expelled from the General Assembly.

Even some of the sponsors of the Albanian resolution have reluctantly noted the growing unwillingness on the part of many supporters of the admission of the People's Republic of China to take this action if it means the expulsion of the Republic of China.

Rationalization of General Assembly Procedures

On November 9 the General Assembly adopted by 88 votes to 0, with 12 abstentions, a resolution sponsored by Canada and 24 other members to deal with the question of rationalizing procedures and organization in the General Assembly.[121] By virtue of the resolution the President of the Assembly will appoint, on the basis of equitable geographic distribution, a 31-member committee which will study and report on the question at the 26th General Assembly.

The United States strongly supported this resolution. The United States has long believed that the procedures and organization of the General Assembly are in need of reform. The United States is particularly concerned at the length of time taken to complete the work of the General Assembly, which often has gone beyond the appointed 3 months. Ambassador

[119] Resolution 2642 (XXV), November 20, 1970.
[120] U.N. document A/L.605, November 20, 1970; text in *Department of State Bulletin*, December 14, 1970, p. 735.
[121] Resolution 2632 (XXV).

[Seymour M.] Finger [U.S. Alternate Representative], in his statement to the General Assembly on this matter,[122] stressed the absolute necessity of completing Assembly work within the agreed time. He furthermore suggested that with more careful planning and organization and with the session attended by more senior government officials, who can make policy decisions, the essential work of the Assembly might be completed within a considerably shorter period than the present 3-month session. The United States expects to be a member of the committee and will participate actively in its deliberations.

COMMITTEE I

Disarmament [123]

*   *   *

Korea

The Assembly again adopted by a large majority a resolution reaffirming the objectives and responsibilities of the United Nations in Korea.[124] The resolution, cosponsored by the United States and 19 other countries, was approved by a vote of 67 (U.S.) in favor, 28 against, with 22 abstentions. As in 1969, the resolution called for cooperation in easing tensions in the area and for the avoidance of incidents and activities in violation of the 1953 armistice agreement.[125]

As in previous years, resolutions were introduced by the supporters of the North Korean regime calling for: (a) the dissolution of the United Nations Commission for the Unification and Rehabilitation of Korea and (b) the withdrawal of all United Nations forces from Korea. Both resolutions were decisively rejected in the First Committee.

Outer Space

The General Assembly adopted four constructive resolutions on outer space on December 16.[126]

One resolution, which deals with the work of the Outer Space Committee on the scientific and technical side, carries forward the President's initiative in 1969 when he undertook to associate

---

122 Text of statement, November 9, 1970, in *Department of State Bulletin,* December 21, 1970, pp. 762–764.
123 For the substance of this section see Documents 8–19.
124 Resolution 2668 (XXV), December 7, 1970.
125 *Documents, 1953,* pp. 289–297.
126 Resolutions 2733 A-D (XXV); details in *U.N. Monthly Chronicle,* January 1971, pp. 35–37.

the United Nations with experimentation with earth resources satellites.[127] As a part of this cooperative effort, scientific panels and other activities are being planned for 1971.

A second resolution calls for urgent action to complete the outer space liability convention, which the United States strongly supports.

A third resolution, a joint Philippine–U.S.–Madagascar–Thai initiative, calls on the World Meteorological Organization to intensify the effort to develop typhoon prediction technology and to take action to minimize the destructive effect of such ocean-generated storms as the recent (November 1970) disaster that struck East Pakistan.

The fourth resolution summarizes the agreed results of an Outer Space Committee study on direct broadcast satellites and notes the potential of this infant technology for improving the telecommunications infrastructure of developing countries; for economic, social, and cultural development in education, agriculture, health, and family planning; and for better understanding among peoples through expanded exchange of information, knowledge, and culture.

The work of the United Nations concerning outer space and space-related activities continues to be extremely positive. We are proud of the leadership of the United States in contributing to and stimulating this work.

Strengthening International Security

The United States is pleased at the outcome of the lengthy negotiations on the Declaration on Strengthening International Security,[128] but as Ambassador Yost stated in his general debate speech on September 30 [129] and in First Committee on December 14, we do not believe that it is worthwhile to devote so much of the time and effort of the United Nations to producing such sweeping hortatory declarations. This is especially so when declarations restate charter provisions or paraphrase previous declarations and resolutions.

"Strengthening international security" was an item introduced by the Soviet Union at the last General Assembly and carried over to this one. It represents the main Soviet initiative in the 24th and 25th sessions. The main Soviet goal was to improve their image as "peacemakers" in the U.N. At the same time they wanted a U.N. "endorsement" of the Brezhnev doctrine of

[127] Cf. *Documents, 1968–69*, p. 475.
[128] Resolution 2734 (XXV), adopted December 16, 1970 by a vote of 120–1 with 1 abstention.
[129] *Department of State Bulletin*, October 19, 1970, pp. 437–445.

limited sovereignty [130] and to produce a document underlining certain provisions of the U.N. Security Council Resolution 242 [131] on the Middle East as a point of departure for propaganda attacks on Israel and the United States.

Attempts to secure General Assembly approval for such a one-sided declaration bogged down last year, and this year competing drafts submitted by Western European, Latin American, and nonaligned countries were submitted. In our view the Western draft, which was the product of much hard work, was clearly preferable to the others. The United States followed closely the intensive negotiations leading to the introduction of the compromise draft approved by the Assembly. As the Soviet Representative himself admitted, the compromise declaration contained less of the Soviet language than that of any of the other groups of cosponsors. The Brezhnev doctrine is laid to rest in operative paragraph 1 of the declaration, which establishes the sovereign equality of states as an absolute principle of international relations. One-sided references to the Middle East have been eliminated or carefully balanced. Several references to peaceful settlement of disputes, peacekeeping operations, and development have been inserted which the Soviet Government strongly opposes. On the whole, the declaration is a good one.

Whatever the merits of the text itself, however, we must consider its cost. Had the efforts expended in producing this document been devoted to solving the real problems of the world community this would have been a more successful session and international peace and security would have been strengthened.

Seabeds and the Law of the Sea [132]

*   *   *

SPECIAL POLITICAL COMMITTEE

Peacekeeping

In delivering the U.S. opening statement in debate on this item [133] Ambassador Yost expressed his deep disappointment that the Special Committee on Peacekeeping and its working group were not able to show progress on questions of substance which

[130] The Brezhnev Doctrine was enunciated by Leonid I. Brezhnev, General Secretary of the Communist Party of the U.S.S.R. in an address to the Fifth Congress of the Polish United Workers' (Communist) Party in Warsaw on November 12, 1968; cf. *Documents, 1968–69*, p. 464.
[131] *Documents, 1967*, pp. 169–170.
[132] For the substance of this section see Documents 79–82.
[133] Text of statement, November 5, 1970, in U.S./U.N. Press Release 158.

would have made possible an agreement on how U.N. peace-keeping efforts should be authorized, established, and carried out. He expressed pleasure at the many statements made by distinguished leaders from all parts of the world in both the general debate and the commemorative session in which they urged that steps be taken now to improve U.N. peacekeeping capabilities. Although virtually all subsequent speakers in the debate in the Special Committee shared Ambassador Yost's concern at lack of progress on guidelines for peacekeeping, no support for seeking even limited agreements was forthcoming. Instead the committee was content to pass unanimously a resolution [134] which instructs the Special Committee on Peacekeeping to intensify its further efforts with a view to completing its report on U.N. military observer missions by May 1, 1971, and to submit a completed report to the 26th session of the General Assembly in September 1971.

In a closing statement Ambassador Yost again expressed U.S. regret that this session had been unable to take any concrete actions to strengthen U.N. peacekeeping.[135] He recalled that he had hoped frankly for an initiative that might have resulted in insuring the readiness and availability of men and facilities for peacekeeping emergencies.

The above resolution was unanimously adopted by the General Assembly on December 8.[136]

United Nations Relief and Works Agency for Palestine Refugees in the Near East

Five resolutions were adopted on this subject. One urged UNRWA to continue its efforts.[137] Another created a working group to try to resolve the serious UNRWA financial crisis.[138] Two resolutions reaffirmed the right of those persons displaced as a result of the 1967 conflict to return to their homes in the occupied territories,[139] and another affirmed that the "people of Palestine" have the right to self-determination and declared that their "inalienable rights" are "an indispensable element in the establishment of a just and lasting peace in the Middle East." [140]

[134] U.N. Document A/SPC/L. 194, November 13, 1970.
[135] Statement of November 13, 1970 in *Department of State Bulletin,* January 18, 1971, pp. 89–92.
[136] Resolution 2670 (XXV).
[137] Resolution 2728 (XXV), December 15, 1970; adopted unanimously.
[138] Resolution 2656 (XXV), December 7, 1970; adopted without objection.
[139] Resolutions 2672 B (XXV) and 2672 D (XXV), December 8, 1970; adopted by a vote of 93–5 with 7 abstentions and 114–1 with 2 abstentions, respectively.
[140] Resolution 2672 C (XXV), December 8, 1970; adopted by a vote of 74–22 with 50 abstentions.

The only controversial resolution was the last, and its most ardent supporters gave to it the interpretation that the "people of Palestine" were entitled to self-determination without any regard for the sovereign rights of Israel or Jordan or any other state in the area, despite the fact that they are members of the United Nations and entitled to full rights under the United Nations Charter. The United States opposed this resolution on grounds that it was intended to call into question Israel's right of existence and to distort Security Council Resolution 242. The advocates of this resolution were those who had refused to participate in the voting on General Assembly Resolution 2628,[141] alleging that Security Council Resolution 242 was antithetical to the rights of the Palestinian people. The Special Political Committee resolution on "inalienable rights" was adopted in plenary by a slim vote of 47 to 22, with 50 abstentions. The vote on a similar resolution at the 24th session of the United Nations General Assembly had been 48 to 22, with 47 abstentions.[142]

*   *   *

Apartheid

The General Assembly adopted seven resolutions dealing with apartheid. The first resolution dealt with the reaffirmation of Security Council Resolution 282 [143] concerning the application of an arms embargo against South Africa. The United States had to abstain on the General Assembly resolution for the same reasons that it expressed in the Security Council when Resolution 282 was adopted. These reasons were that the United States believed that Resolution 282 contained sweeping provisions to which the United States could not commit itself.[144]

Regarding the resolution concerning the decision to expand the membership of the Apartheid Committee,[145] the United States, because it had not supported the original resolution establishing the committee, was unable to support its expansion.

The United States was pleased after modifications were made by the cosponsors to vote in favor of the resolution calling for assistance in the economic, social, and humanitarian fields to oppressed people of South Africa.[146]

---

[141] Document 32.
[142] Resolution 2535 (XXIV), December 10, 1969.
[143] Document 61 (a).
[144] Cf. Document 61 (b).
[145] Resolution 2671 A (XXV), December 8, 1970; adopted by a vote of 105–2 with 6 abstentions.
[146] Resolution 2671 B (XXV), December 8, 1970; adopted by a vote of 111–2 with 1 abstention.

With respect to the resolutions on dissemination of information on apartheid [147] and on convening of a seminar on apartheid by the trade unions,[148] the United States was unable to support these resolutions because of some of the provisions contained in them.

As in previous years, the United States voted in favor of the resolution dealing with the South Africa Trust Fund.[149]

On the general question of apartheid, the United States found it necessary to vote against this resolution [150] because it gave much stronger emphasis to sanctions under chapter VII of the charter. The position of the United States with regard to apartheid in general is well known in that it continues to unequivocally oppose the practice of apartheid in South Africa.

COMMITTEE II

International Development Strategy for the Second U.N. Development Decade [151]

*   *   *

United Nations Volunteers

Another major accomplishment of the Second Committee was the adoption of the resolution recommended by the 49th session of the Economic and Social Council which established the U.N. volunteers effective January 1, 1971.[152] The resolution requested the Secretary General to designate the administrator of the U.N. Development Program as administrator of an International Volunteer Corps and to appoint a coordinator of these volunteers. The Secretary General is also requested to invite governments and interested organizations to contribute to a special voluntary fund for the support of the activities of the volunteers.

By adopting this resolution, the General Assembly completed the necessary legislative action within the U.N. system to authorize the setting up of a practical and viable solution for creating "a legion of volunteers in the service of mankind" as proposed

[147] Resolution 2671 C (XXV), December 8, 1970; adopted by a vote of 107–2 with 6 abstentions.

[148] Resolution 2671 D (XXV), December 8, 1970; adopted by a vote of 106–2 with 7 abstentions.

[149] Resolution 2671 E (XXV), December 8, 1970; adopted by a vote of 111–2 with 1 abstention.

[150] Resolution 2671 F (XXV), December 8, 1970; adopted by a vote of 91–6 with 16 abstentions.

[151] For the substance of this section see Documents 77–78.

[152] Resolution 2659 (XXV), December 7, 1970; adopted by a vote of 91–0 with 12 abstentions.

2 years ago by the Shah of Iran [Muhammad Reza Pahlavi]. This initiative has had the strong support of the U.S. Government.

United Nations Development Program

An important sequel to the strategy for the Second Development Decade as a milestone in the history of U.N. activity in the economic and social development field was the adoption by the Second Committee of ECOSOC Resolution 1530 (XLIX) on the capacity of the U.N. development system.

This resolution incorporated the comprehensive "consensus" which had been carefully worked out at the 10th session of the Governing Council of the UNDP as a result of the recommendations contained in the Jackson capacity study.[153] The major features of the consensus were the formulation of the UNDP country programming procedures based on indicative planning figures, the elimination of remaining distinctions between Special Fund and technical assistance resources, provisions for overall disposition of resources, and the strengthening and reorganization of the program at the country and at headquarters level.

Although there were some aspects of the consensus which the United States believed could stand improvement, we considered it to be the best compromise that could be achieved at this time, and as a consequence we were successful in our efforts to see the statement adopted without change by the General Assembly.[154]

International University

Further significant progress on the question of the establishment of an international university was made in the Second Committee as a result of the adoption of a resolution inviting UNESCO to prepare studies of the educational, financial, and organizational aspects of such a university. It also authorized the Secretary General to establish, in due course, a panel of 10 government-sponsored and 5 U.N.-sponsored experts for the purpose of assisting him in his further consultations and studies concerning the establishment of an international university. A possible jurisdictional conflict between the Secretary General and UNESCO was averted by the careful wording of the resolution, which received wide support.[155]

---

153 Cf. note 42 to Document 75. The Governing Council of the U.N. Development Program held its 10th session in Geneva June 9–30, 1970.
154 Resolution 2688 (XXV), December 11, 1970; adopted without objection.
155 Resolution 2691 (XXV), December 11, 1970; adopted by a vote of 94–0 with 11 abstentions.

World Population Year

The Second Committee held an extended debate in connection with the consideration of a resolution [156] recommended for adoption by ECOSOC designating the year 1974 as World Population Year and requesting the Secretary General to prepare a detailed program of activities in this connection. The final version of the resolution adopted by the committee, with an unusually high number of abstentions, had been revised by qualifier statements in several paragraphs to reflect the concern of many developing countries over the trend toward considering population as a key factor to economic and social development. Statements made in the committee by Latin Americans, Francophone Africans, and the Soviet bloc revealed that the attitudes of these countries were hardening in opposition to the need for U.N. activities in the field of population control.

U.N. Conference on the Human Environment

The debate in the Second Committee on the U.N. Conference on the Human Environment to be held in Stockholm in June 1972 was somewhat overshadowed by the holding of a 2-day informal meeting of the preparatory committee for the conference just 2 weeks previously. Nevertheless, as the result of Second Committee action, the General Assembly adopted a resolution [157] requesting the Secretary General to convene the second and third sessions of the preparatory committee February 8–19, 1971, and September 13–24, 1971, at Geneva and New York, respectively. At the insistence of the developing countries, led by Brazil and Chile, what was to be essentially a procedural resolution was amended to include paragraphs recommending the inclusion in the agenda of the forthcoming sessions of the preparatory committee of items relating to economic and social aspects as they affect the environmental policies and development plans of developing countries. It also recommended that the preparatory committee consider in its preparations for the conference the financing of possible activities for the protection of the human environment in developing countries.

Most developed countries, including the United States, voted for the resolution despite their opposition to the financing provision. Opposition to this controversial paragraph was based to a large extent on the confrontation tactics used by the developing countries to secure their views. As a result of this clash of views,

---

[156] Adopted as General Assembly Resolution 2683 (XXV), December 11, 1970 by a vote of 71–8 with 31 abstentions.

[157] Resolution 2657 (XXV), December 7, 1970; adopted by a vote of 86–0 with 10 abstentions.

it was clearly evident that much remained to be done to persuade the developing countries that their concern that environmental activities would detract from development objectives was unfounded.

Committee III

High Commissioner for Human Rights

Establishment of the post of High Commissioner for Human Rights was given highest priority last year by the 24th General Assembly, when the question was deferred to this year's General Assembly. Actual debate on the issue in this Assembly, however, was prevented by a manifest filibuster by its opponents throughout the Third Committee debates. Thus, although the High Commissioner item was fourth on the agenda of 15 items, the committee did not commence the debate until the last week of the session. It began only after several confusing and delaying sessions during which the committee decided to allot only five of the remaining meetings to the High Commissioner item.

The debate was marked by long and tendentious speeches by opponents of the establishment of the Office of High Commissioner. The United States was unable to speak because of lack of time. Canada moved to close the debate in order to permit a vote on a resolution agreeing in principle to the creation of the post. A motion by Ceylon to adjourn the debate without voting on any resolution was adopted, however, by a vote of 54 to 38 (U.S.), with 15 abstentions. Thus, action was deferred for at least a year.

The United States will continue to support the proposal to establish a High Commissioner for Human Rights, and we hope that it will be adopted at the 26th General Assembly.[158]

We attach special importance to this proposal since we believe it is an important step to further respect for human rights everywhere in keeping with the human rights provisions of the charter.

Humane Treatment of Prisoners of War

During consideration of an agenda item on human rights in armed conflict, Senator Claiborne Pell, speaking for the United States, made a major statement calling for humane treatment of all prisoners,[159] and in particular of American captives held prisoners of war in North Viet-Nam and Southeast Asia. The Senator stressed the importance of strict compliance with the 1949 Geneva Convention Relative to the Treatment of Prisoners

---

158 On December 14, 1970, the General Assembly agreed to defer this item until its 26th session.
159 *Department of State Bulletin,* January 4, 1971, pp. 8–11.

of war.[160] He said mere assertions of humane treatment of captive U.S. citizens by North Viet-Nam could be no substitute for inspection of places of detention of the prisoners by the International Committee of the Red Cross or by a neutral government or humanitarian organization. The Senator cited provisions of the Geneva Convention requiring the application of internationally agreed minimum standards of humane treatment to all prisoners of war. He said that humane treatment was not a political issue but a human rights question, one behind which all segments of opinion could unite.

In addition, a specific resolution sponsored by the United States, along with Belgium, Dahomey, the Dominican Republic, Greece, Haiti, Italy, Madagascar, New Zealand, the Philippines, Thailand, and Togo called for strict compliance with the Geneva Convention. The resolution was adopted by the General Assembly on December 9 by a vote of 67 (U.S.) to 30, with 20 abstentions.[161] Key provisions stress the obligations to permit inspections of all places of detention and to repatriate seriously sick and wounded prisoners. In addition, the resolution endorses the continuing efforts of the International Committee of the Red Cross to secure effective application of the Convention, urges the Secretary General to exert all efforts to obtain humane treatment of prisoners of war, urges humane treatment for those captives who do not meet all the requirements of the definition of prisoners of war, and in general urges compliance with international humanitarian instruments applicable to armed conflict.

The United States also supported other human rights in time of armed conflict resolutions calling for humane treatment of civilians and of journalists,[162] a resolution put forward by France, as well as a procedural resolution [163] asking, among other things, for governments to comment on the Secretary General's reports [164] on human rights in armed conflict and for the 26th General Assembly to consider the reports and the comments.

Narcotics Control

President Nixon, in his address to the commemorative session, stressed the need for international cooperation to curb narcotics

---

[160] Signed at Geneva August 12, 1949; text in United Nations, *Treaty Series*, vol. 75 (1950), No. 972.

[161] Resolution 2676 (XXV); cf. Document 46.

[162] Resolution 2673 (XXV), December 9, 1970; adopted by a vote of 85–0 with 32 abstentions.

[163] Resolution 2677 (XXV), December 9, 1970; adopted by a vote of 111–0 with 4 abstentions.

[164] U.N. documents A/7720 and A/8052.

traffic and abuse. In keeping with this initiative the General Assembly adopted two strong resolutions on this question.

One resolution strongly endorses the decision of ECOSOC for the establishment of a program of action on drug abuse including the creation of a United Nations Fund for Drug Abuse Control.[165] The other resolution [166] calls on members of the U.N. and appeals to nonmembers to "consider seriously the possibility of enacting adequate legislation providing severe penalties for those engaged in illicit trade and trafficking of narcotic drugs."

The United States expressed its pleasure at this constructive action toward a problem which affects many nations.

Committee IV

Colonial and Racial Issues

The problems of Southern Africa, Rhodesia, the Portuguese territories, and Namibia commanded more than two-thirds of the Fourth Committee's time.

As in recent years, most of the Assembly's resolutions dealing with colonial problems contained provisions calling for measures which prevented the United States from fully supporting them. Regarding the resolutions on Namibia, the United States was able to vote for the creation of a Namibia fund to aid Namibians,[167] and it was pleased that the cosponsors made certain modifications to that resolution so that the United States could vote affirmatively. Unfortunately, on the general resolution on Namibia,[168] the United States was unable to support it because of its failure to recognize the actions of the Security Council [169] and its call for the invoking of chapter VII of the U.N. Charter. Other resolutions, on Southern Rhodesia,[170] for example, called for condemnatory measures which under the charter are clearly within the competence of the Security Council. As such they were unacceptable to the United States, and we were compelled to vote against them.[171]

Resolutions against activities of foreign economic and other

165 Resolution 2719 (XXV), December 15, 1970; adopted by a vote of 106–0 with 8 abstentions.
166 Resolution 2710 (XXV), December 15, 1970; adopted unanimously.
167 Resolution 2679 (XXV), December 9, 1970; adopted by a vote of 102–2 with 8 abstentions.
168 Resolution 2678 (XXV), December 9, 1970; adopted by a vote of 95–5 with 14 abstentions.
169 Document 62.
170 Resolution 2652 (XXV), December 3, 1970; adopted by a vote of 79–10 with 14 abstentions.
171 Cf. Documents 59–60.

interests said to be impeding the implementation of the Declaration on the Granting of Independence to Colonial Countries and Peoples [172] and calling for implementation of that declaration by the specialized agencies were likewise unacceptable to the United States. The first resolution [173] was based on false assumptions regarding private foreign investment. The second [174] called upon the specialized agencies and international institutions to take actions which in many cases are inconsistent with their own statutes and with their agreements with the U.N.

The United States continued to make clear its unswerving opposition to colonialism and racial discrimination in all of its forms. We remain convinced, however, that the U.N. can best contribute to progress against these evils by actions which are intrinsically sound, widely supported, and within the capacity of the U.N. to carry out.

COMMITTEE V

1971 Budget and Scale of Assessments

Responsive to the wishes of member governments concerned with the issue of economy, the Secretary General in introducing his budget estimates for 1971 announced that he had decided to review his estimates with the objective of reducing the total requirements from an estimated $200 million projected for 1971 to the level of $193 million. This saving of $7 million would represent a reduction in the percentage increase of the 1971 budget over 1970 from 18.8 percent to 14.8 percent.

In projecting a level of $193 million, the Secretary General took into account an 8-percent salary increase effective January 1 for professional and hired staff which had been recommended by the International Civil Service Advisory Board, amounting to $8.8 million, and an estimated $3 million for new construction costs in 1971. During the course of the Assembly, the salary increase was reduced through deferment of the effective date of the increase from January 1 to July 1, 1971, with a savings to the budget of $4.4 million. The cost of new construction, however, was increased from $3 million to $4 million, and additional appropriations unforeseen in the Secretary General's initial estimates and resulting from decisions reached by the Gen-

[172] *Documents, 1960,* pp. 575–577.
[173] Resolution 2703 (XXV), December 14, 1970; adopted by a vote of 85–11 with 12 abstentions.
[174] Resolution 2704 (XXV), December 14, 1970; adopted by a vote of 83–4 with 21 abstentions.

eral Assembly resulted in a total budget for 1971 of $192.1 million,[175] an increase of 14 percent over the budget for 1970.

Believing that this rate of growth was excessive and that the 8-percent salary increase was not fully justified, the United States for the first time in 25 years did not vote in favor of the U.N. budget, but instead abstained. The United States abstention was designed to emphasize the urgent need for certain measures of reform in United Nations fiscal, budgetary, and programing policies and procedures.

The General Assembly approved a new scale of assessments [176] for contributions from member states to the regular budget for the 3-year period 1971–73. The U.S. assessment rate under this new scale was reduced from its previous level of 31.57 percent to 31.52 percent.

Committee VI

International Court of Justice

The United States joined with 11 other delegations in requesting inscription of this item on the agenda. The cosponsors requested inscription of this item in the belief that the International Court of Justice has not been used as fully as it might be and that it would be useful to focus international attention at the 25th anniversary session on the principal judicial organ of the U.N. We believe the Court has a greater contribution to make to the peaceful settlement of disputes than it has been enabled to do so far.

Speaking for the United States, Senator Jacob Javits,[177] a member of this year's U.S. delegation, said he was pleased that the General Assembly discussed this matter in a serious and positive manner and decided to commence a review of the role of the International Court of Justice.[178] We believe the comments which will be received from governments and from the International Court itself, if it deems it advisable, will be a further positive contribution and will enable the General Assembly at its next session to take further steps in the review process, including the establishment of an ad hoc committee to explore the matter in depth.

[175] Resolution 2738 A (XXV), December 17, 1970; adopted by a vote of 97–10 with 7 abstentions. For further background on the decisions of Committee V see Document 76.

[176] Resolution 2654 (XXV), December 4, 1970.

[177] Text in *Department of State Bulletin,* January 25, 1971, pp. 122–123; related material in same, pp. 116–121.

[178] Resolution 2723 (XXV), December 15, 1970; adopted unanimously.

Declaration on Friendly Relations

One of the highlights of the 25th General Assembly and in particular the anniversary celebration was the adoption by the General Assembly of the Declaration on Principles of International Law concerning Friendly Relations and Co-operation among States in accordance with the Charter of the United Nations.[179]

The declaration, which is the product of 6 years of work, represents the contemporary view of states on the following vital charter principles of international law: the prohibition of the threat or use of force, the obligation to settle disputes by peaceful means, the duty not to intervene in matters within the domestic jurisdiction of any state, the duty to cooperate, the principle of equal rights and self-determination of peoples, good faith in fulfillment of obligations, and the sovereign equality of states.

The declaration represents a positive and balanced legal clarification of the rights and duties of states contained in the charter. We believe the long search for agreement on the definition of these principles was an important contribution to the vigor and health of the United Nations organization and the charter upon which it is based.

Interference With Civil Aviation (Hijacking)[180]

*   *   *

Charter Review

The General Assembly discussed the question of charter review, which had been carried over from last year. Several delegations, in particular the Philippines, made concrete proposals for charter revision. Other delegations, particularly the Soviet Union, strongly opposed any consideration of the matter.

The United States is not opposed to the principle of charter review. We suggested in the course of the debate that charter review is not the sole means of enhancing the capacity of the United Nations and urged that states not be distracted by the less immediate goal of charter review from the work of existing committees on such matters as peacekeeping and the functioning of the General Assembly.

The United States believes the decision to seek government comments and to inscribe the item on the agenda of the 27th

179 Cf. note 106, above.
180 For the substance of this section see Documents 83–85.

General Assembly was an appropriate method of handling the matter at this time.

We shall examine with interest the comments governments will be submitting on this important matter between now and 1972.

X.
INTERNATIONAL ECONOMIC AND FINANCIAL AFFAIRS

A. America in the World Economy.

(88) The Economic Report: Message by President Nixon to the Congress Transmitting the Annual Report of the Council of Economic Advisers, February 2, 1970.[1]

(Excerpt)

To the Congress of the United States:

*　　*　　*

Strengthening the World Economy

The achievement of greater balance and stability in our own economy is also important for international finance and trade. The dollar is not only our currency; it provides the principal vehicle for world trade and payments. We are the world's largest exporter and importer, and instability in the United States— whether it involves inflation or recession—has unsettling effects on the world economy. Inflationary pressures arising in the United States have added to inflationary problems in other countries in recent years. The long inflation has also weakened our trading position. However, with the restraining of excessive demand in 1969, the deterioration in our trade balance has been arrested.

I am particularly gratified to note improvements in the international monetary scene during the past year with the introduction of Special Drawing Rights[2] and with the realignment of several important currencies. In cooperation with other coun-

---

[1] Text from *Weekly Compilation of Presidential Documents*, February 9, 1970, pp. 103–151; for the context see *The United States in World Affairs, 1970*, Section 39.

[2] Cf. note 17 to Document 2.

tries, we are actively investigating other ways to make the international monetary system more stable and orderly, and to give more attention to international coordination and synchronization in the management of domestic economic policies.

Although a high and rising level of international trade can add to the prosperity of the United States and other countries, imports from time to time may cause domestic dislocations. Since the gains from international trade are enjoyed by the country as a whole, it is appropriate that the costs of trade-associated dislocations be spread more evenly. The trade bill presented to the Congress in November [3] contains practical adjustment assistance and escape-clause provisions that would soften the impact of import competition in cases where it harms our own workingmen. It also includes the repeal of the American selling price method of tariff evaluation, a step which is important in reducing the nontariff barriers to U.S. exports.

Trade is vital to the progress of the less developed countries of the world. With other industrialized nations, the United States is exploring ways of enabling less developed nations to participate more in the growing volume of international trade.

* * *

RICHARD NIXON

February 2, 1970

(89) Meeting of the Boards of Governors of the International Monetary Fund and the International Bank for Reconstruction and Development, Copenhagen, September 21–25, 1970: Statement by David M. Kennedy, Secretary of the Treasury, September 22, 1970.[4]

(Excerpt)

* * *

The year since we last met together has been marked by important accomplishments. Special drawing rights have begun to play a useful role among the complex of reserve assets.[5] We

[3] For text of President Nixon's message to the Congress, November 18, 1969, see *Documents, 1968–69,* pp. 522–530; see also Document 91, below.
[4] Department of the Treasury Press Release, September 22, 1970; text from *Department of State Bulletin,* October 12, 1970, pp. 431–435. For the context see *The United States in World Affairs, 1970,* Section 37.
[5] The International Monetary Fund allocated $3.4 million in Special Drawing Rights on January 1, 1970; cf. note 17 to Document 2.

look forward to sizable increases in Fund quotas. The World Bank Group [6] has passed an historic milestone in becoming the largest source of development finance. Its vigor is further reflected in imaginative efforts to bring its funds to bear more directly on pressing development problems. The agreement looking toward replenishment of the resources of the International Development Association at a level of $800 million a year should help to assure the availability of funds to maintain this forward momentum. Progress of our institutions has been accompanied by vigorous growth in trade, a marked reduction in exchange market pressures, and substantial repayments of the short-term and emergency credits accumulated in earlier years.

These are substantial achievements. Yet events of the past year have also clearly exposed basic challenges to the financial stability and liberal trading order upon which the success of the Fund and the Bank must ultimately rest.

PROGRESS IN BRAKING U.S. INFLATION

Inflation is the first of those challenges. In nearly every industrialized country, wage and other income claims are rising faster than capacity to expand real goods and services. As a consequence, the foundations of orderly economic progress are undermined.

I believe our actions have demonstrated the central importance we in the United States have attached to dealing with inflation. We did not shrink from the painful task of applying the tested instruments of firm budgetary control and strong monetary restraints.

I should point out, too, that—alongside the general program of restraint—the determined efforts of President Nixon to scale down the Viet-Nam conflict have set the stage for a decline in defense spending projected at more than $5 billion during the current fiscal year.[7] Manpower and budget resources are being released for more productive use in areas of high social and economic priority. We are thus beginning to reverse a process that contributed so strongly to the buildup of inflationary momentum in the second half of the 1960's.

Eliminating excess demand and braking inflation exacted a cost: By the turn of the year, real economic growth in the United States had been temporarily brought to a standstill. As pressures on the labor market subsided, the unemployment rate

[6] Includes, in addition to the International Bank for Reconstruction and Development, the International Development Association and the International Finance Corporation.
[7] Cf. Document 4.

this summer rose to about 5 percent—considerably higher than would be appropriate over any extended period of time.

However, considerable evidence is also accumulating that the needed adjustments in expectations and actual pricing behavior are underway. The most encouraging sign is that industrial wholesale prices—normally a good barometer of the pricing environment—rose at a seasonally adjusted annual rate of barely more than $2\frac{1}{2}$ percent over the summer, substantially less than the 4-percent rate experienced in 1969. Productivity growth seems to be resuming, helping manufacturers to absorb higher labor costs. The rise in consumer prices has also begun to slow.

At the same time, we fully recognize that the inflationary process in the United States, as in the world at large, is not yet under full control. As elsewhere, the response has been slower than experience or theory would have led us to expect. In these circumstances, I believe we could all profit from intensive consideration of recent experience in the Fund and in the Organization for Economic Cooperation and Development or other forums, looking toward both effective and mutually satisfactory solutions.

For our own part, we are determined to maintain cautious and responsible financial policies. We are willing to accept some budgetary deficit this year when the economy is not under demand pressure. We are also willing to see some rebuilding of private liquidity. Our money and capital markets already reflect some easing of tensions, and we now see signs of a resumption of economic growth.

Our progress in guiding the economy toward reasonable price stability without lapsing into serious recession is, I believe, a noteworthy achievement. But we are as fully aware of the danger of too fast expansion and renewed over-heating as we were of deep recession. We mean to keep Government spending below the limits set by our revenue potential at high levels of income and employment. We will not encourage an expansion of money and credit of proportions that could fuel an excessive burst of demand. A steady, rather than precipitous, advance offers the best prospect for combining fuller employment with greater price stability.

U.S. BALANCE OF PAYMENTS

The process of internal adjustment has been accompanied by sharp crosscurrents in our external accounts. Our current account has improved rather substantially. Indeed, helped by a considerable expansion in exports, transactions in nonmilitary goods and services were generating net receipts at an annual rate of nearly $7½ billion during the first half of the year, more than $2½ billion higher than a year ago. On the other hand, continued heavy Government expenditures overseas required for security and for aid and other purposes were practically as large as that surplus. At the same time, there was a sharp reversal of the extraordinarily favorable pattern of capital flows in recent years, throwing our overall accounts into substantial deficit. In the first 6 months, we recorded a deficit on official settlements of some $4½ billion, an amount slightly exceeding the surplus accumulated over the 2 previous years.

I believe sizable short-term swings in our payments position must be anticipated in a world of relatively free markets and volatile capital movements. I believe we have the capacity to handle those swings so long as they take place within the context of a strengthening current surplus. The current recovery in our trade account, while favorably affected by cyclical developments, points in the right direction. But I recognize it can only be a start.

The steady growth in earnings on our foreign investment account—which nearly tripled in the past decade—is a long-term element of strength. As interest rates return to more normal levels, we should also be able to look forward to some lightening of the extraordinary burden that interest payments have placed on our position. The phasing down of the Viet-Nam conflict—as well as a more equitable sharing of the costs of mutual security in other areas—could help reduce our foreign exchange outlays for defense. But, fundamentally, our effort must rest on a solid competitive position arising from much better domestic price performance. In that respect, our domestic and balance-of-payments goals coincide.

TRADING RELATIONS AMONG NATIONS

The growing friction and concern about trading relations among nations are a third major challenge. In my own country, protectionist sentiments have been increasingly expressed by elements in labor and industry, and restrictive legislation has considerable congressional support.[8]

President Nixon has made clear his commitment to resist these pressures.[9] We mean to preserve and expand the enormous benefits flowing from free and competitive world commerce. In developing measures to meet our own trading problems, we have emphasized measures to support the efforts of our own

[8] Cf. Document 90.
[9] Cf. Document 91.

industry to look outward and compete abroad on a fair and equal basis.

But it is clear that success in maintaining a liberal trading environment can be achieved only by means of a worldwide effort.

Those countries in a strong position, but with markets heavily protected by outmoded quantitative restrictions, should accept a special responsibility to reduce and eliminate import barriers. Agricultural policies that artificially but effectively close markets to more efficient producers urgently require review. Temptations to achieve trading advantage through discriminatory trading arrangements at odds with broader international obligations should be resisted, for they can only be divisive and provoke protectionist reactions elsewhere. The important efforts underway to open markets more freely to the poorer countries, and to free aid from special procurement restrictions, can succeed only as all industrial countries are ready to cooperate fairly and fully.

In the best of circumstances, the way ahead will not be smooth and easy. The danger is that we all could be swept into a self-defeating spiral of efforts to defend particular interests. The only answer can be to reassert—forcefully and widely—the primacy of our strong mutual interest in freer and multilateral trade.

Exchange Rate Relationships and Practices

In the international financial area, our successes in reducing restrictions and freeing markets have brought a different set of problems. International flows of liquid funds have become enormous. They are highly sensitive to differences in cyclical circumstances and monetary policy in individual countries. As a result, independent national monetary policies must often work within narrow limits. At the same time, we have learned that gradual divergences of trends in costs, prices, and incomes can, over longer periods of time, produce exceedingly difficult problems of balance-of-payments adjustment.

It is in this context that I welcome the very useful report of the Executive Directors on the Role of Exchange Rates in the Adjustment of International Payments.[10] That report, and the discussions that have contributed to it, have done much to clarify and advance our thinking. Indeed, I believe it is fair to say that while important differences of opinion remain, the re-

[10] International Monetary Fund, *The Role of Exchange Rates in the Adjustment of International Payments: A Report by the Executive Directors* (September 1970).

port rather clearly points toward an evolving consensus of official thinking in important respects.

The authors wisely emphasize the value of a broad stability in exchange rate relationships and practices. At the same time, the report seems to me to recognize that there are circumstances in which more flexible techniques and practices, within the general context of the Bretton Woods system,[11] could make a practical and useful contribution to maintaining the basic conditions for free trade and orderly markets. For the present, judgment is suspended as to the desirability or form of a particular amendment to the articles to define more specifically the range of possible and desirable actions.

These conclusions imply, I believe, a desire to test the possible need for formal amendments against the evolving situation. We will be particularly interested to see whether national and Fund decisionmaking, within the considerable latitude of the present articles, can and will benefit from the new thinking and new techniques reflected in the report. The Executive Directors may also want to examine more precisely the forms an amendment might take, should our objectives and experience subsequently make it desirable to move in that direction.

As I indicated a year ago, I do not believe the techniques of limited exchange flexibility can provide any kind of a substitute for effective policies on our part to deal with our inflation and balance of payments.[12] As in the past, the dollar must be strong and stable to play its key role in the monetary system, alongside gold and now SDR's. I know of no exchange rate mechanism that can change that fundamental need.

MULTILATERAL DEVELOPMENT ASSISTANCE

President Nixon only last week, in a special message to the Congress, stressed the determination of the United States to respond positively to the challenge of reshaping foreign assistance to meet the needs of the 1970's.[13] As a fundamental part of sweep-

[11] Articles of Agreement of the International Monetary Fund, opened for signature December 27, 1945 and entered into force December 27, 1945; text in *Documents, 1943–1944*, pp. 338–373. Articles of Agreement of the International Bank for Reconstruction and Development, opened for signature December 27, 1945 and entered into force December 27, 1945; text in Senate Document 123, 81st Congress, 1st Session, *A Decade of American Foreign Policy: Basic Documents, 1941–49* (Washington: G.P.O., 1950), pp. 251–273.
[12] For Secretary Kennedy's statement before the 24th annual meeting of the Boards of Governors of the International Monetary Fund and the International Bank for Reconstruction and Development September 29–October 3, 1969 see *Department of State Bulletin,* October 5, 1969, pp. 353–358.
[13] Document 97.

ing changes in the U.S. approach to development finance, he emphasized our commitment to an increasingly multilateral approach—the approach epitomized by the World Bank Group. We aim to increase substantially our support for the international lending institutions. Our remaining bilateral development assistance will be restructured, with the objective of concentrating more fully on longer range needs and working more closely with other providers of funds.

I am glad to report that major legislation is already progressing through the Congress that will help flesh out these intentions with fresh commitments of funds to the World Bank, the Inter-American Development Bank, and its Fund for Special Operations, and the Asian Development Bank.[14] We plan to submit legislation for IDA replenishment early in the next session.

The new thrust of our own program helps highlight some emerging problems of foreign aid programing. It is commonplace today for a primary donor to be joined by other country donors —for one institution to work with or through sister or companion institutions—and for official assistance to take place side by side with private-sector participation. These efforts of donor countries must be integrated with the critically important efforts of the developing countries to enlarge their own savings and to employ them effectively. Rising debt burdens among many developing countries need to be appraised, and the implications more consciously considered, before crisis situations disrupt the development process.

These and other elements bearing upon the question of an appropriate level and composition of development lending are further complicated by the long time horizon in generating fresh flows of resources. For instance, the initial planning for the IDA replenishment took place in 1969.[15] The approval process is not likely to be completed much before 1972. The funds will not be fully committed until 1975, and the disbursements will extend into the early 1980's.

In the face of these complexities and the long time perspective, we cannot escape the requirement for longer range planning. We want to retain the strength that flows from the diversity and flexibility inherent in a variety of aid sources. Nevertheless, we do, it seems to me, need a better framework for setting priorities, for assessing available resources against needs over a period of years, and for dividing responsibilities sensibly.

With its special competence at the center of development

---

[14] Cf. note 7 to Document 66.
[15] Cf. *Documents 1968–69*, p. 547 at note 63.

finance, the World Bank has properly begun to provide some of the elements essential to a sensible planning process. I refer particularly to its long-range country studies and expanded program for economic missions. I hope the Bank will build on these efforts, collaborating closely, as desirable, with the Fund, the regional financial institutions, United Nations and other development agencies, and individual donor countries.

Obviously, planning alone cannot meet the needs of the 1970's. The multilateral institutions must be able to demonstrate their capacity to use sharply augmented funds effectively, and with appropriate balance, if they are to retain the support of sometimes skeptical legislatures. For that reason, I welcome the efforts of the Bank to broaden the scope of its internal auditing activity and to work toward better measurement of achievements against goals.

Our own progress in channeling more aid through the multilateral institutions will be dependent upon willingness of other countries to keep pace, thus appropriately spreading the burden. The broadening contributions to the Special Funds of the Asian Development Bank,[16] the search for a satisfactory mechanism for special contributions for the African Development Bank, and the possibility of added members in the Inter-American Development Bank—all open new opportunities.

I must also emphasize the importance we attach to enlisting the full energies of private citizens—whether in donor or receiving countries—in the development process. We look to the International Finance Corporation to play an increasing role. We would also urge an early agreement to proceed with an International Investment Insurance Agency, and I hope that it will have support from both investing countries and developing countries.

Finally, the President has made clear that the United States is ready to participate fully in those important aspects of development policy—including untying and generalized tariff preferences [17]—that complement financial aid. I would note particularly his proposal for a U.S. International Development Institute. The Institute would focus precisely on those areas—including population planning—where technological breakthroughs could potentially contribute enormously to the development process.

In reviewing the challenges that seem to press in on us so strongly from many directions, I am struck by the interaction

[16] Cf. Document 49.
[17] Cf. Documents 92 and 98.

among them. The problems of inflation, exchange markets, trade, capital movements, and aid cannot be kept in tight compartments.

The Bank and the Fund were founded on a vision of a free and prosperous community of nations, each sharing fairly in the enormous benefits that flow from multilateral trade, financial stability, and rapid development. That vision of the common good must shine as brightly today if it is to guide our way through the maze of difficulties before us. My country means to do its part. We mean to do so first of all by restoring a balance in prices, production, and income in our own economy. We propose to provide our fair share of assistance, public and private. We want to pay our way by competing fairly in world markets—and we expect markets to be open to us.

I believe these are goals that all can share. And by working together, they can be achieved.

B. United States Trade Policy.

(90) *The Rise of Protectionist Sentiment: Address by Ambassador Joseph A. Greenwald, United States Permanent Representative to the Organization for Economic Cooperation and Development, Malmö, Sweden, October 30, 1970.*[18]

(Complete Text)

In recent years there has been a rise of protectionist sentiment in the United States. This has caused much concern to our trading partners, with accompanying criticism and condemnation.

I would like to be able to tell you today that this is mainly smoke and that no real fire lies behind it. If I did, it would be misleading and perhaps dangerous. I believe the most useful service I can perform at this stage is to try to explain the forces at work in the United States and the confluence of factors which have led to the present situation. My aim is to contribute to a better appreciation of the U.S. scene, on the traditional assumption that understanding of a problem is the necessary first step toward constructive action to deal with it. I hope to provide the basis for thinking about current trade policy issues which

[18] Text from *Department of State Bulletin*, December 14, 1970, pp. 724–729; for the context of this and the following document see *The United States in World Affairs, 1970*, Section 38.

goes beyond the exchange of slogans—however self-righteous and satisfying that may be. I also propose to make some specific suggestions as to what might be done to improve the prospects for a continuation of the liberal trade policies followed by successive American administrations over the past 35 years.

Before analyzing the forces at work today which affect current U.S. trade policy attitudes, I would like to review briefly the historical background. My purpose is not to boast about the previous praiseworthiness of the United States but to give the present situation a longer term context.

With relatively little backsliding, six U.S. administrations have consistently followed a policy of trade liberalization since Cordell Hull launched the reciprocal trade agreements program in 1934. In the postwar period, the United States has taken the initiative in every major effort to dismantle trade barriers. We played a major role in the construction of the GATT [General Agreement on Tariffs and Trade] [19] and other international institutions dealing with trade and payments. Sweden and many other countries have supported these efforts.

The concrete result has been a significant reduction of customs tariffs and a massive expansion of world trade. Following a series of multilateral negotiations under GATT auspices,[20] the average level of American tariffs has been reduced by four-fifths from a 1930 peak of 50 percent to 9 percent when the Kennedy Round cuts are fully implemented in 1972. Other participating countries have, of course, made similar tariff concessions, but until convertibility of European currencies was achieved in 1958,[21] the use of import quotas for balance-of-payments reasons by other countries made a large part of the tariff concessions inoperative for U.S. exports. We accepted this temporary nonreciprocity and went further. Under the Marshall plan, for example, we used our missions abroad to find ways of promoting European exports to the United States. In fact, when our own balance-of-payments difficulties emerged in the sixties, it was necessary to launch a retraining program to get members of our Embassies thinking in terms of promoting U.S. exports.

In short, the United States has followed liberal trade policies for more than a third of a century. When the Nixon administration took office in January 1969, careful consideration was given to trade policy along with a wide range of other issues. President Nixon reaffirmed U.S. policy in the following terms: ". . . the

---

[19] Signed at Geneva October 30, 1947; cf. *Documents, 1947*, pp. 424–425.
[20] Cf. *Documents, 1962*, pp. 474–482; same, *1967*, pp. 451–453.
[21] Cf. *The United States in World Affairs, 1958*, pp. 172 and 408.

interest of the United States and the interest of the whole world will best be served by moving toward freer trade. . . ." [22]

Despite President Nixon's clear pronouncements in favor of continuing liberal trade policies, positions taken by key legislative figures and important groups in the United States have raised the question: Is America going back on its longstanding policy? Those who are familiar with the American Constitution know that congressional support and authority are necessary for the reduction of U.S. tariffs and other trade barriers. And this support depends in turn on the attitudes of the general public as well as specific interest groups. To answer the question, then, one must turn to an examination of the forces and factors which affect U.S. opinion on trade policy issues.

Developments in the United States

As Deputy Under Secretary of State [for Economic Affairs Nathaniel] Samuels pointed out in a recently published interview, a liberal trade policy still has tremendous intellectual support in the United States. Even the most vocal proponents of import restrictions seldom are willing to be described as protectionists. They usually argue the special case of a particular industry, the proposition that only the United States abides by the international rules and provides an open market to imports (especially from Japan), the need for restrictions to offset wage differentials or to correct the balance-of-payments deficit, etc.

There are a number of developments in the United States which have led to defection from or decline in support for the liberal trade forces.

The first change was the deterioration in the U.S. trade account. The reasons for the drastic drop in our large trade surplus, which has contributed substantially to our overall payments deficit, can be—and are—argued at great length. Regardless of the reasons, this development has had a major impact on thinking in the United States. Just as the postwar dollar gap looked permanent, so some people are now convinced that the United States has lost its ability to compete in world markets. Inevitably this leads to questions about the need for reconsideration of trade policy.

A second economic development is the increase in U.S. investment abroad and the growth of the multinational enterprise. Again, such a significant new factor leads people to question existing trade and investment policies. This foreign investment

[22] *Weekly Compilation of Presidential Documents*, February 10, 1969, p. 230.

phenomenon may soon loom larger for other countries as they become direct investors in the United States as well as recipients of U.S. investment. It appears that, for the first time, in 1969 Europeans moved faster than Americans in the growth of their investment abroad. The value of net assets owned by Europeans in the United States rose by a fifth, while the value of U.S. investment in Europe increased by just over a tenth. Interestingly, most of this European investment appears to be financed by raising funds in U.S. markets, just as U.S. firms are financing an increasing amount of their foreign direct investment by resort to foreign sources. U.S. investment is still twice as much as European investment, but the trend is clearly shifting from a one-way flow. The result is even greater economic interdependence and, as an American expert on the multinational enterprise puts it, one more "contributory cause to the increasing sense of nakedness and exposure to international forces that many advanced countries have begun to feel."

The third characteristic of the current trade policy environment affects all countries, but perhaps with differing intensities. This is the increased rate of change in technology and competitive conditions. The movement of science and technology has accelerated tremendously. And the flow across national borders has speeded up. This development in turn contributes to the rapidly changing competitive conditions, with some of the low-income countries leading the way. The increase in the pace of change forces relatively rapid adjustments on certain individuals, certain industries, and certain communities. These greater tensions are common to most advanced industrial societies, and some have been more successful than others in smoothing the adjustment process.

The final development is noneconomic in nature but influential nevertheless. There is a tendency in the United States today to be preoccupied with domestic problems. Through weariness and frustration, people are inclined to pay less attention to international affairs—to the extent to which they can be avoided. In many fields, Americans seem to be questioning their role in the world. Such thinking often colors the approach to international trade policy issues.

POLICIES AND ACTIONS BY OUR TRADING PARTNERS

In addition to these factors operating directly in the United States on trade policy attitudes, there are a number of policies and actions by our trading partners which have conjoined to feed the protectionist mill. Perhaps the best known is the common agricultural policy (CAP) of the European Communities.

The United States has from the start supported measures toward European integration. We favor the development and enlargement of the European Communities.[23] We also recognize that a common agricultural policy is an integral part of the Community complex. At the same time, we believe the common policy can be so constructed and applied as to have a less restrictive effect on the trade of the United States and other outside countries.

And the international trade impact of the CAP is not limited to imports into the EC. One consequence of the excessive support of uneconomic domestic production has been the piling up of surplus products produced in Europe. These surpluses, with the aid of massive subsidies, are moving into new markets at the expense of traditional U.S. trade. It's bad enough, our agriculturists feel, to pay variable levies; it's intolerable to have these levies used to pay subsidies to take away your markets elsewhere.

The real pity is that European agricultural policies are more restrictive as the United States is moving in the other direction. The new domestic legislation being sought by the Nixon administration [24] is designed to put the U.S. agricultural economy on a market basis. As Secretary of Agriculture Hardin has described it:

Farm legislation now proposed would provide for loans set at a relatively low level so that the market would "clear" in most years. This program would be "market-oriented" to a greater degree than any other program developed since the early 1930's.

Our learning process seems to be out of phase with the Europeans. They do not seem able to profit from our experience.

Another policy area giving rise to the feeling in the United States that our trading partners are not playing by the rules is the proliferation of association agreements entered into by the European Communities. These arrangements not only have a direct impact on U.S. trade, but they also appear to be undermining the basic principles of the GATT. Furthermore, to some U.S. observers they seem to be a backward step from postwar multilateral efforts.

What makes it even harder for people in the United States to understand the network of special deals negotiated by the European Communities is the fact that the work on a system of generalized preferences is nearing a successful conclusion. In a

23 Cf. note 66 to Document 26.
24 Agricultural Adjustment Act of 1970 (Public Law 91–524), approved November 30, 1970; for text of President Nixon's statement on signing the measure see *Weekly Compilation of Presidential Documents*, December 5, 1970, p. 1616.

major initiative to promote economic development, President Nixon has urged the acceptance of the concept that all industrialized countries should give substantially the same duty-free tariff treatment to all developing countries.[25] It has been agreed that these preferences should be granted on a nonreciprocal basis. The generalized preference scheme has been endorsed by the U.N. General Assembly as one of the key elements of the strategy for the Second Development Decade.[26]

In these circumstances, why does the EC continue to enter into special arrangements with individual developing countries? And why, contrary to the principle of nonreciprocity for the developing countries, should the EC still be asking for preferential treatment (called "reverse" preferences) for its trade? These reverse preferences are not in the interests of the developing countries and cannot be accepted by the United States. We could not ask the Congress for authority to grant preferential treatment to countries which discriminate against U.S. trade.

Turning away from Europe (but only for a moment—I wouldn't want to let such a distinguished captive audience off so lightly), I should like to mention developments in Japan. The growth of the Japanese economy has been both remarkable and gratifying. Exports have been increasing at an incredibly rapid rate, and until recently Japan has also been accumulating substantial reserves from its balance-of-payments surplus. Everyone in Europe, as well as the United States, recognizes that the toughest competitor in the world is Japan. With Japanese goods as the archetype of effective competition, how can we explain in the United States that Japan maintains a substantially larger number of import quotas than any other industrialized country? And that, in addition, the Japanese Government does not permit foreign investment to enter freely? The U.S. business community understandably takes the position that we should insist on the same access in the Japanese market for trade and investment that the Japanese enjoy in the United States. The Japanese have recently announced a program for the reduction of import restrictions and the relaxation of investment controls. But it will take some time, in view of the continuing complex of controls in Japan, for the American business community to feel that it is getting a fair shake.

NONTARIFF BARRIERS TO TRADE

The last factor affecting U.S. trade policy attitudes which I would like to discuss is nontariff trade barriers. Perhaps the

[25] Cf. Document 97.
[26] Document 78.

impact of these barriers on international trade has been over-sold. The fact remains that at the present time nontariff barriers loom large in the minds of American businessmen and they feel that clever Europeans have found ways of frustrating the tariff concessions we negotiated.

The possible exaggeration of the significance of nontariff trade barriers goes both ways. They tend to become symbols of perfidy and to be given weight beyond their actual trade effect. On the European side, the American Selling Price system of valuing certain benzenoid chemicals was blown up as a major issue in the Kennedy Round, although the area of trade covered is relatively insignificant. Similarly, the advent of the tax on value added has been taken by American traders as a devious effort by our European partners to raise the border charges against U.S. goods and thus take away the benefits of the Kennedy Round.

Government procurement practices have been the subject of complaint on both sides. The United States has legislation which requires a differential to be applied in favor of American products. This margin is currently 6 percent normally, and 12 percent for firms in areas of substantial unemployment. Despite these preferential margins, the U.S. Government bought abroad 46 million dollars' worth of heavy electrical equipment in 1967, as compared with 40 million dollars' worth of such equipment purchased from abroad by all other OECD countries combined. Furthermore, the bulk of the latter figure is accounted for by countries which have no domestic heavy electrical equipment production. The United States, which has a major domestic industry, nevertheless did over 50 percent of its Government procurement of these products abroad.

Formally, the European countries and Japan state that they have no preferences for domestic suppliers. The catch is that procurement procedures are not open in these countries and that the "buy-national" objective is achieved by informal means. Evidence of this situation is the fact that both the EFTA [European Free Trade Association] and EC have found it necessary to consider special rules to insure nondiscrimination in governmental procurement. Despite the insistence that no "buy-national" differential exists, EC and EFTA firms apparently felt they were not getting equal treatment under the buying procedures of other member states.

A third nontariff barrier that has contributed to the feeling in the United States that we are getting the short end of the deal is the recent development of technical standards and quality certification relating to electronic products. A group of European countries met to draw up an agreement. The failure to invite all interested countries from the outset led to the suspicion that a new barrier might be erected.

How have these developments affected various interested groups in the United States? Except for certain industries which have been in difficulties during almost the whole of the postwar period, U.S. industry and labor have generally supported liberal trade policies. Under the weight of the factors I have described, this support has recently been seriously eroded.

U.S. producers and exporters feel that Japanese restrictionism, EC association arrangements, and nontariff trade barriers applied by other countries have resulted in the United States being the only truly open market and the only country abiding by the international trade rules. This conclusion can obviously be argued both ways. But it is a fact that the cumulative impact of all these developments and factors I have discussed has been to cause defections of American business from the liberal trade camp.

Labor unions, at the national level, have also been supporters of freer trade in the past. However, as imports have increased significantly and quickly in particular areas like textiles, as U.S. investment abroad has grown rapidly, and as more rapid adjustments are required in a dynamic world economy, the unions are drifting away. They fear that continued investment abroad will mean a substantial loss of jobs in the United States. The union representatives argue that improving skills and technology abroad (particularly in the low-wage countries) means that they can no longer rely on higher U.S. productivity to offset higher U.S. wages. This reaction is intensified in the current economic climate in the United States.

The other strong element in the liberal trade coalition has been agriculture. The agricultural community still feels that it can produce efficiently and compete in world markets. But as restrictionism abroad increases and unfair competition takes place in third markets, our agricultural supporters may conclude that freer trade in agriculture is a lost cause.

Add to these specific factors the rising concern over domestic problems relative to the interest in international cooperation, and you have the setting within which protectionism in the United States has reached its current high level. Nevertheless, the administration continues to support liberal trade policies and hopes that various developments will make it easier for the United States to continue the policies it has followed for so long.

Steps Toward Improvement

What are the actions which could help modify the attitudes I have described? Some measures affect the U.S. domestic situation and can be taken only by the United States. Others affect the international climate and require action by our trading partners.

Obviously the most important step the United States can take is to get inflation under control and thereby to improve our balance-of-payments situation. President Nixon has recognized the priority of this issue and has initiated a program which we believe will succeed. There can be no doubt but that excess demand has been eliminated in the United States. There is increasing evidence that prices and costs are beginning to respond. Our foreign trade surplus has begun to move back up. Effective domestic measures should continue to have a favorable impact on our external position as the economy shifts to orderly growth.

The necessity for looking at the new factors affecting trade policy and for educating the public on these issues has also been recognized. While proposing interim legislation [27] to hold the line on trade policy, President Nixon also established a Commission on Trade and Investment to examine the longer term trade policy questions.[28] With the help of the private groups which still support liberal trade, it should be possible to reverse the trend in our country.

But it will also be essential for our trading partners to act in the fields I have mentioned. If the European Communities could look at their common agricultural policy and their system of preferential association arrangements in terms of the impact on outside countries, a major step forward would be taken in insuring continuing support for liberal trade policies in the United States. The general support for the Communities and their enlargement still exists in the United States, but the concerns about the trade impact on the United States would be substantially lessened if there could be a European initiative for another step in the attack on tariffs and other trade barriers. We believe that the Communities are now strong enough so they need not look upon trade discrimination against the outside world as the cement required to hold them together. Further trade liberalization would also help to resolve many of the problems for countries which are concerned primarily about the commercial aspects of European integration.

27 Cf. Document 91.
28 Cf. note 34 to Document 91.

In sum, the picture is not one of unrelieved gloom. President Nixon's pledge to freer trade provides an important rallying point. The concern which has been registered about some provisions of the current version of the trade legislation has focused attention on the problem. The domestic economic situation in the United States will be improving; the trade figures are already much better this year. Some evidence of constructive initiatives from our trading partners would help greatly to put everyone back on the right road.

(91) The Proposed Trade Expansion Act: Letter from President Nixon to Wilbur D. Mills, Chairman of the House Ways and Means Committee, May 11, 1970.[29]

(Complete Text)

Dear Mr. Chairman:

It is gratifying to me that you are today beginning hearings on trade legislation.[30] The Administration welcomes the chance to testify on behalf of the trade bill which I submitted last November,[31] passage of which we believe to be necessary to provide a start in adjusting U.S. trade policy to meet the problems of the 1970s. These hearings will also be useful in giving all interested citizens a chance to explain their views on a subject which is of great economic and foreign policy significance for this country.

I urge speedy enactment of the proposals which I have sent to the Congress. The proposals are modest in scope, but they provide needed flexibility for U.S. trade policy in a number of significant ways. They would:

—Restore the authority needed by the President to make limited tariff reductions. This authority is not intended for major negotiations, but rather to permit minor adjustments, such as would be required to extend compensation to other countries hurt by U.S. escape clause actions—thereby avoiding retaliation against U.S. exports.

—Recognize the very real plight of particular industries, com-

---

[29] Text from *Weekly Compilation of Presidential Documents,* May 18, 1970, pp. 635–637.
[30] House Report 14870, 91st Congress. The 91st Congress expired January 3, 1971 without having taken final action on the President's proposals; cf. President Nixon's letter to Senators Mike Mansfield and Hugh Scott in *Weekly Compilation of Presidential Documents,* December 14, 1970, pp. 1656–1657.
[31] *Documents 1968–69,* pp. 522–530.

panies and workers faced with import competition, by providing for a readier escape clause and adjustment assistance relief where justified.

—Eliminate the American Selling Price system of customs valuation, a major obstacle impeding progress toward the reduction of non-tariff barriers.

—Strengthen the hand of the President in his efforts to ensure fair treatment for U.S. exports.

Since I submitted this legislation to the Congress in November, there have been a number of developments which add to its urgency. I cite only the important decisions taken by the European Communities on the future evolution of that great trading area,[32] and the consideration by the Congress of new U.S. farm legislation,[33] which would further increase the importance of our access to foreign markets. At a time of rapid movement in international trade relations and patterns, the U.S. will find itself at a disadvantage unless we have the added flexibility which I have requested.

Progress toward freer trade should continue. We must encourage it. Without the strong support of the United States, the world's largest trader, this progress could falter. Passage of the legislation I have submitted will keep us headed in the right direction.

FOR THE FUTURE

The legislation proposed by the Administration represents an interim step toward developing the flexible trade policies needed for the world of the 1970s. For the long range, it is important to reexamine our entire approach. Changes in production, trade and investment patterns, and the rapid progress in communications, transportation and technology impel us toward a basic reassessment of our trade policy. I have recently announced the appointment of the chairman [Albert L. Williams] of my Commission on International Trade and Investment Policy, which will assist in this reexamination, and I will shortly announce its full membership.[34] The Commission is charged with examining the entire range of our trade and related policies, and of preparing recommendations for the next decade.

We need more information regarding the competitive position

32 Cf. note 66 to Document 26.
33 Cf. note 24 to Document 90.
34 Texts of White House announcements of April 7, 1970 and May 21, 1970 in *Weekly Compilation of Presidential Documents*, April 13, 1970, p. 500 and same, May 25, 1970, p. 671, respectively.

of U.S. industries. So that we will have an adequate factual base, I am requesting that the Tariff Commission make a broad survey of the competitiveness of particular industries. I believe that such a broad study, which the Tariff Commission is best suited to conduct, will be of great assistance to us in our future policies and trade actions and in the work of my Commission on International Trade and Investment Policy.

It is my intention to marshal the forces of the executive branch to expedite efficient adjustment to economic changes brought about by increased imports. I intend to activate the Trade Adjustment Assistance Advisory Board called for in the Trade Expansion Act of 1962 [35] to lead a broad coordinated executive effort to make adjustment assistance more effective in opening opportunities for workers and firms. I also intend to request additional funds for adjustment assistance as they are needed.

Certain aspects of our trading relations have been of particular concern in recent years. The decline in our trade surplus, from about $7 billion in 1964 to only $0.8 billion in 1968, and $1.3 billion in 1969, stems from a variety of causes: the inflationary forces which have dominated our economy in the late sixties; the growing economic strength and technological progress of our trading partners; the increase in agricultural self-sufficiency abroad; and the increasing demand of American consumers for goods made in other countries. As I mentioned in my balance of payments statement of April 1969,[36] it is appropriate to deal with fundamental problems by the use of fundamental remedies. One of the required fundamental remedies has been the reduction of inflationary pressures. With the steps we have taken to gain control of inflation, there has been some modest evidence of improvement of our trading position. As our anti-inflationary policies continue, we expect a further improvement. At the same time, it is important to take vigorous steps to improve our exports.

One of the most disquieting trade developments has come in the field of agricultural trade. Although there has been a general reduction in trade barriers in recent decades, there have been contrary trends in agricultural trade. In particular, high trade barriers in a number of countries, used to protect high domestic prices, have created difficulties for our agricultural exports. We have protested against these measures as each new barrier has

[35] Official summary of the Trade Expansion Act of 1962 in *Documents, 1962*, pp. 496–508.
[36] Same, *1968–69*, pp. 506–509.

been raised and have on occasion been reluctantly forced to threaten or to actually take retaliatory measures.

During the past decade, there has been a major integration of the economies of Western Europe. We see ahead the prospect of an enlargement of this community. We wish our friends in Europe well in their efforts toward economic and political unity and will watch their steps toward this end with sympathetic interest—remaining alert, however, to the need for respect for our commercial interests. We would expect, of course, that in the process of enlargement of the European Community, due regard will be given to the rights and interests of the United States and other third countries.

IMPROVED EXPORT PERFORMANCE

For a number of reasons it is possible that American industry has been less export-minded than that of other major competing industrialized countries. Attractive alternatives to export sales development—in our very large domestic market for example, and in the alternative of direct foreign investment abroad for manufacture of products in locations closer to the foreign markets being served—have existed for American industries to a greater degree than for foreign companies. Furthermore, our tax laws tend to favor sales by foreign subsidiaries of U.S. corporations over exports from the United States. Administration witnesses will submit a legislative proposal to improve the tax situation for income earned on exports.

United States exports have increasingly shown a concentration in capital goods and other technologically advanced products. It is customary in domestic as well as international trade in such items for the seller to provide credit on comparable conditions with those provided by his competitors. Important steps have been taken by the Export-Import Bank in the past year to make U.S. Government export credit and guarantee programs as flexible and useful as possible to a wide range of American producers. These steps include a complete revision of the commercial bank discount program to encourage banks throughout the country to respond favorably to financing requests from exporters on a continuing basis, and initiation of an advance commitment procedure that has been most useful to buyers, suppliers and manufacturers.

Significant steps also have been taken to assist U.S. engineering and contracting firms in achieving contract awards for major projects. Money sources from outside the United States have been attracted to finance American exports as a result of the extension of the Export-Import Bank's guarantee authority. Special attention has been given to small business and agriculture through modification of the export insurance operations and through specific program assistance. The American aircraft industry and nuclear power developments have been substantially aided through the actions of the Bank. The key aspect of the Export-Import Bank's new look is greater cooperation and flexibility. Our exporters can look forward to continued expansion of Export-Import Bank activities.

The export programs I have just described, when taken together with the stepped up trade promotion programs of the Department of Commerce and the opening up of foreign markets through the reduction in foreign tariffs and other obstacles to trade, provide strong incentives for American industry to export more. These programs take into account the advice received from all segments of American business, both large and small, as represented by the National Export Expansion Council, as well as other groups. The benefits of an increase in exports should be felt throughout our entire economy. One statistic alone makes this point very strongly: in 1969, about 2.7 million jobs were attributable to U.S. exports.

As you begin hearings on this most important legislation, I want to express my appreciation for your careful attention and my high hope for results that will greatly enhance the U.S. trade position.

Sincerely,

RICHARD NIXON

(92) The United States Stand on Trade Preferences: Statement by Edwin M. Cronk, Deputy Assistant Secretary for International Trade Policy, Before the Special Preferences Committee of the United Nations Conference on Trade and Development, Geneva, March 31, 1970.[37]

(Complete Text)

I should like to use this opportunity to explain in some detail how we in the United States see a generalized scheme of preferences, how we determined the elements of the scheme we have laid before you, and what we hope will be accomplished at this meeting. We hope this background will make it easier for you

[37] Text from *Department of State Bulletin*, May 11, 1970, pp. 612–615; for the context see *The United States in World Affairs, 1970*, Section 39.

to understand our scheme and the answers we have given and will give here to your questions. We also hope this approach will encourage many of you from developing countries to present your views and concerns in an equally frank manner.

We are fully aware of the urgent need to improve the trading opportunities of the developing countries; and in recognition of the magnitude of the problem, we have tried to develop a liberal scheme—one that will yield substantial results. We have sought to get other developed countries to adopt the same approach. As President Nixon said in his report to the Congress on foreign policy for the 1970's: [38]

This proposal (that is, the generalized preference proposal) is designed to meet one of the world's major economic and political problems—the struggle of the developing countries to achieve a satisfactory rate of economic development. Development can be promoted by aid, but aid cannot and should not be relied on to do the whole job. The low-income countries need increased export earnings to finance the imports they need for development. They need improved access for their products to the massive markets of the industrialized nations. Such export increases must come largely in manufactured goods, since the demand for most primary commodities—their traditional exports —grows relatively slowly. And these countries are at early stages of industrialization, so they face major hurdles in competing with the industrialized countries for sales of manufactured goods.

President Nixon personally made the decision on our preference proposal and has stated he would submit, when appropriate, legislation to our Congress to seek authorization for the United States to extend preferences.[39]

The United States came to adopt its present position on preferences only after long and careful study. I am sure most of you here think we took much too long, but I think that the type of scheme we developed as a result of this deliberation made the delay worthwhile.

We made our decision in light of the continued lag of developing-country exports which has seriously limited their ability to accelerate their rates of economic development. I looked at some trade figures the other day and found that between 1960 and 1968 total exports of the developed countries increased by 100 percent while exports of the developing countries increased by only 60 percent. I made a rough calculation of what would have happened if exports of the developing countries had kept pace

[38] Document 2.
[39] Cf. note 31 to Document 91.

with exports of the developed countries between 1960 and 1968; that is, if they had doubled rather than increased by only 60 percent. I found that developing-country exports in 1968 would have been $11 billion more than they actually were. I also noted that the developing countries' share of world trade has declined from 25 percent in 1955 to 21 percent in 1960 to 18 percent in 1968. Facts like these—with which you are all familiar —speak for themselves. They have helped convince us of the urgent need to do something to stimulate developing-country exports. Unless trading opportunities are significantly expanded for the developing countries, their rates of economic development will continue to lag.

We have no illusions that a system of generalized preferences alone, no matter how liberal, is going to solve this problem. It is not a panacea but only one of a number of steps which need to be taken—many of them in the developing countries themselves. But we do want to make the best possible use of this opportunity to provide a useful external stimulus, and hence we have tried to devise as liberal a preference scheme as possible. We have proposed a preference scheme which would eliminate tariffs over the broadest possible commodity range and without limits on preferential imports. We have also pressed other developed countries to do the same.

Our proposal is based on our conviction that any changes in the world trading system should make it less complex—should reduce, or at least not increase, the administrative and other procedural complications of trading. We have labored hard to remove administrative controls on trade over the past years; and we are now, in another forum,[40] concentrating intense attention on other so-called nontariff barriers as well. Certainly, in taking steps to help the developing countries, we do not want to introduce new complexities into the trading system. Not only might such complexities limit the utility of preferences, but they could also lead to potential new frictions among trading countries.

Under our proposal, there would in effect be a two-tier most-favored-nation policy, one applicable to more developed countries, and another, a temporary addition, applicable to less developed countries. There would be no quotas, ceilings, licensing, or other complexities which, however well intentioned, would set the precedent and build the administrative machinery which might in another context threaten to undermine the progress we have made in trade liberalization during the past three dec-

[40] Cf. Documents 93–94.

ades. Moreover, we have built into our system proposals to take advantage of this major change in trading policy to reduce the extent of regional trading arrangements which have been an undesirable element in world trade.

For many years we have based our trade policy on the principle of MFN treatment for free economies, and we believe there should be no more than minimum deviation from this principle. One logical consequence of following the MFN principle is the elimination of the discrimination that many developing countries face in some developed-country markets and the discrimination we, and other developed countries, face in some developing-country markets. Our proposal, and that of other donors, for duty-free treatment and broad product coverage will go a long way in eliminating special preferences on products covered by the scheme.

Also, in line with our belief in MFN, we are seeking the elimination of existing reverse preferences; that is, preferences extended by some developing countries to developed countries. These reverse preferences distort trade patterns, increase the foreign exchange costs of imports by the developing countries, and result in a loss of revenue to them from import duties. Finally, our proposal, if adopted by all donors as a common system, would assure equitable burden-sharing among the major preference-giving countries and thus help create public and legislative support for preferences.

While we believe our proposal is responsive to the needs of the developing countries, we have, of course, taken into account our responsibilities to avoid serious disruption of our domestic industries. We feel we have done so by limiting our exceptions to petroleum and petroleum products, textiles, and shoes and by providing for use of our standard escape-clause and adjustment assistance procedures.

Petroleum and petroleum products are excluded for national security reasons. And petroleum, in any case, is not a manufactured or semimanufactured commodity. Textiles and shoes are excluded because our industries are already undergoing a difficult adjustment process due to sharply increased import competition. United States imports of textiles and clothing have increased from $866 million in 1960 to $1,817 million in 1968 and $2,125 million in 1969—a 17-percent increase in 1969 alone. According to GATT [General Agreement on Tariffs and Trade] statistics our textile imports are increasing faster than those of any other developed country. Many developing countries are already highly competitive in textiles and clothing, and developing countries are substantial contributors to the very rapid increase in U.S. imports of these products. In 1968, over 35 percent of our imports of textiles and clothing came from developing countries. Moreover, the developing-country share of U.S. textile and clothing imports has increased in recent years.

United States shoe imports have likewise increased sharply. Our imports of shoes rose from $148 million in 1960 to $388 million in 1968 and to $488 million in 1969. We could not responsibly propose to our Congress that existing tariff protection for these industries be removed for imports from developing countries in view of the difficulties already being experienced by our domestic industries.

Were we to extend preferences in these areas we would have an unfortunate concentration of adjustment to preferences in just a few U.S. industries. And one could argue that, to some degree, a similar disadvantage would arise in developing countries. New investment and export effort would be heavily concentrated on these products where there is already substantial production in many developing countries, instead of the industrial structure being diversified into new fields to take advantage of preferences. The amount of capital and management skills available to the developing countries is limited, and we believe broadening the industrial base is a better use of these resources than expansion in already well-established industries. At the end of the preferences period the result of such diversification of export effort and investment will be a broader and healthier industrial sector more capable of continued growth.

The other safeguard mechanism we intend to employ is the standard escape clause and adjustment assistance embodied in our general trade legislation. If the escape-clause provisions should be modified (as President Nixon has proposed), the modified provisions would become the "standard escape clause" in the U.S. preference proposal. I would like to describe briefly the escape-clause and adjustment assistance procedures to make clear how rigorous the conditions are for the application of the escape clause.

When a firm, trade association, or labor union petitions for tariff adjustment or adjustment assistance, the Tariff Commission undertakes an investigation to determine whether, as a result in major part of concessions granted under trade agreements, an article is being imported into the United States in such increased quantities as to cause, or threaten to cause, serious injury to the domestic industry or to the workers in that industry.

In the course of such investigations the Tariff Commission after reasonable notice holds public hearings and affords interested parties, including foreign exporters, an opportunity to be present, to produce evidence, and to be heard at such hearings.

The Tariff Commission proceeds carefully to make a full investigation and to consider the facts fully. It has 6 months in tariff adjustment cases to report its judgment to the President.

After receiving a Tariff Commission report containing an affirmative finding, the President may provide tariff adjustment for the industry in question or provide that firms or workers in the industry may apply for adjustment assistance, or any combination of such actions. By way of explanation I would like to say that adjustment assistance can be provided by the Government to an industry, firm, or group of workers to help them adjust to increased import competition by increasing their competitiveness or moving into new products or work. This provision of our law enables us, in some instances, to deal with the problems of adjustment caused by increased imports without resorting to measures affecting trade.

I think the seriousness with which we view escape-clause action and the stringent conditions required for its use are shown by the fact that only two escape-clause actions have been taken since 1962 and only 20 since 1948. Most of these have been revoked.

To sum up, we believe our proposal is sound. It would result in a significant stimulus to exports of the developing countries and thereby contribute to their economic development. It is responsive to the justifiable demands of the developing countries. And it is a fair proposal—fair to the developing countries since it would eliminate discrimination among them and fair to the developed countries since we would all be engaged in a common endeavor.

Before closing let me spend a moment on what we hope will be done at this meeting. First, this meeting provides an opportunity for developing countries to ask questions of the preference-giving countries face to face. Second, this meeting provides an opportunity for the developing countries to express their views on preferences in general and on various specific aspects of a generalized preference system. Third, we hope to learn something of the Socialist countries' plans to take measures to increase their imports of manufactures and semimanufactures from the developing countries.

We welcome this opportunity to answer questions and we shall try to do so to the best of our ability. We cannot speculate on the agreement that will eventually be reached among the preference-giving countries, but we can explain in detail how any aspect of the proposal we have made will work.

I want to make it clear that we have not overlooked the section of Resolution 21 (II)[41] and other UNCTAD resolutions dealing with the least developed among the developing countries. We realize that some developing countries, because of their lower level of development, believe that special measures to assist them are needed if they are to take advantage of preferences. We are sympathetic to this idea, and we are now studying the question in depth. Since our scheme would reduce tariffs to zero for products covered by the scheme and impose no quantitative limits, we find it difficult to devise special measures going beyond that. It's a difficult and important question, and we want to hear your suggestions on this aspect of preferences, both on the measures which the least developed believe would be helpful to them and on the way in which those eligible for any such special treatment would be determined. We note that Resolution 21 (II) represents agreement that the preference scheme be nondiscriminatory. We hope the relationship of this condition to the need for special measures for the relatively least developed can be explored more fully at this meeting.

Before closing I would like to note the progress we have all made and the importance of allowing enough additional time to build a preference system which gives the developing countries the greatest possible benefits.

Preferences were first proposed in UNCTAD in 1964.[42] We have now reached a point where all major countries have presented concrete proposals. It took us 5 years, but we have made significant progress and are on the threshold of success. Now that we approach this final stage, we should be careful to allow sufficient time to build the best possible system. It was only last November that the proposals were placed before the developing countries. The views of the developing countries relative to these proposals have not yet been heard. That is the purpose of this meeting. These views, certainly, should be considered carefully before final decisions are taken. We must keep in mind the importance of the step we are taking. It would be a mistake to make hasty decisions when it will so critically affect so much of great importance to all countries, both developed and developing. This is not to say we do not consider establishing a system of preferences a matter of urgency. It is a matter of extreme ur-

41 The Second U.N. Conference on Trade and Development was held in New Delhi February 1–March 29, 1968; text of Resolution 21 (II), March 26, 1968 in *Proceedings of the United Nations Conference on Trade and Development, Second Session* (U.N. Publication, Sales No.: E.68.II. D.14), p. 38.
42 The First U.N. Conference on Trade and Development was held in Geneva March 23–June 16, 1964; excerpts from the "Preamble and Recommendations of the Final Act," adopted June 15, 1964 in *Documents*, 1964, pp. 432–452.

gency. We intend to push forward with our work, with the help of your views expressed in this conference.

C. The Organization for Economic Cooperation and Development.

(93) Ministerial Meeting of the Council of the O.E.C.D., Paris, May 20–22, 1970: Statement by Nathaniel Samuels, Deputy Under Secretary for Economic Affairs, May 22, 1970.[43]

(Complete Text)

At the outset, I wish to thank the Secretary General [Emile Van Lennep of the Netherlands] and the Trade Committee for the reports on where we stand in our work on preferences. These reports set forth very clearly the major issues which need to be resolved.

As President Nixon indicated last October 31,[44] the United States supports the establishment of a liberal system of generalized preferences for all developing countries. We consider it essential that the system provide maximum benefits to the developing countries and that all developed countries offer comparable access to their markets for all developing countries. We also believe that "reverse preferences" are not consistent with the philosophy of generalized preferences and should be eliminated in the shortest time possible.

The United States originally proposed that we all adopt a common system involving broad product coverage and no ceilings on preferential imports. As the reports before us indicate, we have sought agreement on commonality intensely during the last 6 months, but without arriving at a common viewpoint. While we have failed to reach agreement on a uniform system of preferences, we all seem to agree—and I hope that this can be recorded in our minutes—that we should all make comparable efforts; that is, that we should all do our fair share in accepting preferential imports from the developing countries. In view of this situation, which is clearly brought out in the Secretary General's paper and in the Trade Committee report, I am authorized to state that we are prepared to accept the general approach of the compromise package proposal in the Secretary

43 Text from *Department of State Bulletin,* June 29, 1970, pp. 811–812; for the context see *The United States in World Affairs, 1970,* Section 33.
44 *Documents, 1968–69,* pp. 429–438.

General's paper as the basis for bringing our work on the preference issue to a successful conclusion. This includes his definition of "a common approach" as one of "purpose and intent." We interpret this to mean that we will all strive to adopt systems of preferences which are harmonized as much as possible and can be expected to yield comparable results but that they need not be uniform in all their technical elements.

We all seem agreed that review machinery should be set up in the OECD to ensure that the various schemes are, in practice, achieving an equitable sharing of the burden. I think this is extremely important, and here again, I hope our agreement on this can be noted in our minutes. While the need for continuing review machinery seems to be accepted, it is clear even now that certain schemes need improvement to ensure comparability of effort. In particular, we consider it important that all schemes be based on the principle of duty-free entry and that ceiling systems be administered in as liberal a manner as possible and applied only to sensitive products. This question will require further examination in the Trade Committee and in bilateral conversations.

On reverse preferences, we continue to believe that these should be eliminated. In saying this, I want to make it clear that we recognize the importance of the political, cultural, and economic relationships which exist between the developed and the developing countries concerned. We believe, however, that there are other and more durable ways of maintaining and increasing relationships between the areas concerned than reverse preferences. It is not our purpose to disturb these longstanding relationships or to impose unreasonable burdens on any parties to these arrangements. At the same time, we believe that reverse preferences impose a cost on the developing countries extending them, that they are discriminatory, and that they tend to distort the patterns of world trade. It would be impossible for us to justify before our Congress the extension of preferences to countries which discriminate against us in this fashion. We would be prepared to accept the Secretary General's proposal on this subject as part of an overall package settlement of outstanding issues. This would involve a declaration by the developed countries concerned that they are ready to see the reverse preferences phased out, without penalty to the developing countries concerned. In return, we would agree that these reverse preferences can be phased out over a reasonable period and that the U.S. preference scheme would be extended to the developing countries involved from the outset. Adequate assurances covering these arrangements would, of course, have to be given prior to the extension of our system to the developing countries concerned. In saying this, I wish again to reiterate our desire to accomplish this in a way which does not impair the basic relationships which exist between these areas.

In sum, we are able to indicate our acceptance, in general, of the Secretary General's paper. It is a good summary of our outstanding problems, and it makes reasonable proposals on how we can get on with this important task. I want to congratulate the Secretary General for his efforts to bring us closer together on this endeavor.

(94) Communiqué of the Ministerial Meeting of the Council of the O.E.C.D., Paris, May 22, 1970.[45]

(Complete Text)

1. The Council of the O.E.C.D. met at Ministerial level in Paris on 20th, 21st and 22nd May, 1970, under the Chairmanship of M. Valéry Giscard d'Estaing, Minister of the Economy and Finance of France.

2. In this first Ministerial Meeting of the O.E.C.D. in the 1970s, Ministers focused attention on the major economic issues facing Governments of Member countries in the new decade with regard to developments in both their own countries and the world economy as a whole.

SHORT-TERM ECONOMIC PROSPECTS

3. As a result of policies to combat inflation, output in the O.E.C.D. area will rise appreciably less rapidly in 1970 than the high rates of the past two years. But for most countries this only represents a return to a normal rate of growth. International trade as a whole will probably also expand at a normal rate.

4. Ministers noted with concern that prices in the O.E.C.D. area are now rising by 5 per cent a year—an unacceptably fast rate which is double the average over most of the past decade. They agreed that priority must be given to the elimination of this heightened inflationary pressure. While Governments are determined to avoid any cumulative downturn of production and employment, Ministers agreed on the need to persevere in most countries with the restrictive demand management policies already adopted. To achieve stability it will also be desirable to combine these policies with other measures of a structural and

45 Text from *Department of State Bulletin,* June 29, 1970, pp. 812–814.

more selective nature. According to circumstances, such measures may include manpower policies, regional and sectoral policies, incomes policies, and efforts to increase competition, nationally and internationally. In this context, Ministers underlined the importance of continued trade liberalisation.

5. Ministers noted that recent parity changes and demand management policies have led to sounder balance-of-payments positions for a number of major countries, though further progress remains to be made. They recognised that in many countries existing high interest rates are an important element in present action against inflation. They also recognised, however, that high rates have certain disadvantages from the economic and social point of view. Ministers noted that as and when opportunities to relax national monetary policies arise, it will be important to see that they remain reasonably in line so as to avoid their being a major source of new international payments difficulties.

ECONOMIC GROWTH—QUANTITATIVE AND QUALITATIVE OBJECTIVES FOR THE 1970s

6. Ministers noted that the growth of real national product in the O.E.C.D. area as a whole of 50 per cent, set by the Ministerial Council in 1961 as a collective target for the decade 1960–1970,[46] will be attained and even surpassed. They agreed that steady and sustainable economic expansion, combined with internal and external stability, remains essential, both as a means of bettering the well-being of the people of their own countries and as a basis for promoting the trade and development of developing countries. They also noted that the developing Member countries attained higher than average rates of growth during the past decade and stressed the importance of a similar achievement during the coming decade.

7. Having considered the potentialities of their economies for future growth, Ministers set an increase in the real national product in the O.E.C.D. area as a whole of the order of 65 per cent as a collective growth objective for the decade 1970–1980, in the sense that such a rate of growth, together with other objectives of policy such as the achievement of better long-term price performance, should constitute the framework within which Member countries will determine their economic policies. They recognised that, in the light of developments over the last decade, the experience of different countries over the coming

[46] Text of communiqué, November 17, 1961, in *Documents, 1961*, pp. 257–261.

decade can be expected to be diverse. Ministers stressed that growth is not an end in itself, but rather an instrument for creating better conditions of life. Increased attention must be given to the qualitative aspects of growth, and to the formulation of policies with respect to the broad economic and social choices involved in the allocation of growing resources. Ministers emphasized that an important risk of O.E.C.D. will be to assist Governments in these aims.

Environmental Problems

8. In modern societies, economic expansion, technological changes and rapid urbanisation are accompanied by new and pressing environmental problems. Over a number of years the Organisation has acquired valuable experience in this field through its work on air and water pollution, noise, transport problems and urban management. Ministers agreed that this work should be pursued along lines proposed by the Secretary-General with a view to assessing the economic and trade implications of environmental policies, relating such policies to qualitative objectives of growth policies and proposing concerted solutions to problems having substantial international implications. Ministers noted that the Secretary-General will shortly put forward proposals to the Council for adapting the Organisation's structures to ensure proper co-ordination of environmental activities.[47]

The Role of O.E.C.D. in the Co-ordination of Economic Policies

9. Ministers stressed the important role played by the Organisation in the co-ordination of economic policies among Member countries and agreed on the need to render this co-ordination more effective. Having noted suggestions put forward to this end, they requested the Secretary-General to submit proposals to the Council as soon as possible for further consideration. Ministers also agreed on the need for continued consultation within the Organisation to ensure that Member countries' balance-of-payments aims are compatible.

Co-operation with the Developing Countries

10. As the international community embarks on the Second Development Decade,[48] Ministers reaffirmed the resolve of Mem-

---

[47] The Committee on the Environment held its first meeting in Paris on November 24–25, 1970.
[48] Cf. Documents 77–78.

ber countries, in conformity with the O.E.C.D. Convention,[49] to play their full part in the development effort for the 1970s.

11. Ministers discussed developments regarding the volume of resource flows to the developing countries. All members of the Development Assistance Committee intend to increase their total flows. Several of the members are already exceeding the 1 per cent of GNP target recommended at the Second UNCTAD [United Nations Conference on Trade and Development] [50] and some of the other members have accepted 1975, or an earlier date, for attainment of the target. Several countries have thus far accepted a supplementary target dealing only with official development assistance. Ministers recognised that it was urgent for their Governments to take appropriate decisions with respect to aid volume and decided that these questions will be further discussed in the D.A.C. with particular reference to current negotiations in the United Nations on the strategy for the Second Development Decade. They recognised also the need to increase the share of the contributions to multilateral organisations in the overall resources devoted to aid, taking account of the growing capacity of these institutions to use funds effectively.

12. Ministers recognised that a policy designed to increase the volume of aid must be accompanied by efforts to improve its conditions. With these two objectives in view, Governments represented in the D.A.C. should consider progressively reducing aid tying, especially where it adds to the cost of goods to developing countries or distorts trading patterns. Member countries indicated their willingness to seek jointly the means to relax aid tying and requested that this question, as well as means to increase the volume of aid, on the Agenda for the D.A.C. High-Level Meeting in Tokyo next September.[51] Moreover, a number of Member countries declared their intention favourably to consider reducing aid tying in appropriate specific cases.

13. Ministers took note of the progress made with regard to the establishment of a mutually acceptable system of generalised tariff preferences in favour of developing countries. They noted the useful consultations which Member countries have held with the developing countries within UNCTAD on this matter. They also recognised the efforts still required to move on to the stage where concerted proposals can be presented to the UNC-

[49] Signed at Paris December 14, 1960, effective September 30, 1961; text and related material in *Documents, 1960,* pp. 332–342.
[50] Cf. note 41 to Document 92.
[51] The Ninth Annual High-Level Meeting of the Development Assistance Committee was held September 14–15, 1970; text of communiqué in *OECD Observer,* October 1970, pp. 3–5.

TAD.[52] Ministers gave general guidance with a view to solving the more important remaining difficulties prior to the coming Session of the Trade and Development Board of UNCTAD. This would enable the General Assembly of the United Nations to take account of the position reached when it takes up the question of the Second Development Decade this coming autumn. Ministers expressed their determination to implement generalised preferences as soon as Governments have obtained the necessary legislative or other sanction.

14. An effective approach to the problem of development requires a coherent policy at both the national and international level. Ministers agreed that the broader and more intensive approach recently adopted within the Organisation for the development of such a policy should be actively pursued, with a view to taking further constructive action to promote growth and diversification in developing countries. They declared the support of Member Governments for the effort to draw up a comprehensive, coherent and integrated International Development Strategy for the Decade.

EAST-WEST CONTACTS

15. Ministers underlined the interest of the Members of the Organisation in contacts between East and West, expressed at the Ministerial Council in 1966.[53] They agreed that the Council should continue to examine the role of the Organisation in this matter on the basis of proposals to be prepared by the Secretary-General, with a view to possible broadening of such contacts.

---

[52] A revised list of tariff preferences that members of the Organization for Economic Cooperation and Development were prepared to grant was presented to the U.N. Conference on Trade and Development on September 15, 1970.

[53] *Documents, 1966*, pp. 160–162.

D. New Initiatives in Foreign Aid.

(95) Report of the Presidential Task Force on International Development, Submitted to President Nixon by Rudolph A. Peterson, Chairman of the Task Force, Released March 8, 1970.[54]

(a) Statement by President Nixon, Key Biscayne, Florida, March 8, 1970.[55]

(Complete Text)

I have just received the report of my Task Force on International Development, chaired by Rudolph Peterson.[56]

The task force has recommended sweeping changes in the foreign assistance programs of the United States: clarification of their fundamental objectives, changes in the overall role of the United States in the international development process, changes in the organization of the U.S. Government to carry out its responsibilities in contributing to that process.

A new U.S. approach to foreign assistance, based on the proposals of the task force, will be one of our major foreign policy initiatives in the coming years. I will propose this new approach in responding to the requirement of the Foreign Assistance Act of 1967 [57] that I reappraise our present assistance effort and recommend changes for the future. Taking into account the discussion which will follow my proposals, including close consultation with the Congress, I will submit legislation in January 1971 to carry out the new U.S. approach.

To contribute to the discussion of this important subject, I am making the Peterson report public immediately. I believe its ideas are fresh and exciting. They can provide new life and a new foundation for the U.S. role in this vitally important area of our relations with the developing countries.

The task force intensively examined our assistance programs of the past and present. Looking to the future, it concluded that "The United States has a profound national interest in cooperating with developing countries in their efforts to improve

---

[54] For the context of this and the following documents see *The United States in World Affairs, 1970,* Section 39.

[55] Text from *Weekly Compilation of Presidential Documents,* March 16, 1970, p. 346.

[56] Appointed September 24, 1969; cf. *Documents, 1968–69,* p. 550.

[57] Public Law 90–137, approved November 14, 1967; excerpts in *Documents, 1967,* pp. 442–450.

conditions of life in their societies." I agree. It is to enable the United States to best pursue that profound national interest that I will propose a new U.S. approach to foreign assistance for the 1970's.[58]

(b) "U.S. Foreign Assistance in the 1970s: A New Approach": Report of the Presidential Task Force, Dated March 4, 1970.[59]

(Excerpt)

INTRODUCTION AND CONCLUSIONS

March 4, 1970

THE PRESIDENT OF THE UNITED STATES

Dear Mr. President:

You asked us to examine U.S. foreign economic and military assistance programs, our trade and investment relations with the developing countries, and the fundamental problems that the United States faces in this area of foreign policy. You instructed us to look carefully into the underlying rationale for these programs, to take nothing for granted, and to recommend policies that will serve the best interests of our Nation through the decade ahead.

Many with whom we consulted are deeply troubled by particular aspects of U.S. foreign assistance programs and by the apathy and misunderstanding that seem to surround the issues. Nevertheless, virtually all believe that the United States has a large stake and serious responsibilities in international development.

This feeling of commitment is natural in view of the distinguished role the United States has played for 25 years in this field. It has been a bipartisan endeavor. Many outstanding Americans have contributed direction, insight, and imagination to these programs in the past—and continue to do so today.

A Time for Change. We believe that the U.S. role in international development will be as important in the future as it has ever been in the past; and prospects for success, if looked at in the perspective of experience, are very favorable.

For the first time in history, it appears feasible to approach

---

58 Document 97.
59 Text from *Department of State Bulletin,* April 6, 1970, pp. 447–467; excerpted material on pp. 448–450.

this world problem on a worldwide basis. International development can become a truly cooperative venture—with the countries that receive help eventually achieving the ability themselves to help others. The Marshall Plan countries and Japan, which join us today in providing assistance, were yesterday the recipients of assistance. And some of the developing countries of a decade ago, no longer needing assistance themselves, are beginning to help others.

This kind of cooperation in international development is not only possible but essential. Only a genuinely cooperative program can gain the necessary long-term public support in donor countries—the United States, as well as others. Only by being cooperative, furthermore, can international development succeed abroad.

What the United States does now through its policies and through its determination to persevere for the long haul will influence what others do—the developing countries, the international organizations, and other industrial countries.

This, therefore, is a time for change, a time for reappraising our programs and designing them for the decade ahead. It is also a time to stake out in the most positive terms America's involvement in the way mankind manages its common problems. In time, U.S. international development policies may well prove to be the most important—and the most rewarding—determinant of America's role in the world.

Conclusions. With these considerations in mind we have reached the following conclusions:

1. The United States has a profound national interest in cooperating with developing countries in their efforts to improve conditions of life in their societies.

2. All peoples, rich and poor alike, have common interests in peace, in the eradication of poverty and disease, in a healthful environment, and in higher living standards. It should be a cardinal aim of U.S. foreign policy to help build an equitable political and economic order in which the world's people, their governments, and other institutions can effectively share resources and knowledge.

This country should not look for gratitude or votes, or any specific short-term foreign policy gains from our participation in international development. Nor should it expect to influence others to adopt U.S. cultural values or institutions. Neither can it assume that development will necessarily bring political stability. Development implies change—political and social, as well as economic—and such change, for a time, may be disruptive.

What the United States should expect from participation in international development is steady progress toward its long-term goals: the building of self-reliant and healthy societies in developing countries, an expanding world economy from which all will benefit, and improved prospects for world peace.

3. The United States should keep to a steady course in foreign assistance, providing its fair share of resources to encourage those countries that show a determination to advance. Foreign assistance is a difficult but not an endless undertaking. Some countries already have become self-reliant and are beginning to help others; U.S. policies should aim at hastening this process.

4. U.S. international development programs should be independent of U.S. military and economic programs that provide assistance for security purposes. Both types of programs are essential, but each serves a different purpose. Confusing them in concept and connecting them in administration detract from the effectiveness of both.

5. All types of security assistance—military assistance grants, use of surplus military stocks, military credits, economic assistance in support of military and public safety programs, budget support for political purposes, and the Contingency Fund—should be covered in one legislative act. The State Department should exercise firm policy guidance over these programs.

6. Military and related economic assistance programs will strengthen military security only to the degree that they help move countries toward greater self-reliance. These U.S. programs should be geared to the resources that the receiving countries ultimately will be able to provide for their own security. In some cases, reduction of U.S. military forces overseas will require temporary offsetting increases in such assistance. The ultimate goal should be to phase out these grant programs.

7. The United States should help make development a truly international effort. A new environment exists: other industrial countries are now doing more, international organizations can take on greater responsibilities, trade and private investment are more active elements in development, and, most important, the developing countries have gained experience and competence. Recognizing these conditions, the United States should redesign its policies so that:

—the developing countries stand at the center of the international development effort, establishing their own priorities and receiving assistance in relation to the efforts they are making on their own behalf;

—the international lending institutions become the major channel for development assistance; and

—U.S. bilateral assistance is provided largely within a framework set by the international organizations.

8. U.S. international development policies should seek to widen the use of private initiative, private skills, and private resources in the developing countries. The experience of industrial countries and of the currently developing nations demonstrates that rapid growth is usually associated with a dynamic private sector.

Development is more than economic growth. Popular participation and the dispersion of the benefits of development among all groups in society are essential to the building of dynamic and healthy nations. U.S. development policies should contribute to this end.

9. While the Task Force shares the aspirations of many who have endorsed high targets for development assistance, we have deliberately decided against recommending any specific annual level of U.S. assistance or any formula for determining how much it should be. We do not believe that it is possible to forecast with any assurance what volume of external resources will be needed 5 to 10 years hence. No single formula can encompass all that must be done—in trade, in investment, and in the quality as well as the amount of assistance. Our recommendation is to establish a framework of principles, procedures, and institutions that will assure the effective use of assistance funds and the achievement of U.S. national interests.

10. The downward trend in U.S. development assistance appropriations should be reversed. Additional resources, primarily in support of international lending institutions, are needed now for a new approach to international development. We believe this, having fully in mind the current financial stringency and urgent domestic priorities in the United States, as well as this country's balance-of-payments position. Over the long term, U.S. assistance for development abroad will be small in relation to expenditures for development at home. Moreover, the two programs can prove to be mutually reinforcing.

11. The United States must be able to respond flexibly and effectively to changing requirements in the developing world, and, in association with other industrial countries, help make possible the progress that individual developing countries show themselves determined to achieve. As the United States cuts back its involvement in Vietnam, reduces its forces abroad, and seeks to scale down the arms race, it can more easily carry such a

policy as far and as fast as the resolve and the purpose of the developing countries can take it.

12. To carry out these policies, the Task Force recommends a new focus for U.S. programs, a new emphasis on multilateral organizations and a new institutional framework consisting of:

—*A U.S. International Development Bank,* responsible for making capital and related technical assistance loans in selected countries and for selected programs of special interest to the United States. Whenever it is feasible, U.S. lending should support cooperative programs worked out by developing countries and the international agencies. The Bank would have assured sources of financing, including authority to borrow in the public market, and a range of lending terms appropriate to the development requirements of each borrowing country. It would be run by a full-time chairman and a mixed public-private board of directors.

—*A U.S. International Development Institute* to seek new breakthroughs in the application of science and technology to resources and processes critical to the developing nations. The Institute would concentrate on research, training, population problems, and social and civic development. It would work largely through private organizations and would rely on highly skilled scientific and professional personnel. It would seek to multiply this corps of U.S. talent and experience by supporting local training and research institutions. The Institute would be managed by a full-time director and a mixed public-private board of trustees.

—*The Overseas Private Investment Corporation (OPIC),* as recently authorized by the Congress,[60] to mobilize and facilitate the participation of U.S. private capital and business skills in international development.

—*A U.S. International Development Council* to assure that international development receives greater emphasis in U.S. trade, investment, financial, agricultural, and export-promotion policies. It also would be responsible for making sure that U.S. assistance policies are effectively directed toward long-term development purposes and are coordinated with the work of international organizations. The Chairman of the Council would be a full-time appointee of the President, responsible for coordinating all development activities under the broad foreign policy guidance of the Secretary of State, and would be located in the White House.

With this new institutional framework, the U.S. Government

[60] Cf. note 50 to Document 4.

would need fewer advisers and other personnel abroad. It could assume a supporting rather than a directing role in international development.

In the sections that follow we discuss the considerations underlying these general conclusions and offer specific recommendations for reshaping U.S. policies, programs, and organization.

*   *   *

(96) Foreign Aid Request for Fiscal Year 1971: Statement by Secretary of State Rogers Before the Foreign Operations Subcommittee of the Senate Committee on Appropriations, September 12, 1970.[61]

(Complete Text)

I am testifying today in support of the President's request for $1.8 billion for economic assistance and $350 million for military assistance.[62]

The economic reasons for our assistance programs have been stated many times. But I think they bear restating. Two-thirds of the people in the world live in less developed countries. Their share of the world's wealth is a small fraction of the amount of goods and services enjoyed by those of us who live in economically developed regions. Their share of the world's economic and social burdens is great. For humanitarian reasons alone, it would be only right that the United States—the most prosperous nation in history—should help them.

It is also prudent to do so as a long-range matter of national interest, because our continued security and prosperity depend on a peaceful world environment. Such an environment can hardly emerge from a world one-third rich and two-thirds poor, where economic divisions provoke political divisions and where it makes no sense for us not to do our fair share. In an increasingly interdependent world community, it is in our broadest interest to help the poorer nations improve their economic lot.

These considerations have persuaded five Presidents of the need for an effective U.S. foreign economic assistance program. The positive results of the combination of essential external help with efforts by the countries themselves are clearly visible

[61] Department of State Press Release 268 (undated); text from *Department of State Bulletin,* August 28, 1970, pp. 356–360.
[62] Cf. Document 4.

today—a rejuvenated Western Europe, an Asia benefited by a revolution in agricultural production, and rising rates of economic growth in many less developed countries. During the decade of the 1960's, less developed countries we have aided surpassed the 5 percent growth rate set as the goal for the First U.N. Development Decade.[63] Today many of the fastest growing economies in the world belong to developing countries.

The United States has played a major role in these successful efforts, but our relative share has diminished recently. We remain by far the largest single donor, but 11 countries now provide more official aid as a percentage of their gross national product than we do. The fiscal 1971 AID appropriation request of $1.8 billion is the lowest in 15 years and $400 million less than we asked for in fiscal 1970.[64] This year's figure represents only about one-fifth of 1 percent of our gross national product —in contrast to the nearly 3 percent of GNP that we provided for economic aid in fiscal 1949 during the Marshall Plan.

We should not necessarily expect our aid contributions this year to meet any particular percentage target in terms of our GNP. Our domestic requirements must be served, and some developing countries have ceased to need large amounts of aid. With some—the Republic of China, for example—we have been able to phase out our economic aid program. But the continuing economic disparity between the rich nations and the poor nations makes a substantial program necessary. As you no doubt have noted, the Peterson Task Force,[65] which reviewed our assistance programs for long-range purposes, recommended that the recent downward trend in aid appropriations be reversed.

At a time when this administration, through the Nixon doctrine,[66] is encouraging more self-reliance on the part of other nations, it is particularly important that we not withdraw—or even appear to withdraw—from our role in the world. We are deliberately lowering our military presence in the belief that Asian countries are increasingly in a position to undertake their own defenses in all but major contingencies. The Nixon doctrine, however, is not a program for U.S. withdrawal from Asia. It is a program of readjustment, which may well mean increased military supplies and increased economic relationships. At the present time substantial economic assistance is still needed in many Asian countries—Indonesia, for example—as a stimulus and

---

[63] *Documents, 1961*, pp. 535–538.
[64] For text of President Nixon's message to the Congress, May 28, 1969, see *Documents, 1968–69*, pp. 543–551.
[65] Document 95.
[66] *Documents, 1968–69*, pp. 329–334.

support to their own efforts. We should maintain this assistance in full.

This administration has also stressed the increased importance of multilateral leadership and institutions in our foreign assistance and has asked for increased appropriations for that purpose. This new emphasis should secure more and better contributions by other donors, but it will do so only if the United States does not slacken its own assistance efforts. However, bilateral efforts will continue to play a major role in foreign economic assistance. Certainly, until new decisions are taken after the President submits his views on the Peterson Task Force report, we must continue our present efforts much as they are today.

Unfortunately, the action taken by the House to cut our appropriation request by over half a billion dollars—more than 25 percent—cripples our entire aid program. The largest cut—almost half of the budget request—is in development loans, which are our primary means of supporting self-help measures by developing countries. We have, in fact, in recent years turned increasingly toward loans on concessionary terms as our primary means of economic assistance.

Until a new aid program based on the President's forthcoming recommendations [67] can be enacted, I believe it is crucial that our present program, which has produced solid successes, be maintained with adequate funds.

VIET-NAM

A substantial part of our appropriation request—$366 million —is for Supporting Assistance to Viet-Nam.

Success of our Vietnamization program [68] will depend not only on South Viet-Nam's growing ability to defend itself militarily but also on the stability of its economy. But the process of Vietnamization is bound to cause, and is causing, economic difficulties. Over the years, South Viet-Nam has met a large part of its needs for foreign exchange from U.S. military spending there. Now U.S. forces are being reduced, and the Vietnamese are taking on more of the burden of their own defense. As a result, U.S. military expenditures in Viet-Nam are declining as the cost of the war to the Vietnamese is growing. Viet-Nam needs substantial economic aid in order to meet these increased costs without imperiling its economic stability.

Moreover, increased military spending by the Government of

[67] Document 97.
[68] Cf. Document 42.

Viet-Nam—which is a consequence of Vietnamization—has boosted the demand for goods and services while increasing numbers of men are taken out of the labor force. The inflationary pressures which have inevitably grown require a high level of imports in order to augment the supply of goods in the market-place.

About half of our worldwide Supporting Assistance Program is proposed for the Commercial Import Program in Viet-Nam, our principal means for countering these inflationary pressures. Another $15 million is requested for the land reform program, a major Vietnamese effort to improve the living conditions of the rural population. If the House cut of $40 million from our Supporting Assistance request is not restored, the goals of Vietnamization will be significantly more difficult to achieve.

Mr. Chairman [Senator William Proxmire], the President in his budget message said that as much as $100 million in additional Supporting Assistance funds might be needed to combat inflationary pressures in Viet-Nam that will arise from the Vietnamization program. We are still trying to meet the essential costs of Vietnamization without seeking additional funds. But at the very least, we will need our full request for Supporting Assistance.

EAST ASIA

In the rest of East Asia, where the Nixon doctrine has already resulted in U.S. troop withdrawals from Thailand and projected withdrawals from South Korea, from the Philippines, and again from Thailand, our economic assistance must continue at adequate levels. Assistance to Indonesia, for example, now undertaken through a multilateral donor group, has helped to reduce inflation from 639 percent in 1966 to less than 10 percent in 1969 in this nation representing half the population and area of Southeast Asia. We must convince our Asian friends that a reduced military presence does not mean we are abandoning them. Our economic assistance program is one of the most effective ways to maintain our credibility as an Asian power.

LATIN AMERICA

Our fiscal 1971 program in this hemisphere is based on the wishes expressed by the Latin American countries themselves. This is the approach announced by President Nixon last October.[69] In our discussions this year, principally in the Inter-American Economic and Social Council,[70] the Latin Americans

69 *Documents, 1968–69*, pp. 329–334.
70 Document 67.

gave highest priority to education, employment, private investment (particularly the export sector), the technological bases of
industry and agriculture, and the need for increased food production for a rapidly growing population.

Our fiscal 1971 program reflects these Latin American concerns. It includes an increase of about $85 million mainly related
to the President's statement of an intention to give greater attention to export and tourism promotion, capital market development, and scientific and technological exchange. The House
reduction by a third of the Alliance for Progress [71] loan request
means that to fulfill the President's intention, which we propose
to do, we would have to cut existing high-priority programs in
agriculture and education.

Near East and South Asia

In the Near East and South Asia, 95 percent of our assistance
continues to be concentrated in India, Pakistan, and Turkey,
with a total population of over 700 million. Our objective is to
make permanent and self-sustaining the recent advances in agriculture all these countries have made. Much of the foreign exchange being provided to finance machinery and new materials
is supporting investment in the private industrial sector, as well
as in agriculture.

Africa

In Africa it is important to arrest the decline in our level of
assistance that began 3 years ago. During my trip to Africa last
February,[72] I was struck by the universal and overriding concern
of African leaders with the economic development problems of
their own nations. Approximately 35 independent countries on
this continent are looking toward external assistance to provide
them with the technology, skills, and financial support required
for sustained economic growth. These countries for the most part
have gained independence only in the last decade and, consequently, have only recently begun to move on the path to development. African nations have shown a determination to help
themselves, but these initiatives require external support. Continued limitations on U.S. assistance could threaten our efforts
to support both the national development and cooperation of
African states and place in question our genuine interest in the
people of Africa.

[71] Cf. note 6 to Document 66.
[72] Document 55.

Multilateral Technical Assistance

The United Nations Development Program (UNDP) plays the central role in the U.N.'s economic and social development activities. We have requested $100 million for the UNDP in fiscal 1971, a sum which represents about 40 percent of the $250 million target for all contributions to the UNDP. However, the House action would leave only $63 million for the UNDP, a drop of $23 million from the sum pledged last year and less than the United States has contributed to the UNDP in any year since 1965. Such a cut runs counter to the administration's policy of sharing responsibility by channeling more assistance through multilateral organs. The UNDP program has been a good one and, with newly proposed reforms, is on its way to becoming a better one. Other nations are ready to expand it. We should do our part.

Another high-priority U.N. need has arisen since the preparation of our budget requests last spring. At our initiative the U.N.'s Commission on Narcotic Drugs will hold a special meeting September 28 to prepare for the General Assembly a worldwide plan of action to fight drug addiction and its causes.[73] We are taking this initiative in the U.N. in the knowledge that our own drug problems require international action as much as they do domestic actions. We expect the Commission to authorize a substantial increase in U.N. drug control activities and to establish a special voluntary fund to finance them. We are proposing to pledge $2 million to the initial operations of the fund, using fiscal 1971 funds appropriated for multilateral technical assistance. I hope the committee will endorse this request on a matter which is of such vital concern to the United States.

Military Assistance and Sales

Mr. Chairman, I would like to conclude with a firm expression of support for our military assistance and military sales programs. If we are to encourage our friends and allies to take on more responsibility for their own defense, and to reduce our own role accordingly, then we will have to help them become more self-reliant militarily. If we reduce our own military presence and at the same time make it more difficult for them to acquire the means to defend themselves, the results will only be to weaken their security and their confidence in us. This is the contrary of our objectives.

[73] Cf. Document 87 at notes 166 and 167.

The President and I have repeatedly stated that we intend to honor our commitments. The military assistance and military sales programs help to maintain our allies' confidence that we mean what we say. They encourage our allies along the road to self-reliance, just as they make it easier for us to withdraw troops and close bases.

The administration requested, as you know, $425 million for the Military Assistance Program for fiscal 1970, but Congress passed a 2-year authorizing act setting an annual ceiling of $350 million. This was the amount appropriated last year.[74] We are requesting the same amount this year.

When I defended this appropriation request before the House Appropriations Committee in April, the fiscal 1971 program was essentially the same as the fiscal 1970 program, with no changed regional emphasis. Subsequent developments in Cambodia,[75] however, have made necessary a change in the distribution of the program. We diverted from the fiscal 1970 program $8.9 million in military assistance to Cambodia; we expect to divert about $40 million to Cambodia from the fiscal 1971 program. This assistance, I would note, does not mean that we are assuming a responsibility for the military defense of Cambodia. We support its objective of neutrality and are not seeking any military association. We do believe it is appropriate, however, to provide Cambodia with material assistance in defending itself against a foreign invader. We hope in the process to protect Vietnamization and our troop withdrawal program.

But the changed Cambodian situation has raised a new problem. The new requirement for Cambodia has compelled us to eliminate a number of elements of our overall military assistance program for other countries for fiscal 1971. I know, Mr. Chairman, General [Robert H.] Warren has supplied you with details on that. The necessary downward adjustments in other allocations make it all the more imperative that the total program be funded for this fiscal year. I urge this committee to support the full amount authorized for fiscal 1971.

As the economies of allied countries have improved, we have been able to shift our military assistance from grants to sales on credit—an obvious saving for the American taxpayer. I realize that the Foreign Military Sales Act is not the responsibility of this committee, but I would like to register my disappointment

---

[74] Foreign Assistance and Related Programs Appropriation Act, 1970 (Public Law 91–194), approved February 9, 1970.
[75] Cf. Documents 38–40.

that we do not yet have this act for either fiscal 1970 or fiscal 1971.[76]

The lack of funds for credit sales, combined with the readjustments in the grant program, is causing serious problems. The Republic of China, which relies more on credits than on grants, and has seen its grant assistance reduced by diversion of funds to Cambodia, is an example of a country particularly affected. So also is Israel, which has been counting on credit facilities to ease the financial burden imposed by its military purchases. We are examining the possibilities of meeting some of Israel's requirements through the authorization the Senate has inserted in the Defense Procurement Bill,[77] should it become law.

Mr. Chairman, the military assistance and sales programs are significant elements of a United States policy which seeks to promote greater military self-reliance on the part of our friends. In this respect they complement our economic assistance policy, which encourages self-reliance in the economic field. Both the economic and the military programs about which I have spoken today are important tools in the conduct of our foreign policy. Mr. Chairman, I urge the support of this committee for them.

(97) Redefining Foreign Aid: Message from President Nixon to the Congress, September 15, 1970.[78]

(Complete Text)

To the Congress of the United States:

FOREIGN ASSISTANCE FOR THE 'SEVENTIES

Today, I am proposing a major transformation in our foreign assistance programs.

For more than two decades these programs have been guided by a vision of international responsibilities conditioned by the aftermath of World War II and the emergence of new nations. But the world has been changing dramatically; by the end of the 'Sixties, there was widespread agreement that our programs for foreign assistance had not kept up with these changes and were losing their effectiveness. This sentiment has been reflected in declining foreign aid levels.

[76] Public Law 91–672, approved January 12, 1971.
[77] Public Law 91–441, approved October 7, 1971.
[78] Text from *Weekly Compilation of Presidential Documents,* September 21, 1970, pp. 1214–1225.

The cause of this downward drift is not that the need for aid has diminished; nor is it that our capacity to help other nations has diminished; nor has America lost her humanitarian zeal; nor have we turned inward and abandoned our pursuit of peace and freedom in the world.

The answer is not to stop foreign aid or to slash it further. The answer is to reform our foreign assistance programs and do our share to meet the needs of the 'Seventies.

A searching reexamination has clearly been in order and, as part of the new Administration's review of policy, I was determined to undertake a fresh appraisal. I have now completed that appraisal and in this message I am proposing a set of fundamental and sweeping reforms to overhaul completely our entire foreign assistance operation to make it fit a new foreign policy.

Such a major transformation cannot be accomplished overnight. The scope and complexity of such an undertaking requires a deliberate and thoughtful approach over many months. I look forward to active discussion of these proposals with the Congress before I transmit my new assistance legislation next year.

Reform #1: I propose to create separate organizational arrangements for each component of our assistance effort: security assistance, humanitarian assistance, and development assistance. This is necessary to enable us to fix responsibility more clearly, and to assess the success of each program in achieving its specific objectives. My proposal will overcome the confusion inherent in our present approach which lumps together these separate objectives in composite programs.

Reform #2: To provide effective support for the Nixon Doctrine,[79] I shall propose a freshly conceived International Security Assistance Program. The prime objective of this program will be to help other countries assume the responsibility of their own defense and thus help us reduce our presence abroad.

Reform #3: I propose that the foundation for our development assistance programs be a new partnership among nations in pursuit of a truly international development effort based upon a strengthened leadership role for multilateral development institutions. To further this objective,

—The U.S. should channel an increasing share of its development assistance through the multilateral institutions as rapidly as practicable.
—Our remaining bilateral assistance should be provided largely

[79] Cf. note 63 to Document 96.

within a framework established by the international institutions.

—Depending upon the success of this approach, I expect that we shall eventually be able to channel most of our development assistance through these institutions.

Reform #4: To enable us to provide effective bilateral development assistance in the changed conditions of the 'Seventies, I shall transmit legislation to create two new and independent institutions:

—A U.S. International Development Corporation, to bring vitality and innovation to our bilateral lending activities and enable us to deal with lower income nations on a business-like basis.

—A U.S. International Development Institute to bring the genius of U.S. science and technology to bear on the problems of development, to help build research and training competence in the lower income countries themselves, and to offer cooperation in international efforts dealing with such problems as population and employment.

Their creation will enable us to phase out the Agency for International Development and to reduce significantly the number of overseas U.S. Government personnel working on development programs.

Reform #5: To add a new dimension to the international aid effort insuring a more permanent and enduring source of funds for the low income countries, I have recently proposed that all nations enter into a treaty which would permit the utilization of the vast resources of the seabeds to promote economic development.[80]

Reform #6: I propose that we redirect our other policies which bear on development to assure that they reinforce the new approach outlined in this message. Our goal will be to expand and enhance the contribution to development of trade and private investment, and to increase the effectiveness of government programs in promoting the development process. A number of changes are necessary:

—I propose that we move promptly toward initiation of a system of tariff preferences for the exports of manufactured products of the lower income countries in the markets of all of the industrialized countries.

—I am ordering the elimination of those tying restrictions on

[80] Document 79.

procurement which hinder our investment guarantee program in its support of U.S. private investment in the lower income countries.

—I propose that all donor countries take steps to end the requirement that foreign aid be used to purchase goods and services produced in the nation providing the aid. Complete untying of aid is a step that must be taken in concert with other nations; we have already begun discussions with them toward that end. As an initial step, I have directed that our own aid be immediately untied for procurement in the lower income countries themselves.[81]

The Foundations of Reform

These are the most fundamental of the many far-reaching reforms I propose today. To understand the need for them now, and to place them in perspective, it is important to review here the way in which we have reexamined our policies in light of today's requirements.

Two steps were necessary to develop a coherent and constructive U.S. assistance program for the 'Seventies:

—As a foundation, we needed a foreign policy tailored to the 1970's to provide direction for our various programs. For that, we developed and reported to the Congress in February the New Strategy for Peace.[82]

—Second, to assist me in responding to the Congress and to get the widest possible range of advice on how foreign assistance could be geared to that strategy, I appointed a distinguished group of private U.S. citizens to make a completely independent assessment of what we should be trying to achieve with our foreign aid programs and how we should go about it.

The Task Force on International Development, chaired by Rudolph Peterson, former President of the Bank of America, drew upon the considerable experience of its own members and sought views from Members of the Congress and from every quarter of U.S. society. In early March the Task Force presented its report to me, and shortly thereafter I released it to the public.[83] The Task Force undertook a comprehensive assessment of the conditions affecting our foreign assistance program and proposed new and creative approaches for the years ahead. Its

[81] Cf. Document 98.
[82] Document 2.
[83] Document 95.

report provides the basis for the proposals which I am making today.

I also have taken into account the valuable insights and suggestions concerning development problems which were contained in the Rockefeller Report on our Western Hemisphere policy.[84] Many of the ideas and measures I am proposing in this message in fact were foreshadowed by a number of policy changes and program innovations which I instituted in our assistance programs in Latin America.

The Purposes of Foreign Assistance

There are three interrelated purposes that the U.S. should pursue through our foreign assistance program: promoting our national security by supporting the security of other nations; providing humanitarian relief; and furthering the long-run economic and social development of the lower income countries.

The national security objectives of the U.S. cannot be pursued solely through defense of our territory. They require a successful effort by other countries around the world, including a number of lower income countries, to mobilize manpower and resources to defend themselves. They require, in some cases, military bases abroad, to give us the necessary mobility to defend ourselves and to deter aggression. They sometimes require our financial support of friendly countries in exceptional situations.

Moreover, our security assistance programs must be formulated to achieve the objectives of the Nixon Doctrine, which I set forth at Guam last year. That approach calls for any country whose security is threatened to assume the primary responsibility for providing the manpower needed for its own defense. Such reliance on local initiative encourages local assumption of responsibility and thereby serves both the needs of other countries and our own national interest. In addition, the Nixon Doctrine calls for our providing assistance to such countries to help them assume these responsibilities more quickly and more effectively. The new International Security Assistance Program will be devoted largely to these objectives. I shall set forth the details of the proposed program when I transmit the necessary implementing legislation to the Congress next year.

The humanitarian concerns of the American people have traditionally led us to provide assistance to foreign countries for relief from natural disasters, to help with child care and maternal welfare, and to respond to the needs of international refugees

---

[84] For President Nixon's statement on release of the Rockefeller Report see *Documents, 1968–69*, pp. 439–441.

and migrants. Our humanitarian assistance programs, limited in size but substantial in human benefits, give meaningful expression to these concerns.

Both security and humanitarian assistance serve our basic national goal: the creation of a peaceful world. This interest is also served, in a fundamental and lasting sense, by the third purpose of our foreign assistance: the building of self-reliant and productive societies in the lower income countries. Because these countries contain two-thirds of the world's population, the direction which the development of their societies takes will profoundly affect the world in which we live.

We must respond to the needs of these countries if our own country and its values are to remain secure. We are, of course, wholly responsible for solutions to our problems at home, and we can contribute only partially to solutions abroad. But foreign aid must be seen for what it is—not a burden, but an opportunity to help others to fulfill their aspirations for justice, dignity, and a better life. No more abroad than at home can peace be achieved and maintained without vigorous efforts to meet the needs of the less fortunate.

The approaches I am outlining today provide a coherent structure for foreign assistance—with a logical framework for separate but interdependent programs. With the cooperation of Congress, we must seek to identify as clearly as possible which of our purposes—security, humanitarianism, or long-term development of the lower income countries—to pursue through particular U.S. programs. This is necessary to enable us to determine how much of our resources we wish to put into each, and to assess the progress of each program toward achieving its objectives.

There is one point, however, that I cannot over-emphasize. Each program is a part of the whole, and each must be sustained in order to pursue our national purpose in the world of the 'Seventies. It is incumbent upon us to support all component elements—or the total structure will be unworkable.

Effective Development Assistance—The Changed Conditions

The conditions that surround and influence development assistance to lower income countries have dramatically changed since the present programs were established. At that time the United States directly provided the major portion of the world's development assistance. This situation led to a large and ambitious U.S. involvement in the policies and activities of the developing countries and required extensive overseas missions to advise governments and monitor programs. Since then the international assistance environment has changed:

First, the lower income countries have made impressive progress, as highlighted by the Commission on International Development chaired by Lester [B.] Pearson,[85] the former Prime Minister of Canada. They have been helped by us and by others, but their achievements have come largely through their own efforts. Many have scored agricultural breakthroughs which have dramatically turned the fear of famine into the hope of harvest. They have made vast gains in educating their children and improving their standards of health. The magnitude of their achievement is indicated by the fact that the lower income countries taken together exceeded the economic growth targets of the First United Nations Development Decade.[86] These achievements have brought a new confidence and self-reliance to people in communities throughout the world.

With the experience that the lower income countries have gained in mobilizing their resources and setting their own development priorities, they now can stand at the center of the international development process—as they should, since the security and development which is sought is theirs. They clearly want to do so. Any assistance effort that fails to recognize these realities cannot succeed.

Second, other industrialized nations can now afford to provide major assistance to the lower income countries, and most are already doing so in steadily rising amounts.

While the United States remains the largest single contributor to international development, the other industrialized nations combined now more than match our efforts. Cooperation among the industrialized nations is essential to successful support for the aspirations of the lower income countries. New initiatives in such areas as trade liberalization and untying of aid must be carried out together by all such countries.

Third, international development institutions—the World Bank group, the Inter-American Development Bank and other regional development organizations, the United Nations Development Program, and other international agencies—now possess a capability to blend the initiatives of the lower income countries and the responses of the industrialized nations. They have made

---

[85] *Partners in Development: Report of the Commission on International Development* (New York: Praeger, 1969). The report, a general appraisal of world development problems, was prepared on invitation of the International Bank for Reconstruction and Development.

[86] Cf. note 63 to Document 96.

effective use of the resources which we and others have provided. A truly international donor community is emerging, with accepted rules and procedures for responding to the initiatives of the lower income countries. The international institutions are now in a position to accelerate further a truly international development effort.

Fourth, the progress made by lower income countries has brought them a new capability to sell abroad, to borrow from private sources, and to utilize private investment efficiently. As a result, a fully effective development effort should encompass much more than government assistance programs if it is to make its full potential contribution to the well-being of the people of the developing nations. We have come to value the constructive role that the private sector can play in channeling productive investments that will stimulate growth. We now understand the critical importance of enlightened trade policies that take account of the special needs of the developing countries in providing access for their exports to the industrialized nations.

Effective Development Assistance—The Program for Reform

To meet these changed international conditions, I propose a program for reform in three key areas: to support an expanded role for the international assistance institutions; to reshape our bilateral programs; and to harness all assistance-related policies to improve the effectiveness of our total development effort.

My program for reform is a reaffirmation of the commitment of the United States to support the international development process, and I urge the Congress to join me in fulfilling that commitment. We want to help other countries raise their standards of living. We want to use our aid where it can make a difference. To achieve these goals we will respond positively to sound proposals which effectively support the programs of the lower income countries to develop their material and human resources and institutions to enable their citizens to share more fully in the benefits of worldwide technological and economic advance.

1. *Expanding the Role of International Institutions*

International institutions can and should play a major creative role both in the funding of development assistance and in providing a policy framework through which aid is provided.

Such a multilateral approach will engage the entire international community in the development effort, assuring that each country does its share and that the efforts of each become part of a systematic and effective total effort. I have full confidence that these international institutions have the capability to carry out their expanding responsibilities.

—I propose that the United States channel an increasing share of its development assistance through multilateral institutions as rapidly as practicable.

We have already taken the first steps in this direction. The Congress is currently considering my proposals for a $1.8 billion multi-year U.S. contribution to the Inter-American Development Bank [87] and a $100 million contribution over three years to the Asian Development Bank.[88] These two requests together with authorizations for increases in our subscriptions to the World Bank and International Monetary Fund are critical to our new assistance approach.[89]

Moreover, I am pleased to note the recent statement by the World Bank that there is widespread agreement among donor countries to replenish the funds of the International Development Association at an annual rate of $800 million for the next three years, beginning in fiscal year 1972. I shall propose that the Congress, at its next session, authorize the $320 million annual U.S. share which such a replenishment would require.

—In order to promote the eventual development of a truly international system of assistance, I propose that our remaining bilateral development assistance be coordinated wherever feasible with the bilateral assistance of other donor countries, through consortia and consultative groups under the leadership of these international institutions. These institutions and groups like the CIAP in Latin America will provide leadership in the development process and work out programs and performance standards with the lower income countries themselves.

Moving in this direction holds the promise of building better relations between borrowing and lending countries by reducing the political frictions that arise from reliance on bilateral contacts in the most sensitive affairs of nation-states. It will enhance the effectiveness of the world development effort by providing for a pooling of resources, knowledge, and expertise for solving development problems which no single country can muster.

2. *Reshaping our Bilateral Programs*

If these worldwide initiatives are to be fully effective, we must also refashion and revitalize our own institutions to assure

---

[87] Cf. note 7 to Document 66.
[88] Cf. note 27 to Document 49.
[89] Cf. note 7 to Document 66.

that they are making their maximum contribution within a truly international development system. This will be neither an easy nor quickly accomplished task; it calls for thorough preparation, and an orderly transition. It is essential to undertake this task if our programs are to reflect the conditions of the 'Seventies.

The administration of bilateral assistance programs is complex and demanding. New institutions are needed so that we can directly focus on our particular objectives more effectively.

U.S. International Development Institute

   —I shall propose establishment of a U.S. International Development Institute, which will bring U.S. science and technology to bear on the problems of development.

The Institute will fill a major gap in the international development network. It will match our vast talents in science and technology with institutions and problems abroad. Research has created the basis for the Green Revolution—the major breakthrough in agricultural production—but continued progress in the 1970's will require the lower income countries to deal with more, and more complex, problems. The Institute will concentrate on selected areas and focus U.S. technology on critical problems. This requires flexibility, imagination and a minimum of red tape. If we can provide this Institute with the operational flexibility enjoyed by our private foundations, we can make a major contribution to the lower income countries at modest expense.

An Institute, so organized, could

   —Concentrate U.S. scientific and technological talent on the problems of development.
   —Help to develop research competence in the lower income countries themselves.
   —Help develop institutional competence of governments to plan and manage their own development programs.
   —Support expanded research programs in population.
   —Help finance the programs of U.S.-sponsored schools, hospitals and other institutions abroad.
   —Carry out a cooperative program of technical exchange and reimbursable technical services with those developing countries that do not require financial assistance.
   —Cooperate in social development and training programs.
   —Administer our technical assistance programs.
   —Permit greater reliance on private organizations and researchers.

Given the long-term nature of the research operation and the need to attract top people on a career basis, the Institute should be established as a permanent Federal agency. To provide the necessary financial continuity, I propose that Congress provide it with a multi-year appropriation authorization.

U.S. International Development Corporation

—I shall propose establishment of a U.S. International Development Corporation to administer our bilateral lending program. It will enable us to deal with the developing nations on a mature and businesslike basis.

This Development Corporation will examine projects and programs in terms of their effectiveness in contributing to the international development process. It will rely strongly on the international institutions to provide the framework in which to consider individual loans and will participate in the growing number of international consortia and consultative groups which channel assistance to individual lower income countries. It should have financial stability through a multi-year appropriation authorization and authority to provide loans with differing maturities and differing interest rates, tailored to the requirements of individual borrowers. The Corporation would also have limited authority to provide grant financed technical assistance for projects closely related to its lending operations.

Both the Institute and the Corporation will be subject to normal executive and legislative review, relating their performance directly to their objectives.

Both these new institutions involve a fundamental change from our existing programs. As I have emphasized, the detailed plans and the complete transition will take time. In the interim, I am directing the administrators of our present development programs to take steps to conform these programs, as much as possible, to the new concepts and approaches I have outlined. For example, our program planning for consortia will be based more on analysis and general guidance developed in country studies prepared by the World Bank and other international institutions. Greater utilization of international institutions will permit us to reduce the number of government personnel attached to our assistance programs particularly overseas and make major changes in our present method of operation.

Overseas Private Investment Corporation

—I am submitting to the Senate my nominations for the members of the Board of the Overseas Private Investment Corporation, which I proposed a year ago [90] to promote the role of the private sector in development and which the Congress approved.[91]

I expect this institution to be an important component of our new bilateral assistance program. The most important efforts of this new agency will be operation of the investment insurance and guaranty program and a strengthened program for assisting U.S. firms to undertake constructive investment in developing countries.

Inter-American Social Development Institute

—A few weeks ago I submitted to the Senate my nominations for the members of the Board of Directors of the Inter-American Social Development Institute,[92] which was authorized by the Congress in the Foreign Assistance Act of 1969.[93]

This Institute will provide grant support for innovative social development programs in Latin America undertaken primarily by private non-profit organizations, and will be aimed at bringing the dynamism of U.S. and Latin American private groups to bear on development problems and at broadening the participation of individuals in the development process.

The keynote of the new approach to our bilateral programs will be effectiveness: We will ask whether a program or individual loan will work before we decide to pursue it—and we will expect the international institutions through which we channel funds to do so as well. We will concentrate our activities in sectors in which we can make a significant contribution and in areas where long-term development is of special interest to the United States.

This Administration has been undertaking for some time a full review of all of our foreign economic policies. Those policies, including our new foreign aid policy and programs, must be closely related and mutually supporting. Therefore, I intend shortly to establish a new mechanism which will plan and coordinate all of our foreign economic policies, including our various foreign assistance programs, to assure that they are all effectively related.

[90] *Documents, 1968–69*, p. 545; for the White House announcement, December 4, 1970, listing the proposed membership of the Overseas Private Investment Corporation see *Weekly Compilation of Presidential Documents*, December 7, 1970, p. 1622.
[91] Cf. note 32 to Document 69.
[92] Document 69.
[93] Cf. note 32 to Document 69.

3. *Promoting Effective Development Through Improved Economic Policies*

In addition to a new emphasis on the role of international institutions and a new shape to our bilateral programs, I propose initiatives that will enhance the public and private sector contribution to the development process.

—To open further the benefits of trade to the lower income countries, I have proposed that the international community initiate a system of tariff preferences for the exports of manufactured and selected primary products of the lower income countries in the markets of all of the industrialized countries.

The lower income countries must expand their exports to be able to afford the imports needed to promote their development efforts, and to lessen their need for concessional foreign assistance.

Market growth for most of the primary commodities which have traditionally been their major sources of export earnings is insufficient to enable them to meet these needs. I will submit legislation to the Congress recommending that we eliminate duties on a wide range of manufactured products purchased from the lower income countries. We will move ahead with this approach as soon as we achieve agreement with the other industrialized countries to join us with comparable efforts.

—I proposed steps to expand the constructive role of private investment in the development process.

In order to eliminate the present tying restrictions on procurement which hinder our investment guarantee program, I am now directing that coverage under the extended risk guarantee program be extended to funds used in purchasing goods and services abroad. This will enhance our support of U.S. private investment in the lower income countries. In addition, we support early inauguration of an International Investment Insurance Agency, under the auspices of the World Bank, to provide multilateral—and thereby more effective—guarantees against expropriations and other political risks for foreign investments. We also support an increase in the scope of operations and resources of the International Finance Corporation, to further promote the role of the private sector—particularly within the lower income countries themselves—in the international development process.

—I propose that all donor countries end the requirement that foreign aid be used to purchase goods and services produced in the nation providing the aid.

Because recipients are not free to choose among competing

nations, the value of the aid they receive is reduced significantly. These strings to our aid lower its purchasing power, and weaken our own objectives of promoting development. Aid with such strings can create needless political friction.

Complete untying of aid is a step that must be taken in concert with other nations and we have begun talks to that end with the other members of the Development Assistance Committee of the Organization for Economic Cooperation and Development. In the expectation that negotiations will soon be completed successfully, I have decided to permit procurement now in the lower income countries under the U.S. bilateral lending program—an expansion of the initial step I took with our Latin American neighbors. In addition to improving the quality of our assistance, this should expand trade among the lower income countries, an important objective in its own right.

—I propose that the United States place strong emphasis on what the Peterson Task Force called "the special problem of population."

The initiative in this area rests with each individual country, and ultimately with each family. But the time has come for the international community to come to grips with the world population problem with a sense of urgency. I am gratified at the progress being made by the new United Nations Fund for Population Activities and propose that it undertake a study of world needs and possible steps to deal with them. In order to cooperate fully in support of this international effort, the proposed U.S. International Development Institute should focus the energy and expertise of this country on new and more effective measures for dealing with the problem of population.

—I also believe that the United States should work with others to deal effectively with the debt service problem.

The successful growth of the past has been financed in part through external borrowings, from private as well as government sources which the borrowers are obligated to repay. Furthermore, a portion of their borrowed resources have gone to build roads, schools and hospitals which are essential requirements of a developing nation but which do not directly generate foreign exchange. The debt incurred has heavily mortgaged the future export earnings of a number of lower income countries, restricting their ability to pay for further development.

This problem calls for responsibility on the part of the lower income countries, cooperation on the part of the lenders, and leadership by the international institutions which must take responsibility for analyzing debt problems and working closely with the creditors in arranging and carrying through measures to meet them. The United States will play its role in such a co-operative effort.

The Funding of Development Assistance

International development is a long-term process. Our institutions—like the multilateral lending institutions—should have an assured source of long-term funding. Foreign assistance involves the activities of many nations and the sustained support of many programs. Sudden and drastic disruptions in the flow of aid are harmful both to our long-term development goals and to the effective administration of our programs.

In the past this country has shown its willingness and determination to provide its share. I confirm that determination and ask the Congress and the American people to assume those responsibilities which flow from our commitment to support the development process.

I agree with the conclusion of the Peterson Task Force that the downward trend of U.S. contributions to the development process should be reversed. I also agree with the Peterson Report that the level of foreign assistance "is only one side of the coin. The other side is a convincing determination that these resources can and will be used effectively."

A determination of the appropriate level of U.S. assistance in any one year will depend on a continuing assessment of the needs and performance of individual developing countries, as well as our own funding ability. It must also be influenced by a further definition of the proposals which I am outlining in this message, the responses of other donors and the performance of the international institutions.

As a long-run contribution to the funding of development, the U.S. will seek the utilization of revenues derived from the economic resources of the seabed for development assistance to lower income countries. I have recently proposed that all nations enter into a treaty to establish an international regime for the exploitation of these vast resources, and that royalties derived therefrom be utilized principally for providing economic assistance to developing countries participating in the treaty.

Foreign assistance has not been the specific interest of one party or the particular concern of a single Administration. Each President, since the end of World War II, has recognized the great challenges and opportunities in participating with other nations to build a better world from which we all can benefit. Members of both political parties in the Congress and individuals throughout the nation have provided their support.

The U.S. role in international development assistance reflects the vision we have of ourselves as a society and our hope for a peaceful world. Our interest in long-term development must be viewed in the context of its contribution to our own security. Economic development will not by itself guarantee the political stability which all countries seek, certainly not in the short run, but political stability is unlikely to occur without sound economic development.

The reforms that I propose today would turn our assistance programs into a far more successful investment in the future of mankind—an investment made with the combination of realism and idealism that marks the character of the American people. It will enable us to enter the 'Seventies with programs that can cope with the realities of the present and are flexible enough to respond to the needs of tomorrow. I ask the Congress and the American people to join me in making this investment.

RICHARD NIXON

The White House
September 15, 1970

(98) Untying Foreign Aid: Statement by the Agency for International Development, September 22, 1970.[94]

(Complete Text)

The Agency for International Development on September 22 made public details of the new policy partially "untying" foreign aid procurement which President Nixon announced in his September 15 message to Congress, "Foreign Assistance for the 'Seventies." [95]

"Tying" of aid by a donor country means the requirement that its foreign assistance be used to purchase goods and services produced in that country. Beginning in late 1960 with a directive from President Eisenhower,[96] U.S. foreign aid was progressively "tied" to U.S. purchases, so that procurement in the United States increased from 41 percent of all AID-financed commodities in fiscal year 1959 to 99 percent in 1969.

In his message, President Nixon said: "Complete untying of

[94] AID Press Release 70–73, September 22, 1970; text from *Department of State Bulletin,* October 19, 1970, pp. 459–460.
[95] Document 97.
[96] *Documents, 1960,* pp. 54–61.

aid is a step that must be taken in concert with other nations and we have begun talks to that end with the other members of the Development Assistance Committee of the Organization for Economic Cooperation and Development." (The DAC, with 12 Western European nations, Australia, Canada, Japan, and the United States, coordinates the aid programs of these nations for developing countries.)

Pending agreement among the donor countries on complete untying, the President in his September 15 message announced his decision to permit foreign aid procurement immediately in most lower income countries.

The President pointed out that this is an expansion of an initial step previously taken with respect to Latin America. Effective last November 1, he ordered that loan dollars provided to Latin America could be used to finance purchases not only in the United States but in Latin America as well.

The President's new decision frees AID development assistance loan dollars for purchases of commodities and services in virtually all lower income countries as well as in the United States.

The new policy, effective immediately for all AID loans to the extent that procurement has not yet been initiated, will permit procurement from any independent country in the free world, excluding the recipient country itself and also excluding the following:

Algeria, Andorra, Australia, Austria, Belgium, Canada, Cyprus, Denmark, Finland, France, Federal Republic of Germany, Greece, Hong Kong, Iceland, Iraq, Ireland, Israel, Italy, Japan, Kuwait, Liechtenstein, Luxembourg, Malta, Monaco, Netherlands, New Zealand, Norway, Portugal, Rhodesia, San Marino, Somalia, South Africa, Spain, Sudan, Syria, Sweden, Switzerland, United Arab Republic, the United Kingdom, Yemen, and Yugoslavia.

The so-called componentry rule, which now provides that at least 90 percent (in value) of components of AID-financed commodites must be from an approved source for the finished commodity, is relaxed to provide that at least 50 percent of the value of finished items must be from eligible sources.

Where U.S.-flag shipping is available, the requirement that 50 percent of AID cargoes to a given country must be transported in U.S. ships still will apply. Where U.S.-flag liner service is not available, blanket determinations will be made to that effect by AID, permitting transport in ships of eligible countries other than the United States. Costs of shipping on carriers of eligible source countries (excluding the recipient country) will be financed under AID loans.

Costs of marine insurance obtained on a competitive basis from insurance firms in any eligible source country will be financed under AID loans, with certain conditions.

The policy of denying shipment on ineligible vessels—such as non-free-world vessels and those which have called at Cuba or North Vietnamese ports—will be continued.

With respect to goods financed under so-called program loans (general commodity loans rather than loans for specific project commodities), the price paid may not exceed the prevailing market price in comparable export sales in the source country and must be lower than the market price prevailing in the United States, calculated on a landed-cost basis.

(99) Request for Supplemental Assistance Funds: Message from President Nixon to the Congress, November 18, 1970.[97]

(Complete Text)

To the Congress of the United States:

In today's world, peace is synonymous with the strength of America and her friends.

Economic and military assistance to free nations willing to defend themselves is central to our new conception of American leadership for the 1970s and is crucial to America's hope of working with other nations to bring about the preconditions for peace in the world.

In my February 1970 Foreign Policy Message,[98] I reported that it was our goal to reduce the level of our direct involvements abroad as the capability of friendly nations to provide for defense of our mutual interests increases. At that time I sought the cooperation of the Congress in this task. The provision of support for our friends is a key element in our national security policy. Such support is essential if our policy is to succeed. This is why I ask today for a supplemental appropriation of economic and military assistance funds.

The first six decades of the Twentieth Century taught us that a stable and tranquil world requires American participation in keeping the peace. For us to abdicate that responsibility would be to magnify the world's instability and turmoil for us as well

[97] House Document, 91–419, 91st Congress, 2nd session; text from *Weekly Compilation of Presidential Documents,* November 23, 1970, pp. 1576–1581.
[98] Document 2.

as for our friends, and American strength remains one pillar of our foreign policy.

The United States is not going to withdraw from the world. But times are changing; for us to fulfill our responsibility now, we must link our efforts more closely with those of our friends to build the foundations of peace.

The decade of the 1960s taught us that it is neither necessary, nor even possible, for the United States to bear the principal burden for the defense or economic progress of all our allies and friends. They are now ready and willing to assume an increasing share of the burden for their own defense, and are developing the strength to do so—but they will continue to need our help as they move toward ultimate self-reliance.

The free world looks to this kind of American leadership in the 1970s. It is an American contribution which will encourage and enable other nations to do their part. It is a role for the United States in the world which will enlist the support of the American people, and which America can—and must—sustain.

It is in America's national interest to support the growing efforts of our friends. The overwhelming evidence of the last 25 years—from the Marshall Plan to Vietnamization [99]—is that a systematic program that helps other nations harness their own resources for defense and development enables them to take on the primary burden of their own defense.

Helping countries that demonstrate the capability to help themselves enables us to reduce our direct overseas involvement; it eases our budgetary and balance of payments burdens; and it lessens the likelihood of the engagement of American forces.

We are already carrying out this policy. Since I took office, we have already lowered our military presence abroad:

—Already, 68 installations abroad have been closed, and 44 more have been reduced.
—By next spring, under present plans, the total number of American military personnel overseas will be at least 300,-000 below the number that were abroad in January of 1969.

But our national security requires that we provide friendly nations the military and economic assistance they need to defend themselves.

The change that the Nixon Doctrine [100] calls for—from bearing the primary responsibility ourselves to enabling our friends to shoulder it much more themselves—is not a simple one to carry

[99] Cf. Document 42.
[100] Cf. note 66 to Document 96.

out. We must make this change in a way that permits our friends to adjust materially and psychologically to the new form and content of American support.

If we were to shift too quickly, without offsetting with assistance what we are taking away in direct American involvement, we would risk undermining our self-confidence. If we were to change too slowly, bearing too much of the burden ourselves too long, we would risk eroding their incentives for self-reliance.

In either case, we would fail to provide our friends with the means and confidence to help themselves, and we might ultimately face the dilemma of either letting them down or asserting a direct presence ourselves.

In the Middle East, we see how crucial it is to preserve the military balance [101] so that those who are already willing and able to defend themselves can continue to do so. The interest of all nations would be best served by limiting the shipment of arms to that explosive region, but until this objective can be achieved, we must help prevent a shift in the military balance that would undermine the chances for peace.

In the Middle East and elsewhere, we must strike a careful balance. While we must understand the limitations of our assistance, we must never underestimate its critical value in achieving and preserving such balance.

The supplemental program which I submit today will help achieve this balance, by responding to critical needs that have arisen since my original request for 1971 foreign assistance funds.[102]

1. MIDDLE EAST

Nowhere is our support more necessary or more closely linked with our efforts to achieve peaceful solutions than in the Middle East. Peace will come to the Middle East when all parties feel secure from the threat of military dominance and recognize that the only permanent way to resolve deepseated differences is by negotiation and never by war.

We must now act to preserve the delicate military balance in this area, which will encourage those negotiations leading to peace.

a. Israel

Israel has demonstrated a strong will to survive in freedom. We had hoped that recent agreements and arrangements in the

[101] Cf. Document 28.
[102] Document 4.

Middle East [103] would lead toward peace and make it unnecessary to provide large amounts of military assistance to any of the belligerents in the area. This hope has not yet been realized.

Continued large scale shipments of military equipment by the Soviet Union are a fact that cannot be denied. The buildup of the surface-to-air missile complex in the cease-fire zone west of the Suez Canal, in disregard of the ceasefire-standstill agreement,[104] requires us to redress the imbalance it has caused.

As authorized by the Defense Procurement Act,[105] *I request that the Congress appropriate $500 million to provide Israel with the credits that will assist her in the financing of purchases of equipment that have been necessary to maintain her defense capability, and to ease the economic strain caused by her expanded military requirements.*

b. Jordan

A stable and viable Jordan is essential if that nation is to make a positive contribution toward working out an enduring peace settlement which would serve the interests of all nations in the Middle East. The Jordanian government has recently demonstrated its determination and capacity to resist aggression by forces which oppose a peace settlement and threaten to weaken the stability of that country. But Jordan, which has previously paid for its military equipment, cannot afford to meet this new defense burden, and has asked us for assistance. *I request that the Congress provide $30 million toward meeting Jordan's request.*

c. Lebanon

Lebanon, which has also been threatened, has taken a moderate stance and a positive approach in the search for peace. To assist Lebanon to maintain a stable domestic base for responsible engagement in the search for peace, *I request the Congress to appropriate $5 million toward meeting Lebanon's request.*

2. EAST ASIA

In July 1969, on my trip through Asia,[106] I reaffirmed our determination to provide security support, while calling upon countries which receive our assistance to assume the primary responsibility for their own defense. Equally important, I em-

---

103 Cf. Document 29.
104 Cf. Documents 30–31.
105 Cf. note 77 to Document 96.
106 *Documents, 1968–69,* p. 161, note 76.

phasized the need to provide the help essential for such nations to assume this responsibility quickly. While reducing the direct participation of our forces we must help these other countries develop the capability to carry out the increased responsibilities they are assuming.

In Asia, this approach has provided the basis for a major reduction in our military presence as well as major long term budgetary and balance of payments savings. Authorized troop levels have been reduced by:

—165,000 in Vietnam; further reductions of 100,000 will be accomplished by next spring ;
—20,000 in Korea;
—6,000 in Thailand; further reductions of 9,800 are in process;
—6,000 in the Philippines.

Let us look at the countries in Asia where our help is required as nations move toward greater self-reliance.

a. Vietnam

United States troop withdrawals in Vietnam mean a reduction in the amount of dollars spent by the Department of Defense, and by our soldiers in Vietnam; and these dollars have been an essential factor in that country's economic stability.

Anticipating that Vietnam would require additional funds this year, my budget message suggested that an extra $100 million might be required. *I am now requesting an amount smaller than that—$65 million—but I regard this smaller sum as most important in insuring the success of our Vietnamization program.* It is important because:

—The Vietnamese, with United States encouragement, have recently begun a significant set of economic reforms which can be effective only if the stability of the Vietnamese economy is maintained.
—The Vietnamese economy will bear an increasing burden of defense as United States troops are removed. That burden could create economic disruption to the point that it would jeopardize that nation's stability, thereby threatening the progress of Vietnamization and future troop withdrawals.

b. Cambodia

The operations in the Cambodian border sanctuaries in May and June [107] helped assure the continued success of Vietnamiza-

---

[107] Documents 38–39.

tion and of our troop withdrawal programs. As we knew at the time would be the case, the operations seriously impaired the enemy's ability to operate in South Vietnam, and contributed to the progress which has reduced our casualties there to the lowest level since 1965. Continuing operations by South Vietnamese and Cambodian forces in the border areas will make possible continued progress.

Cambodia itself has mobilized its own manpower and resources in defense of its independence and neutrality. The Cambodian armed forces have grown from some 40,000 before North Vietnam's invasion in April to more than 150,000 today. It is essential that we supplement Cambodia's own efforts by providing resources which are critically needed to enable it to continue to defend itself. Its ability to do so is a vital element in the continued success of Vietnamization.

Cambodia's needs have been urgent, and as Congress has been informed, I have directed that funds be transferred from other already severely limited programs to meet these critical needs. *I am requesting $100 million to restore funds to such vital programs as those for Taiwan, Greece and Turkey.*

The need for these programs—to support our NATO allies and to assure stability in the Mediterranean and in East Asia— are no less urgent today than when I originally requested the funds to implement them; it was only because of the extraordinary urgency of Cambodia's needs that I directed this temporary transfer.

To meet Cambodia's urgent needs for the remainder of this fiscal year, *I request that the Congress provide $155 million in new funds to be directly allocated to the Cambodian program ($70 million for economic support; and $85 million for military assistance).* Seventy percent of the military assistance will be for ammunition.

c. Korea

I have announced our intentions to reduce by 20,000 the authorized level of United States forces in the Republic of Korea. This has placed a greater defense burden on the Koreans.

Our present assistance to Korea is mostly in the form of operation and maintenance items for their military forces. These items do not help to modernize the Korean force structure as we must do if we are to help Korea improve its own defense capability. *I therefore request authority to transfer to Korea equipment currently being utilized by United States forces scheduled to be withdrawn.*

Additional assistance is required this year as part of Korea's major five-year program to modernize its defense forces and to enable it to effectively meet outside threats as we reduce the level of direct US involvement. These funds are needed now to insure that the needed equipment will be delivered in good time. *I request that the Congress provide $150 million in support of this modernization of South Korea's defense.*

3. OTHER PROGRAMS

There are two additional needs for the military assistance program that have arisen since the Congress considered my request earlier in the year.

First, I directed that the Indonesian program be increased by $13 million from the previous level of $5 million for fiscal year 1971. Indonesia—with its population of over 110 million—occupies a key position for the future peace of Southeast Asia, and has shown a strong determination to resist threats to its security and stability. It is in our interest to support such encouraging developments in a nation which can play a key role in the stability of its entire region.

Second, anticipated recoveries of funds from past years' programs in various parts of the world are not materializing; a shortage of $17 million in these resources is now expected. These funds are needed to continue our assistance programs at necessary levels, and have been recognized as such by the Congress. Any shortfalls in these recoveries therefore would require reductions in already severely limited programs, and must be offset.

I request that this $30 million be restored to the military assistance program.

———

The funds requested represent a considerable sum. But the growing strength of our friends and their willingness to accept a greater responsibility for their own defense will mean increased effectiveness of our own efforts, and a lessened possibility that our men will have to risk their lives in future conflicts.

At this time, in light of certain extraordinary needs and in order to continue the success of the approach outlined in the Nixon Doctrine, we must provide additional resources to those of our friends whose security is threatened. The expenditures are essential to the support of our national security goals and our foreign policy interests, as we reduce our direct involvement abroad.

We must signal clearly to the world, to those who threaten freedom as well as those who uphold freedom, that where our interests are involved the United States will help those who demonstrate their determination to defend themselves. Our foreign policy cannot succeed without clear evidence that we will provide such help.

I believe the American people deeply understand the need for secure friends and allies to provide the foundation for a stable peace.

I believe the American people are prepared to accept the costs of assistance to these nations, to reduce the political and economic cost of maintaining a direct United States presence overseas—and thereby to avoid a possible cost of American lives.[108]

RICHARD NIXON

The White House
November 18, 1970

---

[108] Congress authorized additional foreign aid through passage of the Special Foreign Assistance Act of 1971 (Public Law 91–652, approved January 5, 1971). For President Nixon's statement on signing the measure see *Weekly Compilation of Presidential Documents,* January 11, 1971, p. 4.

CUMULATIVE INDEX, 1966–1970

The following pages provide a detailed listing of all documents appearing in the annual volumes of *Documents on American Foreign Relations* for the five years 1966–1970, thus supplementing the five-year indexes for 1963–1967 and 1964–1969 which appeared in *Documents, 1967* and *Documents, 1968–69* respectively. Each document for the 1966–1969 period is listed under (1) its official name, if any; (2) its main subject and principal subordinate subjects; (3) the name of the originating country, organization, or individual, and of the addressee or recipient where appropriate; and (4) its place of origin when this is deemed historically significant. *Not* listed are names and subjects occurring in the body of a document but falling into none of the above categories.

Within each entry, the year is listed at the left and the description of the document, with inclusive page numbers, at the right. Documents for 1966 and 1967 will be found in the annual volumes for those years; documents for 1968 and 1969 will be found in the two-year volume, *1968–69*, while documents for 1970 will be found in the present volume. Explanations of abbreviations used within the index are included in the general alphabetical sequence.

Entries under the heading "United States" are limited to general statements of policy, pronouncements on organizational matters, and the like. Material on the specialized aspects of U.S. foreign relations, including such matters as defense and the balance of payments, should be sought under the appropriate topical headings. Acts and resolutions of the Congress will be found under the heading "Congress (U.S.)," where they are listed both by subject and, where appropriate, by Public Law or Resolution number.

Resolutions of the U.N. General Assembly are listed for each session by subject and also by resolution number; those of the U.N. Security Council are listed by year, subject, and resolution number.

CUMULATIVE INDEX, 1966–1970

Disarmament *(cont.)*

10), 115–18; resolution on same (Dec. 16), 119–22; on suspension of nuclear tests (Dec. 16, excerpt), 122–4; Nixon address (Sept. 18), 472–3; Yost review (Dec. 16), 489–90

Strategic Arms Limitation Talks (Helsinki, Nov. 17–Dec. 22); Nixon message (Nov. 17), 125–6; US-USSR joint communiqué (Dec. 22), 126–7

1970 Nixon remarks on entry into force of the nonproliferation treaty (Mar. 5), 66–8;

CCD (ENDC) meetings (Feb. 17–Sept. 3): report to UN (Sept. 11, excerpts), 43–59; US-USSR second revised draft treaty on barring nuclear weapons from the seabed (Sept. 1), 69–73

UNGA meeting (25th session, Sept. 15–Dec. 15): resolution on barring nuclear weapons from the seabed (Dec. 7, excerpt), 74; on chemical-biological warfare (Dec. 7), 77–80; on general and complete disarmament (Dec. 7), 80–2; on suspension of nuclear tests (Dec. 7, excerpt), 82–3

SALT (Vienna, Apr. 16–Aug. 4; Helsinki, Nov. 2–Dec. 18): Smith statement (Aug. 14), 60–1; Semenov statement (Aug. 14), 61–2; joint communiqué (Aug. 14), 62–3; Smith statement (Nov. 2), 63–4; Semenov statement (Nov. 2), 64–5; joint communiqué (Dec. 18), 65–6

See also Chemical and biological warfare; Missile race

Dominican Republic

1966 Tenth Meeting of Consultation (Buenos Aires, opened May 1, 1965): resolution withdrawing IAPF (June 24), 325–6

Draft U.S. Convention on the International Seabed Area

1970 Summary (Aug. 3), 334–41

East Asia, *see* Asia, Pacific, and regional and country entries

East-West Center for Cultural Exchange (Honolulu)

1966 Johnson address (Oct. 17), 284–91

East-West relations

1966 Johnson remarks (May 3), 53–7; same (June 15), 65–9; same (Oct. 7), 73–80

1967 Johnson-Kosygin meetings (Glassboro, N.J., June 23, 25): Johnson toast (June 23), 52–4; Johnson-Kosygin remarks (June 23), 54–5; Johnson remarks (June 25), 55–6; Johnson report (June 25), 56–8; Kosygin statement (June 25), 58–9

Europe, Western *(cont.)*

1967 Rusk address (New York, Dec. 2), 89–97

1969 Nixon visit (Feb. 23–Mar. 2): Nixon statement (Feb. 6), 143–4; remarks to NATO Council (Brussels, Feb. 24), 144–8; Rogers address (Brussels, Dec. 6), 173–80

1970 Rush address, 115–26

See also country, topical, and organizational entries

Faisal (Faysal) of Saudi Arabia

1966 Statement with Johnson (June 22), 174

Far East, *see* Asia, Pacific, and regional and country entries

First Solidarity Conference of the Peoples of Asia, Africa, and Latin America (Havana, Jan. 1966)

1966 OAS resolution, 323–5

FOBS, *see* Fractional Orbital Bombardment System

Food for freedom, *see* Food for peace program (U.S.)

Food for Peace Act of 1966 (P.L. 89–808, Nov. 11)

1966 Johnson message (Feb. 10), 450–9

Food for peace program (U.S.)

1966 Johnson address (Omaha, June 30), 231–2; Goldberg report (Nov. 7), 367; Johnson remarks (Independence, Mo., Jan. 20, excerpt), 423–4; Johnson message (Feb. 10), 450–9

See also India

Foreign aid program (U.S.)

1966 Johnson message (Feb. 1), 425–37

1967 Johnson message (Feb. 9), 429–42; message on increased aid to Latin America (Mar. 13), 319–28; Foreign Assistance Act (Nov. 14, excerpts), 442–9; signature statement (Nov. 15), 449–50

1968 Johnson message (Feb. 8), 530–43

1969 Nixon message (May 28), 543–51

1970 Peterson report (Mar. 4, excerpt), 417–22; Nixon statement (Mar. 8), 416–17; Rogers statement (Sept. 12), 422–9; Nixon message (Sept. 15), 429–44; AID statement (Sept. 22), 444–6; Nixon request for supplemental aid, 446–53

Foreign Assistance Act of 1966 (P.L. 89–583, Sept. 19, 1966)

1966 Johnson message (Feb. 1), 425–37

Foreign Assistance Act of 1967 (P.L. 90–137, Nov. 14, 1967)

1967 Johnson message (Feb. 9), 429–42; excerpts from act, 442–9; signature statement (Nov. 15), 449–50

Foreign Assistance Act of 1968 (P.L. 90–554, Oct. 8, 1968)

1968 Johnson message (Feb. 8), 530–43

Javits, Jacob K.
  1970 Statement on 2nd UN Development Decade (excerpt), 320–3
Jerusalem, *see* Palestine problem
Johnson, Joseph E.
  1969 Statement on UNRWA, 219–25
Johnson, Lyndon B.
  1966 Messages and communications to Congress: on state of union
    (Jan. 12), 1–11; on budget (Jan. 24, excerpts), 20–4; on food
    for India (Mar. 30), 183–8; on Vietnam (Jan. 22), 198–9; on
    Asian Development Bank (Jan. 18), 260–3; on economic report
    (Jan. 27, excerpts), 417–22; on foreign aid (Feb. 1), 425–37; on
    international education and health (Feb. 2), 437–50; on food
    for freedom (Feb. 19), 450–9

  Addresses and remarks: on foreign policy (Denver, Aug. 26),
    12–18; epilogue to "This America" (Oct. 3), 18–20; on US and
    Eastern Europe (May 3), 53–7; on East-West contacts (June
    15), 65–9; on US and USSR (Arco, Idaho, Aug. 26), 69–73; on
    East-West relations (New York, Oct. 7), 73–80; on French with-
    drawal from NATO (Mar. 23), 115–19; on NATO 17th anni-
    versary (Apr. 4), 123–4; on Vietnam (Jan. 31), 202–4; same
    (Feb. 23, excerpts), 217–21; same (June 18), 224–7; same
    (Omaha, June 30, excerpt), 230–9; on US Asian policy (July
    12), 276–82; same (Honolulu, Oct. 17), 284–91; report on Far
    East (Nov. 2), 293–7; on Africa (May 26), 298–304; on Alli-
    ance for Progress (Mar. 14), 326–9; on Latin America (Mexico
    City, Apr. 15), 330–5; on same (Washington, Aug. 17), 335–
    42; on outer space (May 7), 375–6; on outer space treaty (Dec.
    8), 390–1; on water for peace (Sept. 3, excerpt), 412–16; on
    education and health (Independence, Mo., Jan. 20, excerpt),
    422–5

  Joint statements and communiqués: with Erhard (Sept. 27),
    143–9; with Faisal (June 22), 174; with Mrs. Gandhi (Mar. 29),
    181–3; with Thieu and Ky (Feb. 8), 211–13; with Holt (July
    14), 282–3

  Other messages and communications: on participation in in-
    ternational organizations and programs (Mar. 15), 26–30; to
    ENDC (Jan. 27), 92–5; exchange with de Gaulle (Mar. 7),
    107–8; letter to de Gaulle (Mar. 22), 113–15; report from
    Humphrey (Mar. 3), 221–4; letter from Goldberg (Aug. 22),
    343–9; report from Goldberg (Nov. 7), 361–8; memorandum to
    Fowler (Dec. 12), 468–9
  1967 Messages and communications to Congress: on state of union
    (Jan. 10, excerpts), 1–10; on budget (Jan. 24, excerpts), 30–7;

on budget and economy (Aug. 3, excerpts), 37–41; on ACDA report (Feb. 17), 48–50; on food for India (Feb. 2), 173–4; on Asian Development Bank (Sept. 26), 252–8; on OAS Charter (June 12), 315–17; on aid to Latin America (Mar. 13), 319–28; on outer space treaty (Feb. 7), 384–9; on economic report (Jan. 26, excerpt), 425–9; on foreign aid (Feb. 2), 429–42; on Kennedy Round (Nov. 27), 454–7

Addresses and remarks: on foreign policy (June 19), 10–17; same (Dec. 4, excerpt), 41–7; on Glassboro meetings (June 23), 52–4; same (June 25), 56–8; on draft nonproliferation treaty (Aug. 24), 59–60; on peaceful nuclear activities (Dec. 2, excerpts), 83–5; on Cyprus crisis (Dec. 5), 114–15; on Middle East crisis (May 23), 123–5; same (June 6), 126–7; same (June 7), 127; same (June 19), 14–17; on food for India (Apr. 1), 186–7; on Vietnam (Jan. 10, excerpt), 5–8; same (Feb. 13), 187–8; same (Nashville, Mar. 15), 207–16; same (Guam, Mar. 20, excerpt), 216–17; same (Guam, Mar. 20), 217–19; on South Vietnamese constitution (Guam, Mar. 20), 219–20; on Guam conference (Andrews Air Force Base, Mar. 21), 222–3; on Vietnam (San Antonio, Sept. 29), 236–44; same (Dec. 4, excerpt), 42–4; same (Dec. 19, excerpt), 246–7; same (Vatican, Dec. 23), 249–50; on Latin America (Punta del Este, Apr. 12), 328–30; same (Apr. 13), 330–5; same (Apr. 14), 358–60; on Alliance for Progress (Aug. 17), 360–2; on IDB (Sept. 22), 362–4; on outer space treaty (Oct. 10), 389–92; on rescue and return of astronauts (Dec. 19), 396–7; on signing foreign assistance act (Nov. 15), 454–7; on special drawing rights (Aug. 28, excerpt), 459–60; on pound devaluation (Nov. 18), 461–2; on economy and balance of payments (Dec. 6), 462–6

Joint statements: with Kosygin (Glassboro, June 23), 54–5; same (June 25), 55–6; with Kiesinger (Aug. 16), 106–7; on completion of Guam talks (Guam, Mar. 21), 220–2; with Thieu (Canberra, Dec. 21), 247–9; with Sato (Nov. 15), 266–73

Other communications and exchanges: to ENDC (Feb. 21), 50–2; with Pope Paul (Feb. 7–8), 195–6; with Ho Chi Minh (Feb. 8–15), 198–202; letter to Mansfield (June 8), 128–30

1968 Messages and communications to Congress: on state of union (Jan. 17, excerpts), 1–9; on foreign aid (Feb. 8), 530–43; on special drawing rights (Apr. 30), 509–15; on proposed Trade Expansion Act (May 28), 515–21; on rescue and return of astronauts (July 15), 446–9

Addresses and remarks: on foreign policy (New Orleans, Sept. 10), 10–20; on non-proliferation treaty (June 12), 56–9;

Johnson, Lyndon B. *(cont.)*
> on Czechoslovak crisis (Aug. 21), 134–5; on Middle East (Sept. 10, excerpt), 192–5; on Vietnam (Mar. 31), 226–36; same (Oct. 31), 243–9; on *Pueblo* incident (Dec. 22), 301–2; on Tlatelolco treaty (Feb. 14), 394–5; on OAS Charter amendments (Apr. 23), 401–4; on IDB (June 4), 405–8; on Central America (San Salvador, July 6), 409–13; on balance of payments (Jan. 1), 498–506
>> Joint statement: with Thieu (Honolulu, July 20), 237–43
>> Other communications and exchanges: to ENDC (July 16), 68–71; with Mobutu (May 25), 354–5; to OAU (Sept. 13), 355–6
> 1969 Statement on Alliance for Progress (Jan. 9), 422–4; message on state of the union (Jan. 14, excerpt), 35–38

Johnson, U. Alexis
> 1970 Address on Far East (excerpt), 220–8

Joint United States-Japan Committee on Trade and Economic Affairs
> 1966 5th meeting: communiqué, 271–6

Jordan
> 1966 State Department statement, 173
> *See also* Palestine problem

Kashmir
> 1966 Goldberg review (Aug. 22), 344–5
> *See also* India-Pakistan conflict

Katzenbach, Nicholas deB.
> 1968 Address on Nigeria, 361–70

Kennedy, David M.
> 1970 Statement to IDB (Punta del Este, Apr. 23, excerpt), 280–2; statement to IBRD/IMF (Copenhagen, Sept. 22, excerpt), 381–9

Kennedy Round (Sixth Round of GATT trade negotiations)
> 1966 Johnson message on Economic Report (Jan. 27, excerpts), 420
> 1967 Summary of agreements (signed Geneva, June 30, excerpt), 451–3; Johnson message (Nov. 27), 454–7

Kiesinger, Kurt Georg
> 1967 Statement with Johnson (Aug. 16), 106–7
> 1969 Statement with Nixon (Aug. 8), 160–3

Korea, Democratic People's Republic of
> 1968 Goldberg statement on *Pueblo* incident (Jan. 23, excerpts), 292–8; State Department statement on same (Dec. 22), 298–9; text of North Korean document (Dec. 22), 299–300; Rusk statement (Dec. 22), 300–1; Johnson statement (Dec. 22), 301–2
> *See also* Korean problem

Palestine problem (*cont.*)

ment on same (June 28), 148; Goldberg statement (July 3), 148–56; resolution on refugees (July 4), 156–8; on status of Jerusalem (July 4), 158; on same (July 14), 158–9; Rusk statement on same (July 14), 159–60; resolution on adjournment of session (July 21), 160; Goldberg statement on same (July 21), 160–4; resolution on completion of session (Sept. 18), 164–5

At UNSC (Oct.–Nov.): resolution on military activities (Oct. 25), 165–6; Goldberg statement (Nov. 9), 166–9; resolution on special Middle East representative (Nov. 22), 169–70; Goldberg statement (Nov. 22, excerpts), 170–2

Other comments by Goldberg, 403–5, 410–11

1968 Battle address (May 16), 184–92; Johnson remarks (Sept. 10, excerpt), 192–5; Rusk statement (Oct. 2), 456–7

1969 Rusk statement (Jan. 3, excerpt), 196–8; Nixon statement (Feb. 6, excerpt), 199; Rogers statement (Mar. 27, excerpt), 199–202; communiqué of 4-power talks (Apr. 3), 202–3; Rogers statement (Apr. 7, excerpts), 203–5; Sisco address (Apr. 11), 205–11; Nixon address (Sept. 18), 471–2; communiqué on resumption of 4-power talks (Dec. 2), 211–12; Rogers address (Dec. 9), 212–19; Yost UNGA review (Dec. 16), 492

1970 Sisco statement (Apr. 24), 127–9; Rogers statement (Mar. 23, excerpt), 129–30; the US peace initiative: Rogers statement (June 25, excerpt), 131; Rogers letter to Riad (released July 22), 132–3; Nixon remarks (San Clemente, July 31), 134–5; State Department statement on cease-fire violations (Aug. 19), 135–6; same (Sept. 3), 136; UNGA resolution (Nov. 4), 137–8; Yost statement (Nov. 4), 138–41; Sisco address (San Francisco, Nov. 6), 141–6

Palmer, Joseph 2nd

1967 Address on Africa, 286–94

1968 Address on Africa, 342–54

Pan American Health Organization

1966 Johnson remarks (Aug. 17), 335–42

Pan American Society

1969 Johnson remarks (Jan. 9), 422–4

Pan American Union

1967 Johnson remarks (Aug. 17), 360–2

1968 Linowitz statement (Apr. 26), 404–5

1969 Nixon remarks (Apr. 14), 425–9

Park, Chung Hee

1969 Statement with Nixon (San Francisco, Aug. 22), 334–6

COUNCIL ON FOREIGN RELATIONS

Recent Publications

FOREIGN AFFAIRS (quarterly), edited by William P. Bundy.

THE UNITED STATES IN WORLD AFFAIRS (annual), by Richard P. Stebbins and William P. Lineberry.

DOCUMENTS ON AMERICAN FOREIGN RELATIONS (annual), by Richard P. Stebbins and Elaine P. Adam.

POWER AND EQUILIBRIUM IN THE 1970s, by Alastair Buchan (1972).

Reforming the Dollar: An International Monetary Policy for the United States, by C. Fred Bergsten (1972).

The Smithsonian Agreement and Its Aftermath: Several Views (1972).

Fifty Years of Foreign Affairs, edited by Hamilton Fish Armstrong (1972).

The Foreign Affairs 50-Year Bibliography: New Evaluations of Significant Books on International Relations, 1920–1970, edited by Byron Dexter (1972).

The West and the Middle East, by John C. Campbell and Helen Caruso (1972).

The United States and the Industrial World: American Foreign Economic Policy in the 1970s, by William Diebold, Jr. (1972).

The World This Year: 1972 Supplement to the Political Handbook, edited by Richard P. Stebbins and Alba Amoia (1972).

American Aid for Development, by Paul C. Clark (1972).

The Caribbean Community: Changing Societies and U.S. Policy, by Robert D. Crassweller (1972).

India, Pakistan, and the Great Powers, by William J. Barnds (1972).

Congress, the Executive, and Foreign Policy, by Francis O. Wilcox (1971).

The Realty of Foreign Aid, by Willard L. Thorp (1971).

Political Handbook and Atlas of the World, 1970, edited by Richard P. Stebbins and Alba Amoia (1970).

Japan in Postwar Asia, by Lawrence Olson (1970).

The Crisis of Development, by Lester B. Pearson (1970).

The Great Powers and Africa, by Waldemar A. Nielsen (1969).

A New Foreign Policy for the United States, by Hans J. Morgenthau (1969).

Middle East Politics: The Military Dimension, by J. C. Hurewitz (1969).

The Economics of Interdependence: Economic Policy in the Atlantic Community, by Richard N. Cooper (1968).

How Nations Behave: Law and Foreign Policy, by Louis Henkin (1968).

The Insecurity of Nations, by Charles W. Yost (1968).

Prospects for Soviet Society, edited by Allen Kassof (1968).

The American Approach to the Arab World, by John S. Badeau (1968).

U.S. Policy and the Security of Asia, by Fred Greene (1968).

Negotiating with the Chinese Communists: The U.S. Experience, by Kenneth T. Young (1968).

From Atlantic to Pacific: A New Interocean Canal, by Immanuel J. Klette (1967).

Tito's Separate Road: America and Yugoslavia in World Politics, by John C. Campbell (1967).

U.S. Trade Policy: New Legislation for the Next Round, by John W. Evans (1967).

Trade Liberalization Among Industrial Countries: Objectives and Alternatives, by Bela Balassa (1967).

The Chinese People's Liberation Army, by Brig. Gen. Samuel B. Griffith II U.S.M.C. (ret.) (1967).

The Artillery of the Press: Its Influence on American Foreign Policy, by James Reston (1967).

Trade, Aid and Development: The Rich and Poor Nations, by John Pincus (1967).

Between Two Worlds: Policy, Press and Public Opinion on Asian-American Relations, by John Hohenberg (1967).

The Conflicted Relationship: The West and the Transformation of Asia, Africa and Latin America, by Theodor Geiger (1966).

The Atlantic Idea and Its European Rivals, by H. van B. Cleveland (1966).

European Unification in the Sixties: From the Veto to the Crisis, by Miriam Camps (1966).

The United States and China in World Affairs, by Robert Blum, edited by A. Doak Barnett (1966).

The Future of the Overseas Chinese in Southeast Asia, by Lea A. Williams (1966).

Atlantic Agricultural Unity: Is It Possible? by John O. Coppock (1966).

Test Ban and Disarmament: The Path of Negotiation, by Arthur H. Dean (1966).

Communist China's Economic Growth and Foreign Trade, by Alexander Eckstein (1966).

Policies Toward China: Views from Six Continents, edited by A. M. Halpern (1966).

The American People and China, by A. T. Steele (1966).

International Political Communication, by W. Phillips Davison (1965).

Alternative to Partition: For a Broader Conception of America's Role in Europe, by Zbigniew Brzezinski (1965).

The Troubled Partnership: A Re-appraisal of the Atlantic Alliance, by Henry A. Kissinger (1965).